Winchester Bibliographies of 20th Century Writers

LEONARD WOOLF
A Bibliography

Leila Luedeking is Curator of Modern Literary Special Collections at Washington State University Libraries, which houses the Woolf Library. She holds degrees from the University of Minnesota and from Washington State University.

Michael Edmonds is Supervisor of Public Services at the State Historical Society of Wisconsin Library. He holds degrees from Harvard University and Simmons College, and is the author of a bibliography of Lytton Strachey published in 1981.

LEONARD WOOLF

A Bibliography

by Leila Luedeking
and Michael Edmonds

ST PAUL'S BIBLIOGRAPHIES · WINCHESTER

OAK KNOLL BOOKS · NEW CASTLE · DELAWARE
1992

First published by St Paul's Bibliographies,
West End House, 1 Step Terrace, Winchester, UK in 1992
as part of the Winchester Bibliographies of 20th Century Writers

Published in North and South America by
Oak Knoll Books, 414 Delaware Street,
New Castle, DE 19720, USA

British Library Cataloguing in Publication Data

Leonard Woolf: Bibliography.—(Winchester
Bibliographies of 20th Century Writers
Series)
   I. Luedeking, Leila   II. Edmonds, Michael
   III. Series
   016.070592

ISBN (UK) 1-873040-10-5
ISBN (USA) 0-938768-41-7

Printed in Great Britain by The Alden Press Ltd., Oxford

Contents

Illustrations

Preface

Today Leonard Woolf is remembered primarily as the husband of Virginia Woolf, and even in that peripheral role he tends to be reduced to either her captor or her saviour. If known at all for his own work, he is likely to be considered simply as the chronicler of Bloomsbury, the person whose autobiography contains the most trustworthy and detailed account of that influential group of early twentieth-century British intellectuals.

During the first half of the twentieth century, however, Leonard Woolf was recognized as an important public figure in his own right, one whose literary and political judgements were respected by a wide public. He was invited to write on history and current affairs by magazine editors and scholarly publishers, consulted by royal commissions and foreign statesmen as an expert on international relations, and asked to lecture on political theory over BBC radio. At the end of the First World War, his treatise *International Government* was one of the foundation blocks of the League of Nations; by relying on it, the British delegates at Versailles ensured that the League (and later the United Nations) would foster cultural and economic co-operation rather than limit itself only to the arbitration of disputes.

Between the wars Leonard Woolf was one of the principal architects of Labour Party foreign policy; at a time when most English citizens cherished a strong sentimental attachment to "their" Empire, Woolf and a handful of others strove to dismantle it peacefully by transferring political and economic power to indigenous peoples around the globe.

At the same time, he held responsible positions on several journals of news and opinion. As an editor for the *International Review*, Woolf pioneered documentary journalism by printing and commenting on the texts of important foreign documents. As literary editor of the *Nation and Athenaeum* and the *New Statesman* in the 1920s, he brought new authors to the attention of the reading public, gave unknown writers work and encouragement, and spoke out against censorship and restrictions on intellectual freedom. With William A. Robson he founded the *Political Quarterly* in 1930 to meet the need for a journal devoted to serious discussion of political events. He served as joint editor until 1958 and was a member of its editorial board until 1969; he was also a director of the *New Statesman* from 1941 to 1954.

The Hogarth Press, the publishing firm which Woolf founded and managed (with Virginia 1917–38, John Lehmann 1938–46, and in association with Chatto & Windus Ltd 1946–69), is best known for its support of the major figures of the modern movement such as Virginia Woolf herself, T. S. Eliot, Stephen Spender and Christopher Isherwood. But it also published the standard English translation of Freud's complete works, pamphlets on current events, and a wide range of titles in history, economics, women's studies, politics and international relations.

The primary purpose of this bibliography is to facilitate access to Woolf's published work in all its variety. Writing was one of his chief pleasures, and one in which he indulged daily for most of his 89 years; in addition, he possessed an almost compulsive desire for hard work. This combination of longevity and productivity has made our task a challenging one. Woolf wrote 43 books which collectively went through more than 100 separate editions or issues, and he contributed to dozens more. His career as a journalist spanned almost seven decades, and many of his hundreds of articles were printed in ephemeral or short-lived radical periodicals.

In the face of these bald statistics, it would be naive for us to claim that we have unearthed all of Woolf's published output, left no letter to an editor or political handbill undiscovered. But with the aid of the Leonard Woolf Papers at the University of Sussex, the Library of Leonard and Virginia Woolf at Washington State University, the many excellent secondary sources, librarians dispersed across two continents, and Woolf's own memoirs, we are confident that we have traced the overwhelming majority of his writings.

Introduction

This bibliography attempts to list all published work by Leonard Woolf, and to describe the major collections of his unpublished papers. Section A contains descriptions of all separately published, English-language books and pamphlets written solely by Woolf; translations of his work into foreign languages are mentioned in the notes to each work. Section B includes all books and pamphlets to which Woolf contributed, except anthologies containing work previously published in book form. These contributions to books and pamphlets include prefaces and introductions, translations of Russian literature, work published by committees on which he served, essays or comments solicited by the editors of composite volumes, reprints of periodical contributions in anthologies, and works edited or compiled by Woolf. Section C contains annotated citations of Woolf's periodical articles, and Section D describes the most important collections of his manuscripts.

Excluded from the bibliography are the following tangential or ephemeral materials: Woolf's unsigned publicity items written for the Hogarth Press, such as their catalogues, circulars and dust jackets; works published by the Hogarth Press which he edited prior to publication, such as the Hogarth Lectures on Literature; quotations from his reviews printed on dust jackets; brief passages or letters quoted in secondary sources; unsigned items that cannot be unequivocally attributed to him.

The initial enumeration of Woolf's works was compiled from universal and national bibliographies such as the *National Union Catalog*, library catalogues such as the *British Library Catalogue*, bibliographic utilities such as OCLC, RLIN and WLN, publishing trade sources such as the *English Catalogue of Books*, subject bibliographies, book dealers' and auction catalogues, periodical indexes, and secondary biographical and critical works. This was supplemented by a search of all periodicals which we knew or suspected Woolf to have written for, by references to his literary career in his published letters and in the Leonard Woolf Papers at Sussex, by examination of his annotated review copies in the Woolf Library at Washington State University, and by correspondence with dealers, librarians, archivists and collectors in Britain and the United States.

The entries in Sections A, B and C are arranged chronologically. Whenever possible, exact publication dates have been taken from publisher's records, but in cases where those records were not available, approximate dates were conjectured from book-trade journals, reviews or library accession records.

Although the primary function of this bibliography is enumerative, we hope that the descriptions in Section A are sufficiently detailed to permit a researcher to identify easily a book in hand and to see where it fits into the work's entire publication history. Descriptions in Section A loosely follow the well-known Rupert Hart-Davis/Oxford University Press Soho Bibliographies. We have not routinely described the myriad physical details (the texture of binding cloth or typefaces used) which may be appropriate for books manufactured in an earlier age or written by modern literary figures of greater importance. The entries contain a title-page transcription, format and pagination details, binding description, and publication data. General notes on the composition, content, publication and reception of Woolf's major works are included after the physical description of each title's various editions. Items not personally examined by one of us are marked with an asterisk. The descriptions in Section B are more concise, with references given whenever possible to descriptive bibliographies where more physical detail can be found. Evidence for the attribution of unsigned items is made clear in the notes. Entries in Section C are arranged chronologically, and include full bibliographic citations; most entries also include annotations summarizing the article's contents. Unsigned articles have been verified using the Woolf Papers at Sussex, the Woolf Library at Washington State University, and secondary sources such as the letters and diaries of Virginia Woolf.

Section D describes the major collections of Woolf's manuscripts and many individual documents or letters in widely scattered repositories. Many of Woolf's letters remain in private hands (see the preface to his *Letters* for a list), and some literary or political manuscripts are probably held by repositories who have not reported holdings to centralized sources such as *National Union Catalog of Manuscript Collections*, the *Location Register of Twentieth-century English Literary Manuscripts*, or the on-line bibliographic utilities. The appendices are intended to provide some historical context for Woolf's hard-to-trace pamphlets and ephemeral writings.

Sections A and B are primarily the work of Mr Edmonds, Section C that of Mrs Luedeking, and Section D is a joint effort. Of course no work like this can be accomplished without the help of individuals too numerous to mention. We would, however, like to acknowledge the encouragement given us in the early stages of our work by Angelica Garnett, Quentin Bell, Mrs Ian Parsons, George Spater, George Rylands and Pat Rosenbaum. We would especially like to thank Frederic Spotts, editor of Leonard Woolf's letters, for calling our attention to archival material in English repositories, and Wayne Chapman and Marilyn Manson, for sharing the results of their research in the marked files of the *Nation and Athenaeum*. Other people who provided essential help included Elizabeth Inglis, curator of manuscripts at the University of Sussex, Ann Wierum and Diane Gillespie of Washington State University, Ellen Burke of the State Historical Society of Wisconsin, and Nick Spurrier of Canterbury, dealer in political books who unearthed many obscure Fabian Society and Labour Party pamphlets for us. Our indebtedness to the editors of Virginia Woolf's letters and diaries (Anne Olivier Bell, Joanne Trautmann, and Nigel Nicolson) will be obvious to every user of the bibliography, and Sir Duncan Wilson's *Leonard Woolf: A Political Biography* contained a wealth of relevant detail as well as helpful summaries of political background. We are also indebted to the excellent bibliographic work done by B. J. Kirkpatrick and J. Howard Woolmer, whose books are often cited in the pages that follow. Although these and many other individuals made contributions to our work, they can in no way be held accountable for the book's inevitable omissions or errors (which we hope readers will point out).

We would finally like to thank our respective spouses, Robert Luedeking and Mary Fiorenza, for their help with research and their patience and understanding during the many hundreds of hours we might otherwise have spent together.

Secondary sources mentioned in the text

Birn, Donald S. *The League of Nations Union, 1918–1945*. Oxford: Clarendon Press; New York: Oxford University Press, 1981.

Braithwaite, R. B. *The State of Religious Belief: An inquiry based on "The Nation and Athenaeum" questionnaire*: London: L. & V. Woolf at the Hogarth Press. 1927.

Carrington, Dora. *Carrington: Letters and Extracts from her Diaries*, ed. by David Garnett. Oxford: Oxford University Press, 1979.

Edmonds, Michael. *Lytton Strachey: A Bibliography*. New York: Garland, 1981.

Edwards, Ruth Dudley. *Victor Gollancz: A Biography*. London: Gollancz, 1987.

Goldsworthy, David. *Colonial Issues in British Politics, 1945–61: from 'Colonial Development' to 'Winds of Change'*. Oxford: Clarendon Press, 1971.

Gupta, Partha Sarathi. *Imperialism and the British Labour Movement, 1914–1964*. New York: Holmes & Meier Publishers, 1975.

Keynes, John Maynard. *The Economic Consequences of the Peace*. London: Macmillan, 1919.

Kirkpatrick, B. J. *A Bibliography of Virginia Woolf*. 3rd ed. Oxford: Clarendon Press, 1980.

Labour Party (Great Britain). *Labour Party Bibliography*. London: 1967.

Location Register of Twentieth-Century English Literary Manuscripts and Letters: A Union List . . . Boston, MA: G. K. Hall, 1988.

Martin, Kingsley. *Editor: a Second Volume of Autobiography, 1931–45*. London: Hutchinson, 1968.

Meyerowitz, Selma S. *Leonard Woolf*. Boston: Twayne Publishers, 1982.

Miller, Kenneth. *Socialism and Foreign Policy. Theory and Practice in Britain to 1931*. The Hague: M. Nijhoff, 1967.

Naylor, John F. *Labour's International Policy: The Labour Party in the 1930's*. London: Weidenfeld & Nicolson, 1969.

Pugh, Patricia. *Educate, Agitate, Organize: 100 Years of Fabian Socialism*. London and New York: Methuen, 1984.

Robson, William, ed. *The 'Political Quarterly' in the Thirties*. London: Allen Lane, 1971.

Rosenbaum, S. P. *The Early Literary History of the Bloomsbury Group*, Vol. 1: *Victorian Bloomsbury*. New York: St. Martin's, 1987.

Spater, George, and Ian Parsons. *A Marriage of True Minds: an Intimate Portrait of Leonard and Virginia Woolf*. London: J. Cape/Hogarth Press, 1977; New York: Harcourt Brace Jovanovich, 1977.

Strachey, Lytton. *Eminent Victorians*. London: Chatto & Windus, 1918.

University of Sussex Library. Manuscripts Section. 'Leonard Woolf Papers, c. 1885–1969', Sussex Ms 13. 1977; 1980

—— 'Monks House Papers Catalogue'. 1972.

Wilson, Sir Duncan. *Leonard Woolf: A Political Biography*. London: Hogarth Press, 1978.

Woolf, Virginia. *The Diary of Virginia Woolf*, edited by Anne Olivier Bell. London: Hogarth Press, 1977–85; New York: Harcourt Brace Jovanovich, 1977–85.

Woolf, Virginia. *The Letters of Virginia Woolf*, ed. by Nigel Nicolson, assistant editor Joanne Trautmann. London: Hogarth Press, 1975–80; New York: Harcourt Brace Jovanovich, 1977–82.

Woolmer, J. Howard. *A Checklist of the Hogarth Press, 1917–1946*. Revised and enlarged ed. Revere, Penn.: Woolmer/Brotherson, 1986 (distributed in the UK by St Paul's Bibliographies, Winchester).

Chronology of Leonard Woolf's life

1880   Born 25 Nov. to Sidney Woolf, Q.C., and Marie Woolf, the third of 9 children. Childhood home in Lexham Gardens, London.

1889   Attended St Paul's Preparatory School.

1890–92   Educated at home by tutor.

1892   Death of father; family moved to Putney.

1892–94   Attended Arlington School, Brighton. Won scholarship to St Paul's School.

1894–99   St Paul's School. Won scholarship to Trinity College, Cambridge.

1899–1904 Trinity College, Cambridge. Elected to the Apostles 1902; took first in classical tripos 1902; took second in classical tripos 1903. Graduated Cambridge 1904. Joined Colonial Civil Service Oct. 1904.

1904–11   Ceylon Civil Service.

1905–07   Cadet at Jaffna 1905; Superintendent at pearl fishery 1906; acting Ass't Government Agent at Mannar 1906.

1907–08   Office Assistant at Kandy.

1908–11   Assistant Government Agent at Hambantota. May 1911 returned to London.

1911   Began *The Village in the Jungle*; moved to Bloomsbury.

1912   Resigned from Colonial Civil Service; married Virginia Stephen 10 August; worked with poor in London's East End, joined women's suffrage movement, began to write for *Co-operative News*; secretary to Second Post-Impressionist Exhibition.

1913   *The Village in the Jungle* published. Met Sidney and Beatrice Webb; joined Fabian Society; moved to Asheham House, Sussex.

1914   Lectured for co-operative movement; war broke out, Aug.; commissioned by Fabian Society to write on international organization. *Control of Industry by Co-operators, Education and the Co-operative Movement, The Wise Virgins* all published.

1915   Moved to Hogarth House, Richmond; journalism for *New Statesman*; joined Union of Democratic Control. *The Control of Industry by the People* and *Co-operation and the War* published.

1916   *International Government* and *Taxation* published. Rejected for military service; joined editorial board of *War and Peace*.

1917   Acting editor, *War and Peace*; with Virginia, established the Hogarth Press; helped organize the 1917 Club. *The Future of Constantinople* published.

1918   Editor, *International Review*; appointed secretary, Labour Party Advisory Committee on International Questions. *After the War* and *A Durable Settlement* published.

1919   Purchased Monks House, Rodmell, Sussex; appointed an editor of *Contemporary Review. Co-operation and the Future of Industry* and *International Economic Policy* published.

1920   Adopted as candidate for Parliament; acting political editor of the *Nation. Mandates and Empire, Economic Imperialism,* and *Empire and Commerce in Africa* all published. First disillusionment with Soviet Communism.

1921   *Stories of the East, Scope of the Mandates,* and *Socialism and Co-operation* published.

1922   Lost election for Parliament; resigned from *Contemporary Review. International Co-operative Trade* published.

1923   Appointed literary editor of the *Nation*; moved to Tavistock Sq., Bloomsbury.

1924   Appointed secretary, Labour Party Advisory Committee on Imperial Questions.

1925   *Fear and Politics: A Debate at the Zoo* published.

1926   Supported General Strike.

1927   Lectured on "Imperialism and the Problem of Civilization" to the U.D.C. *Hunting the Highbrow* and *Essays* published.

1928   *The Way of Peace* and *Imperialism and Civilization* published.

1929   With William Robson and others, established the *Political Quarterly;* first issue appeared early in 1930.

1930   Resigned as literary editor of *Nation and Athenaeum.*

1931   Co-editor, the *Political Quarterly*; appointed to Executive Committee of New Fabian Research Bureau, and head of its International Section. *After the Deluge,* vol. I, published.

1935   *Quack, Quack!* published.

1936   Helped found Association for Intellectual Liberty. *The League and Abyssinia* published.

1938   Appointed to Civil Service Arbitration Tribunal; took John Lehmann as partner in Hogarth Press when Virginia sold her share.

1939   Moved to Mecklenburgh Square, Bloomsbury; war declared 3 Sept. *After the Deluge,* vol. II, *The Hotel,* and *Barbarians At the Gate* published.

1940   Tavistock Square home destroyed and Mecklenburgh Square home badly damaged by bombs; moved to Monks House; appointed chairman, Fabian Society International Bureau; became sole editor of the *Political Quarterly. The War for Peace* and *The Future of International Government* published.

1941   Virginia Woolf committed suicide, 28 March. Appointed to Executive Committee of Anglo-Soviet Public Relations Committee.

1942   Elected a director, *New Statesman*; moved back to damaged home in Mecklenburgh Square.

1943   Moved to 24 Victoria Square.

1944   *The International Post-War Settlement* published.
1945   Resigned from Labour Party Advisory committees.
1946   Sold remaining interest in Hogarth Press to Chatto & Windus.
1947   *Foreign Policy: The Labour Party's Dilemma* published.
1953   *Principia Politica* published.
1959   Retired as co-editor of the *Political Quarterly*, but remained its
      literary editor.
1960   Visited Ceylon. *Sowing* published.
1961   *Growing* published.
1962   Retired as literary editor of the *Political Quarterly*.
1963   *Diaries in Ceylon* published.
1964   Awarded honorary doctorate from Sussex University. *Beginning
      Again* published.
1965   Resigned from board of *New Statesman*.
1966   Visited Canada and United States; arranged for Virginia Woolf's
      papers to go to the Berg Collection, New York Public Library.
1967   *Downhill All the Way* published.
1969   Died at Monks House, 14 August. *The Journey Not the Arrival
      Matters* published.

A Separately published books and pamphlets

a. first edition, first issue: Arnold, 1913

THE VILLAGE | IN THE JUNGLE | BY | L.S. WOOLF | LONDON | EDWARD ARNOLD | 1913 | *ALL RIGHTS RESERVED*

Format: [iv] 308 pp. 7⅛ × 5 in.

Pagination: [i] title page as above; [ii] blank; [iii] dedication; [iv] blank; [1] 2–307 text; [308] blank. 16-page catalogue of Arnold's 'Spring Announcements' dated February 1913 sewn in before end-papers.

Binding: Deep blue cloth. Spine blocked in gold: The | Village | in the | Jungle | L.S. | Woolf | ARNOLD. Front cover in gold: [within blind-stamped border] The Village | in the Jungle | L.S. Woolf. Blind-stamped border around back cover. Dust jacket not seen.

Publication: February 1913, at 5s.; the number of copies issued is not known, as publisher's records destroyed.

Notes: 1. 'Printed by T. and A. CONSTABLE, Printers to his Majesty | at the Edinburgh University Press', at foot of p. 307.

2. A second impression (of 'a few hundred copies', according to LW; see General Notes, below) was issued the same year; 'second impression' is stated on the title page, and the undated advertisements contain quotations from reviews of the book. A third impression, also stated on the title page, was printed at the end of 1913 and issued in 1914. Both are bound as above. The exact number of copies of these later impressions is not known, as the publisher's records were destroyed.

b. first edition, second issue: Hogarth Press, 1931

THE VILLAGE IN | THE JUNGLE | LEONARD WOOLF | NEW EDITION [*sic*] | PUBLISHED BY LEONARD & VIRGINIA WOOLF AT THE HOGARTH PRESS, | LONDON, W.C. 1 | 1931

Format: [iv] 308 pp. 7¼ × 4¾ in.

Pagination: [i] title page as above; [ii] *First published 1913* | *Second Impression 1913* | *Third Impression 1913* | *New Edition 1925* | *New Edition 1931*; [iii] dedication; [iv] blank; [1] 2–307 text; [308] blank.

Binding: Medium green cloth. Spine blocked in gold: THE VILLAGE | IN THE JUNGLE | LEONARD | WOOLF | THE | HOGARTH | PRESS. Dust jacket cream paper printed in green.

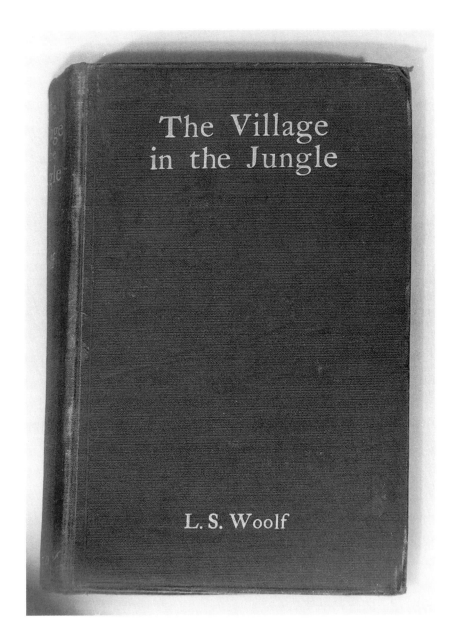

Publication: September 1931, at 7*s.* 6*d.*; 1200 copies were printed.

Notes: 1. PRINTED IN GREAT BRITAIN BY | LOWE AND BRYDONE (PRINTERS) LTD., LONDON, at foot of p. 307.

   2. Woolmer 277.

c. first edition, third issue: Chatto & Windus New Phoenix Library, 1951

THE VILLAGE IN THE JUNGLE | LEONARD WOOLF | [series logo: phoenix, 1¼ × ⅞ in.] | THE NEW PHOENIX | [ornamental 2¼ in. rule] | LIBRARY

Format: [viii] 312 pp. 7⅛ × 4⅝ in.

Pagination: [i-ii] blank; [iii] half-title; [iv] blank; [v] title page as above; [vi] Published by | CHATTO & WINDUS | in association with | THE HOGARTH PRESS LTD | LONDON | * | CLARKE, IRWIN & CO. LTD | TORONTO | Printed in Great Britain by | Lowe and Brydone Printers Limited, | London, N.W. 10 | First published 1913 | Reprinted 1913 (twice), 1925, 1931 | First published in this Library 1951 | All Rights Reserved; [vii] dedication; [viii] blank; [1] 2–307 text; [308–312] blank.

Binding: Light blue cloth. Spine: [purple oval panel 1½ × ⅞ in. bordered in gold on upper spine, on which is in gold:] THE | VILLAGE | IN THE | JUNGLE | [scroll-shaped ornament] | Leonard | Woolf | [at foot: publisher's device ⅝ × ½ in.] | NEW | PHOENIX | LIBRARY. Publisher's device within a 1 in. diameter circle in gold on front cover. White dust jacket printed in red and black.

Publication: 19 March 1951, at 5*s.*; 8080 copies were printed: 4800 were issued in 1951 in this series, 2500 more at 7*s.* 6*d.* in November 1961 bound in pink paper blocked in gold, and the remaining 750 were issued in December 1971 at £1.25 (binding not seen).

d. first edition, fourth issue: Hansa Publishers, 1972

THE VILLAGE | IN THE JUNGLE | LEONARD WOOLF | [publisher's device ½ in. diameter] | 1972 | HANSA PUBLISHERS LIMITED | 'HANSA HOUSE' 26 CLIFFORD AVENUE | COLOMBO 3

Format: [viii] 308 pp. 7 × 4⅞ in.

Pagination: [i-ii] blank; [iii] half-title; [iv] list of works by Woolf; [v] title page as above; [vi] Originally published by | Hogarth Press Ltd | London | First Published 1913 | This Hansa edition 1972 | © M.T. Parsons, 1913 [*sic*] | [5-line reservation statement] | Printed in England; [vii] dedication; [viii] blank; [1] 2–307 text; [308] blank.

Binding: Plain pale blue cloth; dust jacket not seen.

Publication: 1972; price and number of copies unknown.

Note: A second impression (mis-identified on p.[vi] as "This Second Hansa Edition", was issued in July 1974; the number of copies printed is not known.

e. second edition, first issue: Arnold, 1925

THE VILLAGE | IN THE JUNGLE | BY | LEONARD WOOLF | LONDON | EDWARD ARNOLD & CO. | 1925 | *[ALL RIGHTS RESERVED]* [brackets in original]

Format: 304 pp. 7½ × 5 in.

Pagination: [1] title page as above; [2] PRINTED IN THE U.S.A. BY | THE QUINN & BODEN COMPANY | RAHWAY, N.J.; [3] dedication; [4] blank; 5–6 introduction by Woolf; 7–301 text; [302–304] blank.

Binding: Light brown cloth. Spine blocked in dark brown: The | Village | in the | Jungle | L.S. Woolf | ARNOLD. Upper cover in dark brown: The Village | in the Jungle | L.S. Woolf. Dust jacket not seen.

Publication: Late in 1925; the sheets were printed in America and supplied before mid-October, according to Harcourt, Brace correspondence files. The price, exact publication date, and number of copies is not known, as the publisher's records were destroyed; this issue does not appear in the publishing trade bibliographies of the time.

Note: Title page is integral.

f. Second edition, second issue: Harcourt, Brace, 1926

THE VILLAGE | IN THE JUNGLE | BY | LEONARD WOOLF | [publisher's device, 7⁄16 in. sq.] | NEW YORK | HARCOURT, BRACE AND COMPANY

Format: 304 pp. 7⅜ × 5 in.

Pagination: [1] title page as above; [2] PRINTED IN THE U.S.A. BY | THE QUINN & BODEN COMPANY | RAHWAY, N.J.; [3] dedication; [4] blank; 5–6 introduction by Woolf; 7–301 text; [302–304] blank.

Binding: Dark blue cloth. Spine blocked in green: 'THE | VILLAGE | IN THE | JUNGLE | [¼ in. rule] | LEONARD | WOOLF | HARCOURT, BRACE | AND COMPANY. At the upper right of front cover is a blind-stamped panel 2¾ × 2⅛ in. blocked in green: THE | VILLAGE | IN THE | JUNGLE | *by* | LEONARD | WOOLF. Dust jacket white paper printed in gold, navy blue and two shades of green.

Publication: February 1926, at $2.50; the exact number of copies is not known, but 800 copies were sold by June 30, according to publisher's correspondence files.

Note: Some copies have cancel title-page, tipped to front free end-paper.

g. Second edition, third issue: B.R. Publishing, 1975

THE VILLAGE | IN THE JUNGLE | BY | LEONARD WOOLF | *FOREWORD BY* | RHOADS MURPHEY | [publisher's device ½ × ⅜ in.] | B.R. PUBLISHING CORPORATION

Format: [viii] 304 pp. 7 × 4¾ in.

Pagination: [i] title page as above; [ii] First published 1926 | Reprinted 1975 |

Published by: | B.R. Publishing Corporation, | 461, Vivekanand Nagar, | Delhi – 110052. | *Printed at:* | Globe Offset Printers, | 1165, Tokriwalan, | Delhi – 110006; [iii] dedication; [iv] blank; [v] vi-viii, 1–4 foreword by Rhoads Murphey; 5–6 introduction by Woolf; 7–301 text; [302–304] blank.

Binding: Pale brown cloth. Spine blocked in silver: WOOLF | [reading head to foot] THE VILLAGE IN THE JUNGLE | [publisher's device as on title page]. Dust jacket white paper printed in orange.

Publication: 1975, at 50 rupees; the number of copies and exact publication date are not known.

Note: A label fixed to verso of title page (p. [ii]) reads: *Exclusively distributed by –* | D. K. PUBLISHERS' DISTRIBUTORS | 1, Ansari Road, N. Delhi – 110002 | Phone: 274819.

h. *Third edition: Oxford University Press, 1981*

LEONARD WOOLF | THE VILLAGE IN THE JUNGLE | [1 in. ornamental rule] | WITH AN INTRODUCTION BY | E.F.C. LUDOWYK | OXFORD NEW YORK TORONTO DELHI | OXFORD UNIVERSITY PRESS | 1981

Format: [2] [xvi] 180 [10] pp. 7¾ × 5⅛ in.

Pagination: [1–2] blank; [i] biographical notes on Woolf and Ludowyk; [ii] blank; [iii] title page as above; [iv] [publisher's addresses in eight lines, italics] | *Copyright M.T. Parsons 1913* | *Introduction © Oxford University Press 1981* | *First published by Edward Arnold Limited 1913* | *First Hogarth Press edition 1931* | *First issued as an Oxford University Press paperback 1981* | [8-line reservation statement, in italics] | [British Library CIP data in 6 lines, italics] | *Printed in Great Britain by* | *Richard Clay (The Chaucer Press) Ltd* | *Bungay, Suffolk*; [v] dedication; [vi] blank; [vii] viii-xv introduction by Ludowyk; [xvi] blank; [1] fly-title; [2] blank; [3] 4–179 text; [180] blank; [8 pages of publisher's advertisements]; [1–2] blank.

Binding: Stiff white paper wrappers. Printed in black and blue with full-colour illustration of the jungle by Mark Edwards on front, spine and back.

Publication: October 1981, at £2.50 in Britain and $6.95 in U.S.; 10,000 copies were printed, of which 2,040 were sent to the U.S.

General Notes: The Village in the Jungle is LW's most highly regarded novel. The Sinhalese jungle and its inhabitants "fascinated, almost obsessed, me in Ceylon," he wrote. "*The Village in the Jungle* was a novel in which I tried somehow or other vicariously to live their lives. It was also, in some curious way, the symbol of the anti-imperialism which had been growing upon me more and more in my last years in Ceylon." [*Beginning Again,* 1974: 47]. It worked as a catalyst in LW's decision to abandon the colonial service: "The more I wrote [it], the more distasteful became the prospect of success in Colombo." [ibid.: 48].

LW gave conflicting accounts of its origins, stating in different places that he began writing it in August or in October 1911 [*Growing,* 1974: 247; *Beginning Again,* 1974: 47]. He continued to work on it while readjusting to life in London over the next few months. It was apparently finished by the summer of 1912, since E. M. Forster read and criticized a draft of it in May [Forster's *Letters,* no. 103] and Virginia referred to his writing it in the past tense in a letter of June of that year [VW, *Letters:* no. 628]. It was accepted by Edward Arnold on 11 November 1912 [LW, *Letters:* 180] and in a letter to Lytton Strachey the next week Virginia said, "Our great event has been that Arnold has taken Leonard's novel with great praise." [ibid.: no. 653]

LW received the proofs at the very end of the year [LW, *Letters:* 181] and when the book appeared in February 1913 it was greeted by favorable reviews. According to LW, "the first edition sold out at once. . . . Arnold did not take a rosy view of the selling prospects of the book, and when the first edition sold out, he printed only a few hundred copies. Rather to his dismay, I think, he sold these immediately and had to reprint for the second time." [*Beginning Again*, 1974: 88].

Demand for the book continued at a sufficiently steady pace to necessitate a second Arnold edition in 1925. Harcourt, Brace, who had been publishing Virginia Woolf and Lytton Strachey in the U.S. since 1921, planned to bring it out in New York early the next year and supplied the sheets to Arnold. Both these issues contained a new, short preface by LW describing his travels in the Hambantota district and his emotional reaction to the ruins of ancient villages over-run by the jungle.

LW received very little money from *The Village in the Jungle*. In *Beginning Again* he wrote: "By 1929 the book had sold 2,149 copies . . . I got 10% royalty on the first 1000 sold and 15% thereafter." [pp. 88–9] At the end of 1921, he had earned £42 from it, and by 1929 only a total of £63 [ibid.: 89–91]. The American issue proved slightly more lucrative. Harcourt, Brace sold at least 800 copies in 1926, for which LW received a royalty of 10% per copy, or $200 [HBJ Correspondence Files, 16 July 1926, 28 Nov. 1934].

The book, however, has remained in demand, with new printings required every decade or so. It has long been considered a classic in Ceylon, where in the late 1970s it was made into a film under the title *Beddegama* (see "Woolf In the Jungle" by John Cunningham, in the Manchester *Guardian* "Guardian Weekend" section, 1 December 1979, p. 11).

A2*   THE CONTROL OF INDUSTRY BY
CO-OPERATORS AND TRADE UNIONISTS   1914

[within double-ruled border] WOMEN'S CO-OPERATIVE GUILD. | [within ruled border] PAPERS FOR GUIDES. | THE CONTROL OF INDUSTRY | BY CO-OPERATORS AND | TRADE UNIONISTS. | BY | L.S. WOOLF | (MEMBER OF EDMONTON MEN'S GUILD). | PRICE 1D. | TO BE OBTAINED FROM THE GENERAL SECRETARY, | WOMEN'S CO-OPERATIVE GUILD, 28, CHURCH ROW, HAMPSTEAD, | LONDON, N.W.

Format: [original not seen; transcription based on a microfilm copy]

Pagination: [1] 2–16 text.

Binding: not seen.

Publication: January 1914, at 1*d*.; the number of copies issued is not known.

General Note: In the "Women's Corner" of *Co-operative News* for 3 January 1914 [vol xlv, n. 1: 26] appears the note that, "We hope shortly to publish a series of seven papers for guides, [including] 'The Control of Industry by Co-operators and Trade Unionists'; [and] 'The Co-operative College,' by Mr. L. S. Woolf...". On 9 May 1914, it is reported that "The Control of Industry..." was read aloud at a North Lancashire meeting to start a discussion on the relations between local co-ops and trade unions. See Appendix 1 for a summary of LW's writings for the co-operative movement.

A3*   EDUCATION AND THE CO-OPERATIVE MOVEMENT   1914

[within double-ruled border 6 × 3¾ in.] WOMEN'S CO-OPERATIVE GUILD. | [within ruled border ½ × 2½ in.] PAPERS FOR GUIDES. | JANUARY, 1914. | EDUCATION AND | THE CO-OPERATIVE | MOVEMENT. | BY | L.S. WOOLF | (MEMBER OF THE EDMONTON MEN'S CO-OPERATIVE GUILD.) | PRICE 1D. | TO BE OBTAINED FROM THE GENERAL SECRETARY, | WOMEN'S CO-OPERATIVE GUILD, 28, CHURCH ROW, HAMPSTEAD, | LONDON, N.W.

Format: 16 pp. 7⅛ × 4¾ in.

Pagination: [1] 2–15 text; [16].

Binding: White paper wrappers printed in black as above.

Publication: January 1914, at 1*d.*; the number of copies issued is not known.

General Note: This pamphlet expands the themes that LW first stated in a two-part essay entitled "The Proposed Co-operative College", published on 24 May and 31 May 1913 in *Co-operative News* [see items C0024 and C0025]. The value of an educational institution for co-operators was regularly debated in the *News* in the years prior to World War One. Some writers felt it would be an improper use of the movement's capital, which they thought should be channelled toward production or dividends. Others, including LW, felt education was a prerequisite for enhancing the revolutionary function of the movement and extending co-operation over a greater portion of the economy. See notes to A2, and Appendix 1.

A4   THE WISE VIRGINS   1914

a. first edition: Arnold, 1914

THE WISE VIRGINS | A STORY OF WORDS, OPINIONS, AND | A FEW EMOTIONS | BY | L.S. WOOLF | AUTHOR OF "THE VILLAGE IN THE JUNGLE" | LONDON | EDWARD ARNOLD | 1914 | *(ALL RIGHTS RESERVED)*

Format: 336 pp. 7⅜ × 5 in.

Pagination: [1] half-title; [2] blank; [3] title page as above; [4] blank; [5] dedication to

Desmond MacCarthy; [6] blank; [7] contents; [8] blank; [9] 10–336 text. 8-page undated publisher's catalogue sewn in at end.

Binding: Light brown cloth. Spine blocked in white panels. Head of spine in black: THE | WISE | VIRGINS | L.S. | WOOLF; foot in black: ARNOLD. Front cover blocked in white panels; at head in black, THE WISE | VIRGINS, and at foot, L.S. WOOLF. Dust jacket not seen.

Publication: October 1914, at 6*s*; the number of copies issued is not known as the publisher's records were destroyed.

Notes: 1. 'The Anchor Press, Ltd., Tiptree, Essex', on p. 336.

2. Loosely inserted in the Cambridge University copy is a publisher's promotional slip (undated) describing seven of 'Mr. Edward Arnold's New Six Shilling Novels', including this one.

b. second edition, first issue: Hogarth Press, 1979

THE | WISE VIRGINS | *A STORY OF WORDS, OPINIONS* | *AND A FEW EMOTIONS* | BY | LEONARD WOOLF | *WITH AN INTRODUCTION* | *BY* | IAN PARSONS | 1979 | THE HOGARTH PRESS | LONDON

Format: xvi 250 pp. 7¾ × 5 in.

Pagination: [i-ii] blank; [iii] half-title; [iv] *By the same Author* | * | THE VILLAGE IN THE JUNGLE; [v] title page as above; [vi] Published by | The Hogarth Press Ltd | 42 William IV Street | London WC2N 4DF | * | Clarke, Irwin & Co. Ltd | Toronto | [7-line reservation statement] | First published by Edward Arnold | London, October 1914 | [British Library CIP data in 5 lines] | [ISBN] | *Text* © *Leonard Woolf* 1914 | *Introduction* © *Ian Parsons* 1979 | Printed in Great Britain by | REDWOOD BURN LIMITED | TROWBRIDGE & ESHER; [vii] dedication; [viii] blank; [ix] contents; [x] blank; xi-xvi introduction; [1] 2–247 text; [248–250] blank.

Binding: Red mottled paper over boards. Spine blocked in gold: THE | WISE | VIRGINS | . [³⁄₁₆ in. rule] . | LEONARD | WOOLF | THE | HOGARTH | PRESS. Dust jacket glossy white paper printed in orange and pale blue.

Publication: 13 September 1979, at £6.50; 2500 copies were issued.

c. second edition, second issue: Harcourt, Brace, Jovanovich, 1979

THE | WISE VIRGINS | *A STORY OF WORDS, OPINIONS* | *AND A FEW EMOTIONS* | BY | LEONARD WOOLF | *WITH AN INTRODUCTION* | *BY* | IAN PARSONS | [publisher's device ¼ × ³⁄₁₆ in.] | HARCOURT BRACE JOVANOVICH | NEW YORK AND LONDON

Format: [2] xx 254 pp. 8⅜ × 5½ in.

Pagination: [1–2] blank; [i] half-title; [ii] blank; [iii] list of LW's works; [iv] blank; [v] title page as above; [vi] [13 lines of copyright and reservation data] | Printed in the

United States of America | [Library of Congress CIP data in 6 lines] | First American edition | B C D E; [vii] dedication; [viii] blank; [ix] contents; [x] blank; [xi] xii-xviii introduction; [xix] fly-title; [xx] blank; [1] 2–247 text; [248–254] blank.

Binding: Pale brown cloth spine, purplish pink paper over boards. Spine lettering black: [reading head to foot] [ornamental ½ in. rule] | [3⅜ in. rule] | THE WISE VIRGINS | [3⅜ in. rule] | [ornamental ½ in. rule] | LEONARD WOOLF | [publisher's device ¼ × ³⁄₁₆ in.] | [at foot, in three lines:] HARCOURT | BRACE | JOVANOVICH. Dust jacket pale brown paper printed in black, brown and pink.

Publication: November 1979, at $9.95; the number of copies issued is not known.

General Notes: LW began his second novel in a Spanish hotel during his honeymoon. In a letter written 4 September 1912, Virginia described him "on a red plush chair about 6 feet away from me, ... writing the first chapter of his new great work, which is about the suburbs." [VW, *Letters:* no. 645] A few months later (11 April 1913), she gave the following account of his work habits to Violet Dickinson: "All the morning we write in two separate rooms. Leonard is in the middle of a new novel [*The Wise Virgins*]; but as the clock strikes twelve, he begins an article upon Labour for some pale sheet, or a review of French literature for the Times, or a history of Co-operation." [ibid.: no. 665]

These steady habits were apparently productive, for by midsummer he had sent a draft to his family – some of whom were alarmed and displeased by its unflattering portraits of LW's mother and her suburban neighbours [LW, *Letters:* 195–97]. By February 1914 Edward Arnold had read the manuscript and offered to publish it if LW would cut out certain passages which the publisher found offensive [ibid.: 199–200]. These difficulties were overcome, and later that month Virginia noted that Arnold had accepted the book [VW, *Letters:* no. 690], and it appeared in October 1914.

"My second novel," LW wrote in *Beginning Again*, "was published in 1914 simultaneously with the outbreak of war. The war killed it dead and my total earnings from it were twenty pounds." [*Beginning Again*, 1974: 91]. Ian Parsons, in his introduction to the 1979 edition, suspects that LW's own feelings may have helped "kill" the book: "There might well have been another figure for his total earnings had he ever reprinted the book under the Hogarth Press imprint, or allowed anybody else to do so. But he resolutely declined to, and seems to have put it firmly and permanently behind him – perhaps out of consideration for his mother, who lived on until 1939." [*The Wise Virgins*, 1979: xii].

The Wise Virgins was not as enthusiastically received as LW's first novel. Virginia, Vanessa Bell, and E. M. Forster all had mixed feelings about it, and the reviewer in *The Times* was downright snide. In *A Marriage of True Minds*, Spater and Parsons state that "Only a small first edition of *The Wise Virgins* had been printed and only a small part of this printing was sold" [p. 82]. If LW's contract with Arnold was similar to his previous one, at least 400 copies must have been sold to bring him £20.

The Wise Virgins did not disappear entirely without a trace. Though perhaps neglected by intellectuals (the Cambridge University copy was still pristine, even containing its loosely-inserted publisher's advertisements, when I examined it in 1981), it did appeal to a certain class of readers: the Bradford Library and Literary Society copy was borrowed no less than 50 times within two years of publication.

A5   THE CONTROL OF INDUSTRY BY THE PEOPLE
THROUGH THE CO-OPERATIVE MOVEMENT   1915

a. first edition: Women's Co-operative Guild, 1915*

WOMEN'S CO-OPERATIVE GUILD. | [within ruled border ½ × 2½ in.] | PAPERS FOR GUIDES, | JANUARY, 1915. | THE CONTROL OF INDUSTRY | BY THE PEOPLE. | BY | L.S. WOOLF. | PRICE 1D. | TO BE OBTAINED FROM THE GENERAL SECRETARY, | WOMEN'S CO-OPERATIVE GUILD, 28, CHURCH ROW, HAMPSTEAD, | LONDON, N.W.

Format: 16 pp. 7⅛ × 4¾ in.

Pagination: [1] 2–16 text.

Binding: Blue paper wrappers printed in black as above. Co-operative Wholesale Society's Printing Works device on back wrapper.

Publication: January 1915, at 1*d*; the number of copies issued is not known.

b. second edition: Co-operative League of America, 1920*

THE CONTROL OF INDUSTRY | BY THE PEOPLE | *THROUGH* THE CO-OPERATIVE MOVEMENT | BY | LEONARD S. WOOLF | PRICE, 10 CENTS | [⅝ in. rule] | REVISED AND PUBLISHED BY | THE CO-OPERATIVE LEAGUE OF AMERICA | 2 WEST 13TH STREET | NEW YORK | 1920 | [printing trades council logo followed by numerals '181']

Format: 20 pp. 7¼ × 4¾ in.

Pagination: [1] title page as above; [2] blank; 3–20 text.

Binding: White self-wrappers printed in black as above.

Publication: 1920, at 10¢; the number of copies issued and the exact publication date are not known.

Note: Stapled through the fold at pp. 10–11.

General Note: In this pamphlet LW analyses the democratic potential of consumers' co-operation, contrasting it with capitalism, state socialism and syndicalism. The revisions in the American edition include the insertion of section titles, the alteration of spelling, and the substitution of "$" for "£". See Appendix 1.

A6*   CO-OPERATION AND THE WAR   1915

a. part one:*

WOMEN'S CO-OPERATIVE GUILD. | [following two lines are within a ruled border ½ × 2½ in.] PAPERS FOR GUIDES, | JANUARY, 1915. |

CO-OPERATION AND | THE WAR. | I. | EFFECTS OF WAR ON COMMERCE | AND INDUSTRY. | BY | L.S. WOOLF. | PRICE 1D. | TO BE OBTAINED FROM THE GENERAL SECRETARY, | WOMEN'S CO-OPERATIVE GUILD, 28, CHURCH ROW, HAMPSTEAD, | LONDON, N.W.

Format: 16 pp. 7 ¹⁄₁₆ × 4¾ in.

Pagination: [1] 2–16 text.

Binding: Green paper wrappers. Front wrapper printed in black as above; inside of both wrappers blank; back wrapper printed with the device of the Co-operative Wholesale Society Printing Works.

Publication: January 1915, at 1*d*.; the number of copies issued is not known.

b. part two:

WOMEN'S CO-OPERATIVE GUILD. | [following two lines within a ruled border ¾ × 2⅛ in.] PAPERS FOR GUIDES, | JANUARY, 1915. | CO-OPERATION AND | THE WAR. | II. | CO-OPERATIVE ACTION IN | NATIONAL CRISES. | BY | L.S. WOOLF. | PRICE 1D. | TO BE OBTAINED FROM THE | GENERAL SECRETARY, WOMEN'S CO-OPERATIVE GUILD 28, CHURCH ROW, | HAMPSTEAD, LONDON, N.W.

Format: 16 pp. 7½ × 5 in.

Pagination: [1] 2–14 text; [15] blank; [16] Co-operative Printing Society logo [different from that on part 1, above].

Binding: Pale green paper wrappers. Front wrapper printed in black as described above; back and inside of both wrappers blank.

Publication: January 1915, at 1*d*.; the number of copies issued is not known.

General Note: These two pamphlets draw on LW's previous essays on co-operation to explain how the democratic control of industry was affected by the war. They restate in a much-expanded form several of the points raised in "The War: The Duty of the Movement", published on 22 August 1914 in *Co-operative News* [C0065], where LW urged price controls in co-ops and joint efforts with private businesses to eliminate profiteering and minimize suffering caused by the interruption of supplies. See also Appendix 1.

A7 INTERNATIONAL GOVERNMENT 1916

a. first edition: Allen and Unwin/Fabian Society, 1916

INTERNATIONAL GOVERNMENT: | TWO REPORTS BY L.S. WOOLF | PREPARED FOR THE FABIAN | RESEARCH DEPARTMENT, TO– | GETHER WITH A PROJECT BY A | FABIAN COMMITTEE FOR A | SUPERNATIONAL AUTHORITY | THAT WILL PREVENT WAR. |

INTERNATIONAL GOVERNMENT:
TWO REPORTS BY L. S. WOOLF
PREPARED FOR THE FABIAN
RESEARCH DEPARTMENT, TO-
GETHER WITH A PROJECT BY A
FABIAN COMMITTEE FOR A
SUPERNATIONAL AUTHORITY
THAT WILL PREVENT WAR.

 PUBLISHED BY THE FABIAN
SOCIETY AT THE FABIAN
BOOKSHOP, 25 TOTHILL
STREET, WESTMINSTER;
AND GEORGE ALLEN AND
UNWIN, LIMITED, 40, MUSEUM
STREET, LONDON, W.C.

[publisher's device at foot, on left; following lines at foot, at right] PUBLISHED BY THE FABIAN | SOCIETY AT THE FABIAN | BOOK-SHOP, 25 TOTHILL | STREET, WESTMINSTER; | AND GEORGE ALLEN AND | UNWIN, LIMITED, 40, MUSEUM | STREET, LONDON, W.C.

Format: 260 pp. 8⅜ × 5½ in.

Pagination: [1] title page as above; [2] *This volume is the outcome of a Committee of the Fabian Research* | *Department* [. . .] | *First published July,* 1916, | *All Rights Reserved.*; [3] preface; [4] blank; [5–6] contents; [7] 8–87 part one; [88] blank; [89] 90–230 part two; [231] 232–255 part three; [256] select bibliography; 257–259 index; [260] text describing the Fabian Research Dept. 12-page catalogue of publisher's advertisements sewn in at end.

Binding: Brilliant blue cloth. Spine lettering gold: INTER | NATIONAL | GOVERN| MENT | WOOLF | FABIAN | RESEARCH | DEPARTMENT | GEORGE ALLEN | AND UNWIN | LIMITED. Dust jacket not seen.

Publication: July 1916, at 6s.; 1500 copies were issued.

Notes: 1. Contents: Part 1, "An International Authority and the Prevention of War" (by LW); Part 2, "International Government" (by LW); Part 3, "Articles Suggested for Adoption by an International Conference at the Termination of the Present War" (by a Fabian Committee, but drafted mainly by Sidney Webb and LW).

2. Pages 216–33 were reprinted with slight omissions in: Waldo R. Browne, *Leviathan in Crisis* (New York: Viking Press, 1946). Pages 231–55 were issued separately at The Hague in 1917 as "The Supernational Authority That Will Prevent War, by a Fabian Committee"; see B4 for details. Pages 335–37 reprinted in: Henry Pelling, *The Challenge of Socialism* (London: A. & C. Black, 1954; second edition, 1968).

b. second edition, first issue: Brentano's, 1916

INTERNATIONAL | GOVERNMENT | TWO REPORTS BY | L.S. WOOLF | PREPARED FOR THE FABIAN | RESEARCH DEPARTMENT | WITH AN INTRODUCTION BY | BERNARD SHAW | TOGETHER WITH A PROJECT BY A | FABIAN COMMITTEE FOR A SUPER-NATIONAL | AUTHORITY THAT WILL PREVENT WAR | BRENTANO'S | NEW YORK | 1916

Format: xxiv 412 pp. 8 × 5¼ in.

Pagination: [i] half-title; [ii] blank; [iii] title page as above; [iv] *Copyright, 1916, by Brentano's*; v-vii contents; [viii] blank; ix-xxiii introduction by Shaw; [xxiv] blank; [1] division title; [2] blank; 3–412 text.

Binding: Very dark greenish-blue cloth. Spine blocked in gold: [double rule] | INTERNATIONAL | GOVERNMENT | [double rule] | L.S. WOOLF | AND | THE FABIAN SOCIETY | [double rule] | BRENTANO'S | [double rule]. Dust jacket not seen.

Publication: September 1916, at $2.00; the number of copies issued is not known.

c. second edition, second issue: Garland, 1971

INTERNATIONAL | GOVERNMENT | TWO REPORTS BY | LEONARD S. WOOLF | WITH AN INTRODUCTION BY | BERNARD SHAW | AND A NEW INTRODUCTION | FOR THE GARLAND EDITION BY | STEPHEN J. STEARNS | [publisher's device ⅞ × ½ in.] | *GARLAND PUBLISHING, INC., NEW YORK* | *1971*

Format: 22 xxiv 414 pp. 8½ × 5½ in.

Pagination: [1] half-title; [2] series title; [3] title page as above; [4] The new introduction for this | Garland Library Edition is Copyright © 1971, by | *Garland Publishing Inc.* | *24 West 45 St., New York, N.Y. 10036* | [1 in. swelled rule] | All Rights Reserved | [1 in. swelled rule] | [ISBN] | [Library of Congress number] | *Printed in the United States of America*; 5–22 introduction by Stearns; [i]-[xxiv] [1]-412 identical to second edition, first issue, above; [413–414] blank.

Binding: Greyish brown cloth. Spine blocked in gold: [double rule across head] | [reading head to foot:] Woolf *International Government* | [publisher's device] | Garland | [double rule across foot].

Publication: 1971; price and exact publication date unknown; 150 copies were issued.

Note: Issued in "The Garland Library of War and Peace" series.

d. third edition: Allen & Unwin, 1923

INTERNATIONAL | GOVERNMENT | TWO REPORTS BY | L.S. WOOLF | PREPARED FOR THE FABIAN | RESEARCH DEPARTMENT | WITH AN INTRODUCTION BY | BERNARD SHAW | LONDON: GEORGE ALLEN & UNWIN LTD. | RUSKIN HOUSE, 40 MUSEUM STREET, W.C.1

Format: xxiv 388 pp. 8 × 5¼ in.

Pagination: [i] half-title; [ii] blank; [iii] title page as above; [iv] *Copyright, 1916, in the U.S.A. by Brentano's*; v-vi contents; [vii] author's note to the second edition [*sic*]; [viii] blank; ix-xxiii introduction by Shaw; [xxiv] blank; [1] division title; [2] blank; 3–367 text [an exact reprint of the 1916 Brentano's edition to this point]; [368] blank; 369–388 chapter on the Danube Commission taken from LW's *The Future of Constantinople* (A9) and not found in any previous edition.

Binding: Deep purplish-blue cloth. Spine blocked in gold: [double rule] | INTERNATIONAL | GOVERNMENT | WOOLF | [at foot] GEORGE ALLEN | & UNWIN LTD | [double rule]. Front cover blind-stamped with double-ruled border.

Publication: July 1923, at 7*s.* 6*d.*; the number of copies issued is not known.

Notes: 1. *Reprinted in Saxony by the "Obral" process* | BY OSCAR BRANDSTETTER, LEIPZIG, p. 388.

2. Reprinted by the same publisher in July 1929; number of copies not known.

General Notes: When the First World War broke out in August 1914, Bernard Shaw suggested that the Fabian Research Department investigate the history of international organizations and suggest some means of preventing future wars. "As practically nobody knew more than bits and scraps of what had actually been done in the way of International Organization," he wrote in the introduction to the American edition, "the Department had to begin by finding an investigator and skilled writer with the necessary qualifications and devotion for the task of preparing a report and suggesting conclusions ... the man was found in Mr. L. S. Woolf, who turned cheerfully from *belles lettres* to the production of the present volume on terms which would certainly have been rejected with emphasis by a dock laborer." [*International Government*, N.Y., 1916: xviii-xix]

In fact, it was Beatrice Webb who formally proposed the job to LW in December 1914; he agreed to write the report for £100 – money given to the Fabian Society for the purpose by Quaker philanthropist Joseph Rowntree. [Wilson, *Leonard Woolf:* 62; and Shaw, above]

The details of the book's composition and the roles played by LW, Sidney Webb, and the members of the Fabian supervisory committee are discussed at length in chapter four of Sir Duncan Wilson's biography of LW (to which this brief summary is much indebted). Though initially so discouraged that he thought of abandoning the task, LW was well under way by the end of January 1915: "He has already grasped his Arbitration – such is the male mind – & will, I see, go through with it straight off," Virginia wrote on January 26th [VW, *Diary*, 1:28 and 1:22]. LW completed part one of the finished book, "An International Authority and the Prevention of War", in the first four months of 1915. It was vetted by the supervising Fabian committee in April, and was approved after a favorable, though not entirely uncritical, discussion.

LW and Sidney Webb then tried to implement its principles in "articles suggested for adoption by an international conference at the end of the present war"; this draft constitution for a supernational authority was published as part three of the book. These two sections, LW's "An International Authority ..." and the draft articles, appeared as a special supplement to the *New Statesman* on 10 July and 17 July 1915 under the title, "Suggestions for the Prevention of War" [see C0078–79].

When these two sections were completed in the spring of 1915, the committee suggested that LW "continue the work by investigating all the non-governmental international structures" already in place [S. Webb to LW, 25 May 1915, quoted in Wilson, *Leonard Woolf:* 75]. These ranged from the Universal Postal Union to an International Association for the Suppression of Useless Noises [*International Government*, New York, 1916: 167]. Working from a variety of government blue books, annual reports, and personal interviews, LW analysed the ways in which international co-operation already functioned. The resulting work, written during 1915 and 1916 and simply called "International Government", was longer than the two earlier sections combined, and was printed as part two of the published book.

All three parts were issued in July 1916 by Allen & Unwin and the Fabian Society under the title *International Government*. The influence of the Fabian plans on the actual structure of the League of Nations is explained in admirable detail by Sir Duncan Wilson. The various other plans suggested by participants at the Versailles conference are printed and discussed in Florence Wilson's *The Origins of the League Covenant: Documentary History of Its Drafting* (London: Hogarth Press, 1928) and John H. Latane's *Development of the League of Nations Idea* (NY: Macmillan, 1932). Translations of LW's book appeared in Paris, Stockholm and Zurich during the peace negotiations, and Colonel Edward M. House, who played a major role in drafting the US proposals, is known to have possessed a copy at the time [Spater and Parsons, 1977: 83n].

The best summary of LW's contribution to the subject is found in a letter by Philip Noel-Baker, recipient of the Nobel Peace Prize, published in *The Times* on 21 August 1969, shortly after LW's death:

> In Dec. 1918, when the Foreign Office was beginning to organise its League of Nations Section, the late Sydney Waterlow 'discovered' Woolf's book.... He condensed the book into a brilliant F.O. 'print', laying emphasis on Woolf's vision of the scope for international co-operation over labour conditions, public health, transport, economic and social planning, etc. Lord Cecil, the head of the section, ... incorporated virtually the whole of Woolf's ideas into the British Draft Covenant which he gave to Woodrow Wilson in Paris. Woolf thus played an important part in giving concrete form to the general ideas about a League then current, and in particular in launching the conception of the League's technical, social, economic and financial work, which has developed into a dozen UN Agencies, from the I.L.O. and the International Bank to the World Meteorological Organisation.

A8*   TAXATION   1916

WOMEN'S CO-OPERATIVE GUILD. | [floral device ⅛ × ¼ in.] | [within double-ruled border 1¾ × 3¾ in.:] TAXATION: | 1. – WHAT IT IS. | 2. – METHODS AND USES. | 3. – PRINCIPLES. | BY | L.S. WOOLF. | [⅞ in. rule] | TO BE OBTAINED, PRICE THREEPENCE, FROM THE WOMEN'S | CO-OPERATIVE GUILD, 28, CHURCH ROW, HAMP-STEAD, N.W. | (SPECIAL TERMS IF MORE THAN 12 ARE ORDERED.)

Format: 52 pp. 7¼ × 4¾ in.

Pagination: [1] division title; [2] blank; [3] 4–50 text; [51–52] blank.

Binding: Grey paper wrappers printed in black as above. Co-operative Wholesale Society's Printing Works device at centre of back wrapper.

Publication: 1916, at 3*d.*; the exact publication date and number of copies issued are not known.

General Note: From 5 to 8 October 1915 the Women's Co-operative Guild held a school for its members at Hampstead. At the meeting of the central committee on 4 and 5 October, it was voted to issue some of the lectures, including LW's three on taxation, as pamphlets. The pamphlet was reviewed favorably and at length by Janet Case in *Co-operative News* (xlvii, 38: 961) on 15 September 1916, where the principal arguments are summarized and several long quotations are printed. See also Appendix 1.

A9   THE FUTURE OF CONSTANTINOPLE   1917

a. first issue: Allen & Unwin, 1917

THE FUTURE OF | CONSTANTINOPLE | BY | LEONARD S. WOOLF | AUTHOR OF "INTERNATIONAL GOVERNMENT" | "THE VILLAGE

IN THE JUNGLE," ETC. | [publisher's device 1¼ in. sq.] | LONDON: GEORGE ALLEN & UNWIN LTD. | RUSKIN HOUSE 40 MUSEUM STREET, W.C.I

Format: 112 pp. 7 × 4¾ in.

Pagination: [1–2] blank; [3] half-title; [4] publisher's advertisements; [5] title page as above; [6] *First published in 1917* | *(All rights reserved)*; [7] quotation from Lord Brooke; [8] blank; 9 contents; [10] blank; 11–109 text; [110–112] publisher's advertisements.

Binding: Reddish brown cloth. Spine blocked in gold: [blind-stamped double rule] | THE | FUTURE | OF | CONSTANTINOPLE | LEONARD S. | WOOLF | GEORGE ALLEN | & UNWIN LTD | [blind-stamped double rule across foot]. Binding variant: Greyish blue cloth. Spine as above in black. At foot of front cover: SPECIAL U.D.C. EDITION | [2¾ in. rule]; a copy in this binding is in the Woolf Collection at Washington State University. Dust jackets not seen.

Publication: June 1917, at 2s. 6d.; 1030 copies were issued.

Notes: 1. *Printed in Great Britain by* | UNWIN BROTHERS, LIMITED, THE GRESHAM PRESS, WOKING AND LONDON, on p. 109.
    2. Advertisements for this issue appeared in Sept. 1917 in LW's *The Framework of a Lasting Peace* (B3).

b. second issue: Macmillan, 1917

THE FUTURE OF | CONSTANTINOPLE | BY | LEONARD S. WOOLF | AUTHOR OF "INTERNATIONAL GOVERNMENT" | "THE VILLAGE IN THE JUNGLE," ETC. | [publisher's device 1¼ in. sq.] | NEW YORK: THE MACMILLAN COMPANY | LONDON: GEORGE ALLEN & UNWIN LTD.

Format: 112 pp. 7 × 4¾ in.

Pagination: Identical to the first issue, above, but for title page [as above].

Binding: Identical to first issue, but at foot of spine MACMILLAN is above blind-stamped double rule. Dust jacket not seen.

Publication: July 1917, at $1.00; 250 copies, imported from England, were issued.

Note: Printer's note on p. 109 is identical to that in the first issue; title page is a cancel; advertisements on pp. [110–112] are for Allen & Unwin titles.

General Notes: Drawing in part on the ideas presented in *International Government*, A7, LW urged that Constantinople be administered after the war by an international regime. The book contained an historical account of the International Danube Commission (founded in 1865) which was later incorporated into the 1923 Allen & Unwin edition of *International Government*. The "Special U.D.C. Edition" was for distribution to members of the Union for Democratic Control, an organization founded in 1914 to combat secret diplomacy, foster disarmament, restrain imperialism and establish some form of international government.

A10*   A DURABLE SETTLEMENT AFTER THE WAR
BY MEANS OF A LEAGUE OF NATIONS   1918

A DURABLE SETTLEMENT | AFTER THE WAR BY MEANS OF | A LEAGUE OF NATIONS.

Format: Broadsheet, printed on both sides. 8½ × 5⅜ in.

Publication: January 1918, by the League of Nations Society; number of copies issued is not known.

Notes: 1. 'League of Nations Society Publication No. 21. | 1, Central Buildings, S.W.1. January, 1918.' at head of recto.

2. HEADLEY BROS., ASHFORD, KENT, & 18 DEVONSHIRE ST., E.C.2. at foot of verso.

3. Signed at end of text, 'L.S. WOOLF, | Hogarth House, Richmond, Surrey.'

4. The only copy which could be located for examination was at the Hoover Institution for the Study of War, Revolution and Peace, at Stanford University, California.

A11*   AFTER THE WAR   1918

[within a ruled border 5⅞ × 3⅝ in.] | AFTER THE WAR. | [3⅛ in. double rule, with a triangular ornament beneath] | HOW THE WORKERS ARE BEING | ASKED TO SET UP THE CO-OP | ERATIVE COMMONWEALTH OF | :: THE HAPPY CAPITALISTS :: | [¾ in. rule] | BY LEONARD WOOLF. | [ornament, ⅜ in. sq.] | REPRINTED FROM THE "CO-OPERATIVE NEWS," NOV. 9TH & 16TH, 1918. | [¾ in. rule] | PRINTED BY THE CO-OPERATIVE NEWSPAPER SOCIETY, MANCHESTER.

Format: 12 pp. 7¼ × 5 in.

Pagination: [1] cover-title as above; [2] blank; [3] 4–11 text; [12] blank.

Binding: Self-wrappers, as above.

Publication: November 1918?; price and number of copies issued are unknown.

Notes: 1. 'Printed by the Co-operative Newspaper Society, Manchester.', at foot of p. 11.

2. The only copy located for examination was at the Hoover Institution for the Study of War, Revolution and Peace, at Stanford University, California.

A12   CO-OPERATION AND THE FUTURE
OF INDUSTRY   1919

a. first issue: Allen & Unwin, 1919

CO-OPERATION & THE | FUTURE OF INDUSTRY | BY | LEONARD S.

WOOLF | AUTHOR OF "THE VILLAGE IN THE JUNGLE," | "INTER-NATIONAL GOVERNMENT," ETC. | [publisher's device 1¼ in. sq.] | LONDON: GEORGE ALLEN & UNWIN LTD. | RUSKIN HOUSE 40 MUSEUM STREET, W.C.I

Format: 144 pp. 7¼ × 4¾ in.

Pagination: [1] half-title; [2] list of LW's works; [3] title page as above; [4] *First published in 1918* [*sic*] | *(All rights reserved)*; [5] preface; [6] contents; 7–138 text; 139–141 index; [142–144] publisher's advertisements.

Binding: Pale blue cloth. Spine blocked in dark blue: [rule across head] | CO-OPERATION | AND THE | FUTURE OF | INDUSTRY | WOOLF | GEORGE ALLEN | & UNWIN LTD | [rule across foot]. Front cover dark blue with a ruled border. Dust jacket of third impression blue grey paper, dark blue lettering.

Publication: January 1919, at 5 shillings; 1300 copies were issued.

Notes: 1. *Printed in Great Britain by* | UNWIN BROTHERS, LIMITED, THE GRESHAM PRESS, WOKING AND LONDON, p. 141.
2. Further impressions were issued in July 1919 (1000 copies), Nov. 1920 (1164 copies), and May 1928 (1500 copies).

b. *second issue: Macmillan, 1919*

CO-OPERATION & THE | FUTURE OF INDUSTRY | BY | LEONARD S. WOOLF | AUTHOR OF "THE VILLAGE IN THE JUNGLE," | "INTER-NATIONAL GOVERNMENT," ETC. | [publisher's device 1¼ in. sq.] | LONDON: GEORGE ALLEN & UNWIN LTD. | RUSKIN HOUSE 40 MUSEUM STREET, W.C.I | NEW YORK: THE MACMILLAN COMPANY

Format: Identical to first issue, above.

Pagination: Identical to first issue but for the title page [as above].

Binding: Identical to first issue but at foot of spine THE | MACMILLAN | COMPANY is above rule across spine. Dust jacket not seen.

Publication: May 1919, at $2.00; the number of copies issued is not known.

Notes: 1. Printer's note on p. 141 is identical to that in the first issue and the title page is a cancel.
2. A comparison of advertisements appears to date this before the second English impression of July 1919.

General Notes: According to correspondence in the Woolf Papers at Sussex, early in 1913 LW proposed a volume on co-operation to the publishers Williams & Norgate, for inclusion in their "Home University Library" series. Virginia's cousin Herbert Fisher was an editor of the series, and their friends Lytton Strachey and G. E. Moore had each recently published books for it. LW's work for the Fabian Society on *International Government* presumably interfered with his progress, however, because he didn't sign a contract until two years later, finally delivering the manuscript in December 1915.

Williams & Norgate delayed publishing the book (ostensibly due to wartime shortages of paper), and throughout 1916 and 1917 LW tried to provoke them into honouring the terms of their contract. When in the spring of 1918 he finally threatened legal action, Williams & Norgate cancelled his contract and returned the manuscript.

LW had meanwhile been in touch with Allen & Unwin, who hoped to bring it out the following year. He corrected the proofs in the autumn of 1918 (commenting 'It will be a nasty looking vol[ume]' [LW, *Letters:* 222]), and the book finally appeared in January 1919 [VW, *Letters:* no. 888]. In 1923 a Swedish translation was published in Stockholm as *Kooperationen och den Ekonomiska Utvecklingen.*

A13   INTERNATIONAL ECONOMIC POLICY   1919

THE LABOUR PARTY. | [1⅝ in. double rule] | INTERNATIONAL | ECONOMIC POLICY | BY | L.S. WOOLF. | [½ in. rule] | PRICE 2D.; POST FREE 2½ D. | [½ in. rule] | 33, ECCLESTON SQUARE, LONDON, S.W.1

Format: 12 pp. 9⅝ × 6⅛ in.

Pagination: [1] 2–10 text; [11] blank; [12] [device of the Co-operative Printing Society, 1¾ × 1¼ in., at centre].

Binding: Pale green paper wrappers. Front wrapper printed in black as above; back wrapper blank.

Publication: 1919? (see below), at 2*d.* ('2½ d post-free; 10s 6d per dozen, carriage paid', according to inside of back wrapper); the exact publication date and the number of copies issued are not known.

Notes: 1. Printed on very poor quality paper; all copies examined were extremely fragile.

2. The Labour Party official file copy is dated in manuscript, "1919–1920?". The text was checked by the Labour Party advisory committee on international questions on 13 October 1919 and a copy was acquired by the Bodleian Library the following March (Gupta, p. 28, note).

3. See Appendix 2.

General Notes: In this forceful, anti-imperialist pamphlet, LW discusses four main questions: protectionism and free trade, economic relations within the British empire, the new international conditions created by the League of Nations, and the possibility of a co-operative international economic order to replace the competitive imperialist one. He opposes protectionism and recommends abolition of imperial preference in trade with the colonies. He urges Labour to demand that throughout the Third World land be declared the inalienable property of the native inhabitants, that no native inhabitants be compelled to work for wages, and that the wealth generated by European exploitation be channelled toward educating the indigenous populations for self-government. He proposes the creation of a League "world economic council" to regulate international credit, monitor and help distribute the world's supply of food in order to prevent famine, foster mutually beneficial treaties between nations, and otherwise facilitate harmonious economic development. In the final paragraph he recommends that the League utilize each nation's co-operative movement in its economic work, and proposes the unification of the various national co-operative societies into a grand international co-operative organization supported by the League.

A14 EMPIRE AND COMMERCE IN AFRICA 1920

a. first issue: Labour Research Dept/Allen & Unwin, 1920

EMPIRE & COMMERCE | IN AFRICA | A STUDY IN ECONOMIC IMPERIALISM | BY | LEONARD WOOLF | [8-line quotation from Montesquieu] | [at foot, left: publisher's device 1¼ in. sq.] | [at foot, right:] PUBLISHED BY THE LABOUR | RESEARCH DEPARTMENT, 34 | ECCLESTON SQUARE, WEST | MINSTER; AND BY GEORGE | ALLEN AND UNWIN, LIMITED, 40 | MUSEUM STREET, LONDON, WC.I.

Format: 384 pp. 8½ × 5⅜ in.

Pagination: [i] half-title; [ii] list of LW's works; [iii] title page as above; [iv] blank; v acknowledgements; [vi] blank; vii contents; viii quotation from Pascal; [1] division title; [2] blank; 3–374 text and index; [375–376] advertisements for the Labour Research Dept. and its publications.

Binding: Green cloth spine, pale green paper over boards. Spine blocked in gold: EMPIRE | AND | COMMERCE | IN | AFRICA | LEONARD | WOOLF | LABOUR | RESEARCH | DEPARTMENT | AND | Geo. Allen & Unwin, Ld. [*sic*]. Dust jacket not seen.

Publication: 14 January 1920, at 20*s*.; the number of copies issued is not known.

Notes: 1. *Printed by* R.&.R. CLARK, LIMITED, *Edinburgh*., on p. 374.

2. Pages 334–35 and 356–58 were reprinted in George Bennett, *The Concept of Empire* (London: A. & C. Black, 1953; second edition, 1962).

b. second issue: Macmillan, 1920

[Title page is identical to that of the first issue but for the imprint at the lower right:] NEW YORK: THE MACMILLAN | COMPANY. LONDON: THE LABOUR | RESEARCH DEPARTMENT, 34 ECCLES | TON SQUARE, S.W.1., AND GEORGE | ALLEN AND UNWIN, LIMITED, | 40 MUSEUM STREET, W.C.1.

Format: 384 pp. 8⅜ × 5⅜ in.

Pagination: Identical to the first issue, above, but for title page [as above].

Binding: Identical to first issue but imprint at foot of spine reads: NEW YORK | THE MACMILLAN COMPANY | LONDON | LABOUR | RESEARCH | DEPART-MENT | AND | Geo. Allen & Unwin, Ld. Dust jacket not seen.

Publication: April 1920, at $7.00; the number of copies issued is not known.

Note: This issue contains the same printer's note on p. 374, and the same advertisements on pp. [375–76], as the first issue.

c. third issue: Hogarth Press, 1925

[Hogarth Press records indicate that they published a "Cheap Edition" in

1925; see Woolmer 80. Although they advertised it in their catalogues and circulars starting in 1926, no copies could be located for examination by either Howard Woolmer or ourselves. The advertisements describe it as demy 8vo and priced at 7s. 6d.]

d. fourth issue: Fertig, 1968

EMPIRE & COMMERCE | IN AFRICA | A STUDY IN ECONOMIC IMPERIALISM | BY | LEONARD WOOLF | [8-line quotation from Montesquieu] | HOWARD FERTIG | [1⅞ in. rule] | NEW YORK [dot] 1968

Format: 390 pp. 8⅞ × 6 in.

Pagination: [1–2] blank; [i] half-title; [ii] blank; [iii] title page as above; [iv] First published in 1920 | HOWARD FERTIG, INC. EDITION 1968 | Published by arrangement with George Allen & Unwin, Ltd. | *All Rights Reserved.* | [Library of Congress card no.] | For sale only in the United States of America and its dependencies | PRINTED IN THE UNITED STATES OF AMERICA | BY NOBLE OFFSET PRINTERS, INC. | [printer's union device]; [v] acknowledgements; [vi] blank; vii contents; [viii] quotation from Pascal; [1] division title; [2] blank; 3–374 text and index; [375–380] blank.

Binding: Dark blue cloth. Spine blocked in gold: [triple rule] | LEONARD | WOOLF | [rule] | Empire | and | Commerce | in | Africa | [triple rule] | HOWARD | FERTIG.

Publication: June 1968, at $9.00; 720 copies issued.

Note: Although this issue was produced in association with Allen and Unwin Ltd., of London, neither publisher's records shed light on the details of the arrangement.

e. fifth issue: Allen & Unwin, 1968

EMPIRE & COMMERCE | IN AFRICA | A STUDY IN ECONOMIC IMPERIALISM | BY | LEONARD WOOLF | [8-line quotation from Montesquieu] | LONDON | GEORGE ALLEN AND UNWIN LTD

Format: 390 pp. 8¾ × 5¾ in.

Pagination: [1–2] blank; [i] half-title; [ii] blank; [iii] title page as above; [iv] First published in 1920 | Reprinted 1968 | [6-line copyright reservation statement] | PRINTED IN THE UNITED STATES OF AMERICA; [v] acknowledgements; [vi] blank; vii contents; [viii] quotation from Pascal; [1] division title; [2] blank; 3–374 text and index; [375–380] blank.

Binding: Dark purple cloth. Spine blocked in silver: [the following two lines reading vertically, head to foot:] EMPIRE AND COMMERCE IN AFRICA | LEONARD WOOLF | [horizontally:] GEORGE | ALLEN | AND | UNWIN. Dust jacket pale orange paper printed in dark brown.

Publication: October 1968, at 50s.; the number of copies issued is not known.

Note: Although this issue was produced in association with Howard Fertig, Inc., in the United States, neither publisher's records shed light on the details of the arrangement.

General Notes: In the autumn of 1916, Sidney Webb decided that the Fabian Society ought to conduct a detailed analysis of international commerce along the lines of LW's *International Government* [Wilson: 112; VW *Diary*, 1: 229n]. In December of that year the Fabian Society Executive approved the commission of such a work and on 23 February 1917 LW signed a contract to produce "a volume on International Trade" [Wilson: 112]. During the summer and autumn of 1917 he began to investigate this enormous subject, with Virginia helping by "copying out relevant statistics from books and reports lent to LW by the library of the London School of Economics" [VW *Diary*, 1: 229n; VW *Letters*, no. 886].

By October 1917 LW had decided to confine the scope of the book to "imperial trade and exploitation"; the Fabian Society agreed, and Sidney Webb suggested that he concentrate especially on Africa and China [Wilson: 113]. About the same time, he engaged Alix Sargant-Florence, soon to marry James Strachey, as a research assistant [VW *Diary*, 1: 716]. In his autobiography LW recalled that "I wrote [it] in 1918 for the Fabian Society . . . and I did a great deal of intensive reading for it." [*Downhill All the Way* (A42): 83]. At the end of that year, Virginia noted in her diary, "L's book is almost done; February will see it finished most likely" [VW *Diary*, 1: 228–29]. By March 1919 it must have been completed since Virginia quotes Sidney Webb's praise of it and comments that "it is to be printed directly by Clark of Edinburgh, & will be out, perhaps, by June" [VW *Diary*: 250].

In fact, publication took much longer. LW was correcting the proofs in August 1919, [VW *Letters*, no. 1075] and Virginia wrote that it might "be out any day now" in October [VW *Letters*, no. 1084]. LW received six advance copies in the last week of December and the book was finally available on 14 January 1920 [VW *Diary*, 1:317, 2:8].

Reviews were mixed along predictable lines, and LW received letters of praise from Goldsworthy Lowes Dickinson and Maynard Keynes. The book contained the most penetrating and pragmatic analysis of imperialism yet published (Hobson's and Lenin's earlier works being largely theoretical), and was couched in an engaging and accessible style that continues to read well. LW's occasional righteous indignation and icy sarcasm echoed Keynes's *Economic Consequences of the Peace* and Strachey's *Eminent Victorians,* which had been published shortly before. Although Philip Noel-Baker claimed that the book "stirred the conscience of the Colonial Powers, and evoked the sense of trusteeship for subject peoples" [Spater & Parsons: 94], its more tangible effect was to refine LW's criticism of imperialism and encourage the growth of his theory of communal psychology as a force in history.

A15   MANDATES AND EMPIRE   1920

a. first issue: League of Nations Union, 1920

MANDATES | AND EMPIRE | BY | LEONARD WOOLF | *THE WRITER OF THIS PAMPHLET IS ALONE RESPONSIBLE | FOR EXPRESSIONS OF OPINION CONTAINED IN IT.* | LONDON: THE LEAGUE OF NATIONS UNION, | 15, GROSVENOR CRESCENT, S.W.1 | 1920

Format: 20 pp. 8¼ × 5½ in.

Pagination: [1] title page as above; [2] blank; [3] list of pamphlets available from the

League of Nations Union; [4] blank; 5–18 text; 19–20 questionnaire and bibliography.

Binding: Orange stiff paper wrappers. Front cover printed in black: [within double ruled border] MANDATES | AND EMPIRE | BY | LEONARD WOOLF | LONDON: | THE LEAGUE OF NATIONS UNION, | 15, GROSVENOR CRESCENT, S.W.1 | 1920 | PRICE – ONE SHILLING NET.

Publication: September? 1920, at 1s.; the exact publication date and number of copies issued are not known.

Note: BRITISH PERIODICALS LTD., *Printers*, Gough Square, Fleet Street, London, E.C.4, at foot of p. 20.

b. second issue: British Periodicals, 1920

[Title page is identical to the first issue, above, but for the imprint, which reads:] LONDON: | BRITISH PERIODICALS, LIMITED, | GOUGH HOUSE, GOUGH SQUARE, | FLEET STREET, E.C.4. | 1920

Format: Identical to the first issue, above.

Pagination: Identical to the first issue, but for title page [as above].

Binding: Orange paper wrappers printed in black: [within double-ruled border:] MANDATES | AND EMPIRE | BY | LEONARD WOOLF | LONDON: | BRITISH PERIODICALS, LIMITED, | GOUGH HOUSE, GOUGH SQUARE, | FLEET STREET, E.C. 4 | 1920 | PRICE – ONE SHILLING NET.

Publication: September? 1920, at 1s.; the exact publication date and number of copies issued are not known.

Notes: 1. The same printer's note appears at foot of p. 20 as in first issue.
2. Reviewed by Janet Case in *Co-operative News,* 25 September 1920.

General Notes: After briefly reviewing the history of modern imperialism and the terms of Article 22 of the League of Nations Covenant (which established mandates for Allied control over former German and Turkish colonies), LW addresses "some of the most important conditions which will be required if the system is to be successfully and honestly carried out." These are, that all land legally and functionally remain the property of the indigenous peoples, that every family own enough land to support itself, that leases of land to Europeans be temporary and do not curtail the general economic development of the community, and that forced labour be prohibited. Further, LW argues that the mandatory nations of Europe must establish a full range of educational institutions for the native populations in order to promote economic development and democratic government by the inhabitants; he also urges that local self-government be established at once, and that power over central governments be transferred as swiftly as possible from Europeans to Africans.

Recognizing that the imperialist powers of Europe are unlikely to subscribe to these conditions and sincerely embrace the mandate system, LW argues that the League must forcefully and directly control, inspect and supervise the administration of mandates. If necessary, the League must revoke the mandates of nations that do not fulfill the terms of article 22. Finally, if events prove that the mandate system works in the former Axis colonies, LW argues that it be extended to the colonies of the Allied powers as well.

A16   ECONOMIC IMPERIALISM   1920

a. first issue: Swarthmore Press | Harcourt, Brace, 1920

ECONOMIC | IMPERIALISM | BY | LEONARD WOOLF | AUTHOR OF
"EMPIRE AND | COMMERCE IN AFRICA," ETC. | 1920 | [at foot, left]
LONDON: | THE SWARTHMORE | PRESS LTD. | 72, OXFORD
STREET, W. 1 | [at foot, right] NEW YORK: | HARCOURT BRACE | &
HOWE | 1, WEST 47TH STREET

Format: 112 pp. 7¼ × 4¾ in.

Pagination: [1–2] blank; [3] half-title; [4] blank; [5] title-page as above; [6] blank; [7]
contents; [8] foreword by series editor; [9] 10–111 text; [112] advertisements for the
series.

Binding: Orange paper wrappers (English copies) or red cloth (American copies).
English copies: Spine printed in black: The | Swarthmore | International | Handbooks
| [vertically, reading head to foot] ECONOMIC IMPERIALISM By L.S. WOOLF | 2/6
| NET | Swarthmore Press. Front cover printed in black: [within ornamental border
6⅜ × 3⅞ in.] *The Swarthmore International Handbooks | Edited by G. Lowes
Dickinson* | ECONOMIC | IMPERIALISM | By L.S.WOOLF | [publisher's device ¾
in. sq.] | *Two Shillings and Sixpence net* | 1920 | [publisher's addresses as on title
page]. Back wrapper is printed with advertisements for titles 1–7 in the series, and the
Swarthmore Press is listed as the sole publisher. *American copies:* Spine black, reading
head to foot: ECONOMIC IMPERIALISM LEONARD WOOLF; front cover:
INTERNATIONAL RELATIONS SERIES | *Edited by* | G. LOWES DICKINSON;
dust jacket grey paper printed in black with advertisements for other titles in the series
and other Harcourt, Brace & Co. books.

Publication: London, November 1920, at 2*s.* 6*d.*; the number of copies issued is not
known; New York, March 1921, at $1.00; the number of copies issued is not known.

Notes: 1. 'Headley Brothers, 18, Devonshire Street, E.C.2 and Ashford, Kent.', at
foot of p. 111.

    2. In the advertisements on p. [112], only seven titles in the series had been
published when this issue appeared and the Swarthmore Press is listed as sole
publisher.

b. second issue: Swarthmore Press | Labour Publishing Co., 1921

ECONOMIC | IMPERIALISM | BY | LEONARD WOOLF | AUTHOR OF
"EMPIRE AND | COMMERCE IN AFRICA," ETC. | 1921 | LONDON: [at
foot, left:] THE SWARTHMORE | PRESS LTD. | 40, MUSEUM STREET,
W.C.1 | [at foot, right:] THE LABOUR PUBLISHING | CO. LTD. | 6,
TAVISTOCK SQUARE, W.C.1

Format: 112 pp. 7¼ × 4¾ in.

Pagination: Identical to first issue, but for the title page [as above].

Binding: Orange paper wrappers printed in black as the first issue, except that the title
on the spine reads foot to head, eight titles (rather than seven) are advertised on the

back wrapper, and the Swarthmore Press and the Labour Publishing Co., Ltd., are given as joint publishers.

Publication: 1921, at 2*s.* 6*d.*; the exact publication date and number of copies issued are not known.

Notes: 1. The same printer's note as in the first issue appears on p. 111.

2. According to the advertisements on p. [112], eight titles in the series had been published when this issue appeared, and the Swarthmore Press and Labour Publishing Co. are listed as joint publishers.

c. third issue: Fertig, 1970

ECONOMIC | IMPERIALISM | *BY* | LEONARD WOOLF | NEW YORK | HOWARD FERTIG | 1970

Format: 112 pp. 7¹⁵⁄₁₆ × 5¼ in.

Pagination: Identical to the first issue, above, but for the title page [as above] and p. [6], which reads: First published in 1920 | Howard Fertig, Inc. Edition 1970 | Published by arrangement with the author. | *All rights reserved.* | [Library of Congress card no.] | PRINTED IN THE UNITED STATES OF AMERICA | BY NOBLE OFFSET PRINTERS, INC. | [Amalgamated Lithographers Union device].

Binding: Dark blue cloth. Spine blocked in silver: [triple rule across head] | [in two lines reading head to foot] LEONARD WOOLF | Economic Imperialism | [triple rule across foot] | [in two lines reading head to foot] HOWARD | FERTIG.

Publication: October 1970, at $7.00; 803 copies issued.

General Note: This extended essay condenses the conclusions reached in *Empire and Commerce in Africa* (A14), and contains LW's earliest detailed articulation of his concept of communal psychology. A Japanese translation, edited by Tadashi Kawata as part of the Todai shakai kagaku kenkyu sosho series, was published in Tokyo in 1961.

A17   SOCIALISM AND CO-OPERATION   1921

a. first issue: National Labour Press, 1921

SOCIALISM AND | CO-OPERATION | BY | LEONARD S. WOOLF | THE NATIONAL LABOUR PRESS, LTD. | LONDON AND MANCHESTER | – 1921–

Format: 138 pp. 7³⁄₁₆ × 4¾ in.

Pagination: [i-ii] blank; [iii] half-title; [iv] *First Published April, 1921.*; [v] title page as above; [vi] blank; [vii] contents; [viii] blank; [1] 2–129 text; [130] blank.

Binding: Plain greyish-white stiff paper wrappers, to which is tipped a greyish-white paper dust jacket printed in red and black. Front wrapper [in red] SOCIALISM AND | CO-OPERATION | [in black] BY | LEONARD S. WOOLF. | [summary of contents within oval border 2 × 3⅛ in.] | THE NATIONAL LABOUR PRESS, LIMITED. | LONDON: 8 & 9, JOHNSON'S COURT, E.C.4 | MANCHESTER: 30, BLACK-FRIARS STREET. | THREE SHILLINGS AND SIXPENCE, NET. Binding variant: Red cloth. Spine blocked in gold: [triple rule blind-stamped across head] | SOCIAL-ISM | AND | CO-OPERATION | WOOLF | NATIONAL | LABOUR | PRESS | [triple rule blind-stamped across foot]. Front cover has similar triple rules blind-stamped across head and foot. Dust jacket not seen.

Publication: April 1921, at 3*s*. 6*d*. (cloth) or 1*s*. 5*d*. (paper); 958 copies were printed, 400 bound in paper and 558 in cloth.

Notes: 1. 'The National Labour Press, Ltd., Manchester and London. 32217' appears at foot of p. 129.
   2. Title page is integral.

b. second issue: Parsons, 1921

SOCIALISM AND | CO-OPERATION | BY | LEONARD S. WOOLF | LONDON | LEONARD PARSONS | DEVONSHIRE STREET

Format: 136 pp. 7⅛ × 4¾ in.

Pagination: [i] half-title; [ii] *First Published April, 1921.* | LEONARD PARSONS, LTD.; [iii] title page as above; [iv] blank; [v] contents; [vi] blank; [1] 2–129 text; [130] blank.

Binding: Red cloth. Spine blocked in gold: [triple rule blind-stamped across head] | SOCIALISM | AND | CO-OPERATION | WOOLF | PARSONS | [triple rule blind-stamped across foot]. Dust jacket not seen.

Publication: April 1921, at 5*s*.; approximately 450 copies were issued.

Notes: 1. Same printer's note appears at the foot of p. 129 as in the first issue.
   2. Title page is integral.
   3. This was advertised as a "New & Forthcoming Publication, Spring 1921", at the price of 6*s*., in Robert Williams, *The New Labour Outlook* (London, Leonard Parsons, 1920).

c. third issue: Independent Labour Party, 1926

[Title page is identical to first issue, above]

Format: 144 pp. 7³⁄₁₆ × 4¾ in.

Pagination: Identical to the first issue, above, but for one blank leaf before pages [i-ii] and two blank leaves following page [130].

Binding: Greyish-white paper wrappers. Spine printed in black: [reading head to foot:] Socialism and Co-operation; front printed in black: [within double ruled ornamental border 6⅛ × 4 in.] SOCIALISM | AND | CO-OPERATION | *By* LEONARD S. WOOLF | [summary of contents in 16 lines] | *One Shilling* | I.L.P. PUBLICATION DEPARTMENT | 14 GT. GEORGE STREET, WESTMINSTER. Back wrapper printed with advertisements for I.L.P. publications.

Publication: January 1926, at 1*s*.; approximately 600 copies were issued.

SOCIALISM
AND
CO-OPERATION

By LEONARD S. WOOLF

Mr. Woolf's thesis is that the immediate object of the Socialist should be to eliminate the Capitalist, and establish a balance of power between producer and consumer," and in this book he examines the relations between co-operation and Socialism, and the part which the co-operative system might play in the Socialist State. The chapters are headed:

THE FOUNDATIONS OF SOCIALISM :
THE CONTROL OF INDUSTRY :
PRODUCTION AND CONSUMPTION :
THE CO-OPERATIVE COMMONWEALTH :
THE TRANSITION TO SOCIALISM

One Shilling

I.L.P. PUBLICATION DEPARTMENT
14 GT. GEORGE STREET, WESTMINSTER

A17*c*

Notes: 1. Same printer's note appears at foot of p. 129 as in the first issue.
   2. Title page is integral.

General Notes: In 1920, Philip Snowden of the Independent Labour Party, working with the National Labour Press on the "Social Studies Series", requested from LW a volume on socialism and co-operation. LW was then an active member of the ILP, which he later called the left wing of the British labour movement [*Downhill All the Way:* 83]. He agreed to accept £50 and 12½% royalty for writing *Socialism and Co-operation* [LW to ILP 2 February 1926, in the ILP Papers, London School of Economics; we are grateful to Frederic Spotts for calling our attention to this correspondence], and wrote it during the autumn of 1920 and spring of 1921 [VW *Diary,* 2: 74; LW *Letters:,* 391]. It was advertised in the 7 April 1921 issue of the ILP weekly, *Labour Leader,* and described in the 27 May issue as available in either paper wrappers or cloth. When the time came to settle the contract, the National Labour Press found itself in financial difficulties and LW agreed to accept only £25 for it [LW to ILP 2 February 1926].

When the ILP unilaterally reissued the book at the start of 1926, LW asked for a statement of his account, claiming that he had never been informed how many copies had been printed or sold and had never received a royalty statement. The correspondence in the ILP Papers during the spring of 1926 reveals that at least 1558 copies were printed, 958 being issued in 1921 and "about 600" more in 1926. No mention is made of the Parsons issue, but the ILP estimated that 2000 copies had been printed in all, suggesting that about 450 were issued by Parsons.

In *Downhill All the Way,* LW reflected that " . . . this book was even more futile than most of my books, yet I still think that what the book said is both true and important". [85]. A summary of its main arguments is printed on pages 85–88 of *Downhill . . .* and its place in the labour movement's discussions of economic organization is related by Sir Duncan Wilson on pp. 100–102 of his biography of LW.

A18   STORIES OF THE EAST   1921

a. first edition: Hogarth Press, 1921

STORIES | OF THE EAST | LEONARD WOOLF | PRINTED AND PUBLISHED BY LEONARD AND VIRGINIA WOOLF | AT THE HOGARTH PRESS, HOGARTH HOUSE, RICHMOND. | 1921

Format: 60 pp. 7½ × 4⅞ in.

Pagination: [1–2] blank; [1–2] blank; [3] title page as above; [4] blank; [5] 6–18 [19] "A Tale Told By Moonlight"; [20] blank; [21] 22–43 [44] "Pearls and Swine"; [45] 46–54 [55] "The Two Brahmins"; [56] advertisements for Hogarth Press books; [57–58] blank.

Binding: Stiff greyish-white paper wrappers with yapped edges. Front cover printed in red with title and LW's name inside an illustration by Carrington of a tiger between palm trees.

Publication: April 1921, at 3s.; 300 copies issued.

Note: Woolmer 16.

STORIES OF THE EAST
BY
LEONARD WOOLF

A18*a*

b. second edition: Hogarth Press, 1963.

[The text of *Stories of the East* was reissued with LW's Ceylon diaries; see A40 for full description.]

General Note: Stories of the East was printed by the Woolfs in their home on the original Hogarth Press handpress [VW *Letters*, no. 1175], with woodcut cover by Dora Carrington [Carrington: 173]. It was reviewed in the *Times Literary Supplement* on 14 April 1921 and praised extravagantly by Hamilton Fyfe in the *Daily Mail* on 2 May; these reviews left the amateur publishers "flooded with orders" [VW *Letters*, no. 1178] and 261 copies (nearly the entire edition) sold out in the first 5 months [LW *Letters*: 281]. It also led to an amusing exchange of letters between LW and the American publisher Henry Holt (recounted in *Downhill All the Way*, pages 88–100), who predicted LW could earn enormous sums if he would write fiction for the American market. A French translation was published in Paris in 1964.

A19* SCOPE OF THE MANDATES 1921

[At head of p. [1]:] SCOPE OF THE MANDATES UNDER THE | LEAGUE OF NATIONS. | BY LEONARD WOOLF, ESQ.

Format: 16 pp. 8½ × 5½ in.

Pagination: [1] 2–16 text.

Binding: Self-wrappers printed as above.

Publication: 1921; the price, exact publication date, and number of copies issued are not known.

Note: LONDON; PRINTED BY C.F. ROWORTH, 88, FETTER LANE, E.C.4., at foot of p. 16.

General Note: The lack of a conventional publisher's imprint suggests that this was printed informally, perhaps as part of LW's candidacy for Parliament in 1920–22. See notes to A20, below, and Appendix 2.

A20* [ELECTION MANIFESTO] 1922

[At head of first page:] *TO THE ELECTORS OF THE | COMBINED ENGLISH | UNIVERSITY CONSTITUENCY.* [LW's portrait within an oval 2½ × 1⅞ in. is centred between the two previous lines]

Format: 4 pp. 10¾ × 8⅝ in.

Pagination: [1] 2–4 text.

Binding: Self-wrappers, as above.

Publication: October 1922, gratis; the number of copies issued is not known.

Note: 'Printed and published by C.F. Hodgson & Son, 2 Newton Street, W.C.2.', at foot of p. 4.

General Note: In June 1920, LW accepted the invitation of the Seven Universities Democratic Association to be a candidate for Parliament in the Combined English University constituency (representing universities in Birmingham, Bristol, Durham, Leeds, Liverpool, Manchester and Sheffield). Although supported by the Labour Party, he conducted a rather half-hearted campaign and polled only 12% of the vote. The bulk of the text of the manifesto was reprinted by LW in *Downhill All the Way* (pp. 131–33); a photograph of the first page is printed in Spater & Parsons on page 79.

A21   INTERNATIONAL CO-OPERATIVE TRADE   1922

FABIAN TRACT NO. 201 | [⅝ in. rule] | INTERNATIONAL | CO-OPERATIVE TRADE | BY | LEONARD WOOLF | PUBLISHED AND SOLD BY | THE FABIAN SOCIETY | BY ARRANGEMENT WITH THE TRUSTEES OF THE SARA | HALL TRUST, IN COMMEMORATION OF THE LIFE AND | WORK OF ROBERT OWEN | PRICE TWOPENCE | LONDON: THE FABIAN SOCIETY, 25 TOTHILL STREET, WEST-MINSTER, S.W.1. | DECEMBER, 1922

Format: 28 pp. 8 × 5⅛ in.

Pagination: [1] title-page as above; [2] blank; [3] 4–25 text; 26 appendix; [27–28] advertisements for the Fabian Society and its publications.

Binding: The only copies located for examination were bound into hardcover volumes without their original wrappers.

Publication: December 1922, at 2*d.*; the number of copies issued is not known.

Notes: 1. 'Printed by Leicester Co-operative Printing Society Limited, 99, Church Gate, Leicester', at foot of p. [28].

2. An unknown number of copies were bound with other Fabian pamphlets on the same subject and issued the next year in *Fabian Essays on Co-operation*, edited by LW, see B12.

3. Reprinted in 1969 by H.P. Kraus in their Fabian Society Publications set.

General Note: LW opened this pamphlet with a history of international co-operative trade and a summary of existing methods by which the co-operative societies of different nations trade with one another. He goes on to examine how these current mechanisms could be strengthened, and to propose new methods of increasing the international activities of co-operators. Chief among these are the creation of an international information bureau to provide data on international trade to co-operative societies, the establishment of an international co-operative wholesale society to work as a purchasing agent in the international marketplace, and the creation of an international co-operative bank which could finance co-operative trade and invest in co-operative manufactures. LW read part of the pamphlet at a conference of co-operators and trade unionists in London at the end of January 1923; a full report of the meeting, including remarks by LW and others, appeared in *Co-operative News* on 3 February 1923 (p. 11).

A22   FEAR AND POLITICS: A DEBATE AT THE ZOO 1925

FEAR AND POLITICS | A DEBATE AT THE ZOO | LEONARD WOOLF |
[publisher's device ¾ in. diameter] | PUBLISHED BY LEONARD AND
VIRGINIA WOOLF | AT THE HOGARTH PRESS, TAVISTOCK
SQUARE, | LONDON, W.C.1 | 1925

Format: 24 pp. 8½ × 5½ in.

Pagination: [1] blank; [2] list of works in series; [3] title page as above; [4] blank; [5]
6–24 text.

Binding: Greyish-white stiff paper wrappers, printed in black with design by Vanessa
Bell on front cover.

Publication: July 1925, at 2s. 6d.; 1000 copies were issued.

Notes: 1. Woolmer 79.
2. Reprinted in 1973 in *In Savage Times* (A44).
3. Number 7 of the "Hogarth Essays", first series.

General Note: In this light-hearted allegory, LW uses zoo animals to voice the
prevailing political attitudes of the day. After observing human society from their
cages, the animals have concluded that "the human political organization is founded
upon fear, and that when men talk about justice and reason and patriotism, they often
really mean panic and terror." The rhinoceros represents the viewpoint of conservatism and fear of change, which it resists with a blind, ignorant rush of terror. The
monkey expresses the view of the Bolsheviks, shows how capitalists have oppressed
workers through fear and compulsion, and supports the Russian revolution that
points the guns in the other direction for a change. The owl shows how patriotism and
nationalism are based on communal fear and rivalry, and represents the internation-
alist viewpoint; and the elephant, summing up, makes a plea for the restraining force
of convention and civilizing values. The pamphlet is an early expression of LW's
dialectical view of history as a perpetual struggle between barbarism and civilization,
which he elaborated in *Barbarians At the Gate* (A32) and *Principia Politica* (A37).

A23   HUNTING THE HIGHBROW   1927

HUNTING THE | HIGHBROW | LEONARD WOOLF | [publisher's device
¾ in. diameter] | *PUBLISHED BY LEONARD & VIRGINIA WOOLF AT
THE | HOGARTH PRESS, 52 TAVISTOCK SQUARE, LONDON, W.C.1*
| 1927

Format: 56 pp. 6½ × 4⅛ in.

Pagination: [1] half-title; [2] list of books in series; [3] title page as above; [4] Printed
in Great Britain by | NEILL & CO., LTD., EDINBURGH.; 5–51 [52] text; [53–54]
list of books in Hogarth Essays, First Series; [55–56] blank.

Binding: Pale green paper over boards. Spine lettering black: [reading head to foot]
HUNTING THE HIGHBROW. By LEONARD WOOLF. Both covers printed in
black with series title within an abstract design.

Publication: March 1927, at 2*s.* 6*d.*; 1000 copies were issued.

Notes: 1. Woolmer 152.
        2. Number 5 in the "Hogarth Essays", second series.

General Note: In this literary essay on the distinction between mass culture and high culture, LW responds to recent attacks in the press and media on "highbrow" critics. He dismisses these attacks for oversimplifying "aesthetic and psychological problems of considerable intricacy and obscurity", and points out that works of art and literature that have immense popularity are almost always forgotten within a generation or two while classics often go unappreciated in their own day. He argues that most great works are difficult to understand and therefore cannot appeal to the majority of readers, and that the exercise of the intellect is unsettling and frightening to the bulk of the population because it threatens the passions and prejudices that most people live by.

A24   ESSAYS   1927

a. first issue: Hogarth Press, 1927

ESSAYS | ON | *LITERATURE, HISTORY, POLITICS, ETC.* | *LEONARD WOOLF* | [publisher's device, ¾ in. diameter] | *PUBLISHED BY LEONARD AND VIRGINIA WOOLF AT* | *THE HOGARTH PRESS, 52 TAVISTOCK SQUARE, LONDON, W.C.* | *1927*

Format: 256 pp. 7¼ × 4¾ in.

Pagination: [i] half-title; [ii] list of LW's works; [iii] title page as above; [iv] *First printed* 1927 | *Printed in Great Britain by* R. & R. CLARK, LIMITED, *Edinburgh.*; v author's note; [vi] blank; vii-viii contents; 9 division title; [10] blank; 11–18 "Ben Jonson"; 19–25 "Hazlitt"; 26–30 "An Englishman"; 31–38 "Herbert Spencer"; 39–43 "The Fall of Stevenson"; 44–56 "Samuel Butler"; 57–71 "Joseph Conrad"; 72–80 "A Traveller in Little Things"; 81–85 "Lord Morley"; 86–90 "Mr. George Moore and the Critics"; 91–105 "The Modern Nightingale"; 106–113 "The First Person Singular"; 114–121 "Winged and Unwinged Words"; [122] blank; [123] division title; [124] blank; 125–148 "The Pageant of History"; 149–152 "A Civilized Man"; 153–169 "International Morality"; 170–188 "Statesmen and Diplomatists"; 189–197 "The Two Kings of Jerusalem"; 198–211 "Please, Sir, It Was the Other Fellow"; 212–217 "Politics In Spain"; 218–222 "John Bright and Liberalism"; [223] division title; [224] blank; 225–234 "The Aristocratic Mind"; 235–239 "The Anatomy of Old Age"; 240–244 "'Look Up There, With Me!'"; 245–249 "Discarnate Spirits"; 250–255 [256] "The Gentleness of Nature".

Binding: Light brown cloth. Spine blocked in gold: ESSAYS | *Leonard Woolf* | *The Hogarth Press.* Dust jacket white paper printed in black.

Publication: May 1927, at 7*s.* 6*d.*; 1000 copies were issued, of which 350 were later pulped.

Note: Woolmer 153.

b. second issue: Harcourt, Brace, 1927

ESSAYS | *ON* | *LITERATURE, HISTORY, POLITICS, ETC.* | *LEONARD WOOLF* | [publisher's device ⁷⁄₁₆ in. sq.] | NEW YORK | *HARCOURT, BRACE AND COMPANY*

Format: 256 pp. 7½ × 5⅛ in.

Pagination: Identical to first issue, but for title page [as above].

Binding: Deep brownish red cloth. White paper spine label printed in black: [rule] | *ESSAYS* | *by* | *Leonard* | *Woolf* | [rule]. Dust jacket tan paper, front printed in red, spine in brown.

Publication: August 1927, at $2.50; 500 copies were issued, and the book was out-of-print by the spring of 1932, according to the publisher's correspondence files.

Note: Title page is integral.

c. third issue: Books for Libraries Press, 1970

ESSAYS | ON | LITERATURE, HISTORY, POLITICS, ETC. | LEONARD S. WOOLF | ESSAY INDEX REPRINT SERIES | [publisher's device ⅜ in. sq. at left of foot; following lines at right of foot:] BOOKS FOR LIBRARIES PRESS | FREEPORT, NEW YORK

Format: 254 pp. 8⅜ × 5⅜ in.

Pagination: [i] half-title; [ii] blank; [iii] title page as above; [iv] First published 1927 | Reprinted 1970 | [ISBN] | [Library of Congress card no.] | PRINTED IN THE UNITED STATES OF AMERICA; [v-vi] contents; [vii] division title; [viii] blank; 11 [*sic*]-255 [256] text.

Binding: Pale blue cloth. 5⅛ in. red panel on spine blocked in silver: [rule] | [in two lines reading head to foot:] ESSAYS ON LITERATURE, | HISTORY, POLITICS, ETC. | [dot] | [reading head to foot:] WOOLF | [rule] | [publisher's device ¾ × ½ in. at foot:]. A different publisher's device 1¼ × 1 in. is blind-stamped at lower right of front cover.

Publication: 1970, at $8.50; the exact publication date and number of copies issued are not known.

Note: Omits the author's note on p. v of first issue.

General Note: "L. is going to make a book of his essays," Virginia noted on 9 June 1926 [VW *Diary*, 3: 90], and in September she told Margaret Llewelyn Davies that "he's putting together a book of his articles, under pressure from me and America" [VW *Letters*, no. 1667]. The majority of the essays were reprinted from *Nation and Athenaeum* or *New Statesman* with little alteration, though a few represent combinations or condensations of several journal articles.

A25   IMPERIALISM AND CIVILIZATION   1928

a. first edition, first issue: Hogarth Press, 1928

IMPERIALISM | AND | CIVILIZATION | LEONARD WOOLF | "MEN
MORALIZE AMONG RUINS" | [publisher's device ¾ in. diameter] |
PUBLISHED BY LEONARD AND VIRGINIA WOOLF AT | THE
HOGARTH PRESS, 52 TAVISTOCK SQUARE, LONDON | 1928

Format: 136 pp. 7½ × 4¾ in.

Pagination: [i] half-title; [ii] list of LW's works; [iii] title page as above; [iv] *First
printed* 1928 | *Printed in Great Britain by* R. & R. Clark, Limited, *Edinburgh.*; v
contents; [vi] blank; 7–134 [135] text; [136] blank.

Binding: Deep brown cloth. Spine blocked in gold: IMPERIALISM | AND |
CIVILIZATION | LEONARD | WOOLF | THE | HOGARTH | PRESS. Dust jacket
white paper printed in black.

Publication: 3 March 1928, at 5s.; 1500 copies were printed, of which 931 were
issued in 1928 and 569 in 1933 (see second issue, below).

Notes: 1. Woolmer 184.

2. Pages 10–16, 46–47, and 67–76 were reprinted in Alain Locke, *When
Peoples Meet: A Study in Race and Culture Contacts* (New York: Progressive
Education Association, 1942; reprinted by Hinds, Hayden & Eldridge, Inc., in 1946).

b. first edition, second issue: Hogarth Press, 1933

[Title page is identical to the first edition, first issue, above, but for *New
Edition* beneath the publisher's device]

Format: 8vo. 136 pp. 7½ × 4¾ in.

Pagination: Identical to first edition, first issue, above, but for title page and addition
of the words *New Edition* [*sic*] 1933 on p. [iv].

Binding: White paper wrappers printed in black: [front:] IMPERIALISM | AND |
CIVILIZATION | *Leonard Woolf* | [publisher's device ¾ in. diameter] | *Published by
Leonard and Virginia Woolf at The* | *Hogarth Press, 52 Tavistock Square, London,
W.C.* [spine:] 'IMPERIALISM | and | CIVILIZATION | Leonard | Woolf | 2s.6d. | The
| Hogarth | Press.

Publication: 21 February 1933, at 2s. 6d.; 569 copies issued.

Note: Title page is a cancel.

c. first edition, third issue: Garland, 1971

IMPERIALISM | AND CIVILIZATION | BY | LEONARD WOOLF |
WITH A NEW INTRODUCTION | FOR THE GARLAND EDITION BY |
SYLVIA STRAUSS | [publisher's device ¾ × ½ in.] | GARLAND PUB-
LISHING, INC., NEW YORK & LONDON | 1971

Format: 152 pp. 8½ × 5½ in.

Pagination: [The preliminaries have a separate Arabic pagination which precedes that of the original 1928 printing:] [1] series title; [2] note on the series; [3] title page as above; [4] The new introduction for this | Garland Library Edition is Copyright © 1971, by | *Garland Publishing Inc.* | *24 West 45 St., New York, N.Y. 10036* | [1 in. swelled rule] | All Rights Reserved | [1 in. swelled rule] | [Library of Congress CIP data in 11 lines] | *Printed in the United States of America*; 5–11 introduction by Strauss; [12] blank; [hereafter identical to the first edition, first issue, above, until:] [136–140] blank.

Binding: Greyish-brown cloth. Spine blocked in gold: [double rule across head] | [reading head to foot:] Woolf *Imperialism and Civilization* | [publisher's device ½ × ⅜ in.] | Garland | [double rule across foot].

Publication: 1971; exact date and price not known; 150 copies were issued.

d. second edition: Harcourt, Brace, 1928

IMPERIALISM | AND | CIVILIZATION | BY | LEONARD WOOLF | "MEN MORALIZE AMONG RUINS" | [publisher's device ⅜ in. sq.] | NEW YORK | HARCOURT, BRACE AND COMPANY

Format: 184 pp. 7¼ × 4⅞ in.

Pagination: [1] half-title; [2] list of LW's works; [3] title page as above; [4] COPYRIGHT, 1928, BY | HARCOURT, BRACE AND COMPANY, INC. | PRINTED IN THE U.S.A. BY | QUINN & BODEN COMPANY, INC. | RAHWAY, N.J.; [5] contents; [6] blank; 7–182 text; [183–184] blank.

Binding: Deep brown cloth. Spine blocked in green: IMPERIALISM | AND | CIVILIZATION | LEONARD | WOOLF | HARCOURT, BRACE | AND | COMPANY. Publisher's device ¾ in. sq. blind-stamped on front cover. Dust jacket printed in black on yellow paper.

Publication: April 1928, at $2.00; the number of copies issued is not known.

General Note: During the autumn of 1927, LW gave a series of six lectures under the auspices of the Union of Democratic Control on "Imperialism and the Problem of Civilization". The first was delivered on 11 October, and two weeks later he offered this volume, based on the lecture series, to Harcourt, Brace. Although the series did not end until December, LW mailed the manuscript of *Imperialism and Civilization* to New York on 24 November [VW *Diary*, 3: 167 n.1; Harcourt, Brace Correspondence Files, 25 October 1927, 24 November 1927].

This book-length essay is LW's most thorough and lengthy anti-imperialist statement. He starts from the assumption that the "belligerent, crusading, conquering, exploiting, proselytizing civilization" of Europe must now face the revolt of the Third World peoples they colonized; solving this massive international problem is, to him, the most pressing issue of the modern world. After surveying the history of imperialism in classical times and contrasting it with modern forms, he describes in detail how Europeans have conquered and exploited Asia and Africa for their own benefit. He concludes by recommending that the League of Nations hold mandatory powers to the terms of Article 22 and act more vigorously to stabilize the politics and finances of colonial areas in an attempt to end imperialism.

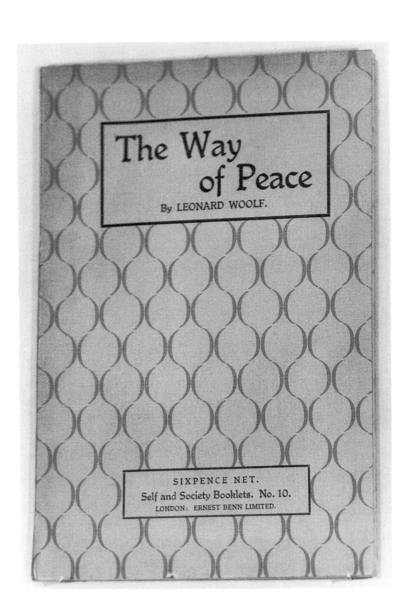

The Way of Peace

By LEONARD WOOLF.

SIXPENCE NET.

Self and Society Booklets. No. 10.

LONDON: ERNEST BENN LIMITED.

A26   THE WAY OF PEACE 1928

SELF AND SOCIETY | THE WAY OF PEACE | BY LEONARD WOOLF |
*AUTHOR OF "THE VILLAGE IN THE JUNGLE," | "INTERNATIONAL
GOVERNMENT," "CO-OPERATION | AND THE FUTURE OF
INDUSTRY," "EMPIRE AND | COMMERCE IN AFRICA," ETC.* | 1928 |
ERNEST BENN LIMITED | BOUVERIE HOUSE FLEET STREET

Format: 32 pp. 7¼ × 5 in.

Pagination: [1] title page as above; [2] *Printed and Made in Great Britain by the | Co-operative Wholesale Society Ltd., Longsight, Manchester*; 3–30 text; [31–32] blank.

Binding: Pale greyish-brown stiff paper wrappers, printed with an abstract pattern in brown and lettering in blue: [within rectangle 3¼ × 1½ in.:] The Way | of Peace | By LEONARD WOOLF. | [within rectangle 2⅝ × ⅝ in. at foot:] SIXPENCE NET. | Self and Society Booklets. No. 10. | LONDON : ERNEST BENN LIMITED.

Publication: November 1928, at 6*d.*; the number of copies issued is not known.

Notes: 1. Reprinted in *In Savage Times* (A44).
           2. See Appendix 1.

General Note: "My argument is that the ordinary economic system, of which the organization and psychology represent the producer's and the profit-maker's interests, makes for international hostility and war, while the consumers' co-operative system represents the consumer's interests and makes for peace." This pamphlet discussing imperialism, international trade, and consumer's co-operation restates facts and arguments previously put forth in *Co-operation and the Future of Industry* (A12) and *Socialism and Co-operation* (A17) and is LW's last separate publication devoted to advancing the cause of the co-operative movement.

A27   AFTER THE DELUGE, VOL. I 1931

a. first edition, first issue: Hogarth Press, 1931

AFTER THE DELUGE | A STUDY OF COMMUNAL PSYCHOLOGY |
LEONARD WOOLF | VOL. I | [7-line quotation from Leibnitz] | [publisher's device ¾ in. diameter] | *PUBLISHED BY LEONARD AND VIRGINIA WOOLF AT | THE HOGARTH PRESS, TAVISTOCK SQUARE, LONDON* | 1931

Format: 348 pp. 8½ × 5½ in.

Pagination: [i] half-title; [ii] list of LW's works; [iii] title page as above; [iv] *First published in* 1931 | *Printed in Great Britain by* R. & R. CLARK, LIMITED, *Edinburgh*; v preface; [vi] blank; vii–xv contents; [xvi] blank; [17] division title; [18] blank; 19–346 [347] text and indexes; [348] blank.

Binding: Light brown cloth. Spine printed in gold: *After | the Deluge |* [five-pointed star] | *Leonard Woolf | The | Hogarth | Press.* Dust jacket not seen.

Publication: 13 October 1931, at 15*s.*; 1000 copies were issued.

Notes: 1. Woolmer 278.
2. Pages 32–40 were reprinted in Michael Curtis, *The Nature of Politics* (New York: Avon Books, 1962; reprinted 1966).

b. first edition, second issue: Harcourt, Brace, 1931

AFTER THE DELUGE | A STUDY OF COMMUNAL PSYCHOLOGY | LEONARD WOOLF | VOL. I | [7-line quotation from Leibnitz] | [publisher's device ⁷⁄₁₆ in. sq.] | NEW YORK | HARCOURT, BRACE AND COMPANY

Format: 348 pp. 8⅝ × 5½ in.

Pagination: Identical to the first issue, above, but for the title page [as above] and p. [iv], which reads: FIRST EDITION, 1931 | PRINTED IN GREAT BRITAIN BY | R. & R. CLARK, LIMITED, EDINBURGH.

Binding: Green cloth. Spine blocked in gold: [within a border composed of dashes] AFTER | THE | DELUGE | — | *LEONARD* | *WOOLF* | [below border of dashes: five-pointed star] | HARCOURT, BRACE | AND COMPANY. Dust jacket not seen.

Publication: January 1932, at $3.50; 500 copies were imported from England, of which only 358 were sold, according to the publisher's correspondence files.

Note: Title page is integral.

c. first edition, third issue: Hogarth Press, 1953

AFTER THE DELUGE | A STUDY OF COMMUNAL PSYCHOLOGY | LEONARD WOOLF | VOL. I | [7-line quotation from Leibnitz] | [publisher's device ¾ in. diameter] | LONDON | THE HOGARTH PRESS | 1953

Format: 348 pp. 8½ × 5½ in.

Pagination: [i] half-title; [ii] list of LW's works; [iii] title page as above; [iv] PUBLISHED BY | THE HOGARTH PRESS LTD. | LONDON | * | CLARKE, IRWIN AND CO. LTD. | TORONTO | FIRST PUBLISHED 1931 | REPRINTED 1953 | ALL RIGHTS RESERVED; v preface; [vi] blank; vii–xv contents; [xvi] blank; [17] division title; [18] blank; 19–346 [347] text and indexes; [348] blank. *Binding:* Pale orange cloth. Spine blocked in gold: AFTER | THE | DELUGE | [ornamental star, ¼ in. diameter] | Leonard | Woolf | *Volume I* | THE | HOGARTH | PRESS'. Dust jacket light grey paper, lettering in black, red rules.

Publication: 8 October 1953, at 21*s.*; 1250 copies were issued, of which 550 were later pulped or remaindered.

Note: PRINTED IN GREAT BRITAIN BY LOWE & BRYDONE (PRINTERS) LIMITED, LONDON, N.W.10, p. [347].

d. second edition: Penguin, 1937

PELICAN BOOKS | AFTER THE DELUGE | A STUDY OF COMMUNAL PSYCHOLOGY | BY | LEONARD WOOLF | [7-line quotation from Leibnitz] | [publisher's device 1⅛ × 1⅜ in.] | PUBLISHED BY | PENGUIN BOOKS LIMITED | HARMONDSWORTH MIDDLESEX ENGLAND

Format: 278 pp. 7⅛ × 4½ in.

Pagination: [i-ii] blank; [iii] half-title, with series note; [iv] publisher's note; [v] title page as above; [vi] First published 1931 | Published in Pelican Books 1937 | MADE AND PRINTED IN GREAT BRITAIN FOR PENGUIN BOOKS LIMITED | BY PURNELL AND SONS, LTD. PAULTON (SOMERSET) AND LONDON; vii preface; [viii] blank; ix-xvi contents; [17] division title; [18] blank; 19–278 text and indexes. 8-page 'Complete list of all Penguin and Pelican books to the end of 1937' and 1 blank leaf bound in at end.

Binding: Stiff paper wrappers printed in blue and black, with a paper dust jacket printed to match. According to the *English Catalogue of Books* this was also issued in boards, but no copy bound in boards could be located for examination.

Publication: Copies in boards, October 1937, at 6*d.*; copies in wrappers, November 1937, at 6*d.*; the number of copies issued in either binding is not known.

Note: Number A18 in the Pelican Books series.

General Notes: The three volumes of *After the Deluge* (1931, 1939 A31, and 1953 A37, volume three bearing the title *Principia Politica*) represent LW's most ambitious attempt at political theory; their principal arguments are recounted in *Downhill All the Way*, pages 196–205. LW recalled there how his research for *International Government* (A7) and *Empire and Commerce in Africa* (A14) led him to examine "communal psychology" as a social force ranking with economic and political power. In the introduction to *Economic Imperialism* (A16) he explained how communal psychology – the complex of beliefs, desires and standards of value that are shared by a community – operate: "It was not God nor kings who for centuries bound Europe in the chains of the feudal system: feudalism was produced by what went on in the minds of dozens of lords and thousands of serfs. . . . It was not the Kaiser or any other 'war criminal' who caused the Great War, but the millions of men and women who read the German, English and French papers, believed what those papers told them to believe and desired what those papers told them to desire." [p. 10]. As can be seen, LW's ideas in some ways parallel those of Antonio Gramsci on cultural hegemony (which were as yet unpublished) and anticipate some of the objections to classical Marxism that would be raised by the New Left thirty years later.

The first volume of *After the Deluge* examined the origin of the communal psychology of liberal democracy in the French and American revolutions, the second traced its spread through England and France in the 19th century, and third (*Principia Politica*) broke the chronological structure to examine the communal psychology of modern totalitarianism. An impartial summary of the work's merits and defects can be found in chapter 14 of Sir Duncan Wilson's biography of LW.

He began to research this subject in 1920 and worked at it sporadically for the next decade [*Downhill All the Way*: 203]. He finished volume one in June 1931 [*VW Diary*, 4: 630] and it was published in October. Though it was praised by some as a masterpiece, LW was disheartened by a mixed review in the *Times Literary*

PELICAN
BOOKS

PUBLISHED BY PENGUIN BOOKS

AFTER THE
DELUGE

LEONARD WOOLF

WITH EIGHT ILLUSTRATIONS

COMPLETE   UNABRIDGED

A27d

Supplement (22 October 1931): "But L. says – & honestly believes – that this puts an end to the book – . . . He says his ten years work are wasted, & that he sees no use in going on. His argument is that he wrote this book for the wider public; that this public is at the mercy of librarians; that librarians take their orders from the Lit. Sup.; that they judge by the length of the review; that no librarian will advise spending 15/- after this review; so that . . . his book is dead; his work wasted . . . his sales won't reach 500 in 6 months, & so on." [VW *Diary*, 4: 51]. Virginia later recorded that it sold more than 400 copies in the first 10 weeks [ibid.: 61], and it was widely distributed as a Penguin paperback several years later.

A28   QUACK, QUACK!   1935

a. first issue: Hogarth Press, 1935

QUACK, QUACK! | LEONARD WOOLF | [publisher's device ¾ in. diameter] | PUBLISHED BY LEONARD AND VIRGINIA WOOLF AT THE | HOGARTH PRESS, 52 TAVISTOCK SQUARE, LONDON, W.C. | 1935

Format: 206 pp. 7 × 4½ in.

Pagination: [1] half-title; [2] list of LW's works; [3] title page as above; [4] *Made in Great Britain. Printed by* R. & R. Clark, Limited, *Edinburgh*; 5 contents; [6] blank; 7 list of illustrations; [8] blank; 9–201 text; [202–206] blank. Four leaves of illustrations tipped in after p. 46.

Binding: Bright green cloth. Spine blocked in gold: *Quack,* | *Quack!* | [five-pointed star] | *Leonard* | *Woolf* | THE | HOGARTH | PRESS. Dust jacket, designed by E. McKnight Kauffer, white paper printed in blue, black and orange, with black and white photographs.

Publication: 27 May 1935, at 7*s.* 6*d.*; 2020 copies were printed, of which 1758 were issued in 1935 and 262 re-issued as a 'Cheap Edition' the following year (see third issue, below).

Note: 1. Woolmer 380.

b. second issue: Harcourt, Brace, 1935

QUACK, QUACK! | BY LEONARD WOOLF | HARCOURT, BRACE AND COMPANY | NEW YORK

Format: 206 pp. 7 × 4¾ in.

Pagination: Identical to first issue, above, but for title page [as above]; p. [4], which reads: COPYRIGHT, 1935, BY | HARCOURT, BRACE AND COMPANY, INC. | [three-line reservation statement in italics] | *first edition* | PRINTED IN THE UNITED STATES OF AMERICA | BY THE POLYGRAPHIC COMPANY OF AMERICA, NEW YORK; and one additional blank leaf at the end. Four leaves of illustrations tipped in following p. 46.

Binding: Brown cloth. Spine blocked in silver: *Quack,* | *Quack!* | [five- pointed star] |

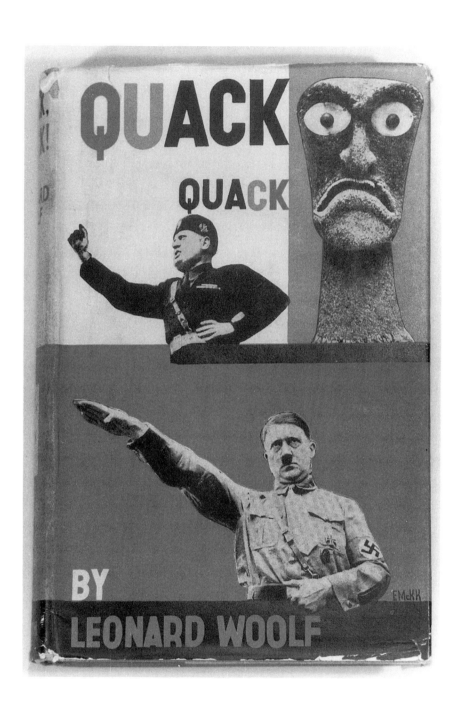

A28*a*

Leonard Woolf | HARCOURT, BRACE | AND COMPANY. Dust jacket pale green paper printed in brown.

Publication: 12 September 1935, at $2.00; the number of copies issued is not known.

c. third issue: Hogarth Press 'Cheap Edition' [sic], 1936

QUACK, QUACK! | LEONARD WOOLF | [publisher's device ¾ in. diameter] | CHEAP EDITION | PUBLISHED BY LEONARD AND VIRGINIA WOOLF AT THE | HOGARTH PRESS, 52 TAVISTOCK SQUARE, LONDON, W.C. | 1936

Format: 194 pp. 7⅛ × 4¾ in.

Pagination: [1] half-title; [2] list of LW's works; [3] title page as above; [4] *First published 1935* | *Cheap Edition 1936* | [printer's note as in first issue, above]; 5 contents; [6] blank; 7 list of illustrations; [8] blank; 9–193 text; [194] blank. Four leaves of illustrations tipped in after p. 46.

Binding: Identical to the first issue, above; dust jacket not seen.

Publication: 5 November 1936, at 2s. 6d.; 262 copies were issued.

Notes: 1. Omits "A Note on Anti-Semitism", which was printed as an appendix to the two previous issues.

    2. 1000 copies were reprinted in 1937, *by the Replika Process in Great Britain by* | PERCY LUND, HUMPHRIES & CO. LTD. [. . .], and bound in grey cloth printed in black as (a) above, with similar dust jacket.

General Notes: This is the first of LW's lengthy polemics on the social issues of the 1930s. It contains some of his most impassioned and amusing arguments against what he considered muddled political thinking, and some of his most eloquent pleas for applying sound reasoning to political life.

    LW began *Quack, Quack!* in 1934, following the Nazi Party's successful rise to power in Germany and perhaps fuelled by the slavish devotion of Nazis displayed at the Nüremberg conference in September of that year (treated on pp. 48–52 of the book). He finished the first part, which is devoted to Fascism, in November [VW *Diary*, 4:262]. According to Virginia, "it [went] along vigorously" throughout that fall and winter [ibid], and in January LW had an encouraging letter from Donald Brace regarding likely American sales [VW *Diary*, 4:273]. In February 1935, LW was "trying to finish" it [LW *Letters*: 324], and finally completed the manuscript on 2 March [VW *Diary*: 284]. It was published at the end of May 1935, and immediately reviewed favorably in the *Times Literary Supplement*; and the edition almost sold out in the first year.

    A sympathetic reader, Dr Charles Singer of London, who was actively engaged in aiding victims of Nazi persecution, urged LW to issue a cheap edition for the masses; he suggested that LW tone down criticisms of the English's own quackery in order to make the book more palatable to a broader audience. LW characteristically rejected the latter idea, but in the autumn of 1936 brought out the unsold first issue sheets at a lower price. These sold quickly, and a reprint of 1000 copies was issued the following year at the reduced price.

A29   THE LEAGUE AND ABYSSINIA   1936

THE LEAGUE AND | ABYSSINIA | LEONARD WOOLF | [publisher's device ½ × ⅝ in.] | PUBLISHED BY LEONARD AND VIRGINIA WOOLF AT THE | HOGARTH PRESS, 52 TAVISTOCK SQUARE, LONDON, W.C. | 1936

Format: 36 pp. 7¼ × 4⅞ in.

Pagination: [1] half-title; [2] list of other titles in series; [3] title page as above; [4] *First published 1936* | PRINTED IN GREAT BRITAIN BY | THE GARDEN CITY PRESS LIMITED | AT LETCHWORTH, HERTFORDSHIRE; 5–35 text; [36] blank.

Binding: Pinkish orange paper wrappers. Front cover printed in black: 'DAY TO DAY PAMPHLETS | No. 31 | THE LEAGUE AND | ABYSSINIA | LEONARD WOOLF | [publisher's device ½ × ⅝ in.] | THE HOGARTH PRESS | *One Shilling Net.*

Publication: March 1936, at 1*s.*; 2200 copies were issued.

Notes: 1. Woolmer 403.
         2. Reprinted in *In Savage Times* (A44)
         3. Number 31 in the Hogarth Press "Day to Day Pamphlets" series.

General Notes: When Italy threatened to invade Ethiopia early in 1935, the Abyssinian government formally petitioned the League of Nations for help. In England the Left was split, some believing in collective, armed security against aggression and others arguing for pacifism; LW was in the first camp. The Italian invasion took place on 2 October 1935, challenging the League and the entire concept of internationalism.

    LW wrote a series of memos for the Labour Party as this issue developed, as well as publishing articles on the subject. This "Day to Day Pamphlet" synthesizes those pieces by reviewing the creation of the League, criticizing the policies of the British government and the Labour Party toward it during the Abyssinian crisis, and urging collective action against aggression via the League.

A30   THE HOTEL   1939

a. first edition: Hogarth Press, 1939

THE HOTEL | LEONARD WOOLF | [publisher's device ¾ in. diameter] | THE HOGARTH PRESS | 52 TAVISTOCK SQUARE, | LONDON, W.C.1 | 1939

Format: 104 pp. 7⅛ × 4⅝ in.

Pagination: [1] half-title; [2] list of LW's works; [3] title page as above; [4] PRINTED IN GREAT BRITAIN BY THE GARDEN CITY PRESS LTD. | AT LETCHWORTH, HERTFORDSHIRE.; [5] dramatis personae; [6] blank; 7–104 blank.

Binding: Pink cloth. Spine blocked in blue: THE | HOTEL | *Leonard* | *Woolf* | THE | HOGARTH | PRESS. Dust jacket pink paper, lettering printed in blue.

Publication: May 1939, at 5*s*.; the number of copies issued is not known, but Spater and Parsons state that fewer than 1000 copies were sold [p. 122]; virtually mint-condition copies were often encountered in the rare book market-place 50 years later.

b. second edition, first issue: Dial Press, 1963

THE | HOTEL | *BY LEONARD WOOLF* | [publisher's device ⅜ × ½ in.] | THE DIAL PRESS NEW YORK 1963

Format: 96 pp. 7⅞ × 5⅜ in.

Pagination: [1] half-title; [2] blank; [3] title page as above; [4] *Copyright* © *1963 by Leonard Woolf* | ALL RIGHTS RESERVED | [Library of Congress card no.] | [six lines of reservation data] | DESIGNED BY ALAN M. HEICKLEN | MANU-FACTURED IN THE UNITED STATES OF AMERICA | BY THE COLONIAL PRESS INC., CLINTON, MASS.; 5–6 introduction by LW; [7] dramatis personae; [8] blank; [9] fly-title; [10] blank; 11–96 text.

Binding: Red cloth. Spine printed in black: [reading head to foot] THE HOTEL *Leonard Woolf* DIAL DRAMA [publisher's device]. Dust jacket white paper printed in black and red.

Publication: 18 February 1963, at $3.75; the number of copies issued is not known.

c. second edition, second issue: Apollo Editions, 1963

[Title page is identical to the second edition, first issue, above]

Format: 96 pp. 7¾ × 5 in.

Pagination: Identical to second edition, first issue, above.

Binding: Stiff white paper wrappers printed in black and red; series title, 'Apollo Editions', and series logo appear on back and front.

Publication: 18 February 1963, at $1.95; the number of copies issued is not known.

General Notes: According to Virginia's diary [5:133 (31 March 1938)], LW had contemplated writing *The Hotel* for more than a decade before putting pen to paper in the spring of 1938. He worked on it throughout that summer and read it to Maynard and Lydia Keynes during the first week of October [VW *Letters*, 6:287; 8 October 1938]. Although Keynes suggested that the Group Theatre might produce it, they turned it down and despite LW's repeated attempts to have it staged, *The Hotel* was never performed [Spater & Parsons, 122].

Many years later, in the introduction to the American edition, LW recollected that "It is a long time since I wrote this play, The Hotel, and it seems even longer. It was written and published in England just before the 1939 war, and Hitler and Stalin and Mussolini – the nazis, communists, and fascists – finally destroyed the world in which it was written. That, after all, is what the play is about; what it prophesied has happened." [5]

A31   AFTER THE DELUGE, VOL. II   1939

a. first issue: Hogarth Press, 1939

AFTER THE DELUGE | A STUDY OF COMMUNAL PSYCHOLOGY | LEONARD WOOLF | VOL. II | 1830 & 1832 | [publisher's device ¾ in. diameter] | THE HOGARTH PRESS | 37 MECKLENBURGH SQUARE, | LONDON, W.C.1 | 1939

Format: 328 pp. 8½ × 5⅜ in.

Pagination: [i] half-title; [ii] list of LW's works; [iii] title page as above; [iv] *First published in* 1939 | Printed in Great Britain by R. & R. CLARK, LIMITED, *Edinburgh*; v preface; [vi] blank; vii contents; [viii] blank; [1] division title; [2] blank; 3–316 [317] text and indexes; [318–320] blank.

Binding: Light brown cloth. Spine blocked in gold: *After* | *the Deluge* | [2 five-pointed stars] | *Leonard Woolf* | *The* | *Hogarth* | *Press*. Dust jacket cream paper, type and decoration printed in dark green.

Publication: 25 September 1939, at 15s.; 1294 copies were printed, 594 of which were issued in 1939, and 700 in 1953 to accompany the publication of vol. 3, *Principia Politica* (A37).

b. second issue: Harcourt, Brace, 1940

AFTER THE DELUGE | A STUDY OF COMMUNAL PSYCHOLOGY | LEONARD WOOLF | VOL. II | 1830 & 1832 | [publisher's device ⁷⁄₁₆ in. sq.] | HARCOURT, BRACE AND COMPANY | NEW YORK | 1940

Format: 328 pp. 8⅝ × 5½ in.

Pagination: Identical to the first issue, above, but for the title page [as above] and p. [iv], which reads only: PRINTED IN GREAT BRITAIN.

Binding: Green cloth. Spine printed in gold: [within a border composed of dashes] AFTER | THE | DELUGE | — | *LEONARD* | *WOOLF* | [below the border of dashes: 2 five-pointed stars] | HARCOURT, BRACE | AND COMPANY'. Dust jacket not seen.

Publication: January 1940, at $3.50; only 260 copies were issued.

Note: 1. Title page is integral.

c. third issue: Hogarth Press, 1953

AFTER THE DELUGE | A STUDY OF COMMUNAL PSYCHOLOGY | LEONARD WOOLF | VOL. II | 1830 & 1832 | [publisher's device ¾ in. diameter] | LONDON | THE HOGARTH PRESS | 1953

Format: 328 pp. 8½ × 5⅜ in.

Pagination: Identical to the first issue, above, but for the title page (as above) and p. [iv] which reads: PUBLISHED BY | THE HOGARTH PRESS LTD. | LONDON | * | CLARKE, IRWIN AND CO. LTD. | TORONTO | FIRST PUBLISHED IN 1939 | PRINTED IN GREAT BRITAIN BY | R. AND R. CLARK, LTD. EDINBURGH | ALL RIGHTS RESERVED.

Binding: Pale orange cloth. Spine blocked in gold: AFTER | THE | DELUGE | [ornamental star, ¼ in. diameter] | Leonard | Woolf | *Volume II* | THE | HOGARTH | PRESS. Dust jacket not seen.

Publication: 8 October 1953, at 15*s.*; 700 copies issued.

General Note: LW returned to the theme of communal psychology in 1935, after finishing *Quack, Quack!* (A28) [VW, *Letters*, 5: 388, 448]. The pressure of practical politics during the late 'thirties prevented him from working at it steadily (at the end of 1936 he confessed that he was "slowly proceeding with the second vol. of my book. But there seem to be incessant interruptions . . ." [LW, *Letters:* 243]). He was finally able to complete it at the beginning of 1939 [VW *Diary*, 5: 197]. It was published in September of that year, but despite praise from Desmond MacCarthy in the *Sunday Times* (19 and 26 November 1939) it sold slowly; in America it sold only about 50 copies in six months [Harcourt, Brace Correspondence Files, 25 April 1940]. The bulk of the printed sheets was not bound until 1953, when they were issued with *Principia Politica* (A37), the final volume of the trilogy. For a general account of the work as whole, see *Downhill All the Way*, 196–206, or Wilson, ch. XIV.

A32   BARBARIANS AT THE GATE   1939

a. first edition, first issue: Left Book Club, 1939

BARBARIANS AT | THE GATE | BY | LEONARD WOOLF | *TRAVAILLONS DONC A BIEN PENSER.* | PASCAL. | LONDON | VICTOR GOLLANCZ LTD | 1939

Format: 224 pp. 7¼ × 4⅞ in.

Pagination: [1] half-title; [2] list of LW's works; [3] title page as above; [4] PRINTED IN GREAT BRITAIN BY RICHARD CLAY AND COMPANY, LTD. (T.U.), | BUNGAY, SUFFOLK.; [5] contents; [6] blank; [7] foreword; [8] blank; [9] 10–221 text; [222–224] blank.

Binding: Pink paper over boards. Spine blocked in black: [within ruled border 1⅜ × ½ in.] BARBARIANS | AT THE | GATE | BY | LEONARD | WOOLF | GOLLANCZ. Front cover printed in black: BARBARIANS AT THE GATE | by | LEONARD WOOLF | [Left Book Club device ⅞ in. sq.] | LEFT BOOK CLUB EDITION | NOT FOR SALE TO THE PUBLIC. Binding variant: identical pink paper and spine, but with front and back boards covered by dull blue paper to obscure the Left Book Club notice; presumably a remainder binding.

Publication: 30 September 1939, at 6*s.*; 37,000 copies were printed, of which 36,250 were bound. According to the publisher, the balance of unbound sheets was possibly lost in bomb damage.

Note: Printed on poor quality paper; pages bulk 10 cm. (approximately ⅜ in.); sewn in gatherings of 16 leaves.

b. first edition, second issue: Victor Gollancz, 1939

[Title page identical to that of first edition, first issue, above]

Format and Pagination: Identical to first edition, first issue, above.

Binding: Black cloth. Spine blocked in gold: BARBARIANS | AT THE | GATE | BY | LEONARD | WOOLF | GOLLANCZ. Dust jacket cream paper, black lettering, magenta thick rule.

Publication: 30 September 1939, at 6s.; 1100 copies were printed, of which 900 were bound. According to the publisher, the balance of unbound sheets was possibly lost in bomb damage.

Notes: 1. Printed on better paper than the first edition, first issue, above; pages bulk 20 cm. (approximately ¾ in.); sewn in gatherings of eight leaves.

2. Although the publisher's records list 30 September as the publication date, LW didn't inscribe a copy to Virginia until 20 November, which suggests a delay of several weeks.

c. second edition: Harcourt, Brace, 1939

BARBARIANS | WITHIN AND WITHOUT | BY LEONARD WOOLF | HARCOURT, BRACE AND COMPANY NEW YORK

Format: 192 pp. 7⅞ × 5⅜ in.

Pagination: [i] half-title; [ii] blank; [iii] title page as above; [iv] COPYRIGHT, 1939, BY | HARCOURT, BRACE AND COMPANY, INC. | [3-line reservation statement] | *First American edition* | *Typography by Robert Josephy* | PRINTED IN THE UNITED STATES OF AMERICA | BY QUINN & BODEN COMPANY, INC., RAHWAY, N.J.'; [v] quote from Pascal; [vi] blank; [vii] publisher's note dated Sept. 1939; [viii] blank; [ix] contents; [x] blank; [1] fly-title; [2] blank; 3–180 text; [181–182] blank.

Binding: Pink cloth. Spine black: *Woolf* | [reading head to foot] BARBARIANS Within and Without | [across foot] *Harcourt, Brace* | *and Company*. Dust jacket printed in orange and black, panels and lettering.

Publication: 26 October 1939, at $1.50; the number of copies issued is not known, but LW was paid royalties reflecting a sale of 380 copies by the end of the year [Harcourt, Brace Correspondence Files, 25 April 1940].

General Notes: Barbarians At the Gate was the second of LW's long political tracts written during the 1930s. In October 1938 the publisher Victor Gollancz invited LW to write a book about the defence of western civilization. He offered £500 for a book on the political ideologies and movements that were driving the continent toward another war [VW *Diary*, 5: 183; Wilson: 197]. Gollancz, Harold Laski and John Strachey were directors of the Left Book Club, a popular and successful venture launched in the mid-thirties to provide inexpensive books on current events, written from a Marxist perspective. LW was fully aware that his liberal views of Soviet authoritarianism might be unwelcome to the directors of the Club, and in his reply to Gollancz he requested (and received) assurance of complete freedom to speak his mind in the book [Wilson: 197–98].

LW completed the manuscript quickly during the winter and spring of 1939, as the fascist states expanded their hegemony in Europe and Stalin tightened his grip on the Soviet Union; he sent the manuscript to Gollancz in June [VW *Diary*, 5:215]. After reading it, Gollancz, Strachey and Laski had strong misgivings about its suitability for the Left Book Club; LW's condemnation of Soviet crackdowns on intellectual and personal freedom struck them as inappropriate for their audience. They tried to delay publication, but at a meeting of all parties on 24 July 1939 (described in *The Journey Not the Arrival Matters* (A43), pp. 11–13) LW successfully defended his position and the book appeared that autumn. It was the first Left Book Club title to openly criticize the Soviet Union and prompted a lively controversy in the Club's newsletter, *Left News* (see Lewis, pp. 116–20; Wilson, 197–98; and Edwards, 296–300, where several letters by LW are quoted).

A33   THE WAR FOR PEACE   1940

a. first issue: Routledge, 1940

THE WAR FOR | PEACE | *BY* | LEONARD WOOLF | LONDON | GEORGE ROUTLEDGE & SONS, LTD. | BROADWAY HOUSE: 68–74 CARTER LANE, E.C.4

Format: 256 pp. 7¾ × 5 in.

Pagination: [i-ii] blank; [iii] half-title; [iv-v] blank; [vi] list of LW's works; [vii] title page as above; [viii] *First published, 1940* | Printed in Great Britain by Butler & Tanner Ltd., Frome and London; ix contents; [x] blank; [xi] fly-title; [xii] blank; 1–244 text.

Binding: Pale greyish yellow cloth. Spine blocked in red: THE | WAR | FOR | PEACE | [diamond-shaped ornament] | LEONARD | WOOLF | ROUTLEDGE. Dust jacket cream-coloured paper printed in red and yellow.

Binding variant: medium yellow cloth, spine red as above; dust jacket cream-coloured paper printed in red.

Publication: August 1940, at 7s. 6d.; the number of copies issued is not known.

b. second issue: Labour Book Service, 1940

THE WAR FOR | PEACE | *BY* | LEONARD WOOLF | LONDON | THE LABOUR BOOK SERVICE | 68–74 CARTER LANE, E.C. 4

Format: 256 pp. 7¾ × 5¼ in.

Pagination: [i] half-title; [ii] blank; [iii] note on the Labour Book Service, including: 'This edition is for members of the Labour Book Service only, and is not available to members of the general public.'; [iv-v] blank; [vi] list of LW's works; [vii] title page as above; [viii] *First published, 1940* | Printed in Great Britain by Butler & Tanner Ltd., Frome and London; ix contents; [x-xii] blank; 1–244 text.

Binding: Brown paper printed in white geometric design, over boards. Spine blocked in five white bands, in brown: THE WAR | FOR | PEACE | WOOLF | LBS.

Publication: August 1940, at 2s. 6d.; the number of copies issued is not known.

Note: 1. Some copies were issued with a loosely inserted publisher's advertisement describing recent titles and recruiting new members.

c. third issue: Garland, 1972

THE WAR FOR PEACE | BY | LEONARD WOOLF | WITH A NEW INTRODUCTION | FOR THE GARLAND EDITION BY | STEPHEN J. STEARNS | [publisher's device $5/8 \times 3/4$ in.] | GARLAND PUBLISHING, INC., NEW YORK & LONDON | 1972

Format: $8\frac{1}{2} \times 5\frac{3}{8}$ in. 264 pp.

Pagination: [1] series title; [2] series note; [3] title page as above; [4] The new introduction for this | Garland Library Edition is Copyright [copyright symbol] 1972, by | *Garland Publishing Inc.* | [7/8 in. swelled rule] | All Rights Reserved | [7/8 in. swelled rule] | [Library of Congress CIP data] | *Printed in the United States of America*; 5–11 introduction by Stearns; [12] blank; [i] half-title; [ii] list of works by LW; [iii] title page of first issue; [iv] verso of first issue title page; [v] contents of first issue (numbered 'ix' at foot); [vi] blank; [vii] fly title; [viii] blank; 1–244 text.

Binding: Greyish brown cloth. Spine blocked in gilt: [double rule] | [reading head to foot:] *Woolf The War for Peace* | [publisher's device $3/8 \times 1/2$ in.] | Garland | [double rule].

Publication: 1972; exact date and price not known; 150 copies were issued.

General Notes: This last of LW's long political tracts from the 1930s was commissioned in 1939 by the Labour Book Service, following the turmoil caused in the Left Book Club by LW's *Barbarians At the Gate* (A32). The Labour Book Service flourished briefly in the early 1940s under the sponsorship of George Routledge and Sons. Its publicity materials emphasized democratic values and tolerance for a diversity of opinions, within a broadly conceived socialist framework; they suggest that it was in open competition with the Left Book Club for members.

LW began to write *The War for Peace* in December 1939 and worked at it almost daily for five months, finishing in May 1940 [Spater & Parsons: 80; VW *Diary*, 5:285]. The book club and trade editions were published simultaneously in August 1940, the Labour Book Service issue being printed and bound with poor quality materials in order to keep the price down; most copies examined were in fragile condition and fine copies are now scarce.

A34   THE FUTURE OF INTERNATIONAL GOVERNMENT   1940

THE | FUTURE OF | INTERNATIONAL | GOVERNMENT | BY | LEONARD WOOLF | [1⅜ in. rule] | PRICE ONE PENNY | [1⅜ in. rule] | PUBLISHED BY | THE LABOUR PARTY | TRANSPORT HOUSE, SMITH SQUARE, LONDON, S.W.1

Format: 12 pp. 8⅜ × 5¼ in.

Pagination: [1] title page as above; [2] PRICES POST FREE. | 1 Copy 1½d. | 12 copies, 9d. | 100 copies 6s. | From | The Labour Publications Dept., | Transport House, Smith Square, London, S.W.1; 3–11 [12] text.

Binding: Self-wrappers, front printed in black as above.

Publication: 1940, at 1*d.*; exact date and number of copies issued are not known.

Note: 'Printed by the Victoria House Printing Co, Ltd (T.U. all Depts.), 55 & 57 Drury Lane, London, W.C. 2. 9|5221.', on p. [12].

General Note: It was typical of LW and his colleagues on the Labour Party Advisory Committee to think to the future of international government at a time when the possibility of its success must have seemed to most people extremely remote. In this short tract, LW lays out the conditions he believes necessary if any international authority is to succeed, and exposes the weaknesses of the League of Nations. He argues that any successor to the League must have the power to enact and enforce its decisions through collective security and peace-keeping forces, while at the same time encouraging national disarmament and international control of weapons.

A35   THE INTERNATIONAL POST-WAR SETTLEMENT   1944

[Front wrapper, black type on deep blue: vertical rule head to foot 1⅛ in. from spine] | THE | INTERNATIONAL | POST-WAR | SETTLEMENT | [two horizontal rules] | BY | LEONARD | WOOLF | FABIAN PUBLICA-TIONS LTD. | PUBLISHED IN CONJUNCTION WITH VICTOR GOLLANCZ LTD. | RESEARCH SERIES NO. 85 | [at right, equal in height to the previous three lines] 6D

Format: 24 pp. 8½ × 5⅜ in.

Pagination: [i] front wrapper, as above; [ii] foreword and publisher's note; 1–21 text; [22] list of Fabian Publications.

Binding: Self-wrappers, as described above.

Publication: September 1944, at 6*d.*; the number of copies issued is not known.

Notes: 1. *Printed by The Hereford Times Ltd. General Printing Works (T.U.). London and Hereford, L 3580,* at foot of back wrapper.

2. Prior to its summer 1944 annual conference, the Labour Party issued an entirely different pamphlet with the same title, a copy of which was sent to LW for his comments.

3. Reprinted in *In Savage Times* (A44), and by Kraus as part of their "Fabian Research Series" in 1972.

General Note: This densely written tract proposes specific policies for a Labour government to support at the close of the war, including: establishment of an effective international authority that will not only settle disputes, but also foster social security and full employment; relinquishing to that authority enough force to defend international law and order from nations that act aggressively; immediate independence for all Third World countries capable of it, and power over the others to be granted not to any European country but to the international authority until self-determination is possible; rejuvenation of the international socialist movement. LW is critical of the first accounts of the Dumbarton Oaks conference and sceptical of the willingness of some belligerent countries to truly support a strong, central, international government.

A36   FOREIGN POLICY: THE LABOUR PARTY'S DILEMMA   1947

[within a ruled border 7⅛ × 4¼ in.] FOREIGN POLICY | THE LABOUR PARTY'S DILEMMA | BY LEONARD WOOLF | WITH A CRITICAL COMMENT BY | W.N. EWER | LONDON, NOVEMBER, 1947 | FABIAN PUBLICATIONS LTD., | 11, DARTMOUTH STREET, SW1 | AND | VICTOR GOLLANCZ LTD., | 14, HENRIETTA STREET, WC2

Format: 36 pp. 8½ × 5⅜ in.

Pagination: [1] title page as above; [2] contents; [3–4] foreword by Harold Laski; [5] 6–26 text by LW; 27–34 comment by Ewer; [35–36] advertisements for the Fabian Society.

Binding: Paper wrappers. Front printed in blue and black: [blue panel ⅝ in. high] | [in black on white] FOREIGN POLICY | The Labour Party's Dilemma | [in black on blue panel 3¾ in. tall] By | LEONARD WOOLF | With a critical comment by | W.N. EWER | Foreword by HAROLD LASKI | [in black on white] FABIAN PUBLICATIONS LTD. | In conjunction with Victor Gollancz Ltd. | RESEARCH SERIES No. 121 | [at right, equal in height to the previous three lines:] 2/-; inside front wrapper printed with notes on the authors; inside back wrapper printed with advertisements for Fabian Society publications; back wrapper blue (unprinted).

Publication: November 1947, at 2s.; the number of copies issued is not known.

Notes: 1. 'Printed by The Hereford Times Ltd., General Printing Works (T.U.), London and Hereford. L 4463', at foot of back wrapper.

2. Reprinted in 1972 by Kraus as part of their "Fabian Research Series" set.

General Notes: As the Cold War commenced, the British Left was divided over which camp to align itself with. Some leaders thought that, as a socialist party, it should ally itself with the Soviet Union despite that nation's authoritarian politics, while others thought that it should support the democratic United States, despite that nation's capitalist economic system; still others argued that Britain should remain non-aligned.

In his foreword, Laski writes that ". . . Mr. Leonard Woolf was asked to set out the different points of view, with their advantages and disadvantages, and to state a policy of his own round which agreement, if possible, might be built." LW concluded that the United Nations as constituted was "a dangerous farce"; that Britain should remain non-aligned and co-operate with both the United States and the Soviet Union whenever individual actions would further democratic socialist goals; that Britain should lead the non-aligned states to prevent the outbreak of war between the two super-powers; and that Britain should immediately reduce its own military forces and imperial obligations.

A37   PRINCIPIA POLITICA   1953

a. first issue: Hogarth Press, 1953

PRINCIPIA POLITICA | A STUDY OF COMMUNAL PSYCHOLOGY | LEONARD WOOLF | [publisher's device ¾ in. diameter] | 1953 | THE HOGARTH PRESS | LONDON

Format: 320 pp. 8½ × 5½ in.

Pagination: [i] half-title; [ii] list of LW's works; [iii] [title page as above; [iv] PUBLISHED BY | The Hogarth Press Ltd. | LONDON | [asterisk] | Clarke, Irwin & Co. Ltd. | TORONTO | PRINTED IN GREAT BRITAIN | ALL RIGHTS RESERVED; v–vi preface; 7–319 text and indexes; [320] PRINTED IN GREAT BRITAIN | BY R. & R. CLARK, LTD., EDINBURGH.

Binding: Pale brownish-orange cloth. Spine blocked in gold: PRINCIPIA | POLITICA | [star-shaped ornament] | Leonard | Woolf | THE | HOGARTH | PRESS. Dust jacket grey paper printed in black and orange.

Publication: 8 October 1953, at 25s.; 3000 copies were issued.

b. second issue: Harcourt, Brace, 1953

PRINCIPIA POLITICA | A STUDY OF COMMUNAL PSYCHOLOGY | LEONARD WOOLF | HARCOURT, BRACE & COMPANY | NEW YORK

Format: 320 pp. 8¼ × 5⅜ in.

Pagination: Identical to first issue, above, except for title page [as above] and p. [iv], which reads: PUBLISHED BY | Harcourt, Brace & Company | NEW YORK | COPYRIGHT 1953 BY LEONARD WOOLF | PRINTED IN GREAT BRITAIN | ALL RIGHTS RESERVED.

Binding: Pale greenish cloth. Spine blocked in dark green: Principia | Politica | [double rule across spine] | LEONARD | WOOLF | Harcourt, Brace | and Company. Dust jacket pale green paper printed in dark green.

PRINCIPIA
POLITICA

A Study of Communal Psychology

Being Volume 3 of

After the Deluge

LEONARD WOOLF

Publication: December 1953, at $5.00; 1000 copies were imported from England, according to the publisher's correspondence files.

Note: According to a slip loosely inserted in review copies, the 'release date for review' was 28 December 1953.

General Notes: Although it broke the chronological framework of the first two volumes of *After the Deluge*, LW conceived *Principia Politica* as the third volume in a trilogy devoted to the communal psychology of the modern world. This final volume explored the psychology of 20th-century totalitarianism, drawing on LW's earlier political tracts and his personal experiences; it is, in some ways, his political autobiography. Copies of all three volumes were bound uniformly and issued simultaneously in the autumn of 1953. See Wilson, pp. 234–40, *Downhill All the Way*, pp. 204–05, and LW's *Letters*, pp. 493–94, for accounts of its negative reception and the effect of that reception on LW.

A38 SOWING   1960

a. first edition, first issue: Hogarth Press, 1960

SOWING | AN AUTOBIOGRAPHY | OF THE YEARS 1880–1904 | BY | LEONARD WOOLF | [publisher's device ¾ in. diameter] | 1960 | THE HOGARTH PRESS | LONDON

Format: 208 pp. 8½ × 5½ in.

Pagination: [1] half-title; [2] list of LW's works; [frontispiece]; [3] title page as above; [4] Published by | The Hogarth Press Ltd | 42 William IV Street | London WC2 | * | Clarke, Irwin & Co Ltd | Toronto | © | Leonard Woolf 1960 | Printed and Bound in England by | Hazell Watson and Viney Ltd | Aylesbury and Slough; [5] dedication; [6] blank; [7] contents; [8] blank; [9] list of illustrations; [10] blank; 11–202 text; 203–205 [206] index; [207–208] blank.

Binding: Brilliant blue cloth. Spine blocked in gold: SOWING | An | Autobiography | of the | Years | 1880–1904 | Leonard | Woolf | THE | HOGARTH | PRESS. Dust jacket pale blue paper printed in dark blue and red.

Publication: September 1960, at 21*s.*; 4000 copies were issued.

Note: Reprinted in 1961, 1967 and 1970.

b. first edition, second issue: Harcourt, Brace, Jovanovich 'Harvest Paperbacks', 1975

SOWING | AN AUTOBIOGRAPHY | OF THE YEARS 1880 TO 1904 | [ornament] | LEONARD WOOLF | [publisher's device ¼ × ⅜ in.] | A HARVEST BOOK | HARCOURT BRACE JOVANOVICH | NEW YORK AND LONDON

Format: 210 pp. 8 × 5¼ in.

Pagination: [1] half-title; [2] list of LW's works; [frontispiece]; [3] title page as above; [4] Copyright © 1960 by Leonard Woolf | [5-line reservation statement] | Printed in the United States of America | [Library of Congress CIP data in 10 lines] | First Harvest edition 1975 | ABCDEFGHIJ; [5] dedication; [6] blank; [7] contents; [8] blank; [9] list of illustrations; [10] blank; 11–206 text and index; [207] advertisements for Harcourt, Brace, Jovanovich paperback issues of LW's autobiography; [208–210] blank.

Binding: Stiff paper wrappers printed in orange, blue, green, white and black.

Publication: October 1975, at $2.95; 10,000 copies were issued, 5000 of which were later used for the five-volume boxed set of LW's autobiography.

Note: Six leaves of illustrations between pp. 102–03.

c. second edition: Harcourt, Brace, 1960

[Ornament ½ × 1½ in.] SOWING | AN AUTOBIOGRAPHY OF | THE YEARS 1880 TO 1904 | BY LEONARD WOOLF [publisher's device ¼ in. sq.] | HARCOURT, BRACE & COMPANY NEW YORK

Format: 224 pp. 8 × 5 in.

Pagination: [1] half-title; [2] list of LW's works; [3] title page as above; [4] [six lines of copyright data, including *First American edition.* and Library of Congress card no.]; [5] dedication; [6] blank; [7] contents; [8] blank; [9] list of illustrations; [10] blank; [11] division title; [12] blank; 13–224 text and indexes.

Binding: Black cloth spine; brown paper over boards. Spine blocked in gold: [in three parallel lines reading head to foot] *SOWING: AN AUTOBIOGRAPHY OF THE YEARS 1880 TO 1904* | [line of small floral ornaments] | *BY LEONARD WOOLF* [publisher's device] *HARCOURT, BRACE AND COMPANY.* Dust jacket white paper printed in black and yellow.

Publication: 28 September 1960, at $4.50; the number of copies issued is not known.

Notes: 1. 'Printed in the United States of America' on p. [4].
          2. Four leaves of illustrations between pp. 160–61.

d. third edition: Readers Union, 1962

SOWING | BY | LEONARD WOOLF | AN AUTOBIOGRAPHY OF THE YEARS 1880–1904 | READERS UNION | THE HOGARTH PRESS | LONDON 1962

Format: 184 pp. 7½ × 4½ in.

Pagination: [i] half-title; [ii] list of LW's works; [iii] title page as above; [iv] [dedication, in three lines] | © LEONARD WOOLF 1960 | *This RU edition was produced in 1962 for sale to its mem-* | *bers only by the Readers Union Ltd at Aldine House, 10–13* | *Bedford Street, London W.C.2* [. . .] | *The book has been reset in* | *12-point Poliphilus type leaded and printed and bound at* | *The Aldine Press, Letchworth. It was first published by* | *The Hogarth Press Ltd.*; v contents; [vi] blank; vii list of illustrations; [viii] blank; 1–176 text.

Binding: Deep blue mottled paper over boards. Spine blocked in gold: [reading head to foot] SOWING *LEONARD WOOLF* | [at foot] RU. Dust jacket light greenish blue paper printed in black.

Publication: February 1962, at 5s. 9d.; number of copies issued not known.

Note: Four leaves of illustrations between pp. 84–85.

General Note: Reprinted in the Oxford University Press two-volume *Auto-biography*; see A45 for more information.

A39   GROWING   1961

a. first issue: Hogarth Press, 1961

GROWING | AN AUTOBIOGRAPHY OF THE YEARS 1904 - 1911 | BY | LEONARD WOOLF | [publisher's device ¾ in. diameter] | 1961 | THE HOGARTH PRESS | LONDON

Format: 256 pp. 8½ × 5½ in.

Pagination: [1] half-title; [2] list of LW's works; [frontispiece]; [3] title page as above; [4] Published by | The Hogarth Press Ltd | 42 William IV Street | London WC2 | [asterisk] | Clarke, Irwin & Co. Ltd | Toronto | © Leonard Woolf 1961 | Printed and Bound in England by | Hazell Watson and Viney Ltd | Aylesbury and Slough'; [5] 8-line motto in French; [6] blank; [7] contents; [8] list of illustrations and maps; [9–10] introduction; 11–252 text; 253–256 index.

Binding: Brilliant blue cloth. Spine blocked in gold: GROWING | *An* | *Autobiography* | *of the* | *Years* | 1904–1911 | Leonard Woolf | THE | HOGARTH | PRESS. Dust jacket pale blue paper printed in red and dark blue.

Publication: 2 November 1961, at 25s.; 4750 copies were issued.

Note: Four leaves of illustrations between pp. 96–97.

b. second issue: Harcourt, Brace and World, 1962

GROWING | AN AUTOBIOGRAPHY | OF THE YEARS 1904–1911 | BY | LEONARD WOOLF | *HARCOURT, BRACE & WORLD, INC. NEW YORK*

Format: 256 pp. 8⅞ × 5⅝ in.

Pagination: Identical to first issue, above, but for title page [as above] and p. [4], which reads: © *1961 by Leonard Woolf* | [4-line reservation statement] | *First American edition 1962* | [Library of Congress card no.] | *Printed in the United States of America.*

Binding: Grey cloth spine; greyish green paper over boards. Spine blocked in gold: [along top half of spine in two lines reading head to foot] *GROWING by LEONARD WOOLF* | *AN AUTOBIOGRAPHY OF THE YEARS 1904–1911* | [panel of dots ½ in. high blind-stamped across spine] | [head to foot] *Harcourt, Brace & World* |

[publisher's device ⅛ in. sq.]. Dust jacket white paper printed in brownish green and yellow.

Publication: 24 January 1962, at $5.95; number of copies issued not known.

Note: Four leaves of illustrations between pp. 96–97.

c. third issue: Harcourt, Brace, Jovanovich 'Harvest Paperbacks', 1975.

GROWING | AN AUTOBIOGRAPHY | OF THE YEARS 1904 TO 1911 | [ornament] | LEONARD WOOLF | [publisher's device ¼ × ⅜ in. sq.] | A HARVEST BOOK | HARCOURT BRACE JOVANOVICH | NEW YORK AND LONDON

Format: 264 pp. 8 × 5¼ in.

Pagination: [1] half-title; [2] list of LW's works; [3] title page as above; [iv] Copyright © 1961 by Leonard Woolf | [five-line reservation statement] | Printed in the United States of America | [Library of Congress CIP data in 12 lines] | First Harvest edition 1975 | ABCDEFGHIJ; [thereafter identical to the first issue, above, until;] [257] advertisements for Harcourt, Brace, Jovanovich paperback issues of LW's autobiography; [258–264] blank.

Binding: Stiff paper wrappers printed in orange, yellow, white and black.

Publication: October 1975, at $3.45; 10,000 copies were issued, of which 5000 were later used for the five-volume boxed set of LW's autobiography.

Note: Four leaves of illustrations between pp. 96–97.

General Note: Reprinted in Oxford University Press two-volume *Autobiography*, A45.

A40   DIARIES IN CEYLON   1963

a. first issue: [as a serial, in the Ceylon Historical Journal, vol. IX nos. 1–4 (July 1959-April 1960, but actually published in February 1962); see C1514. 500 sets of these sheets were issued by the Hogarth Press with their own title page (see A40b).]

b. second issue: Hogarth Press, 1963

LEONARD WOOLF | [3¹⁵⁄₁₆ in. double rule] | DIARIES IN CEYLON | 1908–1911 | RECORDS OF | A COLONIAL ADMINISTRATOR | *BEING THE OFFICIAL DIARIES* | *MAINTAINED BY LEONARD WOOLF* | *WHILE ASSISTANT GOVERNMENT AGENT OF* | *THE HAMBAN-TOTA DISTRICT, CEYLON* | *DURING THE PERIOD AUGUST 1908 TO MAY 1911* | EDITED WITH A PREFACE BY | LEONARD WOOLF | & | STORIES FROM THE EAST | THREE SHORT STORIES ON CEYLON BY | LEONARD WOOLF | 1963 | THE HOGARTH PRESS | LONDON

Format: 366 pp. 8½ × 5⅝ in.

Pagination: [frontispiece]; [iii: sic] title page as above; [iv] Published by | The Hogarth Press Ltd | 42 William IV Street | London WC2 | [asterisk] | Clarke, Irwin & Co Ltd | Toronto | *First published by* | *The Ceylon Historical Journal* | © *February, 1962* | Printed in Colombo, Ceylon; [v] contents; [vi] illustrations; vii-lx introduction; lxi-lxxiii glossary; lxxiv list of abbreviations; lxxv-lxxx preface by LW; 1–244 text of Diaries; 245–250 index to Diaries; [folding map]; [251–252] blank; 253 division title; [254] blank; 255–286 text of Stories from the East; [287] blank; [288] printer's note as below.

Binding: Green cloth. Spine blocked in gold: DIARIES IN | CEYLON | 1908–1911 | AND | STORIES | FROM THE | EAST | [½ in. rule] | LEONARD | WOOLF | [½ in. rule] | THE | HOGARTH | PRESS. Dust jacket pale blue paper printed in dark green.

Publication: April 1963, at 30*s.*; 500 copies were issued.

Notes: 1. '[. . .] Printed at Metro Printers, 19, Austin Place, | Colombo [. . .]', on p. [288].

      2. Some copies were bound without the final leaf (pp. [287–288]).

c. third issue: Tisara Press, 1983

LEONARD WOOLF | DIARIES | IN | CEYLON | 1908–1911 | RECORDS OF A COLONIAL ADMINISTRATOR | *BEING* | *THE OFFICIAL DIARIES MAINTAINED* | *BY LEONARD WOOLF WHILE ASSISTANT* | *GOVERNMENT AGENT OF THE HAMBAN-* | *TOTA DISTRICT,* *CEYLON, DURING THE* | *PERIOD AUGUST 1908 TO MAY 1911* | EDITED WITH A PREFACE BY | LEONARD WOOLF | AND | STORIES FROM THE EAST | THREE SHORT STORIES ON CEYLON | BY | THE CEYLON HISTORICAL JOURNAL | VOL. IX – JULY 1959 TO APRIL 1960 – NOS. 1–4

Format: 366 pp. 8¼ × 5½ in.

Pagination: [i-ii] blank; [frontispiece]; [iii] title page as above; [iv] *First edition* [*sic*] .. *February* 1962 | *Second edition* [*sic*] .. *September* 1983 | *Printed at the* | *TISARA PRESS* | *Dutvgemunu Street, Dehiwala, Sri Lanka*; [v] contents; [vi] illustrations; vii-lx introduction; lxi-lxxiii glossary; lxxiv list of abbreviations; lxxv-lxxx preface by LW; 1–244 text of Diaries; [folding map]; 245–250 index to Diaries; [251–252] blank; 253 division title; [254] blank; 255–286 text of Stories from the East; [287] blank; [288] printer's note as below.

Binding: Brilliant blue cloth spine, with pale blue paper over boards. Spine printed in black as follows [single line, reading head to foot]: CEYLON HISTORICAL JOURNAL VOL 9 JULY 1959—APRIL 1960. Front and rear free end-papers are followed by one blank leaf of similarly heavy paper, then stiff glossy paper leaves printed in brown and black with information about this book and other Tisara Press reprints. The placing and design of these stiff glossy leaves suggest that this issue may also have been available separately bound in paper wrappers, although no such copy was found for examination.

Publication: September 1983, at 300 'Rs/'; number of copies not known.

Notes: 1. Printer's note on p. [288]: Printed by K. Hemachandra at the Tisara Press, 135, | Dutugemunu Street, Dehiwala for Tisara Prakasakayo Ltd., Dehiwala, | Sri Lanka.

2. 'Introduction to the Second Edition [*sic*]', pp. xlv-xlvii, is an expanded list of surviving records from kachcheries around the island; it replaces the 'postscript' found on the same pages in the 1962 issue.

General Note: These official diaries are part of a series kept by colonial administrators in Ceylon that span the years 1808–1941; all surviving volumes are now in the National Archives at Colombo. Although they were meant to be concise accounts of government affairs and intended primarily to inform superiors of his activities, LW's official diaries nevertheless contain much vivid description and frequent expressions of emotion and opinion. They document not only the day-to-day working of British imperialism, but LW's personal reaction to the people and physical environment of Sri Lanka. When he returned on a visit to the island in February 1960 he was presented with a copy of the diaries; the frustrating process of getting them published is chronicled in LW's correspondence with Shelton Fernando, in the Woolf Papers at Sussex University. Part of LW's preface is reprinted in *The Journey Not the Arrival Matters*, pp. 202–04.

A41　BEGINNING AGAIN　　　　　　　　1964

a. first issue: Hogarth Press, 1964

BEGINNING | AGAIN | AN AUTOBIOGRAPHY | OF THE YEARS 1911–1918 | BY | LEONARD WOOLF | [publisher's device ¾ in. diameter] | 1964 | THE HOGARTH PRESS | LONDON

Format: 260 pp. 8½ × 5½ in.

Pagination: [1] half-title; [2] list of LW's works; [frontispiece]; [3] title page as above; [4] Published by | The Hogarth Press Ltd | 42 William IV Street | London WC2 | [asterisk] | Clarke, Irwin & Co. Ltd | Toronto | *First Published May 1964* | © Leonard Woolf 1964 | Printed in Great Britain by | T. & A. Constable Ltd | Hopetoun Street, Edinburgh; [5] dedication; [6] blank; [7] quotation from Rilke; [8] blank; [9] contents; [10] blank; [11] list of illustrations; [12] blank; [13] foreword; [14] blank; 15–259 [260] text and index.

Binding: Brilliant blue cloth. Spine blocked in gold: BEGINNING | AGAIN | *An Autobiography* | *of the* | *Years* | 1911–1918 | Leonard | Woolf | THE | HOGARTH | PRESS. Dust jacket pale blue paper printed in green and orange.

Publication: 7 May 1964, at 30*s.*; 4550 copies were issued.

Notes: 1. Eleven leaves of photographs dispersed throughout the text.

2. Printing history: further impressions were issued in August 1964 (1600 copies), August 1965 (1500 copies), April 1968 (1500 copies), September 1972 (1250 copies), and March 1978 (500 copies).

3. Excerpts relating to the Hogarth Press were reprinted in Bill Henderson, *The Publish-It-Yourself Handbook* (Yonkers, N.Y.: The Pushcart Book Press, 1973).

4. Kirkpatrick B12a.

5. The index in this issue was compiled by LW (1979 ed. of *Wise Virgins*, p. x), and is far less thorough than that in the American issue which followed.

b. second issue: Harcourt, Brace and World, 1964

BEGINNING | AGAIN | [ornamental rule] | *AN AUTOBIOGRAPHY OF THE YEARS 1911 to 1918* | [ornamental rule] | LEONARD WOOLF | HARCOURT, BRACE & WORLD, INC. | [slash in original] *NEW YORK* | [publisher's logo, ¼ in. sq.]

Format: 264 pp. 8 × 5½ in.

Pagination: [1] half-title; [2] list of LW's works; [3] title page as above; [4] © 1963, 1964 by Leonard Woolf | [3-line reservation statement] | first American edition | [Library of Congress card no.] | Printed in the United States of America; [5] dedication; [6] blank; [7] contents; [8] blank; [9] list of illustrations; [10] blank; [11] quotation from Rilke; [12] blank; [13] foreword; [14] blank; 15–263 text and index; [264] blank.

Binding: Spine covered in dark red cloth; boards in brown paper. Spine blocked in gold: [two lines reading head to foot] BEGINNING AGAIN [publisher's device ¼ in. sq.] LEONARD WOOLF | *Harcourt, Brace & World.* Dust jacket white paper printed in black, red and gold.

Publication: 9 September 1964, at $6.95; 3200 copies were issued.

Notes: 1. Twelve leaves of illustrations are dispersed throughout the text.

2. Further impressions were issued in October 1964 (1500 copies), January 1965 (2200 copies), and August 1971 (1000 copies).

3. The index in this issue contains approximately twice as many entries as that in the first issue.

c. third issue: Harcourt, Brace, Jovanovich 'Harvest Paperbacks', 1972

BEGINNING | AGAIN | AN AUTOBIOGRAPHY | [1|2 in. ornamental rule] | LEONARD WOOLF | [publisher's device ¼ × ⅜ in.] | *A HARVEST BOOK* | HARCOURT BRACE JOVANOVICH | NEW YORK AND LONDON

Format: 264 pp. 7¼ × 5 in.

Pagination: [1] half-title; [2] list of LW's works; [3] title page as above; [4] Copyright © 1963, 1964 by Leonard Woolf | [5-line reservation statement] | Printed in the United States of America | [Library of Congress CIP data] | First Harvest edition 1972 | ABCDEFGHIJ; [5] dedication; [6] blank; [7] contents; [8] blank; [9] list of illustrations; [10] blank; [11] 9-line quotation from Rilke, in German and English; [12] blank; [13] foreword; [14] blank; 15–257 text; [258] blank; 259–263 index; [264] advertisements for the paperback issues of the five volumes of LW's autobiography, and the boxed set.

Binding: Stiff paper wrappers printed in orange, brown, white and black, with a photograph of Leonard and Virginia on their wedding day on front.

Publication: 15 March 1972, at $3.45; 5966 copies were issued.

Notes: 1. There was a subsequent impression of 10,271 copies in October 1975; these were bound in multi-coloured stiff paper wrappers, and 5000 were issued in the boxed set of LW's autobiography.

    2. Twelve leaves of illustrations are dispersed throughout the text.

General Note: Reprinted in the Oxford University Press two-volume *Autobiography*, A45.

A42   DOWNHILL ALL THE WAY   1967

a. first issue: Hogarth Press, 1967

DOWNHILL | ALL THE WAY | AN AUTOBIOGRAPHY | OF THE YEARS 1919–1939 | BY | LEONARD WOOLF | [publisher's device ¾ in. diameter] | 1967 | THE HOGARTH PRESS | LONDON

Format: 260 pp. 8½ × 5½ in.

Pagination: [1] half-title; [2] list of LW's works; [frontispiece]; [3] title page as above; [4] Published by | The Hogarth Press Ltd | 42 William IV Street | London WC2 | * | Clarke, Irwin & Co. Ltd | Toronto | © Leonard Woolf 1967 | Printed in Great Britain by | T. & A. Constable Ltd | Hopetoun Street, Edinburgh; [5] quotation from St Luke; [6] blank; [7] contents; [8] list of illustrations; 9–259 text and index; [260] blank.

Binding: Brilliant blue cloth. Spine blocked in gold: DOWNHILL | ALL THE | WAY | An | Autobiography | of the | Years | 1919–1939 | Leonard | Woolf | THE | HOGARTH | PRESS. Dust jacket white paper printed in blue and black, with a black and white photograph of LW on the front wrapper.

Publication: 27 April 1967, at £1 15s.; 5000 copies were issued.

Notes: 1. Five leaves of illustrations dispersed throughout the text.

    2. Subsequent impressions of 1750 copies in May 1967, 1500 copies in February 1968, 1500 copies in July 1970, and 1250 copies in May 1975.

    3. Kirkpatrick B14a.

b. second issue: Harcourt, Brace and World, 1967

DOWNHILL | ALL THE | WAY | AN AUTOBIOGRAPHY OF | THE YEARS 1919–1939 | LEONARD WOOLF | [publisher's device ¼ in. sq.] | HARCOURT, BRACE & WORLD, INC. | NEW YORK

Format: 272 pp. 8 × 5⅜ in.

Pagination: [i-ii] blank; [iii] half-title; [iv] blank; [frontispiece]; [v] list of LW's works; [vi] blank; [vii] title page as above; [viii] Copyright © 1967 by Leonard Woolf | [4-line reservation statement] | First American edition | [Library of Congress card no.] | Printed in the United States of America; [1] quotation from St. Luke; [2] blank; [3]

contents; [4] blank; [5] list of illustrations; [6] blank; [7] fly-title; [8] blank; 9–259 text and index; [260–264] blank.

Binding: Blue cloth spine, light blue paper over boards. Spine blocked in silver in two lines reading head to foot: DOWNHILL ALL THE WAY [dot] LEONARD WOOLF | An Autobiography of the Years 1919–1939 [publisher's device ¼ in. sq.] HARCOURT, BRACE & WORLD. Dust jacket printed in blue, purple, reddish purple, white and black, with photograph of LW on front wrapper.

Publication: 25 October 1967, at $5.95; 5100 copies were issued.

Notes: 1. Four leaves of illustrations follow page 128.
  2. Subsequent impression of 2000 copies in August 1968.
  3. Kirkpatrick B14b.

c. third issue: Readers Union, 1968

DOWNHILL | ALL THE WAY | AN AUTOBIOGRAPHY | OF THE YEARS 1919–1939 | BY | LEONARD WOOLF | READERS UNION | THE HOGARTH PRESS | LONDON 1968

Format: 256 pp. 7⅝ × 5 in.

Pagination: [1] half-title; [2] list of LW's works; [3] title page as above; [4] © LEONARD WOOLF 1967 | This RU edition was produced in 1968 for sale to its members only | [. . . 5 lines regarding the Readers Union book club, including: . . .] This book | has been printed by the Hollen Press, Slough. It was first | published by The Hogarth Press, London.'; [5] quotation from St Luke; [6] blank; [7] contents; [8] list of illustrations; 9–254 text; [255–256] blank.

Binding: Brilliant blue paper-covered boards. Spine blocked in gold: [reading head to foot, in a single line] DOWNHILL ALL THE WAY Leonard Woolf | [across foot:] RU. Dust jacket violet paper printed with deep blue concentric circles, with text in white.

Publication: June 1968, at 8s.; the number of copies issued is not known.

Note: 1. Five leaves of illustrations dispersed throughout the text.

d. fourth issue: Harcourt, Brace, Jovanovich 'Harvest Paperbacks', 1975.

DOWNHILL | ALL THE | WAY | AN AUTOBIOGRAPHY OF THE YEARS 1919 TO 1939 | [ornament ½ in. long] | LEONARD WOOLF | [publisher's device ¼ × ⅜ in.] | A HARVEST BOOK | HARCOURT BRACE JOVANOVICH | NEW YORK AND LONDON

Format: 262 pp. 8 × 5¼ in.

Pagination: [1] half-title; [2] list of LW's works; [frontispiece]; [3] title page as above; [4] Copyright © 1967 by Leonard Woolf | [5-line reservation statement] | Printed in the United States of America | [Library of Congress CIP data in 11 lines] | First Harvest edition 1975 | ABCDEFGHIJ; [5] contents; [6] blank; [7] list of illustrations; [8] quotation from St Luke; 9–259 text and index; [260] blank; [261] advertisement for Harcourt, Brace, Jovanovich paperback issues of LW's autobiography; [262] blank.

Binding: Stiff paper wrappers printed in orange, purple, brown, white and black.

Publication: October 1975, at $3.45; 10,000 copies were issued, of which 5000 were part of the five-volume boxed set of LW's autobiography.

Note: Four leaves of photographs follow p. 128.

General Note: Reprinted in Oxford University Press two-volume *Autobiography* (A45).

A43   THE JOURNEY NOT THE ARRIVAL MATTERS   1969

a. first issue: Hogarth Press, 1969

THE JOURNEY | NOT THE ARRIVAL | MATTERS | AN AUTOBIO-GRAPHY | OF THE YEARS 1939–1969 | BY | LEONARD WOOLF | [publisher's device ¾ in. diameter] | 1969 | THE HOGARTH PRESS | LONDON

Format: 218 pp. 8½ × 5⅜ in.

Pagination: [1] half-title; [2] list of LW's works; [3] title page as above; [4] Published by | The Hogarth Press Ltd | 42 William IV Street | London W.C.2 | * | Clarke, Irwin & Co. Ltd | Toronto | © Leonard Woolf 1969 | Printed in Great Britain by | T. & A. Constable Ltd., | Hopetoun Street, Edinburgh; [5] contents; [6] blank; [7–8] list of illustrations; 9–217 text and index [217 is recto of free end-paper].

Binding: Brilliant blue cloth. Spine blocked in silver: THE | JOURNEY | NOT THE | ARRIVAL | MATTERS | *An* | *Autobiography* | *of the Years* | 1939–1969 | Leonard Woolf | THE | HOGARTH | PRESS. Dust jacket white paper printed in red and black, with black and white photograph of LW in Monks House garden on front.

Publication: 16 October 1969, at £1.75; 5500 copies were issued.

Notes: 1. Eight leaves of illustrations are dispersed throughout the text.
        2. Subsequent impressions of 1500 copies in November 1969 and June 1970, and 1250 copies in September 1973.
        3. Kirkpatrick B14a.

b. second issue: Harcourt, Brace and World, 1970.

THE JOURNEY | NOT THE | ARRIVAL MATTERS | AN AUTOBIO-GRAPHY | OF THE YEARS | 1939–1969 | *LEONARD WOOLF* | HARCOURT, BRACE & WORLD, INC. | NEW YORK

Format: 224 pp. 8 × 5⅜ in.

Pagination: [i] half-title; [ii] blank; [iii] list of LW's works; [iv] blank; [1] title page as above; [2] *Copyright* © *1969 by Leonard Woolf* | [6-line reservation statement] | *First American edition* | [Library of Congress card no.] | *Printed in the United States of America* | [publisher's device]; [3] contents; [4] blank; [5] list of illustrations; [6] blank; [7] fly-title; [8] blank; 9–217 text and index; [218–220] blank.

Binding: Pale yellowish brown cloth spine, orange paper over boards. Spine blocked in silver in two lines reading head to foot: *The Journey Not the Arrival Matters* [dot] *Leonard Woolf* | AN AUTOBIOGRAPHY OF THE YEARS 1939–1969 [publisher's device] HARCOURT, BRACE & WORLD. White dust jacket printed in orange, light brown and black.

Publication: 25 March 1970, at $5.95; 5100 copies were issued.

Notes: 1. Four leaves of illustrations follow p. 124.
2. Subsequent impression of 2000 copies in July 1970.
3. Kirkpatrick B15b.

c. *third issue: Harcourt, Brace, Jovanovich 'Harvest Paperbacks', 1975*

THE JOURNEY | NOT THE | ARRIVAL MATTERS | AN AUTOBIO-GRAPHY | OF THE YEARS 1939–1969 | [ornament ½ in. long] | LEONARD WOOLF | [publisher's device ¼ × ⅜ in.] | A HARVEST BOOK | HARCOURT BRACE JOVANOVICH | NEW YORK AND LONDON

Format: 224 pp. 8 × 5¼ in.

Pagination: [1] half-title; [2] list of LW's works; [3] title-page as above; [4] Copyright © 1969 by Leonard Woolf | [5-line reservation statement] | Printed in the United States of America | [Library of Congress CIP data in 10 lines] | First Harvest edition 1975 | ABCDEFGHIJ; [5] contents; [6] blank; [7] list of illustrations; [8] blank; 9–217 text and index; [218] blank; [219] advertisement for the Harcourt, Brace, Jovanovich paperback issues of LW's autobiography; [220–224] blank.

Binding: Stiff paper wrappers printed in orange, green, black, gold and white.

Publication: October 1975, at $3.25; 10,000 copies were issued, of which 5000 were part of the five-volume boxed set of LW's autobiography.

Note: Four leaves of illustrations follow page 44.

General Note: Reprinted in the Oxford University Press two-volume *Autobiography* (A45).

A44 IN SAVAGE TIMES 1973

IN SAVAGE TIMES | LEONARD WOOLF ON PEACE AND WAR | CONTAINING FOUR PAMPHLETS BY LEONARD WOOLF | FEAR AND POLITICS: A DEBATE AT THE ZOO | THE WAY OF PEACE | THE LEAGUE AND ABYSSINIA | THE INTERNATIONAL POST-WAR SETTLEMENT | WITH A NEW INTRODUCTION | FOR THE GARLAND EDITION BY | STEPHEN J. STEARNS | [publisher's device] | GARLAND PUBLISHING, INC., NEW YORK & LONDON | 1973

Format: 130 pp. 8⅞ × 5⅜ in.

Pagination: [1] series title; [2] series note; [3] title page as above; [4] [3-line copyright notice] | All Rights Reserved | [⅞ in. rule] | [Library of Congress CIP data in 14 lines] | *Printed in the United States of America*; 5–13 introduction; [1] 2–24 Fear and Politics; [one leaf of coloured paper]; [1] 2–30 The Way of Peace; [one leaf of coloured paper]; [1] 2–35 [36] The League and Abyssinia; [one leaf of coloured paper]; [i-ii] 1–21 [22] The International Post-War Settlement.

Binding: Greyish brown cloth. Spine blocked in gold: [double rule across head] | [reading head to foot] Woolf *In Savage Times* [publisher's device at foot] | Garland | [double rule across foot].

Publication: 30 June 1973, at $37.50; 150 copies were issued.

Note: Each title is separately paginated.

A45   AN AUTOBIOGRAPHY   1980

AN AUTOBIOGRAPHY | LEONARD WOOLF | [⅝ in. double rule] | [in vol. 1 only:] WITH AN INTRODUCTION BY QUENTIN BELL | VOLUME 1 [2] | 1880–1911 [1911–1969] | OXFORD NEW YORK TORONTO MELBOURNE | OXFORD UNIVERSITY PRESS | 1980

Format: 320 pp. 7¾ × 5⅛ in.

Pagination, vol. 1: [i] half-title; [ii] list of LW's works; [iii] title page as above; [iv] [publisher's locations in 6 lines] | © *M.T. Parsons, 1960, 1961* | *First published as* Sowing *and* Growing *by* | *The Hogarth Press Limited 1960, 1961* | *First published as an Oxford University Press paperback 1980* | *at the suggestion of Kate Bath* | [12-line reservation statement] | [British Library CIP data in 9 lines] | *Note: References to what was the present at the time of* | *writing have not been updated in the paperback edition* | *Typeset by Blackmore Press, Shaftesbury, and printed in* | *Great Britain by Cox & Wyman Ltd, Reading*; [v] contents; vi list of illustrations; vii-xiv introduction by Bell; [1] division title; [2] dedication; 3–130 text of *Sowing*; [131] division title; [132] 8-line quotation; 133–301 text of *Growing*; 302–306 index.

Pagination, vol. 2: [i] half-title; [ii] list of LW's works; [iii] title page as above; [iv] identical to vol. 1 except: © *M.T. Parsons 1964, 1967, 1969* | *First published in three volumes as* Beginning Again, Downhill all the Way, *and* The Journey not the Arrival Matters; [v] contents; [vi] blank; [vii-viii] list of illustrations; [1] division title; [2] dedication and 9-line quotation; [3] foreword; [4] blank; 5–187 text of *Beginning Again*; [188] blank; [189] division title; [190] 3-line quotation; 191–376 text of *Downhill All the Way*; [377] division title; [378] blank; 379–515 text of *The Journey Not the Arrival Matters*; [516] blank; 517–527 index; [528] blank; [four leaves of publisher's advertisements follow].

Binding: Vol. 1: Grey stiff paper wrappers printed in black, white and blue with full-colour portrait by Henry Lamb of LW as a young man on front cover. Vol. 2: Pale greyish-purple stiff paper wrappers printed in black, white and blue with a full-colour portrait of LW by Vanessa Bell on front cover.

Publication: Vol. 1 May 1980, at £3.50; 10,000 copies were printed, of which an unspecified number were wasted in 1982. Vol. 2 October 1980, at £5.95; again, 10,000 were printed and an unknown number were wasted in 1982. Both volumes were declared out-of-print in Sept. 1991.

Note: Four leaves of illustrations follow p. 82 and p. 210 in vol. 1, and sixteen leaves of illustrations follow page 264 in vol. 2.

General Notes: LW began to contemplate writing his autobiography not long after Virginia's death in 1941. His "Memoirs of an Elderly Man", written in 1945 for Cecil Day Lewis and Rosamond Lehmann's first issue of *Orion* (C1032), recount his journey to Ceylon and the people he met there; names of real people and places were disguised. Soon after, he resigned his posts in the Labour Party, turned over most of the responsibility for the Hogarth Press to Chatto & Windus, and focused his attention on *Principia Politica*, which contains much autobiographical material. In March 1953, with that volume completed, LW began the first of the five volumes of his autobiography [Guide to LW Papers: 15]. The hostile reception given to *Principia Politica* later that year coincided with LW's abandoning his autobiography for five years.

He resumed work on his memoirs briefly in 1958 and in January 1959 began to work steadily on them once again, completing the manuscript of *Sowing* in December [Spater & Parsons: 187; Guide to LW Papers: 16]. Two months later, in February 1960, he visited Ceylon for three weeks, presumably motivated at least in part by the desire to recapture scenes of his youth there before writing *Growing*; during this visit the government presented LW with a copy of his official diaries while a civil servant there 1904–11 which provided another source for the second volume of memoirs. After returning to England, LW wrote the text of that volume between June 1960 and March 1961 [Guide to LW Papers: 16].

The last years of LW's life were largely given to finishing the autobiography. *Beginning Again* was written between January 1962 and June 1963, and published in May 1964; *Downhill All the Way*, between November 1964 and July 1966, and published in April 1967; and *The Journey Not the Arrival Matters*, between August 1967 and February 1969. LW was correcting the proofs that spring when he apparently suffered a stroke; he recovered partially and was able to finish them before dying on 14 August 1969. The final volume of his autobiography appeared eight weeks later.

A46   LETTERS   1990

a. first issue: Weidenfeld and Nicolson, 1990

LETTERS OF | LEONARD | WOOLF | [2 in. swelled rule] | EDITED BY | FREDERIC | SPOTTS | WEIDENFELD AND NICOLSON | LONDON

Format: 656 pp. 9⅛ × 6 in.

Pagination: [i] half-title; [ii] blank; [iii] title page as above; [iv] [acknowledgement for permission to publish Strachey and Forster letters, in 5 lines] | Letters copyright © 1989 the Estate of | Leonard Woolf | Introduction and notes copyright © 1989 | Frederic Spotts | First published in Great Britain in 1990 by | George Weidenfeld and Nicolson Limited | 91 Clapham High Street | London SW4 7TA | [6-line reservation statement] | [British Library CIP data in 8 lines] | Printed and bound in Great Britain by | Butler & Tanner Ltd, Frome and London; v contents; [vi] blank; vii-viii illustrations; ix-xiv preface; xv-xxi sources and acknowledgements; [xxii] blank;

xxiii-xxv note on editing; [xxvi] blank; [xxvii] Woolf family tree; [xxviii] blank; xxix-xxxvi chronology of LW's life; [xxxvii] blank; [xxxviii] reproduction of letter to Lytton Strachey; [1] division title; [2] blank; 3–573 text of letters; [574] blank; 575–586 biographical appendix; 587–616 index; [617–618] blank.

Binding: Brilliant red paper over boards. Spine blocked in gold: LETTERS OF | [reading head to foot:] LEONARD WOOLF | EDITED BY | FREDERIC | SPOTTS | Weidenfeld | & Nicolson. Dust jacket red paper printed in yellow and black, with 2 different portraits of LW by Vanessa Bell.

Publication: 1 March 1990 at £30; 1250 copies were printed.

Note: In addition to p. [xxxviii], there are eight leaves of illustrations following p. 282.

b. second issue: Harcourt, Brace, Jovanovich, 1990

LETTERS OF | LEONARD | WOOLF | [2 in. swelled rule] | EDITED BY | FREDERIC | SPOTTS | HARCOURT | BRACE | JOVANOVICH | SAN DIEGO NEW YORK LONDON

Format: 656 pp. 9⅛ × 6 in.

Pagination: [i] half-title; [ii] blank; [iii] title page as above; [iv] [publisher's logo ¼ in. sq.] | Letters copyright © 1989 by the Estate of Leonard Woolf | Introduction and Notes | copyright © 1989 by Frederic Spotts | [7-line reservation statement] | [5-line note on reprint permission policy] | [6-line acknowledgement for permission to print Strachey and Forster letters] | Library of Congress CIP data in 12 lines, including ISBN 0–15–150915–8; see note to paperbound issue, below] | Designed by Michael Farmer | Printed in the United States of America | First Edition | ABCDE; [remainder of pagination follows first issue, above, exactly].

Binding: Dark blue cloth spine, deep blue paper over boards. Spine blocked in gold: EDITED BY | FREDERIC SPOTTS | [following three lines reading head to foot:] LETTERS OF | LEONARD | WOOLF | HBJ | HARCOURT | BRACE | JOVANO-VICH. Dust jacket glossy coated paper printed with a background of various shades of blue, against which text is printed in white and black with full-colour painting of LW by Vanessa Bell (c. 1938).

Publication: 1990, at $29.95; the number of copies and exact publication date were not released by the publisher.

c. third issue: Harcourt, Brace, Jovanovich, 1991

LETTERS OF | LEONARD | WOOLF | [2 in. swelled rule] | EDITED BY | FREDERIC | SPOTTS | HARCOURT | BRACE | JOVANOVICH | SAN DIEGO NEW YORK LONDON

Format: 656 pp. 9 × 5½ in.

Pagination: [i] half-title; [ii] blank; [iii] title page as above; [iv] [publisher's logo ¼ in. sq.] | Letters copyright © 1989 by the Estate of Leonard Woolf | Introduction and Notes | copyright © 1989 by Frederic Spotts | [7-line reservation statement] | [5-line note on reprint permission policy] | [6-line acknowledgement for permission to print Strachey and Forster letters] | Library of Congress CIP data in 12 lines; see note below on ISBN number] | Designed by Michael Farmer | Printed in the United States of America | First Edition | ABCDE; [remainder of pagination follows first issue, above, exactly].

Binding: Multi-coloured stiff paper wrappers with text and illustrations as the dust jacket of the American hard-cover issue, A46b. A blank leaf of heavy white paper is bound in between the outer wrappers and the printed leaves.

Publication: 1991, at $18.95; the number of copies and exact publication date were not released by the publisher.

Note: The ISBN printed on p. [iv] of this paperbound issue is that for the hard-cover issue (A46b, above). The ISBN of the paperbound issue, printed on the back wrapper, is 0–15–650879–6. This fact, together with the reappearance of Harcourt, Brace, Jovanovich's printing history code 'ABCDE' unchanged, suggests that this paper-bound issue was composed of sheets of the hardcover issue trimmed slightly and bound up in paper wrappers; these have quotations from English and American reviews of the earlier issues.

General Note: According to editor Frederic Spotts, LW received more than 40,000 letters during his lifetime; he presumably wrote approximately the same number, either to initiate the correspondence or in reply. Of those *c.* 40,000 letters, Spotts estimated that about 8,000 survive; 600 (spanning the years 1900–69) are printed in this edition, including all surviving letters to Virginia.

B Contributions to books and pamphlets

B1 EUPHROSYNE 1905

EUPHROSYNE | A COLLECTION OF VERSE | [ornament] | PUBLISHED AND SOLD BY | ELIJAH JOHNSON, 30 TRINITY STREET, CAMBRIDGE | LONDON AGENTS: MESSRS. A. & F. DENNY, 147 STRAND | [rule] | 1905

9½ × 5⅞ in. 92 pp. Grey paper wrappers printed in silver. Issued in the summer of 1905 at 1s. See Edmonds, *Lytton Strachey*, B2.

Poems by LW: "The Song of the Beasts", p. 8; "Dead Leaves", pp. 20–21; and "Dreams", pp. 42–44.

B2 TWO STORIES 1917

PUBLICATION NO. 1 | [rule] | TWO STORIES | WRITTEN AND PRINTED | BY | VIRGINIA WOOLF | AND | L.S. WOOLF | HOGARTH PRESS | RICHMOND | 1917

8⅞ × 5⅝ in. [ii], 34 pp. Various different coloured paper wrappers printed in black. Issued in July 1917 at 1s. 6d. See Kirkpatrick A2 and Woolmer 1.

"Three Jews", pp. [5]-18, by LW.

B3 THE FRAMEWORK OF A LASTING PEACE 1917

THE FRAMEWORK | OF A LASTING PEACE | EDITED BY | LEONARD S. WOOLF | [publisher's device] | LONDON: GEORGE ALLEN & UNWIN LTD. | RUSKIN HOUSE 40 MUSEUM STREET, W.C.1

8⅜ × 5⅜ in. 160 pp. Dark green cloth blocked in gold. Issued in September 1917 at 4s. 6d.

Contains an introduction (pp. 9–58) LW wrote in the winter of 1916–17 and which originally appeared in *War and Peace* in March 1917 (C0149); also contains the Fabian Society's draft plan written by LW and Sidney Webb for an international authority, published in *International Government* (A7). This volume also contains schemes prepared by other organizations. It was reprinted by Garland Publishing Inc., New York, in March 1971.

B4   SUPERNATIONAL AUTHORITY THAT WILL PREVENT WAR   1917

CENTRAL ORGANISATION FOR A DURABLE PEACE. | (HEAD-QUARTERS: RAAMWEG 24, THE HAGUE.) | [4 in. rule] | INTER-NATIONAL CONGRESS FOR THE STUDY | OF THE PRINCIPLES OF A DURABLE PEACE. | BERNE 1916. | [1½ in. rule] | THE SUPER-NATIONAL AUTHORITY | THAT WILL PREVENT WAR | BY | A FABIAN COMMITTEE | [publisher's logo ¾ in. diameter] | THE HAGUE | MARTINUS NIJHOFF | 1917

9 × 6 in. 40 pp. Grey stiff paper wrappers printed in black as above. Issued in 1917; exact date and price not known. Written by LW and Sidney Webb, and originally published in *International Government*; see general notes to A7 for more information.

B5   REMINISCENCES OF TOLSTOI   1920

REMINISCENCES OF | LEO NICOLAYEVITCH TOLSTOI | BY | MAXIM GORKY | AUTHORIZED TRANSLATION FROM THE RUSSIAN | BY | S.S. KOTELIANSKY | AND | LEONARD WOOLF | PUBLISHED BY LEONARD & VIRGINIA WOOLF AT | THE HOGARTH PRESS, PARADISE ROAD, RICHMOND | 1920

7¼ × 5 in. 72 pp. Green marbled paper wrappers with white label printed in black. Issued in July 1920 at 5s. A second edition bound in purple wrappers was published in January 1921 but dated 1920; see Woolmer 10. An American edition was published in New York in 1920 by B.W. Huebsch; a second printing followed in July 1921. The text was also reprinted in B27, below.

B6   THE EMPIRE IN AFRICA   1920

THE LABOUR PARTY. | [double rule] | THE EMPIRE IN AFRICA: | LABOUR'S POLICY. | [rule] | PRICE 2d.; POST FREE, 2½d. | [rule] | 33, ECCLESTON SQUARE, LONDON, S.W.1

9½ × 6⅛ in. 12 pp. Pale orange wrappers printed in black. Issued in September 1920 at 2d. The *Labour Party Bibliography* lists the publication date as 1921 (item 21/5) and its official file copy is dated "1921" in manuscript; but the draft of the text was approved by the Party in January 1920 and it was reviewed in *Co-operative News* on 25 September 1920.

Written by LW and E. D. Morel (see Gupta, p. 77, quoting Morel's letter of 12 May 1924); in his autobiography LW says his co-author was Charles Roden Buxton. B15 is closely based on this text. See Appendix 2.

B7   REMINISCENCES OF CHEKHOV   1921

REMINISCENCES OF | ANTON CHEKHOV | BY | MAXIM GORKY, ALEXANDER KUPRIN | AND I.A. BUNIN | TRANSLATED BY | S.S. KOTELIANSKY AND LEONARD WOOLF | [publisher's device] | NEW YORK B.W. HUEBSCH, INC. MCMXXI

7⅜ × 5⅛ in. xii, 116 pp. Reddish brown cloth over spine, with paper label; grey paper-covered boards. Publication date and price not known; reprinted in B27, below. Gorky's reminiscences of Chekhov were published by The Hogarth Press in April as part of *The Note-books of Anton Tchekhov* (B8).

B8   THE NOTE-BOOKS OF ANTON TCHEKHOV   1921

THE NOTE-BOOKS OF | ANTON TCHEKHOV | TOGETHER WITH | REMINISCENCES OF TCHEKHOV | BY MAXIM GORKY | TRANS-LATED BY | S.S. KOTELIANSKY AND LEONARD WOOLF | PUB-LISHED BY LEONARD AND VIRGINIA WOOLF AT | THE HOGARTH PRESS, PARADISE ROAD, RICHMOND | 1921

7¼ × 4⅞ in. 108 pp. Red marbled paper or blue paper over boards, with printed label. Issued in April 1921 at 5s. An American edition (lacking the separately-published reminiscences by Gorky, B7) was published in New York by B. W. Huebsch in 1921. See Woolmer 14.

B9   LABOUR INTERNATIONAL HANDBOOK   1921

THE LABOUR | INTERNATIONAL | HANDBOOK | EDITED BY | R. PALME DUTT | [...] | LONDON | THE LABOUR PUBLISHING COM-PANY, LTD. | 6 TAVISTOCK SQUARE W.C. | AND | GEORGE ALLEN & UNWIN, LTD. | 40 MUSEUM STREET W.C.

7¼ × 5¾. x, 322 pp. Black cloth printed in gold. Issued in May 1921 at 12s. 6d. "The League of Nations", pp. 19–34, by LW.

B10   THE GENTLEMAN FROM SAN FRANCISCO   1922

THE GENTLEMAN FROM | SAN FRANCISCO | AND OTHER STORIES | BY | I.A. BUNIN | TRANSLATED FROM THE RUSSIAN BY | S.S. KOTELIANSKY AND LEONARD WOOLF | PUBLISHED BY LEONARD & VIRGINIA WOOLF AT | THE HOGARTH PRESS, PARADISE ROAD, RICHMOND | 1922

7¼ × 4¾ in. 86 pp. Multi-coloured paper boards with printed label. Issued in May 1922 at 4s. An erratum note tipped-in states that D. H. Lawrence and S. S. Koteliansky translated the title story, and that LW and Koteliansky translated the others. A new impression was issued in 1934, and the text was combined with other stories and re-issued by Chatto & Windus in 1975. An American edition was published in New York by Thomas Seltzer in 1923 and reprinted later the same year. See Woolmer 19.

B11   THE AUTOBIOGRAPHY OF COUNTESS TOLSTOI   1922

THE AUTOBIOGRAPHY OF | COUNTESS SOPHIE TOLSTOI | WITH PREFACE AND NOTES BY | VASILII SPIRIDONOV | TRANSLATED BY | S.S. KOTELIANSKY AND LEONARD WOOLF | PUBLISHED BY LEONARD & VIRGINIA WOOLF AT | THE HOGARTH PRESS, PARADISE ROAD, RICHMOND | 1922

7⅜ × 4⅞ in. 128 pp. Blue and yellow paper boards with printed spine labels. Issued in June 1922 at 4s. An American edition was issued in New York the same year by B. W. Huebsch. See Woolmer 25.

B12   ENCYCLOPAEDIA BRITANNICA   1922

[The 12th edition of the *Encyclopaedia Britannica*, issued in various formats in New York and London, contained an article by LW entitled "Co-operation" (volume xxx, pp. 745–50)].

B13   FABIAN ESSAYS ON CO-OPERATION   1923

FABIAN ESSAYS | ON CO-OPERATION | EDITED BY | LEONARD WOOLF | PRICE 2S. NET | FABIAN SOCIETY, 25 TOTHILL STREET, WESTMINSTER, LONDON, S.W. | 1923

8¼ × 5¼ in. 140 pp (but separately paginated). Brilliant blue cloth printed in black. Issued in 1923 at 2s.

A collection of lectures given in the autumn of 1922, later issued as tracts, and here bound together with a short preface by LW; also contains the text of his *International Co-operative Trade* (A21). See Appendix 2.

B14   BRITISH LABOUR SPEAKS   1924

BRITISH LABOUR | SPEAKS | EDITED AND ARRANGED | BY | RICHARD W. HOGUE | [publisher's device] | BONI AND LIVERIGHT | PUBLISHERS :: :: NEW YORK | 1924

8¼ × 5½ in. [4], 284 pp. Deep brownish red cloth printed in gold. Issued in November 1924 at $2.00.

Transcript of "Labour and Foreign Affairs", a lecture given by LW, on pp. 167–87.

B15   LABOUR AND THE EMPIRE: AFRICA   1926

LABOUR AND THE EMPIRE | AFRICA | PREFACE BY | THE RT. HON.
J.H. THOMAS, M.P. | PUBLISHED BY THE TRADES UNION CON-
GRESS AND THE LABOUR PARTY, 32–34, ECCLESTON SQUARE,
WESTMINSTER, | LONDON, S.W.I.

7⅛ × 4⅛ in. 28 pp. Stiff black paper wrappers with printed label. Issued in December
1926 at 6*d*.

Written jointly by LW and Norman Leys (see Gupta, 74–76, 81; *Labour Party
Bibliography* 26/9). The text is a slightly revised version of B6, and portions of it were
repeated almost verbatim in section V ("The Colonial Problem") of the *Reports and
Proceedings* of the Third Congress of the Labour and Socialist International
(published in London and Zurich, 1928). See Appendix 2.

B16   BOOKS AND THE PUBLIC   1927

BOOKS AND THE | PUBLIC | BY | [list of 10 contributors] | [publisher's
device] | PUBLISHED BY LEONARD & VIRGINIA WOOLF AT THE |
HOGARTH PRESS, 52 TAVISTOCK SQUARE, LONDON, W.C.I | 1927

7¼ × 4⅞ in. 72 pp. Green paper wrappers printed in black. Issued in September 1927
at 2*s*.; a second impression (dated 1927) was issued the following year. See Woolmer
134.

A series of articles originally published in the *Nation and Athenaeum* in the spring of
1927, including "On Advertising Books" by LW on pp. 48–53.

B17   THE HOGARTH ESSAYS   1928

THE HOGARTH ESSAYS | [publisher's device] | DOUBLEDAY, DORAN
& COMPANY | INC. GARDEN CITY, NEW YORK 1928

8 × 5½ in. viii, 336 pp. White paper over boards with design by Vanessa Bell, grey
cloth spine with paper label. Issued in March 1928 at $3.00. Reprinted in 1970 by
Books for Libraries Press, of Freeport, NY.

LW's essay "Hunting the Highbrow" on pp. 133–59; see A23.

B18   THE ENCYCLOPAEDIA OF THE LABOUR
MOVEMENT   1928

THE | ENCYCLOPAEDIA | OF THE | LABOUR MOVEMENT | EDITED
BY | H.B. LEES-SMITH | [...] | [publisher's device] | [volume number] |
CAXTON PUBLISHING COMPANY, LIMITED | CLUN HOUSE,
SURREY STREET, LONDON, W.C.2

9¼ × 6¼. Three volumes: 352; 326; & 352 pp. All volumes bound in red cloth and blocked in gold. Probably issued in 1928; price not known.

Articles by LW: "Empire – Subject Peoples", vol. 1: pp. 257–62, and "Oil", vol. 2: pp. 304–08.

B19   ESSAYS OF OUR TIME   1928

[within ruled border] | ESSAYS OF OUR TIME | SELECTED AND EDITED | BY | SHARON BROWN | BROWN UNIVERSITY | [publisher's device] | SCOTT, FORESMAN AND COMPANY | CHICAGO ATLANTA NEW YORK

7¾ × 5¼ in. 424 pp. Green cloth spine, with paper label; light green paper-covered boards. Issued in 1928 at $2.00.

Biographical notice of LW on p. 399 and his essay "Please, Sir, It Was the Other Fellow" on pp. 400–10.

B20   THE MODERN STATE   1933

THE MODERN STATE | BY | LEONARD WOOLF | [et al.] | EDITED BY | MARY ADAMS | LONDON | GEORGE ALLEN & UNWIN LTD | MUSEUM STREET

7¼ × 4⅞ in. 320 pp. Deep brownish red cloth printed in gold. Issued in March 1933 at 7s. 6d. A new impression was published in May 1945 (for the armed services). American issues were published in New York by the Century Co. in 1933 and by the Kennikat Press in 1969.

This collection of talks, originally broadcast by the BBC, includes the following by LW: "What is Democracy?", pp. [15]-27; "Happiness", pp. [28]-39; "Equality", pp. [40]–51; "Liberty", pp. [52]–63; "Gods or Bees?", pp. [64]–75; "Citizens of the World", pp. [76]–86.

B21   THE INTELLIGENT MAN'S WAY TO
PREVENT WAR   1933

EDITED BY | LEONARD WOOLF | [rule] | THE | INTELLIGENT MAN'S | WAY TO | PREVENT WAR | BY | [list of seven contributors] | LONDON | VICTOR GOLLANCZ LTD | 14 HENRIETTA STREET COVENT GARDEN | 1933

7¼ × 5 in. 576 pp. Brilliant red cloth printed in black. Issued on 18 September 1933 at 5s. Gollancz issued a "cheap edition" at 2s. 6d. in 1936, and an American issue was published in New York by Garland Publishing Inc. in March 1973.

Introduction by LW on pp. 7–18.

B22   SOME MAKERS OF THE MODERN SPIRIT   1933

SOME MAKERS OF THE | MODERN SPIRIT | A SYMPOSIUM | EDITED BY | JOHN MACMURRAY | [publisher's device] | METHUEN & CO. LTD. | 36 ESSEX STREET W.C. | LONDON

7¼ × 5 in. viii, 188 pp. Light blue cloth printed in dark blue. Issued in September 1933 at 3s. 6d. An American issue was published in New York by Books for Libraries Press in 1968.

This collection of talks originally broadcast by the BBC in the spring of 1933, includes "Rousseau" by LW, on pp. 98–110. This essay was later reprinted on pp. 533–44 of volume 2 of *Readings in the History of Civilization*, edited by Harry H. Kimber and Stebelton H. Nulle (East Lansing, Michigan State College Press, 1948).

B23   THE COLONIAL EMPIRE   1933

[Cover title; in a panel surrounded by photographs:] THE | COLONIAL | EMPIRE | [rule] | THE LABOUR PARTY | PRICE TWOPENCE

9⅝ × 6⅛ in. 24 pp. Thin paper wrappers. Issued in November 1933 at 2d.

Written by the Labour Party Advisory Committee on Imperial Questions, on which LW, as secretary, played a leading role. A draft version entitled "The Colonies" (dated August 1933) was printed and circulated prior to the Labour Party Annual Conference held in October 1933; this privately issued draft differs significantly from the final version published in November. See *Labour Party Bibliography* 33/4. See Appendix 2.

B24   REVISION OF TREATIES   1934

REVISION | OF | TREATIES | AND | CHANGES IN INTERNATIONAL LAW | A REPORT OF THE INTERNATIONAL | SECTION OF THE BUREAU UNDER | THE CHAIRMANSHIP OF | MR LEONARD WOOLF | LONDON | VICTOR GOLLANCZ LTD | 14, HENRIETTA STREET, COVENT GARDEN, W.C.2 | AND | THE NEW FABIAN RESEARCH BUREAU | 17, JOHN STREET, W.C.1

8¼ × 5¼ in. 20 pp. Stiff white paper wrappers printed in red. Issued in January 1934 at 6d.

Written by a committee LW chaired. See Appendix 2.

B25   LABOUR'S FOREIGN POLICY   1934

LABOUR'S | FOREIGN | POLICY | PROPOSALS FOR DISCUSSION PUT | FORWARD BY THE INTERNATIONAL | SECTION OF THE BUREAU

UNDER | THE CHAIRMANSHIP OF | LEONARD WOOLF | LONDON | VICTOR GOLLANCZ LTD | 14 HENRIETTA STREET, COVENT GARDEN, W.C. 2 | AND | THE NEW FABIAN RESEARCH BUREAU | 17, JOHN STREET, W.C.1

8½ × 5½ in. 26 pp. Stiff white paper wrappers printed in black. Issued in July 1934 at 6*d*.; reprinted by H.P. Kraus in their "Fabian Research Series".

Written by a committee LW chaired. See Appendix 2.

B26   ESSAYS OF THE YEAR 1933–1934   1934

ESSAYS | OF THE YEAR | 1933–1934 | [publisher's device] | PUBLISHED AT THE OFFICES OF | THE ARGONAUT PRESS | 175 PICCADILLY, LONDON, W.1

7¼ × 5 in. xvi, 424 pp. Green cloth printed in black. Issued in October 1934 at 5*s*.

"A Happy Anniversary" by LW, on pp. 85–91.

B27   REMINISCENCES OF TOLSTOY, CHEKHOV AND ANDREEV   1934

REMINISCENCES OF | TOLSTOY, CHEKHOV | AND ANDREEV | BY | MAXIM GORKY | AUTHORIZED TRANSLATION FROM THE RUSSIAN BY | KATHERINE MANSFIELD, S.S. KOTELIANSKY | AND LEONARD WOOLF | [publisher's device] | PUBLISHED BY LEONARD AND VIRGINIA WOOLF AT THE | HOGARTH PRESS, 52 TAVISTOCK SQUARE, LONDON, W.C. | 1934

8½ × 5⅜ in. 192 pp. Blue cloth printed in gold. Issued in October 1934 at 7*s*. 6*d*. Reprinted by the Hogarth Press in 1948 and 1968. An American paperback edition was published in New York by the Viking Press in 1959, and reprinted in 1966; the text was included with others in an edition of Gorky's reminiscences published by Dover Publications, New York, in 1946.

The texts of Gorky's *Reminiscences of Tolstoi* (see B5), *Reminiscences of Chekhov* (see B7), and *Reminiscences of Andreev* (translated by Katherine Mansfield and S. S. Koteliansky and issued in a limited edition by Heinemann in 1931).

B28   DOES CAPITALISM CAUSE WAR?   1935

DOES | CAPITALISM | CAUSE WAR ? | WITH A FOREWORD BY | VISCOUNT CECIL | [list of eight contributors] | EDITOR | HENRY BRINTON | PUBLISHED BY H. & E.R. BRINTON | 102|5 SHOE LANE, E.C.4 | AND MAIDSTONE | BY ARRANGEMENT WITH THE NEW STATESMAN AND NATION

7⅞ × 4¾ in. 64 pp. Brilliant yellowish orange paper wrappers printed in black and red, or boards (not seen). Issued in 1935 at 1s. in wrappers or 2s. 6d. in boards.

This reprint of a series of letters in the *New Statesman and Nation* contains LW's comments on pp. 20–23.

B29   THE DEMAND FOR COLONIAL TERRITORIES   1936

[Cover title; at head, in white against a black background:] THE DEMAND FOR | COLONIAL TERRITORIES AND | EQUALITY OF ECONOMIC | OPPORTUNITY

8½ × 5½ in. 52 pp. Thin paper wrappers. Issued in August 1936 at 4d.

LW wrote the initial draft of this pamphlet for a special joint committee of the Labour Party in October 1935 (see Gupta, pp. 228, 238–39, 261 note 169). See Appendix 2.

B30   THE FUTURE OF THE LEAGUE OF NATIONS   1936

THE FUTURE | OF THE | LEAGUE OF NATIONS | THE RECORD OF A SERIES OF DISCUSSIONS | HELD AT CHATHAM HOUSE | THE ROYAL INSTITUTE OF INTERNATIONAL AFFAIRS | CHATHAM HOUSE, ST. JAMES'S SQUARE, LONDON, S.W.I | OXFORD UNIVERSITY PRESS | NEW YORK

8⅞ × 6 in. 188pp. Plain green cloth spine; white paper printed in blue over heavy boards. Issued in September 1936 at 3s. 6d. in England and $1.00 in the United States.

Notes and comments by LW on pp. 9, 17, 62–63, 69, 83, 89, 124–27, & 165–66. LW was not present at the discussions, but submitted his comments in writing.

B31   FROM ANNE TO VICTORIA   1937

[ornament] | FROM | ANNE TO VICTORIA | ESSAYS BY VARIOUS HANDS | EDITED BY | BONAMY DOBREE | [publisher's device] | CASSELL | AND COMPANY LIMITED | LONDON, TORONTO, MELBOURNE | AND SYDNEY

8⅜ × 5⅜ in. x, 630 pp. Red cloth blocked in gold. Issued 18 February 1937 at 10s. 6d. An American issue printed in Britain was published in New York the same year by Charles Scribner's Sons; another American issue was published in Freeport, NY, by Books for Libraries Press in 1967.

LW's essay "Tom Paine" on pp. 504–14.

B32   AUTHORS TAKE SIDES ON THE SPANISH WAR   1937

AUTHORS TAKE SIDES | ON THE SPANISH WAR | LEFT REVIEW | 2 PARTON STREET | LONDON | W.C.1

9¾ × 6⅛ in. Unpaginated [but 32 pp]. Yellow paper wrappers printed in red. Issued in December 1937 at 6*d*.

Terse comment by LW on p. [27]: "I am for the legal Government and people of Republican Spain and civilisation; I am against Franco, Fascism, and barbarism."

B33   CONSUMERS' CO-OPERATION IN GREAT BRITAIN   1938

CONSUMERS' CO-OPERATION | IN GREAT BRITAIN | AN EXAMIN-ATION OF THE | BRITISH CO-OPERATIVE MOVEMENT | BY | A.M. CARR-SAUNDERS | P. SARGANT FLORENCE | ROBERT PEERS | IN CONSULTATION WITH | [list of nine other contributors, including LW] | LONDON | GEORGE ALLEN & UNWIN LTD.

8½ × 5½ in. 560pp. Reddish brown cloth blocked in gold on spine. Issued 25 January 1938 at 15*s*., reprinted later the same year and in 1940; a "student's edition" priced 5*s*. was issued in 1939 by the Co-operative Union, and an American issue was published by Harper & Brothers, New York, in 1938.

The extent of LW's contribution to this volume has not been established. See Appendix 1.

B34   POPULATION MOVEMENTS   1938

POPULATION MOVEMENTS | A STUDY IN MIGRATION | BY | LOUIS GINSBURG | WITH AN INTRODUCTION BY | LEONARD WOOLF | LONDON | VICTOR GOLLANCZ LTD | 14 HENRIETTA STREET COVENT GARDEN WC2 | AND | THE NEW FABIAN RESEARCH BUREAU | 37 GREAT JAMES STREET WC1

8½ × 5½ in. 36pp. Red stiff paper wrappers printed in black. Issued in January 1938 [?] at 6*d*. (publisher's note dated December 1937).

Brief preface by LW on p. [4]. See Appendix 2.

B35   REVIEWING   1939

REVIEWING | VIRGINIA WOOLF | WITH A NOTE BY LEONARD WOOLF | [publisher's device] | THE HOGARTH PRESS | 37 MECKLEN-BURGH SQUARE, | LONDON, W.C.1 | 1939

7¼ × 4⅞ in. 32 pp. Greyish green paper wrappers printed in purple. Issued 2 November 1939 at 6*d*. An American issue was published by Folcroft Library Editions, Folcroft, Penn., on 16 June 1977. See Kirkpatrick A24.

"Note" by LW on pp. 27–31.

B36 HITLER'S ROUTE TO BAGDAD   1939

HITLER'S ROUTE | TO BAGDAD | PREPARED FOR THE INTER- NATIONAL | RESEARCH SECTION OF THE | FABIAN SOCIETY | BY | [list of five co-authors] | INTRODUCTION BY | LEONARD WOOLF | MAPS BY | J.F. HORRABIN | LONDON | GEORGE ALLEN & UNWIN LTD

8½ × 5½ in. 360 pp. Red cloth with a black panel on spine blocked in gold (there is a variant binding which lacks the black panel and has the gold blocked directly on red). Issued 7 November 1939 at 10*s*. 6*d*. An American issue was published by Books for Libraries Press, Freeport, NY, in 1971.

Short introduction by LW on pp. 9–11. See Appendix 2.

B37 BETWEEN THE ACTS   1941

BETWEEN THE ACTS | VIRGINIA WOOLF | THE HOGARTH PRESS | 37 MECKLENBURGH SQUARE, | LONDON, W.C.1 | 1941

7⅛ × 4¾ in. 256 pp. Brilliant blue cloth blocked in gold. Issued 17 July 1941 at 7*s*. 6*d*. An American edition was published by Harcourt, Brace & Co., New York, later the same year, and many subsequent printings in both countries have followed; see Kirkpatrick A26 for full printing history.

Editorial note by LW on p. [5].

B38 SOCIALISM: NATIONAL OR INTERNATIONAL   1942

SOCIALISM | NATIONAL OR INTERNATIONAL | BY | FRANZ BORKENAU | LONDON | THE LABOUR BOOK SERVICE | 68–74 CARTER LANE, E.C.4

7¾ × 5 in. 184pp. Deep green paper-covered boards printed in white.

Introductory note by LW on pp. [v-vi] is not found in the trade edition published by George Routledge & Sons in March 1942. See general notes to *The War for Peace* (A33) for information on the Labour Book Service.

B39   THE DEATH OF THE MOTH   1942

THE DEATH OF THE MOTH | AND OTHER ESSAYS | VIRGINIA
WOOLF | [publisher's device] | THE HOGARTH PRESS | 37 MECKLEN-
BURGH SQUARE | LONDON, W.C.1 | 1942

8½ × 5⅜ in. 160 pp. Brilliant blue cloth blocked in gold. Issued 9 June 1942 at 9s. An
American edition was published by Harcourt, Brace & Co., New York, later the same
year, and many subsequent printings in both countries; see Kirkpatrick A27 for full
printing history.

Editorial note by LW on pp. 7–8.

B40   LETTERS ON INDIA   1942

MULK RAJ ANAND | LETTERS ON INDIA | LONDON | THE LABOUR
BOOK SERVICE | 68–74 CARTER LANE, E.C. 4

7¼ × 4⅞ in. xii, 160 pp. Brown paper over boards, printed in white. Issued in
September [?] 1942; price not known.

Introduction by LW on pp. vii-ix (not found in the trade edition published by George
Routledge & Sons in January 1943). See general notes to *The War for Peace* (A33) for
information on the Labour Book Service.

B41   TWENTIETH CENTURY AUTHORS   1942

[This reference work edited by Stanley Kunitz contains an autobiographical letter by
LW on pp. 1547–48. A slightly revised version was printed in the first supplement to
the work, issued in 1955.]

B42   THE COLONIES   1943

[Cover title:] THE LABOUR PARTY | THE | COLONIES | THE LABOUR
PARTY'S | POST-WAR POLICY | FOR THE AFRICAN AND | PACIFIC
COLONIES. | PRICE THREEPENCE | TRANSPORT HOUSE, SMITH
SQUARE, LONDON, S.W.1

9½ × 6 in. 24 pp. Thin white paper wrappers, as above. Issued in March 1943
at 3d.

LW wrote the first draft of this policy statement in September 1941, and the final text
embodies the comments of Norman Leys, Sir John Maynard, and J. F. N. Green (see
Gupta, p. 275, note 1). See Appendix 2.

B43   WARTIME HARVEST   1943

WARTIME HARVEST | AN ANTHOLOGY OF PROSE AND VERSE | SELECTED BY | STEFAN SCHIMANSKI | AND | HENRY TREECE | [publisher's device] | JOHN BALE AND STAPLES LIMITED | 83–91 GREAT TITCHFIELD STREET LONDON WI

7¼ × 4¾ in. xvi, 154 pp. White cardboard printed in blue and black. Issued in August 1943 at 3*s*. 6*d*.

This anthology of work from the literary magazine *Kingdom Come*, founded at Oxford by John Waller, includes LW's essay "Society and the Work of Art" on pp. 13–18.

B44   WHEN HOSTILITIES CEASE   1943

WHEN HOSTILITIES CEASE | PAPERS ON RELIEF AND RECON-STRUCTION | PREPARED FOR THE FABIAN SOCIETY | BY | [list of seven contributors] | WITH A FOREWORD BY | PHILIP NOEL-BAKER | AND AN INTRODUCTION BY | LEONARD WOOLF | LONDON | VICTOR GOLLANCZ LTD | 1943

7¼ × 4¾ in. 124 pp. Blue cloth blocked in gold. Issued 25 October 1943 at 4*s*. There were two printings before publication and new impressions in January and May 1944.

Introduction by LW on pp. 11–17. See Appendix 2.

B45   KENYA: WHITE MAN'S COUNTRY?   1944

– KENYA – | WHITE MAN'S COUNTRY ? | REPORT | TO THE | FABIAN COLONIAL BUREAU | WITH A PREFACE BY | LEONARD WOOLF

8¾ × 5½ in. 32 pp. Pictorial paper wrappers printed in black and blue. Issued in January 1944 at 1*s*.

Preface by LW on pp. [3–4]. See Appendix 2.

B46   A HAUNTED HOUSE   1944

A HAUNTED HOUSE | AND OTHER STORIES | VIRGINIA WOOLF | THE HOGARTH PRESS | 37 MECKLENBURGH SQUARE | LONDON, W.C. 1 | 1943

7¼ × 4⅞ in. 128 pp. Pale red cloth blocked in gold. Issued 31 January 1944 at 7*s*. 6*d*. An American edition was published by Harcourt, Brace, New York, later the same year. Many subsequent printings occurred in both countries; see Kirkpatrick A28 for full printing history.

Foreword by LW on pp. 7–8.

B47   FABIAN COLONIAL ESSAYS   1945

FABIAN | COLONIAL ESSAYS | BY | [list of 12 authors, including LW] | WITH AN INTRODUCTION BY | A. CREECH JONES, M.P. | EDITED BY RITA HINDEN | [publisher's device] | LONDON | GEORGE ALLEN AND UNWIN LTD

7⅛ × 4¾ in. 264 pp. Medium blue cloth printed in white. Issued 27 February 1945 at 8*s. 6d.*

"The Political Advance of Backward Peoples" by LW on pp. [85] – 98. See Appendix 2.

B48   MORALITY AND HAPPINESS   1945

MORALITY | AND HAPPINESS | BY | LAN FREED | WITH A FORE-WORD BY | LEONARD WOOLF | LONDON | WILLIAMS AND NORGATE LTD. | GREAT RUSSELL STREET

7¼ × 5 in. 80 pp. Light blue cloth blocked in black. Issued in April 1944 at 5*s.*; second impression 1945.

Foreword by LW on pp. 5–6.

B49   CO-OPERATION IN THE COLONIES   1946

CO-OPERATION | IN THE | COLONIES | A REPORT | FROM A SPECIAL COMMITTEE | TO THE | FABIAN COLONIAL | BUREAU | WITH A PREFACE BY | C.F. STRICKLAND | [publisher's device] | [rule] | LONDON: GEORGE ALLEN & UNWIN LTD

8⅜ × 5⅜ in. 208 pp. Bright blue cloth blocked in white. Issued 21 February 1946 at 10*s. 6d.*

Written by a committee on which LW served; all sections are unsigned, and it is impossible to identify the extent of his contributions. See Appendix 2.

B50   THE PARADOX OF NATIONALISM   1947

THE PARADOX | OF NATIONALISM | AN EPILOGUE TO THE NUREMBERG TRIALS | COMMON-SENSE REFLECTIONS IN | THE ATOMIC AGE | BY JULIUS BRAUNTHAL | WITH AN INTRODUCTION BY | LEONARD WOOLF | [publisher's device] | ST. BOTOLPH PUBLISH-ING CO., LTD. | 5 LITTLE BRITAIN | LONDON E.C.1 | 1946

8¼ × 5⅛ in. 104 pp. Bright green cloth blocked in black. Issued in April 1947 at 5*s.*

Introduction by LW on pp. 7–8.

B51   MAN AND THE STATE   1947

MAN AND THE | STATE | MODERN POLITICAL IDEAS | EDITED BY
WILLIAM EBENSTEIN | ASSOCIATE PROFESSOR OF POLITICS |
PRINCETON UNIVERSITY | RINEHART & COMPANY, INC. |
PUBLISHERS NEW YORK

9⅛ × 6 in. xvi, 784 pp. Red cloth blocked in black and gold. Issued in June 1947 at
$6.50. There was a second printing the same month and a third in 1953. A much-
revised edition appeared in 1954 under the title, *Modern Political Thought*.

"Utopia and Reality" by LW on pp. 631–41; originally published in the *Political
Quarterly* (see C1215).

B52   THE MOMENT   1947

THE MOMENT | AND OTHER ESSAYS | VIRGINIA WOOLF | [pub-
lisher's device] | LONDON | THE HOGARTH PRESS | 1947

8 × 5 in. 192 pp. Red cloth blocked in gold. Issued 5 December 1947 at 10*s*. 6*d*.
Several subsequent printings in England and America; see Kirkpatrick A29 for a
complete printing history.

Editorial note by LW on pp. 7–8.

B53   TURNSTILE ONE   1948

TURNSTILE | ONE | A LITERARY MISCELLANY FROM | THE NEW
STATESMAN AND NATION | EDITED BY | V.S. PRITCHETT | [pub-
lisher's device] | TURNSTILE PRESS | 10 GREAT TURNSTILE, LONDON,
W.C.1.

8⅜ × 5⅜ in. x, 254 pp. Grey cloth blocked in red and gold. Issued in March 1948 at
10*s*. 6*d*.; "cheap edition" October 1951.

"The Economic Determination of Jane Austen" by LW (C1263) on pp. 54–59.

B54   THE WEBBS AND THEIR WORK   1949

THE WEBBS | AND THEIR WORK | [rule] | EDITED BY | MARGARET
COLE | LONDON | FREDERICK MULLER LTD | 29 GREAT JAMES
STREET | W.C.1

8⅜ × 5½ in. xvi, 304 pp. Black cloth, with a light brown panel on spine blocked in
gold. Issued in September 1949 at 12*s*. 6*d*. Reprinted in 1974 by the Harvester Press,
Brighton, and Barnes & Noble, New York.

"Political Thought and the Webbs" by LW on pp. 251–64.

B55   FLOWER OF CITIES   1949

FLOWER OF CITIES | A BOOK OF | LONDON | STUDIES AND
SKETCHES | BY TWENTY-TWO AUTHORS | [...] | 1949 | MAX
PARRISH LONDON

8⅞ × 6¼ in. 324 pp. Pale blue cloth blocked in gold. Issued October 1949 at 18s. 6d.
American issue published by Harper & Brothers, New York, on 19 July 1950.
"Bloomsbury" by LW on pp. 176–84.

B56   THE CAPTAIN'S DEATH BED   1950

THE CAPTAIN'S | DEATH BED | AND OTHER ESSAYS | BY | VIRGINIA
WOOLF | HARCOURT, BRACE AND COMPANY | NEW YORK

8 × 5⅜ in. viii, 248 pp. Blue cloth blocked in gold. Issued 4 May 1950 at $3.00.
Several subsequent printings followed in England and America; see Kirkpatrick A30
for full printing history.
Editorial note by LW on pp. vii-viii.

B57   CHAMBERS'S ENCYCLOPAEDIA   1950

[*Chambers's Encyclopaedia*, published in New York and London in 1950 and
reprinted in 1955, contains an article by LW entitled "Imperialism", in volume vii, pp.
404–08. A slightly expanded version appeared in the "New Revised" edition, volume
vii, pp. 399–403, published in Oxford and New York in 1967 and reprinted in 1973.]

B58   SHAW AND SOCIETY   1953

SHAW AND SOCIETY | AN ANTHOLOGY AND A SYMPOSIUM |
WITH CONTRIBUTIONS BY | [list of five authors, including LW] |
EDITED BY C.E.M. JOAD | (FOR THE FABIAN SOCIETY) | [publisher's
device] | ODHAMS PRESS LIMITED | LONG ACRE [dot] LONDON

8¼ × 5¼ in. 280 pp. Pale blue cloth blocked in gold. Issued in Sept. 1953 at 16s.
"The Early Fabians and British Socialism" by LW on pp. 39–53. See Appendix 2.

B59   A WRITER'S DIARY   1953

A | WRITER'S DIARY | BEING EXTRACTS FROM THE DIARY OF |
VIRGINIA WOOLF | EDITED BY | LEONARD WOOLF | [publisher's
device] | 1953 | THE HOGARTH PRESS | LONDON

8¾ × 5½ in. x, 374 pp. Orange cloth blocked in gold. Issued 2 November 1953 at 18s. Several further printings in both Britain and America; see Kirkpatrick A31 for a full printing history.

Preface by LW on pp. vii-x; reprinted in *Praise from Famous Men: An Anthology of Introductions*, edited by Guy R. Lyle and published by Scarecrow Press, Metuchen, New Jersey, in 1977.

B60   RAYMOND AND I   1956

RAYMOND AND I | [rule] | ELIZABETH ROBINS | WITH A FORE-WORD BY | LEONARD WOOLF | 1956 | THE HOGARTH PRESS | LONDON

8½ × 5½ in. 344 pp. Black cloth blocked in gold. Issued in September 1956 at 21s. American issue published by the Macmillan Co., New York, the same year.

Foreword by LW on p. v.

B61   VIRGINIA WOOLF & LYTTON STRACHEY: LETTERS   1956

VIRGINIA WOOLF | & | LYTTON STRACHEY | [ornament] | LETTERS | EDITED BY LEONARD WOOLF & JAMES STRACHEY | THE HOGARTH PRESS | [ornament] | CHATTO AND WINDUS

8½ × 5½ in. 124 pp. Tan cloth blcoked in gold. Issued 14 November 1956 at 18s.; reprinted in 1969. An American edition was also issued in 1956. See Kirkpatrick A32 or Edmonds B7 for full printing history.

Foreword by LW and James Strachey on pp. 7–8.

B62   COMING TO LONDON   1957

COMING TO | LONDON | BY [list of 14 authors, including LW] | [publisher's device] | PHOENIX HOUSE LTD | LONDON

7⅛ × 4½ in. 176 pp. Red cloth blocked in silver. Issued in September 1957 at 12s. 6d.

"Coming to London" by LW on pp. 27–35.

B63   GRANITE AND RAINBOW   1958

GRANITE | AND RAINBOW | ESSAYS BY | VIRGINIA WOOLF | [publisher's device] | 1958 | THE HOGARTH PRESS | LONDON

8⅝ × 5½ in. 240 pp. Blue cloth blocked in gold. Issued 16 June 1958 at 18s. Several subsequent printings in England and America; see Kirkpatrick A34 for a full printing history.

Editorial note by LW on pp. [7–8].

B64   HOURS IN A LIBRARY   1958

HOURS | IN | A LIBRARY | BY VIRGINIA WOOLF | HARCOURT, BRACE AND COMPANY | NEW YORK | [publisher's device]

7⅝ × 4⅞ in. 24 pp. Black cloth boards; blue cloth spine blocked in gold. Issued 1 January 1958 as a gift to friends of the publishers. See Kirkpatrick A33.

Brief prefatory note by LW on pp. 7–9.

B65   80TH BIRTHDAY BOOK FOR
ERNEST DARWIN SIMON   1959

80TH | BIRTHDAY BOOK | FOR | ERNEST DARWIN SIMON | LORD SIMON OF WYTHENSHAWE | B. 9TH OCTOBER 1879 | PRINTED FOR PRIVATE CIRCULATION | AT THE CLOISTER PRESS LTD | HEATON MERSEY STOCKPORT | OCTOBER 1959

8½ X 5¾ in. 64 pp. Bound in white vellum with front cover blocked in gold. Edited by Simon's wife, Shena, and issued in October 1959 for friends.

Tribute by LW on pp. 35–37.

B66   INTO THE TENTH DECADE   1962

INTO THE 10TH | DECADE | TRIBUTE TO BERTRAND RUSSELL

11⅛ × 8⅞ in. Unpaginated (40 pages). Stiff paper wrappers. Issued in 1962 as a tribute to Bertrand Russell on his 90th birthday. Full publishing details and price unknown.

Brief tribute to Russell from LW on p. [xl].

B67   NEW STATESMANSHIP   1963

NEW | STATESMANSHIP | AN ANTHOLOGY | SELECTED BY | EDWARD HYAMS | [publisher's device] | LONGMANS

8½ × 5½ in. 302 pp. Red cloth blocked in gold. Issued 18 April 1963 at 25s.; a second printing followed in April 1963. American issue published by Books for Libraries Press, Freeport, New York, in 1970.

"The Prehistoric 'N.S. & N.'" by LW on pp. 219–23.

B68   ALDOUS HUXLEY: A MEMORIAL VOLUME   1965

ALDOUS HUXLEY | [2 in. rule] | 1894–1963 | [2 in. rule] | A MEMORIAL VOLUME | EDITED BY | JULIAN HUXLEY | 1965 | CHATTO & WINDUS | LONDON

8⅜ × 5⅝ in. 176 pp. Blue cloth blocked in gold. Issued in October 1965 at 25s. A second printing followed in 1966, and American edition published by Harper & Row, New York, in 1966.

Memoir by LW on pp. 34–38.

B69   COLLECTED ESSAYS, VOLUME ONE   1966

COLLECTED | ESSAYS | BY | VIRGINIA WOOLF | VOLUME ONE | [publisher's device] | 1966 | THE HOGARTH PRESS | LONDON

7¾ × 5 in. [8], 364 pp. Dark brown cloth blocked in gold. Issued 20 October 1966 at £1 15s. Several subsequent printings occurred in both England and America; see Kirkpatrick A37 for full printing history.

Editorial note by LW on p [v].

B70   NURSE LUGTON'S GOLDEN THIMBLE   1966

NURSE LUGTON'S | GOLDEN THIMBLE | BY | VIRGINIA WOOLF | WITH PICTURES BY | DUNCAN GRANT | [publisher's device] | 1966 | THE HOGARTH PRESS | LONDON

7¾ × 6 in. iv, 20 pp. Violet paper boards blocked in gold. Issued 8 December 1966 at 6s. See Kirkpatrick A38.

Brief foreword by LW on p. [4].

B71   A CALENDAR OF CONSOLATION   1967

A | CALENDAR OF | CONSOLATION | A COMFORTING THOUGHT | FOR EVERY DAY IN THE YEAR | SELECTED BY | LEONARD WOOLF | [publisher's device] | 1967 | THE HOGARTH PRESS | LONDON

8 × 5⅜ in. 104 pp. Grey cloth blocked in gold. Issued in February 1967 at 15s. An American edition, with a slightly different sub-title, was published by Funk & Wagnall's, New York, the following year.

An anthology of brief quotations from many writers, arranged as a calendar and edited by LW.

B72   AUTHORS TAKE SIDES ON VIETNAM   1967

AUTHORS | TAKE SIDES ON VIETNAM | TWO QUESTIONS ON THE WAR IN VIETNAM | ANSWERED BY THE AUTHORS OF SEVERAL NATIONS | EDITED BY | CECIL WOOLF AND JOHN BAGGULEY | [publisher's device] | PETER OWEN [dot] LONDON

8½ × 5½ in. [2], 234 pp. Black cloth blocked in silver. Issued in September 1967 at 37s. 6d. An abbreviated American edition (lacking LW's response) was published by Simon & Schuster, New York, the same year.
LW's response on pp. 47–48.

B73   MUGGERIDGE THROUGH THE MICROPHONE   1967

MALCOLM MUGGERIDGE | MUGGERIDGE THROUGH | THE MICROPHONE | BBC RADIO AND TELEVISION | EDITED BY CHRISTOPHER RALLING | WITH DRAWINGS BY TROG | BRITISH BROADCASTING CORPORATION

8¼ × 5⅛ in. 168 pp. Green cloth blocked in gold. Issued in December 1967 at 21s.
"Looking Back with Leonard Woolf: Remembering Virginia", on pp. (67)-71.
This is a transcript of a small portion of the 60-minute programme broadcast by the BBC in September 1966. Muggeridge interviewed LW for approximately 24 hours in preparation for this programme (see *Downhill All the Way*: 159–60).

B74   NANCY CUNARD   1968

NANCY CUNARD | BRAVE POET, INDOMITABLE REBEL, 1896–1965 | EDITED BY HUGH FORD | CHILTON BOOK COMPANY | PHILA-DELPHIA NEW YORK LONDON

9⅛ × 6⅛ in. xv, 386 pp. Purple cloth blocked in gold. Issued in April 1968 at $12.50.
Brief memoir of Cunard by LW on pp. 58–59.

B75   LETTERS FROM NORTH AMERICA   1969

LETTERS | FROM NORTH AMERICA | AND THE PACIFIC | 1898 | CHARLES PHILLIPS TREVELYAN | WITH A FOREWORD BY | LEONARD WOOLF | 1969 | CHATTO & WINDUS | LONDON

8½ × 5½ in. xviii, 238 pp. Issued in November 1969 at 55s. An American edition, with the title *The Great New People*, was published by Doubleday, New York, in 1971.
Foreword by LW on pp. ix-xvii.

B76   THE PELICAN BOOK OF ENGLISH PROSE   1969

THE PELICAN BOOK OF | ENGLISH | PROSE | VOLUME 2 | FROM 1780 TO THE PRESENT DAY | EDITED BY | RAYMOND WILLIAMS | [publisher's device] | PENGUIN BOOKS | BALTIMORE [dot] MARYLAND

7⅛ × 4¼ in. 512 pp. Stiff paper wrappers printed in blue, red, black and white. Issued in 1969 at $2.25.

"The Gentleness of Nature" by LW on pp. 323–25; see C0144.

B77   VIRGINIA WOOLF'S LIGHTHOUSE   1970

VIRGINIA WOOLF'S | LIGHTHOUSE | A STUDY IN CRITICAL METHOD | [swelled rule] | MITCHELL A. LEASKA | 1970 | THE HOGARTH PRESS | LONDON

8½ × 5½ in. 224pp. Red cloth blocked in gold. Issued in January 1970 at £1.80. American issue published by Columbia University Press, New York, in 1970.

Foreword by LW on pp. 9–12.

B78   THE POLITICAL QUARTERLY IN THE THIRTIES   1971

THE POLITICAL QUARTERLY | IN THE THIRTIES | EDITED BY | WILLIAM A. ROBSON | ALLEN LANE THE PENGUIN PRESS

8⅝ × 5¼ in. 256 pp. Green cloth blocked in gold, or a variant binding of yellow cloth blocked in black. Issued in February 1971 at £3.15.

"Meditation on Abyssinia" and "De Profundis" by LW, on pp. 158–74 and 239–50, respectively.

B79   DICTIONARY OF NATIONAL BIOGRAPHY, 1951–1960   1971

[An article by LW, "Moore, George Edward" appeared in the *Dictionary of National Biography, 1951–1960* (London and New York: Oxford University Press, 1971) on pp. 745–48].

B80   E. M. FORSTER: THE CRITICAL HERITAGE   1973

E. M. FORSTER | THE CRITICAL HERITAGE | EDITED BY | PHILIP GARDNER | ASSOCIATE PROFESSOR OF ENGLISH | MEMORIAL UNIVERSITY OF NEWFOUNDLAND | [rule] | ROUTLEDGE & KEGAN PAUL: LONDON AND BOSTON

8½ X 5½ in. 518 pp. Pale blue cloth blocked in gold. Issued in Dec. (?) 1973 at £7.50.
LW's review of Forster's *A Passage To India* on pp. 204–06.

B81   THE BLOOMSBURY GROUP   1975

THE BLOOMSBURY GROUP | A COLLECTION OF MEMOIRS, COM-
MENTARY | AND CRITICISM | EDITED BY | S.P. ROSENBAUM |
CROOM HELM LONDON [or:] [publisher's device] | UNIVERSITY OF
TORONTO PRESS | TORONTO AND BUFFALO

8½ × 5⅜ in. 480 pp. Dark grey cloth blocked in gold, or multi-coloured paper
wrappers (American issue only). English issue published in March 1975 at £7.95;
American issue published 31 May 1975 at $25 in cloth or $10 in paper (a second issue
bound in paper wrappers was issued in 1976).

LW's obituary notice of Lytton Strachey on pp. 177–81, and selections from his
autobiography on pp. 92–123.

C   Contributions to periodicals

Sources for entries for Leonard Woolf's contributions to periodicals are primarily the University of Sussex Library in England. and the Library of Leonard and Virginia Woolf at Washington State University, Pullman, WA, USA. The amount of material at Sussex suggests that Leonard Woolf never threw away anything. His files included drafts of articles, copies of the published article, a list of early articles with copies made by Virginia Woolf, and correspondence pointing the way to a great many other publications. The Woolf Library at WSU, Pullman, houses the books which belonged to the Woolfs. Review slips and copies of notes from publishers of books or editors of periodicals abound. LW's practice of making notes on the endpapers of his books also provided valuable leads.

Books about the activities of many of the organisations in which LW participated contain valuable references and leads. Among the most useful are Donald Birn's *League of Nations Union;* David Goldsworthy's *Colonial Issues;* P. S. Gupta's *Imperialism and the British Labour Movement;* Kenneth Miller's *Socialism and Foreign Policy;* John F. Naylor's *Labour's International Policy,* which includes a "Bibliographical Essay", pp. 315–24; and Patricia Pugh's *Educate, Agitate, Organize: 100 Years of Fabian Socialism;* as well as books dealing specifically with LW and his friends and associates. Details of publication are given in "Secondary Sources ...".

Included among the entries are a number of letters signed by several people, including LW. He did not write all of these, but he did join his name with others in a number of causes. Also included are entries from an incomplete run of the marked files of the *Nation & Athenaeum* at City University London. Among them are a few longer reviews, many short reviews in "Books in Brief", and other regular features to which Leonard Woolf contributed as editor. These are even more topical than his other writing. "From Alpha to Omega", signed Omicron, gives information about plays, operas, concerts and exhibitions, and often ends with a paragraph on "Things to see and/or hear in the coming week." "On the Editor's Desk" is just a list, and "Gramophone Notes" is not much more. Although few of these have much interest for many of today's readers they do show the multiplicity of LW's activities and something of his eclectic interests. No doubt more unsigned or anonymous contributions could be found in a complete run of the *N & A.*

Not included are the parliamentary reports LW says he wrote in 1916 for the *Labour Monthly.* None of these is signed, and no more information has been found. A run of reviews in the *Daily Herald* in the mid 1920s signed L.W. may be by Leonard Woolf, or they may be by Lewis Wynne who was also writing longer reviews for the paper at the time. Excerpts from LW's reviews included in the *Book Review Digest* are not noted. The reader can find a large number of these beginning about 1924.

Entries in the C section are listed in chronological order of their publication, in the following order: exact date; monthly; quarterly; annual. Unless otherwise stated the place of publication of periodicals is London.

Differences in spelling of words such as civilisation/civilization; organisation/organization abound. This is not just a reflection of English versus American practice. Different periodicals used different conventions, and a periodical might vary its spellings. Books that LW reviewed included titles with different spellings. I have tried to follow the spelling used in the publication of the specific article.

Abbreviations used include:

BA	*Beginning Again*
DAW	*Downhill All the Way*
DVW	*Diaries of Virginia Woolf*
LW	Leonard Woolf
LVW	*Letters of Virginia Woolf*
N & A	*Nation & Athenaeum*
NS & N	*New Statesman and Nation*
PQ	*Political Quarterly*
TLS	*Times Literary Supplement,* London
VW	Virginia Woolf
WOB	THE WORLD OF BOOKS

1901

C0001 2 A.M. *Cambridge Review,* XXIII (24 October 1901), 25.
A poem, signed L.S.W. Five 3-line stanzas followed by one 4-line stanza.
A play on the lines:
> I've done with all philosophies
> And bowed to Mephistopheles.

C0002 DREAMS. *Cambridge Review,* XXIII (7 November 1901), 55.
A poem, signed L.S.W. Seven numbered 8-line stanzas.
Reprinted in *Euphrosyne,* 1905, B1, pp. 42–44.

1902

C0003 3 A.M. *Cambridge Review,* XXIII (13 February 1902), 188.
A poem, signed L.S.W. Five 3-line stanzas followed by one 4-line stanza.
A play on the lines:
> In Life's supreme inanity
> And all we do is vanity.

C0004 DEAD LEAVES. *Cambridge Review,* XXIII (29 May 1902), 347.
A poem, signed L.S.W. Eight 4-line stanzas.
Reprinted in *Euphrosyne,* 1905, pp. 20–21.

1903

C0005 SONG OF THE BEASTS. *Cambridge Review,* XXIV (26 February 1903), 214.
A poem, signed L.S.W. Three 8-line stanzas.
Reprinted in *Euphrosyne,* 1905, p. 8.

1904

C0006 VOLTAIRE. *Independent Review,* I (January 1904), 680–84.
Review of *The Life of Voltaire,* by S. G. Tallentyre [Evelyn Beatrice Hall].
2 vols signed L. Sidney Woolf.
> Mr. Tallentyre fails to bring out "the real relation of Voltaire's life and work with his time and ours." In his insistence upon the right to freedom of thought Voltaire was a revolutionary, but as a man of his time he thought Rousseau's introspection insane.

1910

C0007 A CEYLON GAME SANCTUARY. *Times of Ceylon*, Christmas Number, 1910, p. 55.
An article, signed Mr. L. S. Woolf, Ceylon Civil Service. With photo "Herd of Deer in Yala Sanctuary".
Description and observations upon the animal life.

1912

C0008 AN ESSAY IN "SCIENTIFIC MANAGEMENT". *Nation*, London, 3 August 1912, 652–54.
Unsigned article.
Clippings kept by Virginia Woolf of Leonard Woolf's works suggest that he wrote this. See Letter to the Editor signed "Employer", *Nation*, 24 August 1912, 766, and some letters, *Nation*, 5 October 1912, 18–19. The points made in this article agree with those in the following three.

C0009 THE SCIENCE OF MANAGEMENT. A NEW METHOD, BASED UPON PRINCIPLES AND LAWS WHICH DEAL WITH EFFICIENCY. *Co-operative News*, Manchester, XLIII (3 August 1912), 956.
The first of 3 signed articles criticizing Taylorism.
Under this theory, reducing work to its component tasks will increase production.

C0010 THE SCIENCE OF MANAGEMENT. HOW IT HAS BEEN DEVELOPED IN AMERICA. II. *Co-operative News*, XLIII (10 August 1912), [981]-982.
Efficiency engineers analyse workers' output by time studies; then they reorganise the work.

C0011 THE SCIENCE OF MANAGEMENT. EFFECT OF THE SYSTEM UPON THE WORKERS. LESSONS FOR CO-OPERATORS. III. *Co-operative News*, XLIII (17 August 1912), [1009]-1010.
The increased efficiency and output of scientific management could help the co-operative movement; or private industry could use scientific management to speed up the work in ways that further exploit the workers.

C0012 [THE PRINCIPLES OF SCIENTIFIC MANAGEMENT]. *Economic Journal*, XXII.87 (September 1912), 471–75.
Untitled review of 4 books, signed L. S. Woolf. *The Principles of Scientific Management*, by Frederick Winslow Taylor (New York: 1911); *Addresses on Scientific Management: Tuck School Conference, Dartmouth College* (Hanover, N.H., 1912); *Increasing Human Efficiency in Business*, by Walter Dill Scott (New York: 1911); and *Fatigue and Efficiency*, by Josephine Goldmark (N.Y.).
Taylor may be too optimistic about the effects of scientific management upon the happiness of the worker. Miss Goldmark's book proves that reducing the work to a few high-speed movements has a "dulling and deadening effect". This may reduce the "minds of all its workmen to that of a squirrel perpetually revolving in a cage."

C0013 ECONOMICS. *New Witness*, I.1 (7 November 1912), 18–19.
Story, signed X, which mentions *Making Both Ends Meet, the Income and Outlay of New York Working Girls*, by Sue Ainslee Clark and Edith Wyatt (New York: 1911).

A Sussex farmer's wife urging her husband to move to the city or to America for higher wages leads X to consider the relationship of efficient production to the welfare of the worker. Neither the book above nor a discussion with an economist convince X that industrial workers fare better than farm workers.

1913

C0014 SYNDICALISM [1]. A SKETCH OF ITS GROWTH AND ITS RELATION TO THE CO-OPERATIVE MOVEMENT. *Co-operative News*, XLIV (11 January 1913), 38.
  The first of two articles. Introduction and background.

C0015 SYNDICALISM [2]. A SKETCH OF ITS GROWTH AND ITS RELATION TO THE CO-OPERATIVE MOVEMENT. *Co-operative News*, XLIV (18 January 1913), 72.
  This and C0014 attempt to allay the popular fear of French Syndicalism.

C0016 SYNDICALISM. *Co-operative News*, XLIV (8 February 1913), 177.
  Letter replying to one from Dr. Haddon, published in the previous issue. Consumers can combine as effectively as producers.

C0017 THE POLITICS OF CO-OPERATION. SHORTER HOURS, LIVING WAGES, DECASUALISATION OF LABOUR. HOW THE "FORCES" CAN WORK TOGETHER. *Co-operative News*, XLIV (8 March 1913), 290. Article, signed L. S. Woolf.
  A plea for co-operation among trade unions, co-operatives, and the Labour Party at the joint meeting.

C0018 PROFIT-SHARING AND CO-PARTNERSHIP. WHY THEY ARE ILLUSORY. *Daily Citizen*, Manchester, Late London ed., 12 March 1913, p. 4, col. 4.
  First of two signed articles.
  Profit-sharing schemes have not proved very lasting. The average gain to the wage-earner has been 5 per cent increase in wages. Employers do not agree that schemes have increased productivity.

C0019 PROFIT-SHARING AND CO-PARTNERSHIP. WHY THEY ARE ILLUSORY [II]. *Daily Citizen*, Manchester, Late London ed., 13 March 1913, p. 4, col. 4.
  Payment in shares of the business rather than in cash has remained at the same level as profit-sharing.

C0020 PSYCHOLOGY AND INDUSTRIAL EFFICIENCY. *Co-operative News*, XLIV (19 April 1913), 491.
  Review of *Psychology and Industrial Efficiency*, by Hugo Münsterberg.
  Woolf summarizes the book and relates it to Taylor's, see C0012.

C0021 "SCIENTIFIC MANAGEMENT". AMERICA'S LABOUR-SAVING INVENTION. *Daily Citizen*, Manchester, 26 April 1913, p. 4, col. 4.
  Signed article based on Münsterberg's *Psychology and Industrial Efficiency*.
  Labour should beware lest the means for increased efficiency in production enrich only the employer.

C0022 STEPHANE MALLARME. *Times Literary Supplement*, London, 1 May 1913, 180–81; hereafter cited as *TLS*.
  Unsigned review of *Poésies*, by Stéphane Mallarmé, and *La Poésie de Stéphane Mallarmé*, by Albert Thibaudet.
  Mallarmé's poetry is obscure, for he is too withdrawn from everyday life, yet it has strange beauty. Thibaudet should have condensed his book.

C0023 CO-OPERATIVE PRODUCTION AND ITS INFLUENCE UPON PRICES. *Co-operative News*, XLIV (10 May 1913), 565.
Signed article.
> Better records should be kept to provide the information needed on production and pricing in the Movement.

C0024 THE PROPOSED CO-OPERATIVE COLLEGE. [1]. HOW WE USE OR MISUSE OUR OPPORTUNITIES. GREAT SYSTEM OF EDUCATION REQUIRED. *Co-operative News*, XLIV (24 May 1913), 652.
First of two signed articles.
> Too little money is used for the education necessary for co-operators.

C0025 THE PROPOSED CO-OPERATIVE COLLEGE. II. WANTED – A YOUNGER, FRESHER AND MORE LIVING SYSTEM OF EDUCATION. *Co-operative News*, XLIV (31 May 1913) 686.
> The college would study statistics, history and the theory of the economics of co-operation; concentrate on current events as examples of economic theory.

C0026 SCIENTIFIC MANAGEMENT AND INDUSTRIAL EFFICIENCY. *New Statesman*, London, 7 June 1913, 270.
Letter to the Editor.
> "Is not the true view of Scientific Management somewhere in between the uncompromising censure of your reviewer and the uncompromising praise of Mr. Scott Maxwell?" Refers to "The Misuse of Science", p. 86–87 of same periodical, 26 April 1913, and letter "Industrial Efficiency," pp. 239–40, published 31 May. Maxwell agreed with Woolf in a letter published 21 June 1913, p. 335.

C0027 A DEMOCRACY OF WORKING WOMEN. *New Statesman*, 21 June 1913, 328–29.
Unsigned article.
> The delegates to the Women's Co-operative Guild Congress held at Newcastle June 10–11 showed remarkable orderliness and common-sense. They discussed minimum wage, trade unions and divorce.

C0028 A PARLIAMENT OF WOMEN. SOCIAL TYPES. *Nation*, 21 June 1913, 456–57.
Unsigned article on the same subject as C0027.
> The 650 working women in this assembly favoured a union of the co-operative movement, trade unions and the Labour Party, and were willing to forego starting a convalescent fund in order to vote for education for themselves and their children. This is the same group which helped to get the minimum wage raised to 17 shillings per week for women.

C0029 THE SPIRIT OF ASSOCIATION. *TLS*, 10 July 1913, 290. (See also C0031).
Unsigned review of *The Spirit of Association, Being Some Account of Guilds, Friendly Societies, Co-operative Movement, and Trade Unions of Great Britain*, by M. Fothergill Robinson.
> The author fails to show how man evolved into a political animal in order to achieve certain ends. The book is just a collection of facts with no generalisations to tie it together.

C0030 "LES COPAINS". FICTION. *TLS*, 7 August 1913, 330. Unsigned review of *Les Copains*, by Jules Romains.
> Romains does not fulfill the promise of his earlier *Morte de Quelqu'un*, a serious book; *Les Copains* is a poor farce. Romains' real interest is in the feelings of people as members of groups rather than as individuals.

Note: B. J. Kirkpatrick lists this in her *Bibliography of Virginia Woolf*, but VW included it with her clippings of works by LW now at the University of Sussex Library. Her illness in the summer of 1913 makes it seem likely that LW wrote this review.

C0031 GUILD AND TRADE UNION. *Nation*, 16 August 1913, 757.
Unsigned review of *The Spirit of Association . . .* by M. Fothergill Robinson (see also C0029).

> This short book provides basic information but fails to throw " 'light upon the impulses which guide the great democratic movements of our own times' ". Robinson gives some history of medieval guilds, but these guilds have no connection with the modern democratic kind.

C0032 TWO CHARACTERS. 1. LADY MATILDA JONES. 2. DOROTHEA. *New Statesman*, 27 September 1913, 787–88.
Sketches signed L. S. Woolf.

> When Lady Matilda Jones, who never did anything wrong, died and went to the place of judgment, nothing written about her could be found. This angered Rhadamanthus who had her consumed by fire. Dorothea, a lady whose mind flits like a butterfly, is a painter who teaches, but tries to forget that she earns her living.

C0033 LEOPARDS AND MONKEYS. EVIDENCE FROM CEYLON. *The Times*, London, 22 November 1913, p. 6, col. 4.
Letter dated Nov. 17, responding to an article entitled "XI. Of Panthers", published November 17, p. 6.

> Report of personal observations. A reply by the writer of the article was also published.

C0034 HOW LEOPARDS CATCH MONKEYS. FASCINATION OF CLICKING TEETH. A JUNGLE STUDY. (Place and date of publication not established).
Excerpt from C0033. Virginia Woolf listed this "Leopards and Monkeys", the title assigned to the letter by *The Times*. LW repeated this in *Growing*, A39, pp. 207–08.

C0035 M. CLAUDEL'S ODES. *TLS*, 18 December 1913, 615.
Unsigned review of *Cinq Grandes Odes Suivies d'un Processional pour Saluer le Siècle Nouveau*.

> Claudel is remarkable for his doctrine of Christian mysticism and the form of his verse. These odes show "the merits and defects of both".

1914

C0036 WAGES AT THE C.W.S. TOBACCO FACTORY. *Co-operative News*, XLV (3 January 1914), 22.
Letter objecting to the refusal of a spokesman at the meeting at Westminster to provide information on wages. Several writers responded that the C.W.S. paid union wages or better.

C0037 THE WORLD OF LABOUR. *Co-operative News*, XLV (10 January 1914), 52.
Review of *The World of Labour; A Discussion of the Present and Future of Trade Unionism*, by G. D. H. Cole.

> "Like all sensible and unbiased men, Mr. Cole is against the capitalist system."

C0038 THE ROAD HOME. *New Statesman*, 21 February 1914, 626–28.
A short story, by L. S. Woolf.

Mr. Brumpy at the age of 56 begins to notice the world around him and thinks he is going mad. A change of scene sets him right.

C0039 TRADE BOARDS AND CO-OPERATION. WHAT THE MOVEMENT HAS TO GAIN BY A RISE IN LOWER-LEVEL WAGES. A DIFFICULT POINT. *Co-operative News*, XLV (28 February 1914), 266–67.
    Article.
    The Co-operative Movement should establish a minimum wage in its system. Representatives of the Movement should be on the trade boards which set the levels.

C0040 Review of *The Story of the C.W.S. The Jubilee History of the Co-operative Wholesale Society, Limited, 1863–1913*, by Percy Redfern. *Economic Journal*, XXIV (March 1914), 112–15.
    This history, which is more complete than any before written, brings out "the romantic interest" which animates the Co-operative Movement.

C0041 THE FREE STATE OF THE FUTURE. WHO WILL CONTROL INDUSTRY? III. By L. S. Woolf. *Labour Leader*, XI.15 (9 April 1914), 16.
    Article in which LW summarizes his vision.
    In the co-operative socialist state everyone will be both a member of a co-operative society and a trade-unionist. All who consume will also produce. Production will be limited to what is needed for consumption. The conditions of employment and wages will be democratically controlled.

C0042 VIRGINIBUS PUERISQUE. *New Weekly*, I.5 (18 April 1914), 151.
    Review of *The Bonds of Society*, by John Sutherland.
    The author's attempt to explain everything by an evolutionary theory does not work.

C0043 C.O.S. [Charity Organisation Society]. *New Weekly*, I.5 (18 April 1914), 154.
    Review of *Social Work in London, 1869–1912*, by Helen Bosanquet.
    Despite good intentions the C.O.S. has proved incapable of dealing with social problems.

C0044 A SYNDICALIST ON SCIENTIFIC MANAGEMENT. *New Statesman*, 9 May 1914, 153.
    Unsigned review of *L'Organisation du Surmenage (Le Système Taylor)*, by Emile Pouget (M. Revière et Cie).
    Pouget mistakes "exaggeration and over-emphasis for argument and persuasion". Labour should recognise that scientific management has possibilities for both good and evil and should insist that the workers have a voice in the application of its principles.

C0045 POVERTY IN EUROPE. *New Weekly*, I.8 (9 May 1914), 249.
    Review of *The Church, the State, and the Poor*, by W. E. Chadwick.
    The book covers early Christian days to the Middle Ages better than it does more recent times. The author should have discussed more thoroughly the "effect upon society of the Church resigning the care of the poor to the State."

C0046 THE PERIL OF TIMIDITY. A REPLY TO MR. GREENING: THE REAL DANGERS CO-OPERATORS HAVE TO FEAR. *Co-operative News*, XLV (23 May 1914), 637.
    Article inspired by "The Peril of Politics", by Edward Owen Greening in the May 16 issue of *Co-operative News*, pp. [605]-606.

Co-operation with other labour organisations will not drive away prospective or current Liberals or Conservatives unless the Movement affiliates itself with the Labour Party, and no one has proposed this. There should be more co-operation and more commitment to social change on a broad scale.

(Greening replied in "The Logic of Facts", May 30, pp. 670–71).

C0047 LUXURIES AND NECESSARIES. *TLS*, 11 June 1914, 279.

Unsigned review of *Poverty and Waste*, by Hartley Withers.

The author's calm and genial approach makes pleasant reading, but his theory that the remedy for the imbalance of wealth lies in consumers buying only necessities is absurd.

C0048 THE CRIMINAL. *New Weekly*, I.13 (13 June 1914), 408.

Review of *Criminology*, by Baron Raffaele Garofalo, translated by Robert Wyness Millar.

The author fails to prove his contention that criminals are born so, and that the only cure is to eliminate them.

C0049 EVERYDAY LIFE. *New Weekly*, I.13 (13 June 1914), 412.

Unsigned review of *The Psychopathology of Everyday Life*, by Sigmund Freud. Authorised English translation, with an Introduction by A. A. Brill.

"Freud... writes with great subtlety of mind, a broad and sweeping imagination more characteristic of the poet than the scientist or the medical practitioner.... His works are often a series of brilliant and suggestive hints." One may need to know all his works to know what he is talking about in any one place. This book will interest the ordinary person. In it Freud relates everyday lapses of memory to dreams and to madness (See C0052).

C0050 THE SCIENCE OF SCIENCES. *New Weekly*, II.1 (20 June 1914), 20.

Review of *Work and Wealth*, by J. A. Hobson (includes a photo of Hobson). (See also C0061).

Hobson is a humanist who attempts to translate economic values to human values by showing to what degree the human effort expended in production benefits the human being. The title of this review is taken from MacQuerdy, who in 1831 called political economy "the science of sciences".

C0051 THE WIRE PULLER. *New Weekly*, II.1 (20 June 1914), 21–22.

Unsigned review of *The War of Steel and Gold: A Study of the Armed Peace*, by Henry Noel Brailsford.

The author's satiric picture of a Turkish railway, built as a concession to European financiers, which covers vast areas but fails to serve any populous areas because it "twists and turns 'in sinuous folds' and 'enormous arcs' so that 'a passing train resembles nothing so much as a kitten in pursuit of its own tail'" does more to indict "the modern system of international finance than all the cogent arguments and reasonings that he advances against it."

C0052 THE DAILY ROUND. *New Statesman*, 20 June 1914, 344–45.

Review of *The Psychopathology of Everyday Life*, by Sigmund Freud. Similar to C0049.

C0053 PARLIAMENT OF MOTHERS. WORKING WOMEN & THEIR PROBLEMS. A REMARKABLE CONFERENCE. *Manchester Guardian*, 24 June 1914, p. 10, col 1.

Report of the Women's Co-operative Congress, Birmingham, June 16 and 17, signed From a Correspondent.

"The Co-operative Movement has made women articulate and eloquent." The women at this conference were more earnest than the men at similar meetings. They agreed to establish maternity centres and to work for women's suffrage. They agreed that mutual consent of partners should be sufficient ground for divorce. Quoted below in C0059.

C0054 WORKING WOMEN'S PARLIAMENT. A STRIKING ASSERTION OF FEMININE DEMOCRACY. *Daily News and Leader*, 25 June 1914, p. 6, col. 4. Article similar to C0053, signed L. S. Woolf.

Woolf's emphasis on the co-operative women's orderly conduct in this article and the preceding one contrasts sharply with the reports of the activities of another group of women, carried in newspapers at the time, the suffragettes.

Quoted below in C0059.

C0055 THE MODERN STATE. *New Statesman*, 27 June 1914, 375–76.

Unsigned review of *The Great Society*, by Graham Wallas, similar to C0066. Wallas has produced a lucid introduction to social philosophy. "He has set out the problem and started us thinking."

C0056 AN EXPERIMENT IN DECASUALISATION: THE LIVERPOOL DOCKS SCHEME. *Economic Journal*, XXIV.94 (June 1914), 314–19. Contents page lists as "The Liverpool Docks Scheme".

Essay about efforts to deal with problems of unemployment and impermanent employment. LW cites two papers by R. Williams. The first was reviewed by R. H. Tawney in the *Economic Journal*, June 1912, p. 263, and the second was called "The First Year's Working of the Liverpool Docks Scheme".

C0057 THREE FREE CITIES. *TLS*, 2 July 1914, p. 320, col. 3.

Review of *Chronicles of Three Cities – Hamburg, Bremen, Lübeck*, by Wilson King.

"The book gives a vivid picture of medieval life. It is full of valuable information about the Hanseatic League." Trade was a civilising element; forming guilds, a move towards a democratic spirit. But the League's members were too exclusive. By closing markets to everyone but itself the League brought about its own failure.

C0058 PLAYS WITH A PURPOSE. *New Weekly*, II.17 (11 July 1914), 117–18.

Review of *Three Plays:* Volume III. *The Fugitive; The Pigeon; The Mob*, by John Galsworthy (Duckworth); and *Three Plays:* Second Series: *Love and Geography; Beyond Human Might; Laboremus*, by Björnstjerne Björnson, tr. by Edwin Björkman (Duckworth).

In plays with a purpose "the artist has capitulated to the teacher or preacher." The best of these six plays, *The Fugitive*, is just "a thesis on marriage", although it contains the elements of a tragedy.

C0059 OUR WOMEN'S PARLIAMENT: WHAT THE NEWSPAPERS HAD TO SAY ON THE GUILD CONGRESS. *Co-operative News*, XLV (11 July 1914), 911–12.

Article with excerpts from LW's articles "Parliament of Mothers", C0053 and "Working Women's Parliament", C0054.

C0060 CO-OPERATIVE TRADITION AND FREEDOM OF DISCUSSION. A CRITICAL STAGE IN THE MOVEMENT'S DEVELOPMENT. *Co-operative News*, XLV (1 August 1914), 990–91.

Article.

A plea for wider political discussion and involvement by the movement based on historical precedents.

C0061 WORK AND WEALTH. *New Statesman*, 1 August 1914, 536–37.
Unsigned review of *Work and Wealth*, by J. A. Hobson. See also C0050.
> Hobson views the production of wealth and the distribution of income "from the standpoint of the organic welfare of the community."

C0062 DIAGNOSIS WITHOUT TREATMENT. *New Weekly*, II.20 (1 August 1914), 213.
Review of *The Future of Work and other Essays*, by L. G. Chiozza Money. Includes a photograph of Mr. Money.
> This well-written book deals with the depressing facts of an industrial system in which those who work are paid less than they need to be able to live well.

C0063 THEORY AND PRACTICE. *New Weekly*, II.21 (8 August 1914), 240.
Review of *Master-Clues in World History*, by Andrew Reid Cowan.
> Mr. Cowan fails to reveal the master-clues "to the understanding of how man has come to be civilised." His clues are to the barbarism of man. He underrates the importance of trade. "It taught men that there were better things in the world than the squalid business of killing one another." It is some consolation that the postman who brought the news of the war is opposed to it.

C0064 THE PLAIN MAN IN POLITICS. *New Weekly*, II.22 (15 August 1914), 273.
Review of *The Story of Mr. Chamberlain's Life*, by Alexander Mackintosh; with photo of Joseph Chamberlain.
> Mackintosh tried to write an impartial biography, but it is not possible to write an honest biography without some bias. Chamberlain was not a complex man; he "knew his own mind" but often changed it.

C0065 THE WAR: THE DUTY OF THE MOVEMENT. *Co-operative News*, XLV (22 August 1914), 1081–82.
Article.
> The C.W.S. must refuse to raise its prices. This will force commercial traders to do the same. The C.W.S. and commercial traders must co-operate in the effort to reduce the suffering in the population which may result from the war.

C0066 Review of *The Great Society*, by Graham Wallas. *War and Peace*, I.1 (August 1914), 331. See C0055.

C0067 SPORT IN CEYLON. *TLS*, 3 December 1914, 537.
Unsigned review of *Jungle Sport in Ceylon*, by Marcus W. Millet.
> The aesthetic sportsman enjoys the best hunting in Ceylon because of the variety of game to be seen. Millet, a simple sportsman who hunts only to kill, sees little. His book is full of mis-spellings and confused terminology, but is still worth reading.

1915

C0068 CEYLON FOLK TALES. *TLS*, 7 January 1915, 3.
Unsigned review of *Village Folk Tales of Ceylon*, collected and tr. by H. Parker. vols II & III.
> These stories are especially interesting to one who knows Sinhalese. Parker tells tales in the native manner, but some of the translation is too literal to be understandable English.

C0069   THE DIPLOMATIC SERVICE. *New Statesman,* 16 January 1915, 359–60.
Review of *The Blue Book Report by the Royal Commission on the Civil Service,* April 29-July 16, signed L.S.W.
This "amusing document" recommends abolishing the property qualification and requiring applicants to obtain the Foreign Secretary's permission to appear before the Board of Selection, but that the Board be retained and that candidates appear before it at the age of 18 – recommendations which insure that the selection will continue to be based on family and wealth, for the only remaining qualification is that the candidates have enough money to keep up appearances.

C0070   IN THE LANDS OF THE SUN. *TLS,* 18 February 1915, 52.
Review of *In the Lands of the Sun. Notes and Memories of a Tour in the East,* by Prince William of Sweden.
Having gone to the East with preconceived ideas, Prince William complained that he missed "the genuine 'Indian' atmosphere." He went in 1912 to attend the coronation of King Maha Vajiravudh of Siam. The most interesting parts of the book concern this king who started a kind of Boy Scout Movement in his country, the Wild Tiger Core.

C0071   M. CLAUDEL IN THE EAST. *TLS,* 8 April 1915, 118.
Unsigned review of *The East I Know,* by Paul Claudel, tr. by Teresa Frances and William Rose Benét.
The author's visions of Asia have beauty and power, but his mysticism and symbolism cause dismay. The translators fail to mention the French title, *Connaissance de l'Est.* By examining the text the reader may observe the difficulties of conveying the original French into English.

C0072   THE CAUTIOUS CO-OPERATOR. *New Statesman,* 5 June 1915, 198–99.
Article about the Co-operative Congress held the previous week at Leicester, signed L.S.W.
In response to agitation by a Catholic organisation, the Board recommended that the Congress override the Women's Co-operative Guild's fight for reform of the divorce laws. The Congress also failed to support the women's move towards a "Fusion of Forces" of co-operative societies and trade unions.

C0073   CONSCRIPTION AND THE CAPITALIST: DESIRE TO GET THE WORKING CLASSES 'DISCIPLINED' AND 'UNDER ORDERS': NEW WEAPON IN THE HANDS OF THE EMPLOYING CLASSES. *Co-operative News,* XLVI (5 June 1915), 764–65.
Conscription is both a denial of basic freedoms and a tactic of class war: "It is the very Prussianized system which we thought we were fighting."

C0074   SOCIALISM AND THE WAR. *New Statesman,* 19 June 1915, 259.
Unsigned review of *Socialists and the War,* by W. E. Walling (New York: Henry Holt).
The book is absorbing. By quoting the words and documents of the Socialists themselves the author shows the tragedy of the International.

C0075   WORKING WOMEN AND THE WAR. *New Statesman,* 26 June 1915, 275–76.
Article on the Women's Co-operative Guild Congress held the previous week at Liverpool, signed L.S.W.
These women discussed the difficulties which arose when the government had workers work too long hours. They advocated equal pay for equal

work, arguing that if women doing war work are exploited, men returning from the war may find their pay lowered.

C0076 WHAT IS WRONG WITH GERMANY? *New Statesman,* 26 June 1915, 283–84.

Review of 3 books: *The World in the Crucible,* by Gilbert Parker; *Changing Germany,* by Charles Tower; and *America and the German Peril,* by Howard Pitcher Okie.

> All three books show prejudice. Sir Gilbert's is "four hundred pages of unmitigated denunciation", Tower's is "thoroughly entertaining", and Mr. Okie has some practical suggestions. All assume that "the root of the German disease lies in the subordination of the individual to the State."

C0077 NATIONALITY AND CONFLICT. *New Statesman,* 10 July 1915, 332.

Unsigned review of *Nationality and the War,* by Arnold Toynbee; and *The Interpretation of History,* by L. Cecil Jane.

> These two books are like "two sides of an imperfect coin". Toynbee's book deals with the future; Jane's with the past. Mr. Toynbee faces the complexity of the world's problems; Mr. Jane does not.

C0078 AN INTERNATIONAL AUTHORITY AND THE PREVENTION OF WAR. *New Statesman,* V.118, 10 July 1915. Special Supplement: Suggestions for the Prevention of War [1], Pp. 24.

"Memorandum prepared by Mr. L. S. Woolf for the International Agreements Committee of the Fabian Research Department."

C0079 PROPOSALS OF THE COMMITTEE FOR THE ESTABLISHMENT OF AN INTERNATIONAL LEGISLATURE AND AN INTERNATIONAL HIGH COURT. *New Statesman,* V.119, 17 July 1915. Special Supplement: Suggestions for the Prevention of War II, Pp. 8.

Draft treaty drawn up by LW and Sidney Webb for the Fabian Society. Includes a Select Bibliography.

This Special Supplement and the one for July 10, with a section by Woolf entitled "International Government", were published as *International Government,* A7, in July 1916. The *New Statesman* frequently advertised the Special Supplements, quoting the price of 6d. each, during November 1915. In December 1915 this price was raised to 1/- each. The Fabian Bookshop ran an ad in The *New Statesman,* 26 August 1916, listing *International Government* at 6/-. *New Statesman* ads for their special supplements continued to appear in September but had ceased by November 1916.

C0080 DO ET DES. *New Statesman,* 17 July 1915, 343–44.

Unsigned article about India's contribution to the war.

> An article in *The Times,* "The Monsoon and the War Loan", says India can give more, but a Blue Book report on the Indian budget makes one doubt this.

C0081 ROUMANIA. *New Statesman,* 17 July 1915, 356.

Unsigned review of *Roumania and the Great War,* by R. W. Seton-Watson.

> A concise and lucid explanation.

C0082 CO-OPERATION AND RAW MATERIALS. *Co-operative News* XLVI, (24 July 1915), 990–91.

Article.

> A recent pamphlet urges the Co-operative Movement to produce the raw materials from which it makes and sells its products. The ways various industries do this should be carefully examined.

C0083   THE PREVENTION OF WAR. *New Statesman*, 24 July 1915, 379–80.
Unsigned review of *Towards International Government*, by J. A. Hobson.
Cf. C0086.

> The proposal for direct popular election of those who constitute
> international government is utopian.

C0084   PERPETUAL PEACE. Headed MISCELLANY. *New Statesman*, 31 July
1915, 398–99.
Signed review of *Perpetual Peace*, by Immanual Kant, tr. by M. Campbell
Smith.

> Kant wrote this book as a parody of the Treaty of Basle, a complicated
> joke. Even so, it endures as the most practical work on the subject,
> establishing the indispensable ingredients for perpetual peace.

C0085   "J'ACCUSE!" *New Statesman*, 7 August 1915, 428–29.
Unsigned review of *J'Accuse!* by a German [Richard Grelling], tr. by
Alexander Gray.

> The work is so heavy, verbose and unorganised that only a German could
> have written it.

C0086   THE INTERNATIONAL MIND. *Nation*, 7 August 1915, 614.
Signed review of *Towards International Government*, by J. A. Hobson.
Cf. C0083.

> Hobson deals only with legislation and settlement of international
> disputes. He recognises that an international mind is necessary to a
> workable international government, but he is too impatient with the
> existing machinery of government, not content to let the international
> mind of the ordinary people convince their representatives.

Hobson replied in a letter dated August 8, that the important changes in
human conduct are not slow, but sudden, catastrophic (*Nation*, 14 August
1915, p. 639). See Woolf's reply, C0088.

C0087   PHILOSOPHICAL NEUTRALITY. *New Statesman*, 14 August 1915, 451.
Unsigned discussion of 3 books: *The International Crisis in Its Ethical and
Philosophical Aspects. Lectures,* by Eleanor M. Sidgwick, Gilbert Murray,
A. C. Bradley, and others; *Evolution and the War,* by P. Chalmers Mitchell;
and *Reflections of a Non-Combatant*, by M. D. Petre.

> Here, at last, are three objective books on the war. They are the more
> remarkable because they deal with the emotions war arouses individually
> and nationally.

C0088   THE INTERNATIONAL MIND. *Nation*, 21 August 1915, 675–76,
Letter replying to Hobson's August 14, see C0086.

> Woolf agrees with Hobson about ends but not about means. The *Nation*
> published several more letters concerning LW's review.

C0089   THE WAR AND INTERNATIONAL LAW. *New Statesman*, 21 August
1915, 474.
Unsigned review of *International Law and the Great War*, by Coleman
Phillipson [spelled Philippson throughout this review], with an Introduction
by Sir John MacDonell. Cf. C0093.

> This is the second serious work on the subject since the outbreak of the
> war. The first, written by Rear Admiral Stockton of the U.S. Navy, scarcely
> discussed the subject. Phillipson discusses it so vigorously that he forgets
> that an international lawyer should be neutral. It is still a good book.

C0090   RIVAL KULTURES. *New Statesman*, 28 August 1915, 499.
Unsigned review of 5 books on nationality: *The Soul of Europe*, by Joseph

McCabe; *L'Esprit Européen*, by Louis Dumont-Wilden, New edition; *Serbia*, by W. M. Petrovich; *The Spirit of the Allied Nations*, ed. with an Introductory Essay by Sidney Low; and *Why Europe is at War*, by Frederic René Coudert, F. W. Whitridge, Edmond von Mach, and others.

McCabe's book is the best; they are all interesting.

C0091 SHORTER NOTICES. *New Statesman*, 28 August 1915, 501.

Untitled, unsigned review of *The History of Twelve Days; July 24th to August 4th, 1914*, by J. W. Headlam; and *Documents Relating to the Great War*, Selected and arranged by G. A. Andriulli, with an Introduction by Prof. G. Ferrero, tr. by T. Okey.

Mr. Andriulli's book is a "judicious selection"; Mr. Headlam's is so detailed that it confuses the reader.

C0092 THE HARVEST OF WAR BOOKS. *New Statesman*, 4 September 1915, 523–24.

Unsigned review of 6 books: *The Meaning of the War*, by Henri Bergson; *The War and After*, by Sir Oliver Lodge; *The German Peril*, by Frederic Harrison; *Some Aspects of the War*, by S. Pérez Triana; *The Holy War – "Made in Germany"*, by Dr. Snouck Hurgronje; *The War Thoughts of an Optimist*, by B. A. Gould.

Modern warfare has silenced the poets. The books listed above show that prose has not fared better. Only Dr. Hurgronje knows his subject.

C0093 WAR AND INTERNATIONAL LAW. *Nation*, 4 September 1915, 742 & 744.

Unsigned review of *International Law and the Great War*, by Coleman Phillipson.

This review differs from C0089. LW again criticises the author for not being impartial. He says the most vital issue of the war is its effect upon the law of nations.

C0094 THE SOUTHERN SLAVS AND ITALY. *New Statesman*, 11 September 1915, 534–36.

Unsigned article, citing *The Balkans, Italy, and the Adriatic*, by R. W. Seton-Watson.

Understanding the Balkan problem is essential to the making of peace.

C0095 NATIONALISM AND THE BALKAN WARS. *New Statesman*, 11 September 1915, 547.

Unsigned review of *Nationalism and the War in the Near East*, by A Diplomatist [Sir George Young], ed. by Lord Courtney of Penwith.

The author's expertise and imagination convey a sense of tragedy.

C0096 THE REALITIES OF WAR. *New Statesman*, 18 September 1915, 571–72.

Review of *A Journal of Impressions of Belgium*, by May Sinclair; *France in War Time, 1914–1915*, by Maud F. Sutton-Pickhard; and *The Irish Nuns at Ypres*, by D. M. C., ed. by R. Barry O'Brien.

The authors of these three books have "too much ego in their cosmos". Miss Sinclair writes well.

C0097 CO-OPERATORS AND THEIR EMPLOYEES: I. THE A.U.C.E. AND TRADE UNIONISM. *Co-operative News*, XLVI (18 September 1915), 1252–53.

First of 3 articles.

A summary of events leading up to the withdrawal of the co-operative employees from the T.U.C., and the kinds of industrial organisations being debated within the Labour Movement.

C0098 MEN AS MACHINES. *New Statesman*, 25 September 1915, 583–84.
Unsigned review of *Fatigue from the Economic Stand-point*, British Association Report, discussed at Manchester.
   Modern industry has turned man into "an appendage or extension of the
   machine". Too long hours cause fatigue and lead to accidents. This report
   presents more facts and sets forth its conclusions more clearly than any
   other work on the subject, including *Fatigue and Efficiency*, by Josephine
   Goldmark.

C0099 THE RIDDLE OF AUSTRIA. *New Statesman*, 25 September 1915, 595.
Unsigned review of *Modern Austria: Her Racial and Social Problems*, by
Virginio Gayda. Abridged translation of *La Crisi di un Impero*.
   This translation rivals what before was the most informative book in
   English on Austria, Steed's *The Hapsburg Monarchy*. Neither author has
   solved the riddle of the hatred between the Austrian Czechs and the
   Austrian Germans.

C0100 CO-OPERATORS AND THEIR EMPLOYEES: II. THE A.U.C.E. AND
THE CO-OPERATIVE MOVEMENT. *Co-operative News*, XLVI (25
September 1915), 1291–93.
   Plurality of smaller union organisations within one large association of
   co-operative employees would ensure representation of the various and
   different workers and trades. Any co-operative employee should be free to
   join any union, not just the A.U.C.E.

C0101 MARTIAL LAW IN CEYLON. *New Statesman*, 2 October 1915, 610–11.
Unsigned article concerning a *Memorandum upon Recent Disturbances in
Ceylon*, presented to the Secretary of State for the Colonies by Mr. Edward
Perera.
   The statements in this memorandum lead to questions about the
   application of martial law after the riots beginning 28 May.

C0102 MAN AND THE MOUNTAINS. *New Statesman*, 2 October 1915, 624–25.
Unsigned review of 2 books: *Geographical Aspects of Balkan Problems in
Relation to the Great European War*, by Marion I. Newbigin; and *Arms and
the Map*, by Ian C. Hannah.
   Hannah's book is too short. Newbigin treats the subject with
   "that extreme conscientiousness which is characteristic of the feminine
   scholar". Geography practically ensures that the Balkans will always be a
   centre for war.

C0103 CO-OPERATORS AND THEIR EMPLOYEES: III. PRESENT DIFFI-
CULTIES. *Co-operative News*, XLVI (2 October 1915), 1324.
   Withdrawal from the T.U.C. is a "grave error"; compromises should be
   made; the co-operative movement as a whole should not take sides in the
   trade union debate.

C0104 CONSTANTINOPLE. *New Statesman*, 16 October 1915, 43–44.
Unsigned review of *Forty Years in Constantinople*, by Sir Edwin Pears; and
Journal d'un Habitant de Constantinople (1914–1915), by Emile Edwards.
   M. Edwards sees the East in the way one sees a cinematograph. Sir Edwin
   has "real knowledge and understanding of men and events, of Eastern
   habits and psychology." Still, he always sees the Turk from a European
   point of view. His book reveals the incompetence of the British Foreign
   Office in which no one knew a single word of Turkish.

C0105 THE GUILD SCHOOL AT HAMPSTEAD. *Co-operative News*, XLVI (16
October 1915), 1394–95.

Article. A summary of LW's lectures on taxation to the Women's Co-operative Guild School, including quotations. The lectures were published in 1916 as *Taxation*, A8.

C0106 TREATIES OF GUARANTEE. *New Statesman*, 23 October 1915, 67.
Unsigned review of *England's Guarantee to Belgium and Luxemburg*, by C. P. Sanger and H. T. J. Norton.
> The vague language used by diplomats has rendered almost impossible these authors' task of analysing the question "Ought we to have intervened?"

C0107 THE WAR AND TAXATION. *Co-operative News*, XLVI (23 October 1915), 1427.
Article quotes and summarises LW's lecture to the Women's Co-operative Guild at Hampstead; it was published as part of the pamphlet *Taxation*, A8.

C0108 INTERNATIONAL MORALITY. *International Journal of Ethics*, XXVI.1 (October 1915), 11–22.
Article concerning the question, What effect have ideas of right and wrong upon the handling of international affairs? Books and articles mentioned include Sidgwick's *Elements of Politics;* Maria Edgeworth's *Moral Tales;* Hobbes; Thucydides; Gladstone's *Bulgarian Horrors;* Fitzmaurice's *Life of Lord Granville; La Politique de l'Equilibre, 1907–1911,* by Gabriel Hanotaux; Baty's *International Law;* and H. Wickham Steed's *Hapsburg Monarchy.*
Reprinted, with changes including up-to-date examples, in *Essays . . . 1927,* A24, pp. 153–69.

C0109 THE PENTECOST OF CALAMITY. *New Statesman*, 6 November 1915, 114.
Unsigned review of 4 books on the war: *The Pentecost of Calamity,* by Owen Wister; *The German Mole,* by Jules Claes; *The War of Freedom and the Unity of Christendom,* by W. Felce; and *Civilisation in the Melting Pot,* by George A. Greenwood, with a Preface by Arthur Ponsonby.
> Wister has "the advantage of a literary style and a practised pen." He is an American who is neither afraid nor ashamed to have ideals. He is open-minded and sympathetic to the Allies.

C0110 THE GERMAN SOCIALISTS. *New Statesman*, 27 November 1915, 187.
Unsigned review of *The Socialist Party in the Reichstag and the Declaration of War,* by P. G. La Chesnais; and *German Socialists and Belgium,* by Emile Royer.
> Both are good books. The German Socialists are no more to blame for the war than British Labour.

C0111 WOMEN'S WAGES. *New Statesman*, 4 December 1915, 199–201.
Unsigned article.
> If women who are doing the same work as men continue to be paid less than men, those men returning to jobs after the war will also receive lower wages. Trade unions should let women join and should insist that men and women are paid the same wages. The concept of " 'equal pay for equal work' provides too many loopholes for the evasive employer."

C0112 ATROCITIES AND HUMANITIES. *New Statesman*, 4 December 1915, 211–12.
An ironic unsigned review of 4 war books: *Germany's Violations of the Laws of War, 1914–15,* compiled under the auspices of the French Ministry of Foreign Affairs, tr. by J. O. P. Bland; *Belgium and Germany. Texts and*

Documents. Foreword by Henri Davignon; *The Prisoners of War Informa-tion Bureau in London*, by R. F. Roxburgh. Introduction by L. Oppenheim; and *The Work of the War Refugees Committee: an Address by Lady Lugard*.
> The first two books show that only iron discipline such as Wellington advocated can prevent military atrocities. The second pair show that some advance has been made in treatment of war prisoners and refugees.

C0113   VIEWS OF THE WAR. *New Statesman*, 18 December 1915, 260–61.
Unsigned review of 4 books: *My Year of the War*, by Frederick Palmer; *A Frenchman's Thoughts on the War*, by Paul Sabatier; *France at Bay*, by Charles Dawbarn; and *In the Hands of the Enemy*, by B. G. O'Rorke.
> These views of the war are "like those of a football match that a small boy gets through a hole in the fence."

C0114   THE FACTORY IN PEACE AND WAR. *New Statesman*, 18 December 1915, Blue Book Supplement, pp. 2–3.
Unsigned review of 3 government reports: *Report of the Chief Inspector of Factories and Workshops for 1914* (Cd. 8051); *Report of the Clerical and Commercial and Employments Committee* (Cd. 8110); and *Report of the "Shops Committee"* (Cd. 8113).
> These reports show the need for vigilance to make factory owners comply with the laws governing safety.

C0115   ROYAL PATRIOTIC FUND. *New Statesman*, 18 December 1915, Blue Book Supplement, p. 10.
Unsigned review of *Royal Patriotic Fund Corporation, 11th Report, for the Year 1914* (Cd. 8026).
> It is ironic that this fund established in 1903 to benefit widows and orphans of the "class which serves in the ranks" is undemocratically administered by the upper classes.

1916

C0116   THE WORKERS' MONEY BOX. *New Statesman*, 1 January 1916, 295–96.
Unsigned article.
> The government should use the techniques already developed by the Co-operative Movement for getting workers to save money rather than flooding the press with untried schemes. Limitations on holdings in the Co-operative Wholesale Society should be removed and war loans should be made from the excess.

C0117   THE NEW JAPAN. *New Statesman*, 1 January 1916, 308–09.
Unsigned review of *Japan, the New World Power*, by Robert P. Porter; and *Japan (Madame Chrysanthème)*, by Pierre Loti, tr. by Laura Ensor.
> Porter's book is a re-issue of *The Full Recognition of Japan*, a large factual book which overlooks the corruption of Japan by foreigners. Loti's book is "mere sentimentality".

C0118   THE GOVERNMENT AND CO-OPERATORS' SAVINGS. *Co-operative News*, XLVII (15 January 1916), 74.
Letter to the Editor.
> To help finance the war the government should use C.W.S. savings rather than commercial loans which ultimately benefit the rich lenders and bankers.

C0119   THE CHINESE REVOLUTION. *New Statesman*, 22 January 1916, 379–80.
Unsigned review of *Through the Chinese Revolution*, by Fernand Farjenel, tr. y Margaret Vivian (Duckworth).

The author's frank and simple eye-witness account of the Chinese Revolution, 1911–13, shows that he prefers democracy, freedom and honesty. For this he has been ridiculed as an "unpractical idealist".

C0120   CROWDS AND THEIR LEADERS. *New Statesman*, 29 January 1916, 398–99.
Review of three books, signed L. S. Woolf: *The Executive and His Control of Men*, by E. B. Gowin; *The Crowd in Peace and War*, by Sir Martin Conway; and *The Psychology of Leadership*, by Abdul Majid.
> All three books generalise too much. The kind of crowd a leader tries to influence determines to some degree his kind of leadership. The main duty of a democratic leader is to get the crowd to think.

C0121   HOSPITALS AND HEROISM. *New Statesman*, 29 January 1916, 403–04.
Unsigned review of *Letters from a Hospital*, by Mabel Dearmer, with a memoir of the author by S. Gwynn; and *Fighting France: From Dunkerque to Belfort*, by Edith Wharton.
> Mabel Dearmer, who views war from a hospital, shows her own personality and her compassion for her patients. Despite her literary sensitivity, Mrs. Wharton's book fails because she too scrupulously keeps blood out of it. She seems determined to see the heroic side of the war.

C0122   ENGLAND v. GERMANY. *New Statesman*, 12 February 1916, 453.
Unsigned review of *War and Civilisation*, by J. M. Robertson, M.P.
> Robertson vigorously refutes Dr. Gustav Steffen's pro-German book *Krieg und Kultur*. His use of certain words and phrases is irritating, but he conducts his controversy with skill and zest.

C0123   THE NEMESIS OF DEMOCRACY. *New Statesman*, 26 February 1916, 499.
Unsigned review of *Political Parties*, by Robert Michels, tr. from the Italian by Eden and Cedar Paul.
> The work is interesting despite the heavy style which reflects the "laborious unimaginativeness of its author". Dealing too exclusively with German democracy, Michels wrongly concludes that every democracy must become an oligarchy.

C0124   CIVILISATION OF STATES. *New Statesman*, 4 March 1916, 524.
Unsigned review of *The Morality of Nations*, by C. Delisle Burns; *The Unity of Western Civilisation*, ed. by F. S. Marvin; and *What is Diplomacy?* by C. W. Hayward.
> The second and third books provide good commentary on "Burns's extraordinarily interesting book". Burns covers the history of states and suggests that their function should be to bring nations together. Because this is exactly the opposite of what they have done in the past he urges a new view of the state. (See also C0142).

C0125   THE RIOTS IN CEYLON. *New Statesman*, 11 March 1916, Blue Book Supplement, pp. 6–7.
Unsigned review of *Ceylon. Correspondence Relating to Disturbances in Ceylon* (Cd. 8163).
> The Blue Book does not give a coherent account of the riots which lasted from 25 May to 5 June and the martial law which continued until 30 August. The riots were blamed on an attack by Buddhist Sinhalese on Mohamedan Moormen out of religious animosity, but economic factors also contributed. The severity of the punishments, which included many

hangings, seems excessive. When E. W. Perera questioned the need to continue martial law for so long the government threatened to prosecute him.

C0126   CONTRABAND OF WAR. *New Statesman,* 11 March 1916, 55l.

Unsigned review of *The Law of Contraband of War,* by H. Reason Pyke.

Pyke provides a good history of the law together with examples of its application. His book shows learning, industry and acumen. Blockade is necessary to full use of sea power.

C0127   THE STUDY OF INTERNATIONAL RELATIONS. *New Statesman,* 18 March 1916, 567.

Letter to the Editor, signed L. S. Woolf.

LW takes issue with the contributor of an article of this title who advocated the balance of power as policy (*New Statesman,* 11 March 1916, 538–40). The Editor commented that "Woolf's analysis of possible alternative meanings of the 'Balance of power' seems to us a piece of mere logomachy." See LW's reply C0128.

C0128   THE STUDY OF INTERNATIONAL RELATIONS. *New Statesman,* 25 March 1916, 592.

Letter to the Editor, signed.

Here LW attempts to clarify his meaning, to differentiate between war policy and peace policy, and to urge international government. The Editor replies that he still does not understand.

C0129   THE RELIGION OF SYNDICALISM. *New Statesman,* 25 March 1916, 599.

Unsigned review of *Reflections on the Violence,* by Georges Sorel, tr. by T. E. Hulme.

The author advocates the General Strike as a means of social change, of revealing Socialism, and of keeping a sense of class war alive in the workers. By refusing to follow the rules of writing he abandons clear thinking.

J. C. Squire requested this review and that of *Above the Battle* in a letter to LW, 3 March 1916.

C0130   THE TRAVELLER IN ASIA. *New Statesman,* 1 April 1916, 624.

Unsigned review of *Perfumes of Araby,* by H. F. Jacob; and *Visits to Monasteries in the Levant,* by Robert Curzon.

Colonel Jacob writes as an Anglo-Indian, one who has chosen to live in the East. Curzon is only a traveller. Although he is a better writer, he does not give as real a picture as Jacob does.

C0131   ABOVE THE BATTLE. *New Statesman,* 1 April 1916, 624–25.

Unsigned review of *Above the Battle,* by Romain Rolland, tr. by C. K. Ogden.

The essays and letters which make up the part of this book from which the title *Au-dessus de la Mêlée* is derived were prevented from appearing in Paris in 1915 because their author hates war more than he hates Germans.

C0132   A CALL FOR A NATIONAL CAMPAIGN: WHY OUR LEADERS SHOULD COME OUT BOLDLY ON BEHALF OF FREE TRADE. *Co-operative News,* XLVII (1 April 1916), 65.

Article.

Proposals in the Northcliffe press for protectionism should be resisted. Tariffs seem to protect jobs and wages, but the profits go to the capitalists and not to the workers.

C0133 FEMININE WAR BOOKS. *New Statesman*, 15 April 1916, 44.
Unsigned review of *War Letters of an American Woman*, by Marie Von Vorst; *A Frenchwoman's Notes on the War*, by Claire de Pratz; *In a French Military Hospital*, by Dorothy Cator; *Diary of a Nursing Sister on the Western Front, 1914–1915;* and *In a French Hospital*, by M. Eydoux-Démains.
> LW severely criticises all but *Diary of a Nursing Sister* which he calls "the real thing" with its vivid colloquial style.

C0134 THE PLATFORM AND THE FLOOR. *Co-operative News*, XLVII (27 May 1916), 543.
Letter to the Editor replying to attacks on the W.C.G. by "A Member of the C.E.C."
> The Guild has the respect and admiration of the Labour Movement.

C0135 THE ENFORCEMENT OF PEACE. *New Statesman*, 3 June 1916, 196–97.
Unsigned article on the significance of President Wilson's speech, 17 May 1916.
> President Wilson defines principles of international relationships which embody the British ideal, and he offers to ally the United States with any association of states formed to defend them.

Clifford Sharp wrote a series of articles based on Wilson's speech and this article, "The Need for Discussion of Peace Terms" (*New Statesman*, August 26, 1916), and five articles headed "An Allied Peace". This series was republished as a *New Statesman* pamphlet, *An Allied Peace*. Edward Hyams quotes from LW's article and calls it and Sharp's writing on the topic "the essence of New Statesmanship" (*The New Statesman: History of the First Fifty Years*, p. 59).

C0136 THE PLATFORM AND THE FLOOR [II]. *Co-operative News*, XLVII (17 June 1916), 636.
Second letter on this subject (see C0134).
> "I am glad that my letter has succeeded in dragging 'A Member of the C.E.C.' just a little bit more into the open, though, not unnaturally, he is still ashamed to sign his name to what he writes."

C0137 THE WOMEN'S CONGRESS. Headed CO-OP. TOPICS. *Labour Leader*, XIII.21, 6 July 1916, p. 5, cols. 3 & 4. Article on the Women's Co-operative Guild Congress at Westminster, by L. S. Woolf.
> "An object lesson in efficient organisation, combined with a natural genius for politics, and the finest working-class spirit . . . the Guild . . . has firmly grasped the necessary elements in a constructive working-class social and political programme."

C0138 THE INHUMAN HERD. *New Statesman*, 8 July 1916, 327–28.
Signed review of *Instincts of the Herd in Peace and War*, by W. Trotter.
> Trotter attributes man's acceptance of herd actions to his gregarious nature. He says policemen are more suggestible than burglars, lunatics, writers, artists and critics. The system of education "works to ensure the acceptance by the individual of the suggested beliefs, the beliefs of the human herd", and the conflicts which result from struggling against these often result in insanity or in people being cast out from the herd.

C0139 THE PROBLEM OF EMPIRE. *Nation*, 19 August 1916, 638 & 640.
Unsigned review of *The Commonwealth of Nations*, Part I, Edited by Lionel Curtis.
> The idealism expressed by the various authors is admirable, but they fail to apply the cold light of reason.

C0140 THE CO-OPERATIVE MOVEMENT AFTER THE WAR. *War and Peace*, III.35, August 1916, 163–64.
Signed article.

> Despite the success of the Co-operative Movement in supplying the needs of its 3 million workers "the co-operator's control of raw materials is extremely limited; he has no control at all of transport: though his manufactures have grown enormously, his industrial system is still largely confined to buying wholesale and supplying himself retail with articles of food and household use." If the House of Commons succeeds in taxing the co-operators' dividend on purchases the result may be to unite co-operators politically.

C0141 THE HISTORY OF THE ENTENTE. *Nation*, 16 September 1916, 766.
Unsigned review of *Histoire de l'Entente Cordiale Franco-Anglaise: Les Relations de la France et de l'Angleterre depuis le XVIe siècle jusqu'à nos jours*, by J. L. de Lanessan.

> The author includes much good information but devotes too much space to some historical periods and too little to others.

C0142 "MAGNA LATROCINA". THE STATE AS IT OUGHT TO BE AND AS IT IS. *International Journal of Ethics*, XXVII (October 1916), 36–49.
Review of The Morality of Nations, by C. Delisle Burns, signed L. S. Woolf.
See also C0124.

> This book is better than Bosanquet's *Theory of the State*, but the author should have decided which state he was discussing. [LW goes on to discuss the history of states in theory and in practice.]

C0143 A BREAK IN THE CLOUDS. *Nation*, 2 December 1916, 325.
Letter signed Leonard S. Woolf, November 29, 1916.

> The German Chancellor's statement that his country is ready to form a union of peoples suggests a reversal of pre-war policy which should not be ignored.

1917

C0144 THE GENTLENESS OF NATURE. *New Statesman*, 6 January 1917, 326–27.
Signed article.

> Under this ironic title Woolf shows the ruthlessness of nature as he observed it in Ceylon. This moving piece is one of his best.

Parts reprinted in "A Painful Mystery", *N & A*, 7 November 1925, C0628; reprinted unchanged in *Essays … 1927*, A24; reprinted in *Asia*, August 1927, C0780; reprinted in *The Pelican Book of English Prose*, vol. II, B76. See also *Diaries in Ceylon*, A40, and *The Village in the Jungle*, A1. Elaborated in *Growing*, A39, pp. 194–98.

C0145 SHALL THE NATIONS ENFORCE PEACE? INTRODUCTION BY L. S. WOOLF. *War and Peace*, IV.40, January 1917, [53]-54.

A consideration of the pros and cons of the use of force as an instrument of international government. This introduces the issue devoted to a discussion by Charles Roden Buxton, Hugh Richardson, Bertrand Russell, J. A. Hobson, Arthur Ponsonby, G. Lowes Dickinson and Henry T. Hodgkin based on their addresses at a conference of the Peace Committee of the Society of Friends at Devonshire House the previous October.

C0146 A POLICY OF CO-OPERATIVE RECONSTRUCTION: V. CO-OPERATION OR STRIKES? *Co-operative News*, XLVIII (3 February 1917), 104–05.

Article including a picture of Mr. L. S. Woolf.

> Subdivision of labour and worker demand for participation in manage-ment will change all industry. Workshop committees should be formed to represent the workers' interests; and conciliation boards, to arbitrate disputes with management.

C0147   INTERNATIONAL GOVERNMENT IN BEING. *War and Peace*, IV.41, February 1917, 83-[84].

Extracts from L. S. Woolf's *International Government* (A7) are printed "to illustrate and substantiate the argument in Section III of the foregoing article."

C0148   THE CHARACTER OF HERBERT SPENCER. *New Statesman*, 10 March 1917, 541–42.

An amusing signed review of *Herbert Spencer*, by Hugh Elliot.

> The author is right to insist upon the "connection between the character of the philosopher and the content of his philosophy." But he makes Spencer too eccentric to be believed. He fails to mention *Home Life with Herbert Spencer* by the ladies with whom Spencer lived for eight years.

C0149   THE FRAMEWORK OF PEACE. *War and Peace*, IV.42, March 1917, [85]-100.

Article.

Reprinted as the Introductory portion of *The Framework of a Lasting Peace*, B3, 1917; reprinted in the Garland edition, 1971.

C0150   THE TWO KINGS OF JERUSALEM. *New Statesman*, 28 April 1917, 85–87.

Signed review of *A Guide to Diplomatic Practice*, 2 vols, by Ernest Satow.

> The author has difficulty defining the terms of this antiquated art because so many of them have double meanings. Traditionally the diplomatic function has fitted Sir Henry Wotton's definition of an ambassador, "an honest man, sent to lie abroad for the good of his country." The diplomatist must be a gentleman, obey protocol, and observe etiquette, but always with a view to outwitting his opponent.

Reprinted in *Essays . . . 1927*, A24.

C0151   OXFORD EXTENSION LECTURES. *Co-operative News*, XLVIII (9 June 1917), 558.

Letter to the Editor.

> The proposed curriculum of the Workingman's Educational Association summer session omits discussion of a League of Nations.

C0152   TCHEHOV [*sic* throughout this review]. *New Statesman*, 11 August 1917, 446–48.

Signed article about volume III of Mrs. Garnett's translations of Tchehov's short stories which includes "The Lady with the Dog" and "The Doctor's Visit".

> Despite his unflinching realism, Tchehov's stories leave the reader with a sense of incompleteness. Tchehov is really a mental stammerer, bewild-ered by life. He masks this by his realism and his detached irony.

C0153   PROGRESS WITHOUT WAR. *The Project of a League of Nations. L. of N. S. Publications*, No. 15, 2nd ed., August 1917 (Westminster, The League of Nations Society), pp. 14–15.

Signed article.

> The world needs an international government with a council of concilia-tion, international legislation, and international conferences to reconcile the differences among nations.

C0154 A LEAGUE OF NATIONS. *Co-operative News*, XLVIII (20 October 1917), 997.
Article.
Explanation of how a League might work and an appeal to Co-operators to support the movement for a League.

C0155 HAZLITT. *New Statesman*, 15 December 1917, 257–58.
Signed review of *Hazlitt, Selected Essays*, edited by George Sampson.
Hazlitt was a good writer, critic and journalist whose ill-nature kept him from being great. His predilection for liberty and equality in an age when everyone else was a conservative made him a minority of one. This made him hate his friends even more than his enemies.

C0156 BALKAN STATES AND BALKAN NATIONS. *War and Peace*, No. 51, December 1917, 155–56.
Unsigned article.
Background about the area and speculation on peace terms relating to it.

C0157 DIE INTERNATIONALE RECHTSORDNUNG NACH DEN VORSCH-LAGEN DER FABIER-GESELLSCHAFT. Gutachten von L. S. Woolf. Entwurf eines Völkervertrages von dem Komitee der Fabier. *Internationale Rundschau*, 3. Jahrgang 1917, Heft 12, pp. 569–622.
Authorized translation of excerpt from *International Government*. Reissued, Zürich: Art. Institut Orell Füssli, 1918.

1918

C0158 PROBLEMS OF THE PEACE. *War and Peace*, No. 55, April 1918, 233–34.
Unsigned review of *Problems of the Peace*, by W. Harbutt Dawson.
Dawson based his book on solid facts and sound judgment, but he apparently wrote it before the peace treaty changed the situation.

C0159 IS INTERNATIONALISM A FAILURE? *U.D.C. [Union of Democratic Control]*, III.8 (18 June 1918), 235.
Signed article.
Although opposed and belittled by nationalists such as Lord Cromer and Lord Milner, internationalisation of services such as the post office, railways, shipping and navigation has proved very successful.

C0160 THE NEMESIS OF SECRET DIPLOMACY. *War and Peace*, No. 57, June 1918, 276 and 278.
Unsigned review of *The Secret Treaties and Understandings, Text of the Available Documents*, with Comments and Notes by F. Seymour Cocks (U.D.C.).
"Diplomacy of war is even more secret and unscrupulous than that of peace." In this valuable, reasonably priced book Mr. Cocks makes it possible for ordinary men to read treaties.

C0161 WINGED AND UNWINGED WORDS. *New Statesman*, 6 July 1918, 272–73.
Article based on *Public Speaking and Debate*, a new (14th) edition, by George Jacob Holyoake, signed Leonard Woolf.
Holyoake "had a perpetually agitated mind. He dances over the surface of his subject as restlessly as a midge upon the surface of a pond." "Oratory is an art, which can exist as an end in itself like a sonnet or a symphony; public speaking is a useful instrument, intended like a pamphlet or a plough, to serve a practical purpose."
Reprinted in *Essays* ... 1927, A24.

C0162 THE DUTCH CONVOY. *New Statesman*, 20 July 1918, 310.
　　　　Signed letter about an article of the same title.
　　　　　　Draws attention to a fact not mentioned in the article (*New Statesman*, 13
　　　　　　July 1918, pp. 283–84).

C0163 AFTER THE WAR – I. HOW THE WORKERS ARE BEING ASKED TO
　　　　SET UP THE CO-OPERATIVE COMMONWEALTH OF THE HAPPY
　　　　CAPITALISTS. STATE SUPPORT OF CAPITALISM. *Co-operative News*,
　　　　XLIX (9 November 1918), 719.
　　　　　　The first of two articles. The report of the Balfour Committee on
　　　　　　commercial and industrial policy after the war proposed state-supported
　　　　　　industrial monopolies and trusts.

C0164 AFTER THE WAR – II. THE ONLY ALTERNATIVE TO THE BALFOUR
　　　　COMMITTEE'S PROPOSALS IS CO-OPERATION. *Co-operative News*,
　　　　XLIX (16 November 1918), 730–31.
　　　　　　The Balfour Committee's suggestions for protectionism in international
　　　　　　trade policy are not compatible with the co-operative assumptions of a
　　　　　　League of Nations. They would enrich private capitalists while driving up
　　　　　　consumer prices.
　　　　This and the previous article were republished as a pamphlet, A11, at the end
　　　　of 1918.

C0165 AN INTERNATIONAL DIARY, OCTOBER-NOVEMBER, 1918. *Inter-
　　　　national Review*, 63, December 1918, 391–93.
　　　　　　The first of LW's monthly articles of this title.
　　　　　　See also C0166, C0170, C0174, C0183, C0191, C0201, C0210, C0215,
　　　　　　C0225, C0228, C0234.

1919

C0166 AN INTERNATIONAL DIARY. (NOVEMBER-DECEMBER, 1918).
　　　　International Review, 64, n.s. 1, January 1919, [1]-8.
　　　　Includes BRITAIN AND THE U.S.A.: THE FREEDOM OF THE SEAS;
　　　　BELGIUM AND HOLLAND; RUSSIA; and THE BALKANS.

C0167 WORLD RATIONING OR WORLD SCRAMBLE? *International Review*,
　　　　64, n.s. 1, January 1919, 14–28.

C0168 THE WORLD OF NATIONS: FACTS AND DOCUMENTS. *International
　　　　Review*, 64, n.s. 1, January 1919, [46]-67. Hereafter THE WORLD OF
　　　　NATIONS.
　　　　The first "World of Nations" feature, made up of excerpts from official
　　　　government documents, speeches and editorial comments both at home and
　　　　abroad. In this first issue the editors included introductory and explanatory
　　　　notes to sections entitled FRANCE; THE JUGO-SLAVS AND ITALY;
　　　　GERMANY; and POLAND.

C0169 DEATH OF LADY RITCHIE. THACKERAY'S DAUGHTER. *The Times*,
　　　　28 February 1919, p. 13, col. 4.
　　　　Obituary article.
　　　　　　Lady Ritchie was heir to the literary background in which her famous
　　　　　　father moved and to his genius. Her touch was too light for sustained
　　　　　　novel-writing, but she wrote important introductions to her father's
　　　　　　works. She showed her real genius in personal relationships and in
　　　　　　autobiographical memoirs of the famous people she knew.

Lady Wolseley wrote to the *The Times* concerning this article, March 1. Her letter was forwarded to LW. She wrote to him March 13 (LW Papers Sussex). See also *DVW* I, p. 251 and note 12.

C0170 AN INTERNATIONAL DIARY. DECEMBER, 1918-JANUARY, 1919. *International Review*, 65, n.s. 2, February 1919, 73–78.

Includes sections on THE PROBLEM OF RUSSIA; POLAND; THE STRUGGLE FOR POWER IN GERMANY; and THE CHILE-PERUVIAN DISPUTE.

C0171 GENERAL SMUTS'S LEAGUE. *International Review*, 65, n.s. 2, February 1919, 102–06.

C0172 THE WORLD OF NATIONS. *International Review*, 65, n.s. 2, February 1919, [113]-139.

Introductory and connecting paragraphs and footnotes to COUNT CZERNIN'S REVELATIONS; FRANCE; ITALY; AND GERMANY.

C0173 COBDEN'S INTERNATIONALISM. *International Review*, 65, n.s. 2, February 1919, 141–42.

Unsigned review of *Richard Cobden: The International Man*, by J. A. Hobson.

C0174 AN INTERNATIONAL DIARY. JANUARY-FEBRUARY, 1919. *International Review*, 66, n.s. 3, March 1919, 145–51.

Includes sections: THE LEAGUE OF NATIONS; COLONIES AND MANDATES; RUSSIA AND ROUMANIA; THE RUSSIAN PROBLEM; THE BERNE CONFERENCE; and THE GERMAN REPUBLIC.

The draft treaty of the League of Nations is ready for the representatives of the nations to consider. Whether it will work in practice depends upon how committed the participants are to its success.

C0175 THE WORLD OF NATIONS. *International Review*, 66, n.s. 3, March 1919, [195]-226.

Introductory paragraphs to COUNT CZERNIN'S REVELATIONS (FINAL PORTION); THE PEACE NEGOTIATIONS IN ROUMANIA; THE TURKISH BULGARIAN QUARREL; THE SUBMARINE WAR; REPUBLIC OR MONARCHY; and THREE MONTHS OF GERMAN-AUSTRIA.

C0176 KORNILOVISM AND BOLSHEVISM. *International Review*, 66, n.s. 3, March 1919, 229–30.

Unsigned review of *The Prelude to Bolshevism: The Korniloff Rebellion*, by A. F. Kerensky.

C0177 A LEGAL VIEW OF THE LEAGUE. *International Review*, 66, n.s. 3, March 1919, 230.

Unsigned review of *The League of Nations and Its Problems*, by L. Oppenheim.

C0178 EDUCATION AND SOCIAL MOVEMENTS. *Athenaeum*, 4 April 1919, 138–29.

Unsigned review of *Education and Social Movements, 1700–1850*, by A. E. Dobbs.

Mr. Dobbs packed his book with interesting facts but failed to organize it in a way "which enables the reader to see through the maze of details the outlines of a complete and living book."

C0179 LENIN'S SPEECHES. THE WORKING OF INDIRECT CENSORSHIP. *Westminster Gazette*, 17 April 1919, p. 6, col. 4.

Letter to the Editor, signed by nine men including Noel Buxton and L. S. Woolf. Cf. C0181 and C0182.

Lenin's speeches were about to be printed in *International Review* but were seized by the censor.

LW repeats this story in *DAW*, A42, pp. 19–21.

C0180 THE RIGHTEOUS QUAKER. *Athenaeum*, 18 April 1919, 207.
Review of *Joseph Sturge; His Life and Work*, by Stephen Hobhouse, signed L.W.

This interesting, if heavy, biography deals with a 19th-century man "who loved righteousness and practised it even in politics."

C0181 THE CENSORSHIP. *Manchester Guardian*, 19 April 1919, p. 8, col. 4.
Letter to the Editor signed by several writers (see also C0179 and C0182).

C0182 METHODS OF CENSORSHIP. *The Times*, 19 April 1919, p. 6, col. 3.
Letter, headed 10 Adelphi Terrace W.C.2, April 16, signed by Noel Buxton and 8 others including LW.

That LW wrote this, C0179 and C0181, seems certain when one compares them with his statement in "An International Diary", C0191 below.

C0183 AN INTERNATIONAL DIARY. FEBRUARY-MARCH, 1919. *International Review*, 67, n.s. 4, April 1919, 233–40.

C0184 THE WORLD OF NATIONS. *International Review*, 67, n.s. 4, April 1919, 301–30.
Introductory paragraphs to THE COVENANT OF THE LEAGUE OF NATIONS; FRANCE; CHINA AND JAPAN; RUSSIA; and ITALY.

C0185 IMPERIALISM. *International Review*, 67, n.s. 4, April 1919, 334.
Unsigned review of *La Paix Coloniale Française*, by C. Fidel (Paris: Sirey).

C0186 Unsigned review of *How France is Governed*, by Raymond Poincaré, tr. by Bernard Miall. *International Review*, 67, n.s. 4, April 1919, 336.

C0187 IMPERIAL CAPITALISM. *New Statesman*, 3 May 1919, 117.
Letter to the Editor, dated Richmond April 19.

Professor Bowley is mistaken in saying that the way the 10 per cent of the national income derived from foreign imports is shared is unimportant. It is wrong to exploit foreign labour.

C0188 THE LEAGUE OF NATIONS COVENANT. HOW A PACIFIC INSTRUMENT IS BEING DISTORTED INTO A MACHINE FOR MAKING FUTURE WARS CERTAIN. *Co-operative News*, n.s. no. 3 (17 May 1919), 1.
Signed article.

The Covenant, as it stands, would exclude Germany and the Soviet Union, concentrate power in the hands of the victorious Allies, lack democratic procedures, and fail to establish an impartial international court of justice. Even so, it provides a framework for an international system, if those who implement it really believe it necessary.

C0189 THE INFANCY OF SOCIALISM. *Athenaeum*, 23 May 1919, 362–63.
Unsigned review of *The Infancy of Socialism*, vol. I, by M. Beer, with an Introduction by R. H. Tawney.

Quotations show this book is extraordinarily good.

C0190 THE PEACE TREATY. *Manchester Guardian*, 24 May 1919, p. 8, col. 7.
Letter to the Editor signed by 40 scholars and public men including Leonard S. Woolf.

It is imperative that the terms of the peace do not inflict such harsh punishment on Germany as to practically ensure another war.

Noted by *The League of Nations Journal and Monthly Report of the League of Nations Union*, June 1919, pp. 199–200, and by Donald Birn, who says it appeared in several newspapers (*The League of Nations Union 1918–1945*, 1981, pp. 17 and 231, note 42).

C0191 AN INTERNATIONAL DIARY. MARCH-APRIL, 1919. *International Review*, 68, n.s. 5, May 1919, 337–43.

The Secret Peace is not in keeping with "President Wilson's 'open covenants of peace, openly arrived at.'"

Paragraph on "The Indirect Censorship," p. 343, on seizure of Lenin's speeches which were to have been published in the April issue. See C0179, C0181 and C0182 for other appearances of this story. LW retold this episode in *DAW*, A42, pp. 18–21.

C0192 THE WORLD OF NATIONS. *International Review*, 68, n.s. 5, May 1919, [389]-419.

Introductory paragraphs to sections entitled WHAT IS HAPPENING IN GERMANY?; GERMANY NATIONALIZES HER COAL INDUSTRY; and THE JUGO-SLAV CLAIM TO FIUME.

C0193 TWO ENGLISHMEN ON BISMARCK. *International Review*, 68, n.s. 5, May 1919, 420–21.

Unsigned review of *Germany, 1879–1899*, vol. III, by Sir Adolphus Ward; and *The German Empire, 1867–1914*, vol. I, by William Harbutt Dawson.

C0194 INTERNATIONAL RIVERS. *International Review*, 68, n.s. 5, May 1919, 422–23.

Review of *International Rivers. A Monograph based on Diplomatic Documents*, by G. Kaeckenbeeck. Grotius Society.

C0195 IS THIS POETRY? *Athenaeum*, 20 June 1919, 491.

Unsigned review of T. S. Eliot's *Poems* by LW and of J. M. Murry's *The Critic in Judgment* by VW.

There is definitely poetry in Mr. Eliot, but it is most evident when he forgets his scientific method of trying to evolve something new from the past.

Note: Virginia Woolf told Philip Morrell and T. S. Eliot that she and Leonard had reviewed these two short books they had themselves published at the Hogarth Press (*LVW* II, pp. 373 and 437).

C0196 THE TRUCE. *International Review*, 69, n.s. 6, June 1919, [425]-434.
Unsigned article.

The peace treaty is nothing but a truce.

Note: There was no "International Diary" article in June.

C0197 THE WORLD OF NATIONS. FACTS AND DOCUMENTS. *International Review*, 69, n.s. 6, June 1919, 470–505.

Introductory and connecting paragraphs to THE PEACE CONFERENCE; CHINA JAPAN, AND THE PEACE CONFERENCE; THE TREATY OF PEACE; LABOUR AND THE PEACE TERMS; and RESPONSIBILITY FOR THE WAR.

C0198 THE PACIFIC. *International Review*, 69, n.s. 6, June 1919, 506.

Unsigned review of *The Pacific: Its Past and Future and the Policy of the Great Powers from the Eighteenth Century*, by Guy H. Scholefield.

C0199 THE LAW OF THE SEA. *International Review*, 69, n.s. 6, June 1919, 507–08.
Unsigned review of *The Declaration of Paris, 1856*, by Sir Francis Piggott.

C0200 BOLSHEVIK RUSSIA. *New Statesman*, 12 July 1919, 373.

Unsigned review of *Six Weeks in Russia in 1919*, by Arthur Ransome.

This straightforward personal narrative makes the official picture of the Red Terror seem exaggerated.

C0201 AN INTERNATIONAL DIARY. MAY-JUNE, 1919. *International Review,* 70, n.s. 7, July 1919, 512–18.

> The treaty Germany was finally asked to sign had an important change, a plebiscite in Silesia. "The frontiers are drawn, not in accordance with right and nationality, but by military strategy."

C0202 "GIRD UP THY LOINS". *International Review,* 70, n.s. 7, July 1919, 519–20.

Unsigned article.

> There is no point lamenting the bad peace. Let us remedy what we can by forming a workable League of Nations.

C0203 BACK TO GROTIUS? *International Review,* 70, n.s. 7, July 1919, 550–51.

Unsigned review of 5 books: *The Three Stages in the Evolution of the Law of Nations,* by C. Van Vollenhoven (The Hague: Nijhoff); *International War: Its Causes and Its Cure,* by Oscar T. Crosby; *National and International Right and Wrong: Two Essays,* by Henry Sidgwick, with a Preface by Viscount Bryce; *Helps for Students of History;* and *Securities of Peace,* by Sir A. W. Ward.

C0204 Unsigned, untitled reviews. *International Review,* 70, n.s. 7, July 1919, 553.

The Evolution of Modern Germany, by William Harbutt Dawson. Rev. ed.; and *Greece Before the Conference,* by Polybius.

C0205 THE WORLD OF NATIONS. *International Review,* 70, n.s 7, July 1919, 555–84.

Introductory paragraphs to the following: THE AMERICAN PEACE AND HUNGARY; SWITZERLAND AND THE BLOCKADE; THE RECOGNITION OF KOLTCHAK; GERMANY; A SECRET TREATY: THE PARTITION OF TURKEY; and CHINA, JAPAN AND THE PEACE CONFERENCE.

C0206 WOMEN'S WAGES. *Athenaeum,* 1 August 1919, 688.

Unsigned review of *The Wages of Men and Women: Should They Be Equal,* by Mrs. Sidney Webb.

> Mrs. Webb wrote her report as "a minority of one". In an attempt to clarify her thoughts "she sacrifices verbal lucidity as well as verbal beauty". Nevertheless, her careful analysis and rejection of the various proposals for adjusting the wages of men and women is a real contribution to the question. She recommends an inquiry into the whole question of inequalities of income.

C0207 INDIA'S PAST TODAY. *Athenaeum,* 1 August 1919, 684.

Unsigned review of *Ceylon and the Hollanders, 1658–1796,* by P. E. Pieris; *India's Nation Builders,* by D. N. Bannerjea; and *The Future Government of India,* by Ernest Barker.

C0208 DILETTANTISMS. *Athenaeum,* 15 August 1919, 751.

Review of *Obiter Scripta* by Frederic Harrison, signed L.W.

> Harrison claims to have worked all his life for the "sacred cause" of labour. He was once a member of the Royal Commission on that question, but he considers anything so revolutionary as the Labour Party to be Bolshevist.

C0209 SAMUEL BUTLER. *Athenaeum,* 29 August 1919, 808–09.

Unsigned review of *The Note-Books of Samuel Butler,* edited by Henry Festing Jones.

> "Samuel Butler made his contribution to thought by glancing sideways at the universe."

C0210 AN INTERNATIONAL DIARY. JUNE-JULY, 1919. *International Review*, II.2, August 1919, 1–6.

> The policy of blockade against governments has caused famine among the peoples. The policy by which powerful governments encourage nationalism among smaller ones has led to the Balkanization of Europe.

C0211 BEGINNING AT HOME. *International Review*, II.2, August 1919, 7–8. Article.

> Instead of complaining about the unclean hands of others, the British should undertake the German colonies as an honourable trust, not for profit.

C0212 THE CONGO AND AFRICA. *International Review*, II.2, August 1919, 33. Unsigned review of *The Belgian Congo and the Berlin Act*, by Arthur Berriedale Keith.

C0213 THE WORLD OF NATIONS. *International Review*, II.2, August 1919, [39]-72.

> Introductory paragraphs to THE FRENCH DEBATE ON RUSSIA; THE FRENCH NAVAL MUTINIES; CONDITIONS IN GERMANY; DEMOCRACY AND THE SOVIET SYSTEM; KOLTCHAK AND THE ALLIES; and INTERNATIONAL LABOUR LEGISLATION: THE GERMAN DRAFT.

C0214 THE BOLSHEVIST REVOLUTION. *Athenaeum*, 19 September 1919, 914. Unsigned review of *Ten Days that Shook the World*, by John Reed (New York: Boni & Liveright).

> Reed does not tell his reader what Bolshevism is, but he does show that it appealed to many people.

C0215 AN INTERNATIONAL DIARY. JULY-AUGUST, 1919. *International Review*, II.3, September 1919, [73]-79.

> Comments on THE FALL OF BELA KUN; INTERNATIONAL ANARCHY; THE PART OF RUMANIA; THE POSITION OF HUNGARY; EUROPE'S DOOM; CONDITIONS IN GERMANY; GERMANY'S FINANCIAL POSITION.

C0216 FREEDOM OF THE SEAS. *International Review*, II.3, September 1919, 108–09. Unsigned review of *The Freedom of the Seas*, by Sir Francis Piggott.

> Even in this book for the specialist Sir Francis takes the position of advocacy.

C0217 SWISS DEMOCRACY. *International Review*, II.3, September 1919, 110. Unsigned review of *La démocratie suisse*, by Félix Bonjour.

> This work by a former president of the Swiss National Council should be translated into English and studied in schools.

C0218 Unsigned review of *The Language Question in Belgium*, by Dr. A. Van de Perre. *International Review*, II.3, September 1919, 111.

C0219 Notice of 4 pamphlets published by the China National Defence League. *International Review*, II.3, September 1919, 112.

> *Law Reform in China*, by Wang Chung-Hui; *The Relations between China and Japan During the Last Twenty-five Years*; *Chino-Japanese Treaties of 1915*; and *The World-Peace and Chinese Tariff Autonomy*.

C0220 THE WORLD OF NATIONS. *International Review*, II.3, September 1919, 113–44.

> Introductory paragraphs to THE BOLSHEVIK ARMY, by L. TROTZKI; GERMANY: STATE CONTROL OF INDUSTRY; AUSTRIA; NATIONAL-

IZATION OF COAL INDUSTRY; HOLLAND AND BELGIUM; MR. WILSON AND CHINA; THE NEW POLAND; and FRANCE: THE WORKERS' RIGHTS.

C0221   LOST AND OTHER CAUSES. *Athenaeum,* 3 October 1919, 971–72.
Review of *My Diaries: Being a Personal Narrative of Events, 1888–1914,* Part I, 1888–1900, by Wilfrid Scawen Blunt, signed L.W. (Part II, 13 Feb. 1920, see C0241).
> "Self-consciousness stands between Mr. Blunt and greatness." When he is in Egypt he has his eye on England and vice versa. Mr. Blunt's cause – that of subject peoples and savage races – "is probably the most hopelessly lost cause of all political causes.... For a knight-errant to be completely successful he must keep his eyes on the dragon."

C0222   LORD GREY'S FOREIGN POLICY. *Athenaeum,* 10 October 1919, 999.
Review of *How the War Came,* by Earl Loreburn, signed L.W.
> Loreburn's thesis is that Viscount Grey's 1905–1914 policy of secret conversations with France led inevitably to war. Loreburn acquits Grey of intentional wrongdoing, yet finds him guilty.

C0223   WHAT IS BOLSHEVISM? *Athenaeum,* 24 October 1919, 1061.
Unsigned review of *Bolshevism. The Enemy of Political and Industrial Democracy,* by John Spargo.
> A judicious attack on Bolshevism from the historical standpoint.

C0224   THE LEAGUE AND THE TROPICS. *The Covenant* (Journal of the League of Nations Union), I.1 (October 1919), 28–32.
Article signed Leonard Woolf.
> Article XXII of the Covenant of the League of Nations is a proposal to eliminate economic imperialism by substituting a system of mandates under which the German colonies will be administrated for their "well-being and development".

C0225   AN INTERNATIONAL DIARY. AUGUST-SEPTEMBER, 1919. *International Review,* II.4, October 1919, 145–54.
> Article on the progress of peace on various fronts.

C0226   THE WORLD OF NATIONS. *International Review,* II.4, October 1919, [191]-220.
> Introductory information to sections on MR WILSON AND THE SENATE; THE FRENCH SOCIALIST CONFERENCE; A MODEL MANDATE FOR AFRICA; and THE CAPITAL LEVY IN GERMANY.

C0227   FAR EASTERN POLITICS. *Athenaeum,* 21 November 1919, 1223.
Review of *The Mastery of the Far East,* by Arthur Judson Brown, signed L.W.
> Brown holds that "'the sorrowful conditions in Korea have been largely due to injustice, oppression and superstition. With good government, a fair chance, and a Christian set of morals I believe that the Koreans would develop into a fine people.' This is a good example ... of Dr. Brown's whole attitude to the volcano in the Far East."

C0228   AN INTERNATIONAL DIARY. SEPTEMBER-OCTOBER, 1919. *International Review,* II.5, November 1919, [221]-228.
> The policy of the Allies in Eastern Europe is leading to disaster. The League of Nations is in danger. Anarchy in Eastern Europe is the result of the Allied "policy of destroying the Soviet Government by force of arms". Military adventurers are taking advantage of it.

C0229   Unsigned review of *A Brief History of Poland,* by Julia Swift Orvis. *International Review,* II.5, November 1919, 265.

C0230 Unsigned review of *The German Empire: 1867–1914*, vol. II, by W. H. Dawson. *International Review*, II.5, November 1919, 266.

C0231 Unsigned review of *The League of Nations: The Principle and the Practice*, ed. by Stephen Pierce Duggan (Boston: Atlantic Monthly Press). *International Review*, II.5, November 1919, 266.

C0232 THE WORLD OF NATIONS. *International Review*, II.5, November 1919, 267–96.

Connecting and explanatory paragraphs which introduce sections entitled IN EUROPE'S HELL; THE WHITE TERROR IN HUNGARY; etc.

C0233 AMRITSAR. *Daily Herald*, 23 December 1919, p. 4, col. 3.

Article, signed Leonard Woolf.

The horrors of Amritsar show clearly the dangers of the religion of imperialism which can lead to such atrocities as General Dyer committed.

C0234 AN INTERNATIONAL DIARY. OCTOBER-NOVEMBER, 1919. *International Review*, II.6, December 1919, [297]-304.

This last entry to the "International Diary" is headed by a notice that the *International Review* will cease, and that "The World of Nations" will continue in the *Contemporary Review*.

The American Senate has rejected the Treaty, partly to limit the president's power. But the Senate had already cut the heart out of the peace.

C0235 Unsigned review of *Red Rubber*, by E. D. Morel. New and rev. ed. (National Labour Press). *International Review*, II.6, December 1919, 336

C0236 THE WORLD OF NATIONS. *International Review*, II.6, December 1919, 337–72.

Introductory paragraphs to information on CAPITAL AND LABOUR IN AMERICA; THE ALLIES AND ROUMANIA; LAND NATIONALIZATION IN EASTERN EUROPE; and THE GERMAN CONSTITUTION.

1920

C0237 SOCIAL HISTORY. *Athenaeum*, 16 January 1920, 75–76.

Review of *Skilled Labourer, 1720–1832*, by J. L. and Barbara Hammond, signed L.W.

The authors give "an infinite number of facts", but fail to interpret or shape them.

C0238 THE WORLD OF NATIONS: FACTS AND DOCUMENTS. *Contemporary Review*, CXVII (January 1920), [101]-132.

Introductory remarks for MR. PLUM EXPLAINS HIS PLAN; and GERMANY IN THE CONFESSIONAL.

C0239 THE PROBLEM OF THE DANUBE. *New Europe*, XIV.173 (5 February 1920), 85–90.

Article similar to the section on the Danube's European Commission in *The Future of Constantinople*, A9, reprinted in *International Government*, 1923, A7d.

The history of the concept of free and equal access to international rivers extends from 1792 to the Paris Conference of 1919. Methods of international administration were established for the Danube. The problems and current solutions will be discussed at the forthcoming international conference.

C0240 THE LEAGUE AND THE TROPICS. *The League of Nations, An International Review*, 2nd year, No. 1, 10 February 1920, pp. 31–35.

Article.

> European economic imperialism caused the greatest miseries in Asia and Africa. The system of mandates is "the crucial test of the League". How Article 22 is carried out will determine the future. The League should see that every native receives enough inalienable land to support himself and his family.

C0241 WOE FOR THE KINGS WHO CONQUER! *Athenaeum*, 13 February 1920, 210.

Review of *My Diaries*, Part II, by Wilfrid Scawen Blunt, signed L.W. (review of Part I, see C0221).

> Part I was amusing, but in part II the reader senses tragedy. "The reader of these pages [gradually] becomes conscious that he is being given a vision of an era of politically tremendous events in which the chief actors have no ideals, no hopes, no beliefs, no principles, no understanding – only personal ambitions, personal vanities, personal loves and hates."

C0242 THE EMPIRE AND THE AFRICAN. *New Statesman*, 21 February 1920, 575–77.

Unsigned article. See sequel, C0253.

> Little by little the white man has been taking over the natives' land. He soon realised that he needed native labour as well. In British East Africa the government is attempting to force the natives to provide this. Would it not be better to treat East Africa as a trust, to aid the natives to the best economic development of their country?

C0243 THE NEW GERMANY. *Daily Herald*, 25 February 1920, p. 8, col. 3.

Review of *The New Germany*, by George Young; and *The Better Germany in War Time*, by Harold Picton.

> Young shows that the birth of a less militaristic Germany is being hindered by the Allies; Picton gives examples of the humanity of Germany.

C0244 THE LABOUR PARTY AND FOREIGN AFFAIRS. *New Europe*, XIV.176, 26 February 1920, p. 4 of the cover.

Letter refuting Mr. Roscoe who said the Labour Party's interest in foreign affairs is limited to Russia.

> The number of Labour Party pamphlets on the subject and the resolutions published by the Executive Committee show its interest in foreign affairs.

C0245 THE WORLD OF NATIONS. *Contemporary Review*, CXVII (February 1920), [253]-284.

Introductory remarks to sections: THE REGIME OF KOLCHAK AND DENIKEN; FIUME AND THE ADRIATIC; BOLSHEVIK INDUSTRY AND FINANCE; THE JUGO-SLAV MINORITIES TREATY; BELGIUM'S INTERNATIONAL POSITION; and THE SECOND BREAK UP OF AUSTRIA.

C0246 SNAKES IN IRELAND. *Daily Herald*, 10 March 1920, p. 8, col. 3.

Review of *Democracy and the Eastern Question*, by Thomas F. Millard.

> There is no democracy in Asia. Mr. Millard blames this entirely on Japan, but other writers have shown that European and even American imperialism are to blame.

C0247 A JEWISH NOVELIST *New Statesman*, 13 March 1920) 682–83.

Unsigned review of *Jewish Children*, from the Yiddish of Shalom Aleichem.

> These stories reveal the Jewish psychology; they show "why it is that the Jew has for centuries been able to meet his environment with a granite resistance."

C0248 AN OLD PROBLEM. *Daily Herald*, 17 March 1920, p. 8, col. 3.
Review of *Le Nationalité et l'Etat*, by W. Lewinsky (Parti Socialiste-Democrate Ukrainien), signed L.W.
    The author's consideration of the theory of the state does not go very deep.

C0249 "GOING IN FOR GOD". *Athenaeum*, 19 March 1920, 365–66.
Review of *William Booth, Founder of the Salvation Army*, by Harold Begbie. 2 vols, signed L.W.
    Mr. Begbie is not objective enough. He "seems to have considered that it was necessary for his official biographer to pray perpetually with the general. . . ."

C0250 TANGIER; A STUDY IN INTERNATIONALISATION. *Round Table: A Quarterly Review of the Politics of the British Empire*, X.38 (March 1920), 348–60.
Unsigned article. Concerns "the effects of international administration as distinguished from international responsibility." – editor's note.
    Foreign governmental intervention on behalf of various European nationals living in Morocco has made the native Moslems miserable.

C0251 THE WORLD OF NATIONS. *Contemporary Review*, CXVII (March 1920), [405]-436.
Introductory remarks for: THE SOVIET LAW OF MARRIAGE AND THE FAMILY; AUSTRIAN REVELATIONS; and PROSECUTION OF GERMAN WAR CRIMINALS.

C0252 CHARLES BRADLAUGH AND GENERAL BOOTH. *Athenaeum*, 2 April 1920, 458.
Letter to the editor.
    Expressing regret that a story he quoted, C0249, about Bradlaugh's last word caused pain to Mrs. Bonner (letter *Athenaeum*, March 26, p. 425), LW points out that he took the story from Begbie's book. He denies her allegation that he used lying rumours against a dead atheist.

C0253 NATIVE LABOUR IN AFRICA. *New Statesman*, 10 April 1920, 7–8.
Unsigned article written as a result of the criticism of his article of 21 February, C0242.

C0254 THE GOOD KIND CAPITALIST FAIRY. *Daily Herald*, 21 April 1920, p. 8, cols. 4–5.
Review of *The Case for Communism*, by Hartley Withers.
    Socialists should read this amusing, urbane book. A model for the controversialist, it is a better case against socialism than for the capitalism the author advocates.

C0255 THE VISION OF LORD KITCHENER. *Athenaeum*, 30 April 1920, 571–72.
Ironic review of *Life of Lord Kitchener*, by Sir George Arthur, 3 vols, signed L.W.
    "It is most unfortunate that the biographer should have considered it to be part of his duty to eliminate all the creases and wrinkles which make character." From these volumes it is "almost impossible to form a judgment upon Kitchener's objective achievements as a General and as an administrator."

C0256 THE WORLD OF NATIONS. *Contemporary Review*, CXVII (April 1920), [557]-588.
Introductory remarks to THE COAL QUESTION BETWEEN FRANCE AND GERMANY; THE FRENCH SOCIALISTS AND THE INTER-NATIONALE; and THE SOVIET LAW OF FAMILY.

C0257   ARTICLE XXII. *New Statesman*, 1 May 1920, 94–95.
Unsigned article.
If England and France do not adhere to the provisions of Article 22 in Syria and Mesopotamia the "mandatory system is nothing but a worthless scrap of paper."

C0258   WHAT WE FOUGHT FOR. *Daily Herald*, 19 May 1920, p. 7, col. 3.
Review of *The War After the War*, by Charles Roden Buxton and Dorothy Frances Buxton.
A diagnosis rather than an indictment of the maladies brought on by the peace following the war. This book is depressing, though judicial and fair and especially good on Bolshevism.

C0259   THE WORLD OF NATIONS. *Contemporary Review*, CXVII (May 1920), [709]-740.
Introductory remarks to THE HUNGARIAN WHITE TERROR AND THE ALLIES; and WHAT IS HAPPENING IN GERMANY.

C0260   THE INDIAN VIEW. *Daily Herald*, 9 June 1920, p. 7, col. 1.
Review of *The Problem of National Education in India*, by Lajpat Rai; and *Indian Nationalism*, by K. M. Panikkar.
The problems presented in these two books would lead one to despair but for the reasonable, impartial presentation of the authors.

C0261   THE WORLD OF NATIONS. *Contemporary Review*, CXVII (June 1920), [861]-888.
Introductory remarks to JUSTICE UNDER BOLSHEVISM; THE FRENCH BUDGET; PRESIDENT WILSON ON THE TURKISH TREATY; and CONGRESS AND THE PEACE TREATY.

C0262   POLITICS AND AFFAIRS. *Nation*, 3 July 1920, 420–24.
Articles titled ANOTHER SCRAP OF PAPER; NEW DOMINION STATUS; and THE RAMROD IN THE MACHINE.

C0263   POLITICS AND AFFAIRS. *Nation*, 10 July 1920, 456–59.
Articles titled THE BREAKING OF THE POLISH BARRIER; AMERICA STANDS ALOOF; and THE PRICE OF MR. CHURCHILL.

C0264   THE CIVIL SERVICE. *Daily Herald*, 14 July 1920, p. 7, cols. 4–5.
Review of *The Public Service in War and Peace*, by Sir William Beveridge.
The author explains the difference between the requirements for public service and for commercial life, and he makes suggestions for improving the Civil Service.

C0265   IMPERIALISM AND SOUTH AFRICA. *Daily Herald*, 14 July 1920, p. 7, col. 5.
Review of *History of South Africa from 1873 to 1884*, by G. M. Theal.
Theal's interest in the trees prevent his seeing the wood. Still, by giving facts without comment he hits on real truths.

C0266   POLITICS AND AFFAIRS. *Nation*, 17 July 1920, 488–92.
Articles titled THE CHOICE IN INDIA; ILLUSIONS AND REALITIES AT SPA; and HOW CAN THE COST OF LIVING BE REDUCED?

C0267   POLITICS AND AFFAIRS. *Nation*, 24 July 1920, 516–19.
Articles titled THE REVOLT OF THE CONSUMER; THE NEW WARS IN THE EAST; and THE BEST MONUMENT OF THE WAR.

C0268   POLITICS AND AFFAIRS. *Nation*, 31 July 1920, 544–47.
Articles titled IRISH REPUBLIC; PEACE IN THE BALANCE; and THE NEW GERMAN ECONOMIC COUNCIL.

C0269 REMINISCENCES OF TOLSTOY. A LETTER, by Maxim Gorki. *London Mercury*, II.9, July 1920, 304–19.
Pre-publication excerpt of a translation by S. S. Koteliansky and LW. Reprinted with additional material and some changes in punctuation in *Reminiscences of Leo Nicolayevitch Tolstoi*, published by L and VW at the Hogarth Press, B5.

C0270 THE WORLD OF NATIONS. *Contemporary Review*, CXVIII (July 1920), [101]-132.
Introductions to sections on NATIONALIZATION AND FRENCH RAILWAYS; THE FRANCHISE IN ALGERIA; JAPAN AND SIBERIA; THE FALL OF CARRANZA; and JUSTICE UNDER BOLSHEVISM.

C0271 INTERNATIONALISM. *Daily Herald*, 4 August 1920, p. 7, col. 5.
Review of *Internationalism*, by C. Delisle Burns, signed L.W.
This "eminently useful book" shows the difference between international policy and foreign policy, international finance and capitalism.

C0272 POLITICS AND AFFAIRS. *Nation*, 7 August 1920, 572–76.
Articles titled EUROPE AND FEISUL; THE WORLD AND ITS FOOD; and A FOOTNOTE TO HISTORY.

C0273 POLAND AND POGROMS. *Daily Herald*, 12 August 1920, p. 7, cols. 3–4.
Review of *Poland and Minority Races*, by Arthur L. Goodhart.
This diary of a journey in Poland gives a vivid picture of conditions a year ago. Military training by French officers and Jew-baiting occupied the time and energy that should have been given to economics. Mr. Goodhart's observations prove that the official position that the Jews massacred people at Minsk is not true. The placid acquiescence of Europeans at the lunacies of their governments in foreign policy causes nine-tenths of the misery.

C0274 POLITICS AND AFFAIRS. *Nation*, 14 August 1920, 600–03.
Articles titled THE VICE OF FRENCH POLICY; THE WORKMEN'S REFUSAL; and THE ISSUES AT MINSK.

C0275 POLITICS AND AFFAIRS. *Nation*, 21 August 1920, 628–31.
Articles titled A NEW VETO ON WAR; THE ISOLATION OF FRANCE; and THE IRISH WAR.

C0276 LABOUR IN AUSTRALIA. *Daily Herald*, 25 August 1920, p. 7, cols. 1 & 2.
Review of *Australian Social Development*, by E. M. Lawson.
The story of the struggle against landlordism and capitalism and the role of the Labour Party in Australia.

C0277 POLITICS AND AFFAIRS. *Nation*, 28 August 1920, 656–59.
Articles titled WANTED – A POLICY; PROCESSIONAL; and RECESSIONAL.

C0278 THE WORLD OF NATIONS. *Contemporary Review*, CXVIII (August 1920), [253]-282.
Introductory remarks to sections on BRITAIN, FRANCE, ASIA AND OIL; JAPAN IN SIBERIA; THE BOLSHEVIKS AND ASIA (Turkey); THE MANDATE STYSTEM; ITALY AND ALBANIA; and THE ALLIES AND AUSTRIA (reparations).

C0279 POLITICS AND AFFAIRS. *Nation*, 4 September 1920, 684–87.
Articles titled THE END OF OUR GOVERNMENT IN IRELAND; THE MINERS AND THE NATION; and THE NEAR EAST.

C0280 ABRACADABRA. *Daily Herald*, 8 September 1920, p. 7, col. 5.
Review of *Industrial Control*, by E. M. Lawson.

The book "is a curious mixture of scientific management and mystic quackery".

C0281 POLITICS AND AFFAIRS. *Nation*, 11 September 1920, 712–15.
Articles titled THE LAST PHASE; and THE DILEMMA OF LABOR [*sic*].

C0282 THEIR BROTHERS' KEEPERS. *Athenaeum*, 17 September 1920, 371.
Unsigned review of *The Egyptian Problem*, by Sir Valentine Chirol; and *The Government of Egypt*, Recommendations by a Committee of the Labour Research Department, With Notes on Egypt by E. M. Forster.
"Sir Valentine Chirol takes three hundred pages to say that he thinks that he ought to be his brother's keeper, and the Labour Committee and Mr. Forster take twelve to say that they don't." Chirol is a knight-errant who cannot believe that the peoples of the East reject the well-meaning intentions of Englishmen to rule them.

C0283 POLITICS AND AFFAIRS. *Nation*, 18 September 1920, 740–45.
Articles titled THE CASE OF THE 'DAILY HERALD'; THE ELEVENTH HOUR; and FRANCE AND OURSELVES.

C0284 REVOLUTION. *Daily Herald*, 22 September 1920, p. 7, col. 5.
Review of *The Principles of Revolution*, by C. Delisle Burns.
Like several others by the same author, this book is too short to be more than superficial.

C0285 POLITICS AND AFFAIRS. *Nation*, 25 September 1920, 772–75.
Articles titled A POSSIBLE WAY OUT; THE GRAND CAUSE OF UN-EMPLOYMENT; and ITALY'S WAY.

C0286 NOTHING NEW. *Daily Herald*, 29 September 1920, p. 7, col. 1.
Review of *The War for Monarchy*, by J. A. Farrer, signed L.W.
This excellent account of the years of the war between 1792 and 1815 is depressing because it shows that there is nothing new under the sun.

C0287 THE WORLD OF NATIONS. *Contemporary Review*, CXVIII (September 1920), [405]-436.
Introductory remarks to sections on PLATFORMS IN U.S.A. PRESIDEN-TIAL ELECTION; CZECHO-SLOVAK CONSTITUTION; FRANCE AND WRANGEL; CZECHO-SLOVAKIA & THE RUSSO-POLISH CONFLICT; RUSSIAN-AUSTRIAN TREATY; A FRENCH AMBASSADOR AT MUNICH; and ITALY'S FOREIGN POLICY.

C0288 THE NEW SLAVE POLICY IN EAST AFRICA. *New Statesman*, 2 October 1920, 700.
Letter to the editor in reply to a letter from Travers Buxton (p. 644). Buxton commented on an unsigned article of this title, published 11 September 1920, p. 615. LW may have written the article as well as this reply. The article refers to earlier articles in this periodical including a paragraph in the "Comments" section, August 14, p. 514. See C0242 and C0253.
The real point of the article is that forced labour is deemed necessary because private employers will not let the government compete with them for labour.

C0289 POLITICS AND AFFAIRS. *Nation*, 2 October 1920, 4–8.
Articles titled THE PROCLAMATION OF ANARCHY; WHITE FRONT IN FRANCE; and THE TWO PATHS.

C0290 POVERTY. *Daily Herald*, 6 October 1920, p. 7, col. 6.
Review of *The Facts of Poverty*, by H. A. Mess (Student Christian Movement), signed L.W.

This straightforward account of the workers in East Ham seems to belie the claim that only capitalism provides the incentive which keeps men at work.

C0291 POLITICS AND AFFAIRS. *Nation*, 9 October 1920, 32–36.
Articles titled A PROPOSAL OF IRISH SETTLEMENT; THE GUILT OF THE GOVERNMENT; and THE LEAGUE OF M. LEYGUES.

C0292 WHAT WAS CHARTISM? *Athenaeum*, 15 October 1920, 516–17.
Review of *A History of the Chartist Movement*, by Julius West.
Although "not the study of Chartism we had hoped for . . . it does provide the raw material for anyone with the patience and ability necessary for the writing of such a study." Unlike earlier studies "it shows the real beliefs and desires of the Chartists" and "the social significance and object of the movement."

C0293 POLITICS AND AFFAIRS. *Nation*, 16 October 1920, 60–63.
Articles titled KILLING NO MURDER; and ANOTHER PUNIC PEACE.

C0294 THE WORLD OF NATIONS. *Contemporary Review*, CXVIII (October 1920), [557]-588.
Introductory remarks to RUSSIA & POLAND; PEACE NEGOTIATIONS; CZECHO-SLOVAK CONSTITUTION; GERMANY & THE SAAR STRIKE; RUSSIA & AUSTRIA; THE BALKAN ENTENTE; and RUSSIA & LATVIA.

C0295 A RUSSIAN STATESMAN. *Athenaeum*, 19 November 1920, 693.
Unsigned review of *The Memoirs of Alexander Iswolsky*, tr. by Louis Seeger.
This is an interesting book even though the author fails in his attempt to exonerate the Tzar of charges of duplicity and betrayal in the treaty with Germany in 1905.

C0296 THE WORLD OF NATIONS. *Contemporary Review*, CXVIII (November 1920), [709]-740.
Introductory remarks to CAPITAL AND LABOUR IN ITALY; THE LITTLE ENTENTE; MAXIM GORKY ON LENIN; THE CZECHOSLOVAK CONSTITUTION; and RUSSIA AND LATVIA.

C0297 BACK TO ARISTOTLE. *Athenaeum*, 17 December 1920, 834–35.
Review of *The Sacred Wood*, by T. S. Eliot.
For Eliot as for Aristotle criticism is a science.

C0298 THE BOLSHEVIK CONTRA MUNDUM. *New Statesman*, 18 December 1920, 342–44.
Unsigned review of *The Practice and Theory of Bolshevism*, by Bertrand Russell; and *Terrorism and Communism*, by Karl Kautsky, tr. by W. H. Kerridge.
Both writers oppose communism because to the Bolsheviks it is a religion.

C0299 GUILD SOCIALISM. *Daily Herald*, 22 December 1920, p. 7, col. 3.
Review of *The Meaning of National Guilds*, by M. B. Reckitt and C. E. Bechhofer; *Guild Socialism Re-stated*, by G. D. H. Cole; and *Guild Socialism*, by G. C. Field.
The first two books state the aims and objects of guild socialism. Mr. Cole's book is the most interesting. He has mellowed since his last book. Field is hostile, but he is fair.

C0300 THE POOR CONSUMER. *Daily Herald*, 22 December 1920, p. 7, col. 4.
Review of *The Consumer's Place in Society*, by Percy Redfern (Co-operative Union), signed L.W.

An admirable book. Only the Co-operator seems to remember that the object of production is consumption.

C0301 THE WORLD OF NATIONS. *Contemporary Review*, CXVIII (December 1920), [857]-888.
Introductory remarks to THE RUSSIAN-POLISH PEACE; COMMUNISTS AND SOCIALISTS IN GERMANY; NATIONALIZATION OF GERMAN MINING INDUSTRY.

C0302 CO-OPERATION AND GUILD SOCIALISM. *Guildsman*, No. 48, December 1920, pp. 3–4.
Article.
"Capitalist psychology " makes man a wolf to man. It must be eliminated if socialism is to succeed.

1921

C0303 WAR AND PEACE. *Daily Herald*, 5 January 1921, p. 7, col. 4.
Review of 3 books published by the Swarthmore Press in the International Handbooks series: *Causes of International War*, by G. Lowes Dickinson; *Unifying the World*, by G. N. Clark; and *Nationalism*, by G. P. Gooch.
Mr. Lowes Dickinson, series editor, has written an excellent study; Mr. Clark examines the effect of modern communications on international relations; Mr. Gooch includes too many examples for the space.
LW's contribution to the series, *Economic Imperialism*, was reviewed by Wat Tyler in the *Daily Herald*, 12 January 1921, p. 7, col. 2.

C0304 THE DEVELOPMENT OF THE C.W.S. *New Statesman*, 15 January 1921, 440–41.
Article signed From a Correspondent but listed in the index as by L. S. Woolf.
The current report from the directors of the C.W.S. shows the amazing growth of this organization, particularly in international trade.

C0305 THE LEAGUE STARTS. *New Statesman*, 22 January 1921, 480 & 482.
Unsigned review of *The League of Nations Starts, An Outline by Its Organisers*.

C0306 THE EMPIRE. *Daily Herald*, 26 January 1921, p. 7, col. 1.
Review of *The British Commonwealth of Nations*, by Duncan Hall, signed L.W.
The author deals with the Dominions and their demand for equality in foreign policy with the imperial government in London, and he proposes a solution.

C0307 THE WORLD OF NATIONS: FACTS AND DOCUMENTS. *Contemporary Review*, CXIX (January 1921), [101]-124.
The monthly "World of Nations" articles, excerpts from articles on foreign affairs taken from foreign newspapers, continued. Subjects during the year included ANGLO-FRENCH RELATIONS; ARGENTINA AND THE LEAGUE; ARMAMENTS; AUSTRIA; BELGIUM; BOLSHEVIKS; BULGARIA; CHINA; CZECHOSLOVAKIA; D'ANNUNZIO; FRANCE; GERMANY; HAPSBURGS; HOHENZOLLERNS; HUNGARY; ITALY AND FASCISTI; JAPAN; KOREA; LEAGUE OF NATIONS; LENIN; LITTLE ENTENTE; POLAND; REPARATIONS; RUSSIA – FAMINE AND RELIEF – PEASANT REVOLT; SAAR; SECRET TREATIES; SYRIA; SWITZERLAND; TURKEY; U.S.A.; WASHINGTON CONFERENCE; and YUGOSLAVIA.

C0308 ANTON TCHEKHOV'S NOTEBOOK 1891–1904. *London Mercury*, January 1921, 285–95.
Selection from the translation by S. Koteliansky and LW published in the spring at the Hogarth Press, B8.

C0309 THE WORLD OF NATIONS. *Contemporary Review*, CXIX (February 1921), [245]-268.

C0310 COAL, IRON, & WAR. *Daily Herald*, 9 March 1921, p. 7, col. 4.
Review of *Coal, Iron and War*, by Edwin C. Eckel, signed L.W.
> This study of the causes and effects of industrialism is based on facts and has some conclusions which will make the reader think whether or not he agrees.

C0311 JOHN STUART MILL (1806–1873). Headed GREAT NAMES. *Daily Herald*, 16 March 1921, p. 7, col. 3.
Review of *On Liberty; On Representative Government; Utilitarianism;* and *Dissertations and Discussions.*
> Mill popularized the theory of utilitarianism, laissez-faire, and individualism by his writings.

C0312 BERNSTEIN IN EXILE. *Daily Herald*, 23 March 1921, p. 7, col. 1.
Review of *My Years of Exile*, by Eduard Bernstein.
> Having left Germany just as Bismarck began persecuting the socialists, the author's trip became an exile. His reminiscences are not bitter, but provide an interesting picture of both the German socialist movement and of England in the 1880s and 90s.

C0313 THE WORLD OF NATIONS. *Contemporary Review*, CXIX (March 1921), [389]-412.

C0314 THE WORLD OF NATIONS. *Contemporary Review*, CXIX (April 1921), [533]-556.

C0315 A SACRED TRUST. *New Statesman*, XVII (14 May 1921) 151–52.
Unsigned article.
> "According to the Covenant the well-being and development of the natives in African territory is 'a sacred trust of civilisation.'" [But in Kenya] "there can be no possible excuse for the way in which the Administration by its acts persistently sacrifices the interest of the natives for the economic advantage of the European settler."

C0316 THE WORLD OF NATIONS. *Contemporary Review*, CXIX (May 1921), [677]-700.

C0317 THE TURBID EAST. *Nation & The Athenaeum*, (hereafter *Nation & Athenaeum*) 4 June 1921, 368–69.
Unsigned review of *China, Japan and Korea*, by J. O. P. Bland.

C0318 WORKING HISTORY. *Daily Herald*, 8 June 1921, p. 7, col. 3.
Review of *Industrial History of England*, by Abbot Payson Usher; and *The Social and Industrial History of Scotland*, by James Mackinnon.
> Unlike the entertaining books of Lytton Strachey, these are academic books, "large, tough, a little bitter, dignified, and dry", but full of facts.

C0319 EMPIRE CONFERENCE. *Daily Herald*, 13 June 1921, p. 4, cols. 4 and 5.
Article. Mentions *The British Commonwealth of Nations*, by Duncan Hall.
> The Dominions want some control over foreign policy which might involve them in a world war. Their demand for equality will probably lead to an imperial cabinet.

C0320 WHAT CO-OPS. CAN DO. *Daily Herald*, 17 June 1921, p. 4, col. 4.

Article.

The Women's Co-operative Guild meeting this week in Manchester is presently working on behalf of international co-operative trade.

C0321 A DEMOCRATIC SYSTEM OF INDUSTRY. FIRST ESSENTIAL: MAN BEFORE MONEY. *Co-operative News*, 18 June 1921, p. 2, cols. 1 & 2.

Signed article, including a photograph of LW, dated San Francisco, May 21st, 1921. Original article from which it was taken not found.

C0322 THE WORLD OF NATIONS. *Contemporary Review*, CXIX (June 1921), [817]-840.

C0323 A PARTNERSHIP THAT PAID. *Daily Herald*, 20 July 1921, p. 7, col. 2.

Review of *A Democratic Co-Partnership*, by E. O. Greening (Leicester Co-operative Printing Society).

This interesting matter-of-fact story of Wigston Hosiers, Ltd. does not bear out the company's claim of being democratic. Its success was due rather to sound financial policy and to demand resulting from the war.

C0324 WHAT'S THE WORLD COMING TO? *Daily Herald*, 27 July 1921, p. 7, col. 2.

Review of *Breaking Point*, by Jeffery E. Jeffery, with a foreword by G. D. H. Cole; and *The Future of Local Government*, by G. D. H. Cole.

Mr. Jeffery just adds an exclamation point to every question. Mr. Cole stimulates the reader to think. This is but a chapter in the social theory towards which he is working in a hasty, impatient manner.

C0325 ECONOMIC IMPERIALISM AND THE "SACRED TRUST". *Labour Monthly*, I.1, July 1921, pp. 51–61.

Signed article.

Two reports by British Government commissions and one by a Belgian commission show that the situation of exploiting the natives which obtained 20 years ago in the Belgian Congo is now the condition of the British colonies in East Africa.

C0326 THE WORLD OF NATIONS. *Contemporary Review*, CXX (July 1921), [101]-124.

C0327 THE FOG OF HISTORY. *Nation & Athenaeum*, 27 August 1921, 762.

Review of *The Evolution of World Peace*, edited by F. S. Marvin, signed L.W. None of the writers included in this volume has really grasped the subject. Each has considered it from the traditional perspective of history, the lifetime of one man, whereas it must be considered from the perspective of eternity.

C0328 THE WORLD OF NATIONS. *Contemporary Review*, CXX (August 1921), [245]-268.

C0329 LENIN AND KENYA. *New Statesman*, 10 September 1921, 615–16.

Unsigned article.

"The notion is fantastic that a few thousand white men, possessed of the crude and narrow ideas which they openly display ... can govern autocratically and exploit economically an African population which outnumbers them by hundreds to one, and also an Indian population which outnumbers them by three or four to one. . . ." It is "the white settlers, not Lenin, who are directly responsible for the agitation among the Indians; the growing unrest among the natives", and the growth of labour unions.

C0330 THE WORLD OF NATIONS. *Contemporary Review*, CXX (September 1921), [389]-412.

C0331 THE WORLD OF NATIONS. *Contemporary Review,* CXX (October 1921), [533]-556.
C0332 THE WORLD OF NATIONS. *Contemporary Review,* CXX (November 1921), [677]-700.
C0333 THE WORLD OF NATIONS. *Contemporary Review,* CXX (December 1921), [817]-840.

1922

C0334 SOCIALISM AND SOCIETY. *Daily Herald,* 11 January 1922, p. 7, col. 6.
Review of *Elements of Social Justice,* by L. T. Hobhouse; and *Socialism: An Analysis,* by Rudolph Eucken.
> Both books are detailed discussions of society. Hobhouse seems at first to oppose Socialism, but as his argument goes on it differs little from its current ideals. Eucken begins by seeming to favour Socialism but ends by turning against it.

C0335 MR. WELLS AND THE WORLD'S PEACE. *Daily Herald,* 25 January 1922, p. 7, col. 6.
Review of *Washington and the Hope of Peace,* by H. G. Wells.
> Here Wells pins his hopes on the Washington Conference. He sees and feels the large and deep currents moulding history, but he is sometimes a bit late to speak out. He changes allegiance rapidly. Yesterday he was all for the League of Nations.

C0336 THE CO-OPERATIVE MOVEMENT. *New Statesman,* 21 January 1922, 452.
Review of *The Consumers' Co-operative Movement,* by Sidney and Beatrice Webb, signed L.S.W.
> The Webbs analyse the Movement scientifically and imaginatively, describing it both as a whole and in detail. In their previous writings they stressed the limitations of the Movement; now they stress its potentialities.

C0337 FOREIGN AFFAIRS. *Contemporary Review,* CXXI (January 1922), [101]-116.
Signed article.
> First of a year-long series based on facts and documents, especially as set forth in the foreign press. Space limitation imposed by the periodical meant that LW had to summarize the articles and documents rather than print abstracts verbatim as in "The World of Nations" articles. Topics covered during the year include ALBANIA, ARMAMENTS, AUSTRIA, BALKANS, BALTIC STATES, BAVARIA, BELGIUM – LANGUAGE QUESTION IN, BULGARIA, CHINA, FRANCE, GERMANY, HAPS-BURGS, HUNGARY, ITALY, JAPAN, THE LEAGUE OF NATIONS, THE LITTLE ENTENTE, POLAND, REPARATIONS, RUSSIA, THE SAAR, SILESIA, TANGIERS, and VILNA.

C0338 IMPERIALISM. *Daily Herald,* 22 February 1922, p. 7, col. 4.
Review of *The Foundations of Imperialist Policy,* by Michel Pavlovitch, signed L.W.
> "An interesting, lucid, and thorough analysis of various theories as to the origin and nature of imperialism."

C0339 FOREIGN AFFAIRS. *Contemporary Review,* CXXI (February 1922), [237]-252.

C0340 FOREIGN AFFAIRS. *Contemporary Review,* CXXI (March 1922), [373]-388.

C0341   WOBBLY IMPERIALISM. *New Statesman,* 1 April 1922, 736.
Review of *The Dual Mandate in British Tropical Africa,* by Sir F. D. Lugard, signed L.S.W.
> The author does not seem to have made up his mind. He attempts a stand for imperialism and against the Labour Party's pamphlet on policy for the empire in Africa, but when he goes into detail about his own theories and actions in Africa he appears to disagree with only one principle of government set forth in the pamphlet; he advocates importing contract labour.

C0342   FOREIGN AFFAIRS. *Contemporary Review,* CXXI (April 1922), [509]-524.

C0343   FOREIGN AFFAIRS. *Contemporary Review,* CXXI (May 1922), [645]-660.

C0344   BOTTOMLEY AND CAPITALISM. *Daily Herald,* 1 June 1922, p. 4, col. 3.
Letter.
> Protests against leading article which held that Bottomley should not have been punished for fraud because "the greatest of all frauds – the exploitation of the workers through Capitalism – is legal" (May 30, p. 4, col. 2). LW says the *Daily Herald* should not condone this false, "sentimental claptrap".

C0345   ANCIENT CLASS WARS. *Daily Herald,* 21 June 1922, p. 7, col. 1.
Review of *Social Struggles in Antiquity,* by M. Beer.
> A short study of an extraordinarily interesting subject, the effects of economics on history in Palestine, Greece and Rome.

C0346   THE LABYRINTH OF DIPLOMACY. *New Statesman,* 29 June 1922, 470.
Review of 2 books, signed L.W.
Let France Explain, by Frederick Bausman; and *Secret Diplomacy*, by Paul S. Reinsch.
> Looking at the same facts, these two intelligent Americans come to opposite conclusions. Bausman is lost in a labyrinth of facts and blind with prejudice. Reinsch is usually sound. He should have included his own experience as a diplomat.

C0347   FOREIGN AFFAIRS. *Contemporary Review,* CXXI (June 1922), [777]-792.
Contains "Dangerous Thought in Japan" (see C0349 below).

C0348   MULTUM IN PARVO. *Daily Herald,* 26 July 1922, p. 7, col. 2.
Review of *A Primer of Social Science,* by Robert Jones.
> A short trial trip through theories of government.

C0349   DANGEROUS THOUGHT IN JAPAN. *Current History: A Monthly Magazine of the New York Times,* XVI.4, July 1922, [629]-30.
Signed article.
> Includes quotation from the *Japan Weekly Chronicle* of the drastic bill against socialism and labour strikes in the House of Peers (see C0347).

C0350   KASIMIR STANISLAVOVITCH, BY IVAN BUNIN. Translated from the Russian by LW and S. S. Koteliansky. *Dial,* Chicago; New York, LXXIII.1, (July 1922), [41]-47.
A short story.
Reprinted as part of the book *A Gentleman from San Francisco*, B10, published by the Woolfs at the Hogarth Press.

C0351   FOREIGN AFFAIRS. *Contemporary Review,* CXXII (July 1922), [101]-116.

C0352   FOREIGN AFFAIRS. *Contemporary Review,* CXXII (August 1922), [237]-252.

C0353 ENGLAND, PAST AND PRESENT. *Daily Herald,* 6 September 1922, p. 7, col. 5.
Review of *England Under Edward VII,* by J. A. Farrer; and *England Today,* by George A. Greenwood.
> These books comprise an analysis of the conditions in England resulting in the Great War and the greatness of Edward VII.

C0354 THREE VIEWS OF THE FAR EAST. *New Statesman,* 23 September 1922, 664 & 666.
Review of *Asia at the Cross Roads,* by E. Alexander Powell; *The Shantung Question,* by Ge-Zay Wood; and *Japan's Pacific Policy,* by K. K. Kawakami, signed L.S.W.
> Each of these authors states the views of his own country. The American Powell is disinterested. The Chinese diplomat Wood makes the most of an unanswerable case. The Japanese journalist Kawakami has written a clever book of pure propaganda which may convince readers who do not know the real facts.

C0355 FOREIGN AFFAIRS. *Contemporary Review,* CXXII (September 1922), [373]-388.

C0356 BREAKING CHINA. *New Statesman,* 28 October 1922, 118.
Review of *The Problem of China,* by Bertrand Russell; *The Washington Conference,* by R. L. Buell (Appleton); and *China at the Conference,* by W. W. Willoughby (Johns Hopkins Press), signed L.S.W.
> Mr. Russell may be too liberal with his ironic wit on this depressing subject.

C0357 FOREIGN AFFAIRS. *Contemporary Review,* CXXII (October 1922), [509]-524.

C0358 THE OLD GAME WITH TURKEY. Headed POLITICS AND AFFAIRS. *Nation & Athenaeum,* 18 November 1922, 275–76.
Article.
> Turkey operates by bluff and by playing one power against another. We must not give in to her demands.

LW began writing articles under the "Politics and Affairs" section before the end of 1922, but just how early is not known. Typescripts for those listed here are in LW Papers Sussex.

C0359 THE OFFICIAL VIEW OF AFRICA. *New Statesman,* 25 November 1922, 246 & 248.
Review of *The Partition and Colonialisation of Africa,* by Sir Charles Lucas, signed L.F.W. [probably a misprint].
> The author's years at Whitehall are evident.

C0360 GERMANY AND ITS GOVERNMENT. Headed POLITICS AND AFFAIRS. *Nation & Athenaeum,* 25 November 1922, 307–08.
Unsigned second leader.
> Two things killed Dr. Wirth's government, the reparations question and the instability of the political parties.

C0361 FOREIGN AFFAIRS. *Contemporary Review,* CXXII (November 1922), [645]-660.

C0362 FOREIGN AFFAIRS. *Contemporary Review,* CXXII (December 1922), [777]-792.

1923

C0363 EVENTS OF THE WEEK. *Nation & Athenaeum*, 6 January 1923, 535–37.

C0364 A PLEA FOR ANGLO-AMERICAN POLICY. Headed POLITICS AND AFFAIRS. *Nation & Athenaeum*, 6 January 1923, 538–39.
Unsigned article.
> The French stand on reparations, no moratorium without pledges, will be ruinous to Germany and to Europe. Britain should back America's proposal that the question be submitted to an international committee of experts.

C0365 EVENTS OF THE WEEK. *Nation & Athenaeum*, 13 January 1923, [567]-569.

C0366 WHAT SHOULD BRITAIN DO? POLITICS AND AFFAIRS. *Nation & Athenaeum*, 13 January 1923, 570–71.
> The breakdown of the Paris Conference and the decision of Poincaré to enforce the terms of the peace treaty by marching into German territory make it necessary that the British get out of Cologne.

C0367 EVENTS OF THE WEEK. *Nation & Athenaeum*, 20 January 1923, [599]-601.

C0368 THE NEXT GREAT WAR BEGINS. POLITICS AND AFFAIRS. *Nation & Athenaeum*, 20 January 1923, 602–03.
> If the British remain in Cologne there is danger that they may become a buffer against the French. They should be aware that the Russian government is mobilizing the Red Army.

C0369 EVENTS OF THE WEEK. *Nation & Athenaeum*, 27 January 1923, [633]-35.

C0370 STOP THE NEW WAR! POLITICS AND AFFAIRS. *Nation & Athenaeum*, 27 January 1923, 636–37.
> *Woodrow Wilson and World Settlement*, by Ray Stannard Baker shows that the French have accomplished by force what they set out to do at the peace conference in 1919. They are now kicking the enemy they have already knocked down and disarmed. The British have adopted a policy of benevolent neutrality. They should insist that the Council of the League of Nations take up the question.

C0371 EVENTS OF THE WEEK. *Nation & Athenaeum*, 3 February 1923, [673]-675.

C0372 THE DANGERS OF NEUTRALITY. POLITICS AND AFFAIRS. *Nation & Athenaeum*, 3 February 1923, 676–77.
> Britain should make clear to France her opposition to that country's policy. It is unwise to take the short view.

C0373 EVENTS OF THE WEEK. *Nation & Athenaeum*, 10 February 1923, [707]-709.

C0374 THE MEANING OF LAUSANNE. POLITICS AND AFFAIRS. *Nation & Athenaeum*, 10 February 1923, 710–11.
> Negotiations for a peace treaty with Turkey have shown the Turks playing off one country against another. There is some evidence that the French have been encouraging the Turks. The British must not be tempted to buy peace with Turkey at the price of assenting to French policy in the Ruhr.

C0375 EVENTS OF THE WEEK. *Nation & Athenaeum*, 17 February 1923, [739]-741.

C0376 FRANCE'S CARE FOR HERSELF. POLITICS AND AFFAIRS. *Nation &*
Athenaeum, 17 February 1923, 742–43.
> Justifications for French policy in the semi-official *Temps* include rumours
> that Germany plans to invade France. France wants no Allied interference
> with her goal of unconditional German surrender to France. Great Britain
> should demand arbitration immediately.

C0377 EVENTS OF THE WEEK. *Nation & Athenaeum*, 24 February 1923, [771]-
773.

C0378 NOT NEUTRALITY, BUT OPPOSITION. POLITICS AND AFFAIRS.
Nation & Athenaeum, 24 February 1923, 774–75.
> If Britain cannot impose arbitration on France, she should use economic
> sanctions.

C0379 OPPRESSED PEOPLES AND THE LEAGUE OF NATIONS. *Labour*
Magazine, I.10, February 1923, 471.
> Signed review of *Oppressed Peoples and the League of Nations*, by Noel
> Buxton and T. P. Conwil-Evans.

C0380 EVENTS OF THE WEEK. *Nation & Athenaeum*, 3 March 1923, [807]-809.

C0381 A SECRET DOCUMENT. POLITICS AND AFFAIRS. *Nation &*
Athenaeum, 3 March 1923, 810–11.
> "[Being the Text of an Undespatched Despatch from H.M. Secretary of State
> for Foreign Affairs to the French Ambassador.]" A summary of the charges
> against France, headed "Foreign Office, February, 1923."

C0382 EVENTS OF THE WEEK. *Nation & Athenaeum*, 10 March 1923, [845]-
847.

C0383 ONCE MORE IN THE SPIDER'S WEB. POLITICS AND AFFAIRS. *Nation*
& Athenaeum, 10 March 1923, 848–49.
> "We are watching to-day the old diplomacy beginning to respin its spider-
> web of armed alliances, ententes, understandings over Europe . . ."

C0384 ENGLAND AND GERMANY. *The Nation*, New York, CXVI.3010, 14
March 1923, 290–91.
> Signed article.
> The English leaders' mistake of going along with French demands after
> the war is making the British side with Germany. The peace treaty may
> have been only the end to the first chapter of the war.

C0385 EVENTS OF THE WEEK. *Nation & Athenaeum*, 17 March 1923, [903]-
905.

C0386 WHY PERISH? POLITICS AND AFFAIRS. *Nation & Athenaeum*, 17
March 1923, 906–07.
> Disillusioned article which cites *War: Its Nature, Cause, and Cure*, by G.
> Lowes Dickinson; and the translation of Maurice Paléologue's *Memoirs*.

C0387 AVENUES TO PEACE. POLITICS AND AFFAIRS. *Nation & Athenaeum*,
17 March 1923, 907–08.

C0388 EVENTS OF THE WEEK. *Nation & Athenaeum*, 24 March 1923, [939]–40.

C0389 THE CAPITALIST SYSTEM. POLITICS AND AFFAIRS. *Nation &*
Athenaeum, 24 March 1923, 942–43.
> Article prompted by anger over the House of Commons Committee's
> sanctioning admission fees to the British Museum and the Natural History
> Museum.

C0390 THE FRENCH HEGEMONY. POLITICS AND AFFAIRS. *Nation &*
Athenaeum, 24 March 1923, 943–45.

C0391 EVENTS OF THE WEEK. *Nation & Athenaeum*, 31 March 1923, [971]-73.

C0392 THE NEW RACE IN ARMAMENTS. POLITICS AND AFFAIRS. *Nation &
Athenaeum,* 31 March 1923, 974–75.
Another plea that international problems be submitted to the Council of the
League of Nations.

From April 1923 to February 1930 Leonard Woolf was Literary Editor of the *Nation
& Athenaeum.*

C0393 POLITICS IN SPAIN. *Nation & Athenaeum,* April 1923, 74–75.
Article headed "Ugijar, April, 1923, By Leonard Woolf".
"There are no politics . . . in the real Spain", but only in Madrid, where the
army is everywhere. The real Spain hates the politicians and military men
who conscript people and send them to be slaughtered.
Reprinted, practically unchanged, in *Essays . . . 1927,* A24, pp. 212–17. In
the book version the place-name is spelled "Ugyar".

C0394 THE WORLD OF BOOKS. *Nation & Athenaeum,* 5 May 1923, 157.
Review of *Men of Letters,* by Dixon Scott, with an introduction by Max
Beerbohm, signed L.W.
Dixon Scott correctly predicted that the work of a number of writers
would not stand the test of time because of the unsuitable uses to which
they put their literary gifts. He included Bernard Shaw, Rudyard Kipling,
Sir James Barrie, H. G. Wells, Arnold Bennett, G. K. Chesterton and John
Masefield.
This article is similar to many of LW's "World of Books" contributions: more
than a review, it includes an overview of literature.

C0395 THE WORLD OF BOOKS. *Nation & Athenaeum,* 12 May 1923, 196.
Review of *On the Margin,* by Aldous Huxley, signed L.W.
Huxley is a first-class literary journalist who writes light, easy, witty
essays despite his "passion for learning and literature. . . . The worst of
good journalism is that its flowers are so bright, so pretty, and so
perishable."

C0396 LORD NORTHCLIFFE ROUND THE WORLD. THE WORLD OF
BOOKS. *Nation & Athenaeum,* 19 May 1923, 226.
Review of *My Journey Round the World,* by Alfred, Viscount Northcliffe,
signed L.W.
Lord Northcliffe's literary artistry is evident in this readable, vividly
descriptive book with its economy of phrase. "He interested me mainly by
his character and the way he brought the flavour of his character into his
book." He was candid, and he had a sense of humour, a respect for
anything big, and an acute sense of observation.

C0397 THE RUSSIANS. THE WORLD OF BOOKS. *Nation & Athenaeum,* 26 May
1923, 271.
Review of 4 books written by Russians: *The Plays of Tolstoy,* tr. by Louise
and Aylmer Maude; *A Russian Gentleman,* by Serghei Aksakoff, tr. by J. D.
Duff; *December the Fourteenth,* by Dmitri Merezhkovsky, tr. by N. A.
Duddington; and *The Diary of Nellie Ptaschkina,* tr. by Pauline de Chary,
signed Leonard Woolf.
Russian literature owes its vitality to a combination of passion and
interminable conversation. The last book listed is especially remarkable
for being the diary of a girl who died at the age of 17.
This is the first of many "World of Books" articles signed "Leonard Woolf".

Subsequent entries in this bibliography indicate only signatures that differ. THE WORLD OF BOOKS will be designated WOB.

C0398　POETRY AND MALARIA. WOB. *Nation & Athenaeum*, 2 June 1923, 304.
　　　　Review of *Memoirs*, by Sir Ronald Ross.
　　　　　　In this book a scientist who wrote poetry reveals his very interesting character.

C0399　MR. DRINKWATER'S DIFFICULTY. Headed THE DRAMA. *Nation & Athenaeum*, 9 June 1923, 343–44.
　　　　Review of the play "Oliver Cromwell" at His Majesty's Theatre, signed L.W.
　　　　　　So long as Drinkwater relied on public records of the speeches and pronouncements of Cromwell and other public figures of his time there was no problem. His difficulty was to put any kind of small talk in the mouths of his characters.
　　　　Francis Birrell, who often wrote the drama column, signed the "World of Books" article for this week.

C0400　FROM HICKEY TO HARDMAN. WOB. *Nation & Athenaeum*, 16 June 1923, 367.
　　　　Review of *Memoirs of William Hickey*, vol. III; and *A Mid-Victorian Pepys: The Letters and Memoirs of Sir William Hardman*, edited by S. M. Ellis.
　　　　　　These two autobiographies reflect the differences between the times of the two authors, Hickey the 18th century and Hardman the 19th. Standards of correctness in the former were replaced by standards of morality in the latter.

C0401　BEN JONSON. WOB. *Nation & Athenaeum*, 23 June 1923, 396.
　　　　Review of *Ben Jonson's Conversations with William Drummond of Hawthornden*, edited by R. F. Patterson.
　　　　　　This book "lifts one out of 1923, carries one straight over three centuries, and deposits one in the middle of 1618." Dr. Patterson's edition is the first to give the full text of the conversations. Reprinted as "Rare Ben Jonson" in *The Living Age*, C0409; reprinted with additions in *Essays ... 1927*, A24, pp. 11–16.

C0402　LONDON TOWN. WOB. *Nation & Athenaeum*, 30 June 1923, 427.
　　　　Review of 5 books: *Historic Streets of London*, by L. & A. Russan; *London and Westminster in History and Literature*, by W. Marston Acres; *Queer Things about London*, by Charles G. Harper; *The London of Dickens*, by Walter Dexter; and *London, Its Origin and Early Development*, by William Page.

C0403　THE ANATOMY OF OLD AGE. WOB. *Nation & Athenaeum*, 7 July 1923, 456.
　　　　Review of *A Green Old Age*, by Alexandre Lacassagne; and *De Senectute*, by Cicero.
　　　　　　"Lacassagne belongs to the same school as Burton, Montaigne and Sir Thomas Browne.... His book is full of digressions, full of quotations...."
　　　　Reprinted with minor changes in *Essays ... 1927*, A24, pp. 235–39.

C0404　BOOKS FOR A HOLIDAY. WOB. *Nation & Athenaeum*, 14 July 1923, 489.
　　　　Notice of 6 books: *Companionable Books*, by Henry Van Dyke; *Masters and Men*, by Philip Guedalla; *The Man of Promise, Lord Rosebery*, by E. T. Raymond; *Adventures in the Near East*, by Colonel A. Rawlinson; *In Many Places*, by Clare Sheridan; and *'Racundra's' First Cruise*, by Arthur Ransome.

C0405 A CHRONICLE OF KINGS. WOB. *Nation & Athenaeum*, 21 July 1923, 520.

Review of *The Glass Palace Chronicle of the Kings of Burma*, tr. by Pe Maung Tin and G. H. Luce.

All lovers of curious books will find this chronicle fascinating. "It tells its stories with a subtle sense of humour which can hardly be unintentional." Like much Asiatic art and literature it combines "two almost contradictory characteristics, a kind of megalomania and a curious form of unworldliness." See Woolf's comment on his remarks here in C0406 below.

C0406 AN ANCIENT CODGER. WOB. *Nation & Athenaeum*, 28 July 1923, 548.

Review of *Tales of Nasr-ed-Din Khoja*, tr. by Henry D. Barnham.

Before beginning his review LW admits that he generalized too much in "A Chronicle of Kings" (C0405).

"To talk, as I did of Asia differing from Europe in its megalomania and unworldliness and its sense of humour, is to put one's foot upon the slippery slope, at the bottom of which lie racialism, nationalism, anti-Semitism. . . ."

"Khoja" means something like codger or queer person. Five centuries ago the Sultan disliked this Khoja's humour and "refused to allow the tales to be published in Turkish and it was only after the Turkish revolution in 1908 that a large collection of them was made and printed in Constantinople." An earlier English translation by George Borrow is called *The Turkish Jester*.

C0407 DISRAELI IN PALESTINE. "TANCRED" AT THE KINGSWAY. Headed THE DRAMA. *Nation & Athenaeum*, 28 July 1923, 554 & 556.

Review of a dramatic adaptation by Edith Millbank [Mrs. Alfred Lyttelton], signed L.W.

The play is "a reshuffling of the conversations and incidents in the novel."

C0408 DRYDEN. WOB. *Nation & Athenaeum*, 4 August 1923, 575.

Review of *Dryden and His Poetry*, by Allardyce Nicoll; and *Dryden's Heroic Plays*, by B. J. Pendlebury.

Dryden's writing is technically excellent "and yet . . . there is something alien and repellent . . . at the core of his writing." Mr. Pendlebury says this is because Dryden and his age took the standard of the day-dream as the standard for life and literature.

There was no "World of Books" article 11 August 1923.

C0409 RARE BEN JONSON. *The Living Age*, 11 August 1923, 281–82.

Reprint of "Ben Jonson", C0401.

C0410 A TRAVELLER IN LITTLE THINGS. WOB. *Nation & Athenaeum*, 18 August 1923, 638.

Review of 3 vols of the re-issue of The Works of W. H. Hudson: *Far Away and Long Ago; Idle Days in Patagonia;* and *A Traveller in Little Things* (Dent).

Hudson and Conrad were writing classic English prose when most English writers of note were more interested in what they were saying than in how they said it. Hudson's works might have been re-issued sooner had he not been "incorrigibly meditative and philosophic".

Reprinted as part of "A Traveller in Little Things", in *Essays . . .* 1927, A24, pp. 72–76, together with the review of 22 December 1923, C0427.

C0411 AN ENGLISHMAN. WOB. *Nation & Athenaeum*, 25 August 1923, 662.
Review of *Rural Rides*, by William Cobbett; and *Cobbett*, selections with
Hazlitt's essay and notes by A. M. D. Hughes.
> "First among Cobbett's virtues I place his English style... plain,
> absolutely unaffected, vigorous and supple, beautiful...." But he has
> faults. "His opinions are nearly always prejudices... springing in a
> peculiarly English way, from a subsoil of 'common sense'.... He always
> has someone and something which he wants to abuse and beat and bully."

Reprinted with some modification in *Essays* ... 1927, A24.

C0412 HERMAN MELVILLE. WOB. *Nation & Athenaeum*, September 1923, 638.
Review of five of Melville's novels: *Moby Dick; Typee; Omoo; White Jacket;*
and *Mardi*, Library edition (Cape).
> Melville must have read Dickens between writing *Omoo* and *Mardi*. His
> early novels are good, plain, vigorous stories of adventure, but his later
> ones are disfigured by exaggerated humour. Despite his execrable English
> style he produced masterpieces.

C0413 THE PILGRIMAGE OF FA-HSIEN. WOB. *Nation & Athenaeum*, 8
September 1923, 715.
Review of *The Travels of Fa-hsien, or Record of the Buddhistic Kingdoms*, tr.
by Professor Giles.
> Fa-hsien made a remarkable walking pilgrimage from China to India to
> the fountain-head of Buddhism 1500 years ago. His book gives interesting
> glimpses of the history and religion of Central India in the fifth century.

David Garnett wrote "WOB" for September 15.

C0414 RUSKIN. WOB. *Nation & Athenaeum*, 22 September 1923, 777.
Review of *Selections from Ruskin*, by A. C. Benson.
> The author fails in his intention to illustrate "the development of
> [Ruskin's] personality and literary style." He neither presents the
> selections chronologically nor dates them. "If I had to give a candid
> judgment from these selections ... I should have to say that Ruskin was a
> very bad writer with an abominable literary style."

LW refers to correspondence about this article in "Samuel Butler", C0422.

C0415 CHARMING MEMORIES. WOB. *Nation & Athenaeum*, 29 September
1923, 808.
Review of *Early Memories: Some Chapters of Autobiography*, by John Butler
Yeats (Dublin: Cuala Press).
> The author of this charming book is a born writer. He recalls childhood
> memories vividly and beautifully.

C0416 THE MAN WITH THE NOSE. WOB. *Nation & Athenaeum*, 6 October
1923, 15.
Review of *Voyages to the Moon and Sun*, by Cyrano de Bergerac, tr. by
Richard Aldington.
> Mr. Aldington keeps the spirit of the original better than most translators.
> "Cyrano tilts against religion, priests, and intolerance; against kings and
> princes and governments; against irrationality and shams.... Behind the
> satire and the buffoonery you can see a mind of no mean quality trying
> fearlessly to see everything exactly as it is and to examine every question
> on its merits."

C0417 LORD MORLEY. WOB. *Nation & Athenaeum*, 13 October 1923, 55.
Article discussing *Politics and History*, a volume in the works of John Morley,
in relation to some of his other works. LW says this is not a review.

Morley lacked "imaginative passion" and purpose in argument. His writing style was excellent, but he was so fair, so open-minded, so temperate that he never let his imagination take over. "He is always guarding and qualifying his propositions. . . ."

Reprinted in *Essays . . .* 1927, A24.

C0418 LORD CURZON'S TRAVELS. WOB. *Nation & Athenaeum,* 20 October 1923, 120.

Review of *Tales of Travels,* by Lord Curzon of Kedleston.

Lord Curzon leaves the reader with the impression that in travelling round the world "he has never met anyone lower in rank than a Maharaja". Unlike Morley, he sometimes uses rhetoric. Like all good travel books, Curzon's provides romance and entertainment while revealing the author's reactions to his experiences.

C0419 "ARABIA DESERTA". WOB. *Nation & Athenaeum,* 27 October 1923, 155.

Review of *Travels in Arabia Deserta,* by Charles Montagu Doughty (Cape and the Medici Society); and of an abridgment, *Wanderings in Arabia* (Duckworth).

This book is too good to be abridged, even though the cost of the whole work is great. The contorted style is "exactly fitted to express the subject matter". It enables the reader to share the experience of the desert and the nomad.

C0420 THE FIRST PERSON SINGULAR. WOB. *Nation & Athenaeum,* 3 November 1923, 188.

Discussion, based on the following: *The Diary of Samuel Pepys,* New ed. in 3 vols; *Myself When Young,* by Alec Waugh; and *The Luck of the Year,* by E. V. Lucas.

The use of the pronoun "I" does not bother the reader of the essays of Pepys and Montaigne because their egos are real, not sham.

Arthur Ponsonby and "A Reader" commented on this in the *Nation and Athenaeum,* 10 November, p. 221.

Reprinted with changes, in *Essays . . .* 1927, A24, pp. 106–08 and 111–13, in combination with part of "Egoism in Print", C0474.

C0421 THE LOST FLUTE. WOB. *Nation & Athenaeum,* 10 November 1923, 222.

Review and critique of two translations of Chinese poems: *The Temple and Other Poems,* by Arthur Waley; and *The Lost Flute and other Chinese Poems,* by Gertrude Laughlin Joerissen.

Mr. Waley's book is scholarly; Miss Joerissen's is not. Waley has translated poems from the "first four centuries A.D.; the other collection draws chiefly from the great poets of the Tang period and the eighth century. . . . The modern poems included in Miss Joerissen's volume seem to show that [the flute which once produced beautiful music in poetry] has been lost even in China."

C0422 SAMUEL BUTLER. WOB. *Nation & Athenaeum,* 17 November 1923, 276.

Discussion of the first two volumes of the Shrewsbury Edition of the Complete Works of Samuel Butler, *Canterbury Settlement; and Other Essays* and *Erewhon.*

It is surprising that so fine a monument has been made to Butler. He will never be popular because his satire is so "extraordinarily unemotional". He is "a humourist who is apparently never amused".

Reprinted, quite changed, in *Essays . . .* 1927, A24.

C0423 THE JOURNALESSAYIST [*sic*]. WOB. *Nation & Athenaeum*, 24 November 1923, 314.
Discussion of the difficulties of writing anything approaching an essay in the limited space allotted to journalists, illustrated by 7 books: *Fantasies and Impromptus*, by James Agate; *The Blue Lion*, by Robert Lynd; *Sparks from the Fire*, by Gilbert Thomas; *Pencillings*, by J. Middleton Murry; *I for One*, by J. B. Priestley; *Streams of Ocean*, by Aubrey de Selincourt; and *Life and I*, by C. Lewis Hind.

C0424 THE DAYDREAM. WOB. *Nation & Athenaeum*, 1 December 1923, 346.
Review of *The Daydream: A Study in Development*, by George H. Green.
The daydream plays important roles in everyday life, from helping one to fall asleep to providing escape through art and literature. Green's book shows that it helps man to overcome his fears. The daydream is essential to romantic literature but not to classical literature.

C0425 MR. CONRAD'S ROVER. WOB. *Nation & Athenaeum*, 8 December 1923, 377.
Review of vols 13 and 14 of the Uniform edition of Conrad's works: *'Twixt Land and Sea* and *Chance* (Dent); and of *The Rover* (F. Unwin).
Mr. Conrad achieves his art by distilling a few simple ideas and a few simple emotions and "eliminating everything which makes life itself and the people in it so subtle, unexpected, confused and sordid." To appreciate Conrad's writing the reader must accept his convention of the melodrama.
Reprinted, with minor changes, as part of "Joseph Conrad" in *Essays . . .* 1927, A24, pp. 61–64. See also C0481 and C0613 below.

C0426 GOSSIP AND HISTORY. WOB. *Nation & Athenaeum*, 15 December 1923, 431.
Review of *Gossip of the Seventeenth and Eighteenth Centuries*, by John Beresford; and *The Diary of the Lady Anne Clifford*, ed. by Vita Sackville-West.
"These books are extraordinarily entertaining, if only because on the back-stairs of history people are, for the most part, much more alive than in the council chambers and on the battlefields where they are introduced to us by the solemn historian."
Part of this reprinted in *Essays . . .* 1927, A24, p. 14.

C0427 W. H. HUDSON. WOB. *Nation & Athenaeum*, 22 December 1923, 463.
Review of 3 books in the The Works of W. H. Hudson: *Nature in Downland; Hampshire Days;* and *The Land's End*, Popular ed.; and *153 Letters from W. H. Hudson*, edited by Edward Garnett (Nonesuch Press).
It is curious that the admirably printed book from the Nonesuch Press has no statement about the printer. The letters reveal Hudson's character. Mr. Garnett attributes their author's bitter querulousness to old age and ill-health. But the letters cast "certain shades and shadows in Hudson's other books which I certainly had never noticed before."
Reprinted with changes as part of "A Traveller in Little Things" in *Essays . . .* 1927, A24, pp. 76–80. See also C0410 above.

C0428 FASCINATION OF CRIME. WOB. *Nation & Athenaeum*, 29 December 1923, 490.
Discussion of the great output of books on the subject.
Two stories from *The Bravo Mystery and Other Cases*, by Sir John Hall show that the fascination of crime may arise from a mystery surrounding

it or from the revelation of the secret thoughts and passions of the criminals. Other recently published books are *Dramatic Days at the Old Bailey*, by Charles Kingston; *Insanity and the Criminal*, by John C. Goodwin; and *The Trial of Frederick Bywaters and Edith Thompson*, by Filson Young.

1924

C0429   THE FALL OF STEVENSON. WOB. *Nation & Athenaeum*, 5 January 1924, 517.
Review of the first ten volumes of the Tusitala Edition of *The Complete Works of Stevenson* (Heinemann); *The Life of Robert Louis Stevenson*, by Rosaline Masson; and *Selected Essays of Robert Louis Stevenson*, ed. by H. G. Rawlinson.
> Stevenson "had nothing original to say" and wrote his essays in "a false literary style". His stories, written without self-conscious attention to style, are good and enjoyable.
Reprinted with little change in *Essays . . .* 1927, A24, pp. 39–43. LW republished this in its original form although it generated such heated controversy that he wrote another article to explain it, see C0447 below.

C0430   SEVENTEENTH-CENTURY BARBER. WOB. *Nation & Athenaeum*, 12 January 1924, 546.
Review of *Master Johann Dietz*, an English translation of *Meister Johann Dietz*, edited by Ernst Constentius.
> This great autobiographer presents a vivid picture of later 17th-century middle-class German life. A son of a rope-maker and chandler, born in Halle in 1665, he had numerous adventures in the army, on a whaling ship, and at the Prussian Court as a barber surgeon.

C0431   THE "PAGEANT" OF HISTORY. WOB. *Nation & Athenaeum*, 19 January 1924, 574.
Review of *Readings in English Social History: from pre-Roman Days to A.D. 1837*, ed. by R. B. Morgan.
> Each extract "is fascinating, but the composite panorama is extra-ordinarily confused and confusing." Some extracts seem to show that there was no change from century to century; others, that there were an infinite number of small changes.
Reprinted, slightly changed, in *Essays . . .* 1927, A24, pp. 127–31.

C0432   THE BUCCANEERS. WOB. *Nation & Athenaeum*, 26 January 1924, 607.
Review of *Esquemeling, The Buccaneers of America, A True Account of . . . Assaults Committed . . . upon the Coast of the West Indies by the Buccaneers of Jamaica and Tortuga*. Written in Dutch by John Esquemeling (first published in Amsterdam in 1678 and in English translation in 1684).
> In his Introduction to this new editon Andrew Lang says the idea that buccaneering is romantic is nonsense. Esquemeling was twice sold into slavery. He bought his freedom but was stranded on the island of Tortuga and became a pirate. Most of the other pirates had backgrounds similar to his. The tortures they imposed upon their Spanish prisoners were too horrible to be printed in the *Nation & Athenaeum*.
Note: WOB for 2 February 2 1924 is by Francis Birrell.

C0433   RABINDRANATH TAGORE. WOB. *Nation & Athenaeum*, 9 February 1924, 669.

Review of *Gora,* a novel by Tagore.

> The book shows "the social, political, and psychological problems which confront the educated Bengali in Calcutta today." It is hard to say whether Tagore has succeeded in raising this novel with a thesis to the level of art.

C0434 MR. MOORE AND THE CRITICS. WOB. *Nation & Athenaeum,* 16 February 1924, 702.

Review of *Conversations in Ebury Street,* by George Moore.

> Mr. Moore delights in sticking out his tongue at the critics. He says that he prefers pure literary art unadulterated by thought; that he prefers Landor's writing to Shakespeare's. He is himself "an artist in words. . . . He cannot think – he has never been able to think – but he can write."

Reprinted in *Essays . . .* 1927, A24.

C0435 BUTLER'S "FAIR HAVEN". WOB. *Nation & Athenaeum,* 23 February 1924, 735.

Review of *The Fair Haven* and *Life and Habit,* by Samuel Butler, Shrewsbury edition (Cape).

> Although Butler's irony in *The Fair Haven* is similar to Swift's in *A Modest Proposal,* many readers misunderstood his real meaning because he designed his satire "to go on fizzling . . . ironically, and never to explode."

Reprinted, almost unchanged, in "Samuel Butler". *Essays . . .* 1927, A24, pp. 48–52. See also C0422 and C0510.

C0436 TOLSTOI'S PLAYS. WOB. *Nation & Athenaeum,* 1 March 1924, 766.

Review of *The Dramatic Works of Lyof N. Tolstoi,* translated by Nathan Haskell Dole.

> Mr. Dole includes a piece not in Mr. and Mrs. Maude's translation, but the Maudes make better use of words. "I cannot believe that, even in America, a peasant would say 'You are too previous in your speech.'" Tolstoi wrote his plays after he had repudiated art in favour of propaganda. "The propagandist almost always defeats and drives out the artist if they attempt to inhabit the same body and use the same pen. . . . In this unequal struggle Tolstoi triumphed as an artist."

C0437 CONFESSIONS. WOB. *Nation & Athenaeum,* 8 March 1924, 798.

Review of *The Chinese Confessions of C. W. Mason.*

> The book is entertaining and unusual. The writer entered the Chinese customs service in 1887 at the age of 20, but joined a secret society which started a revolution in 1891. For this he went to prison. A check of available facts proves the truth of some of the author's statements. The book is successful as the picture of a life and as a story, but the author should not have tried to analyse his own psychology.

Note: A Letter to the Editor, signed K. S., describes Mason as "a very crabby, strange old man" who said "Mr. Woolf has a disconcerting – I mean a discerning, eye. He might have gone a little further than saying 'at least two' of the names mentioned by me are real names" (*Nation & Athenaeum,* 26 April 1924, 109–10).

C0438 THE HARVEST OF SPRING. WOB. *Nation & Athenaeum,* 15 March 1924, 834.

Estimate of the quality of books about to be published.

C0439 DAEDALUS AND ICARUS. WOB. *Nation & Athenaeum,* 22 March 1924, 890.

Review of *Daedalus, or Science and the Future*, by J. B. S. Haldane; and *Icarus, or the Future of Science*, by Bertrand Russell.

> The authors take opposite views about the prospects of science for the happiness of mankind.

C0440   A REAL HISTORIAN. WOB. *Nation & Athenaeum*, 29 March 1924, 922. Discussion of two works by Frederick Arthur Simpson: *The Rise of Louis Napoleon;* and *Louis Napoleon and the Recovery of France, 1848–1856*.

> "Mr. Simpson knows his subject and period, but does not obtrude his learning . . . [He] is not only a real historian, but a very original, lively and witty writer."

C0441   FROM ALPHA TO OMEGA. *Nation & Athenaeum*, 5 April 1924, 16. Paragraph beginning "Mr. Sutro's comedy 'Far above Rubies' at Comedy Theatre . . ." and "Things to see or hear in the coming week."

LW and VW frequently contributed to "From Alpha to Omega", a regular column on current events, signed Omicron.

C0442   BOOKS IN BRIEF. *Nation & Athenaeum*, 5 April 1924, 26. Short unsigned reviews of *Far Eastern Jaunts,* by Gilbert Collins; and *Misadventures with a Donkey in Spain,* by Jan Gordon and Cora J. Gordon.

C0443   A GREAT AUTOBIOGRAPHY. WOB. *Nation & Athenaeum*, 5 April 1924, 17.

Review of *The Memoirs, My Past and Thoughts*, by Alexander Herzen, tr. by Constance Garnett.

> This work is more complete than J. O. Duff's translation published earlier in the year. Herzen "stands out of his pages as a man of great intelligence and extraordinary charm." He gives a vivid description of his extremely interesting life. An enlightened liberal, Herzen shows the horrors of Tsarist Russia.

C0444   FROM ALPHA TO OMEGA. *Nation & Athenaeum*, 12 April 1924, 50. "Things to see and hear in the coming week."

C0445   THE ROMANCE OF A DROWNED PARROT. WOB. *Nation & Athenaeum*, 12 April 1924, 51.

Review of *The Conquest of the River Plate*, by R. B. Cunninghame Graham.

> This interesting book shows the futility of the lives of the conquistadors. All that the main character had to show for twenty years of hardship in South America were some parrots. The parrots and all the people except him were drowned on the way home to Bavaria.

C0446   BOOKS IN BRIEF. *Nation & Athenaeum*, 12 April 1924, 62. Short unsigned reviews of *The French Revolution in English History,* by Philip Anthony Brown; *A Short History of the French Revolution,* by I. H. Humphrys; *Benham's Book of Quotations,* by W. Gurney Benham; and *Debrett's House of Commons and Judicial Bench 1924*.

C0447   THE FALL OF STEVENSON. II. WOB. *Nation & Athenaeum*, 19 April 1924, 86. Discussion occasioned by the publication of the second ten volumes of the Tusitala Edition of Stevenson's complete works.

> Correspondents had alleged Woolf's earlier review, C0429, was unfair. He says, "It is practically impossible for any one person to make another understand exactly what he means." But he tries.

C0448   MR. GARNETT'S SECOND. WOB. *Nation & Athenaeum*, 26 April 1924, 115. Review of *A Man in the Zoo*, by David Garnett.

Mr. Garnett wrote *Lady into Fox* in a style borrowed from Defoe. His second book, written in his own style, is better. Behind the fantastic narratives there seems to be a second meaning, but Mr. Garnett does not seem to have decided what it is.

C0449 BOOKS IN BRIEF. *Nation & Athenaeum*, 26 April 1924, 126.
Short unsigned reviews of: *Studies in Tidal Power*, by Norman Davey; *Time Measurement*, by L. Bolton; *A Song to David* ... chosen by Edmund Blunden; *A Short History of Birkbeck College*, by C. Delisle Burns; *Prohibition Inside Out*, by Roy A. Haynes; *A Social History of the American Negro*, by Benjamin Brawley; *"The Studio" Year Book of Decorative Art, 1924*; *Ernest Gimson: His Life and Work*; and *English Homes I: Early Tudor*, by H. A. Tipping.

C0450 THE ROAD TO IMMORTALITY. WOB. *Nation & Athenaeum*, 3 May 1924, 146.
Review of *The Diary of a Country Parson: The Reverend James Woodforde, 1758–1781*, edited by John Beresford.
"The diary ... enables you to watch Mr. Woodforde and his relations and parishoners living the daily life of an eighteenth-century village; it admits you into close intimacy with Mr. Woodforde's mind and soul from hour to hour through half a century."

C0451 LAWYERS AND CRIMINALS. WOB. *Nation & Athenaeum*, 10 May 1924, 178.
Review of three books on crime: *Famous Crimes and Criminals*, by C. L. McCluer Stevens; *Judgment of Death*, by E. Bowen-Rowlands; and *Seventy-two Years at the Bar, A Memoir*, by E. Bowen-Rowlands.
These three books "illumine one another and the subject of law and crime". The first book is too crowded with stories. The second is full of information about capital punishment but is not a good book because the author's mind goes "all over the place". But the third, a memoir of Sir Henry Bodkin Poland written as a series of interviews with Mr. Bowen-Rowlands, gives a vivid vision of the characters of both men and of the LAW [in capital letters]. After reading it and contemplating the frontispiece portrait of Sir Henry Poland one is more horrified of the LAW [*sic*] than of the criminal.

C0452 BOOKS IN BRIEF. *Nation & Athenaeum*, 10 May 1924, 186.
Short unsigned reviews of *Social Aspects of Psycho-Analysis*, edited by Ernest Jones; *An Anthology of English Verse*, by John Drinkwater; *How to be Healthy*, by a Physician; and *North Wales*, by M. J. B. Baddeley & S. C. Ward.

C0453 MRS. CARLYLE. WOB. *Nation & Athenaeum*, 17 May 1924, 206.
Review of *Jane Welsh Carlyle: Letters to Her Family, 1839–1863*, edited by Leonard Huxley.
Mrs. Carlyle wrote some of her best letters to her cousin, Jeannie Welsh. They show that she could have been a great novelist, but also that she was "a difficult and, in some ways, a disagreeable character.... The undercurrent of the letters is a thwarted and starved ambition.... [O]ne can see now that Mrs. Carlyle was enmeshed in the conventions and rules of her time ...".

C0454 FROM ALPHA TO OMEGA. *Nation & Athenaeum*, 24 May 1924, 261.
"Things to see or hear ..."

C0455 GEORGE BORROW. WOB. *Nation & Athenaeum*, 24 May 1924, 262.
Review of *The Works of George Borrow*. Norwich edition (Constable).
"In binding, type and paper it is exactly what an edition of 'Complete Works' should be." But the amount of new material exceeds its quality. "Now that we have Borrow complete in sixteen volumes, he still remains the author of only four books."

C0456 THE RUSSIAN RIDDLE. *Nation & Athenaeum*, 24 May 1924, 268.
Unsigned review of *The Russian Soviet Republic*, by Edward A. Ross; *The Bolshevik Persecution of Christianity*, by Captain Francis McCullagh; and *Impressions of Soviet Russia*, by Charles Sarolea.
Ross, an American professor of sociology, who was in Russia in 1917, is biased against the Russian émigrés and their allies. Captain McCullagh, journalist and author, is indignant against the Bolsheviks, but does not know much history. Professor Sarolea has more experience of both pre- and post-war Russia, but wears "heavily tinted anti-Bolshevik spectacles".

C0457 BOOKS IN BRIEF. *Nation & Athenaeum*, 24 May 1924, 270.
Short unsigned reviews of *A Publisher's Confession*, by W. H. Page; *Genesis: Twelve Woodcuts* by Paul Nash; *A Handbook of Garden Irises*, by W. R. Dykes; *Chambers's Encyclopaedia*, New edition, vols III & IV; and *The Education Authorities Directory 1924–25.*

C0458 THE APOTHEOSIS OF TORYISM. WOB. *Nation & Athenaeum*, 31 May 1924, 294.
Review of *A History of the Tory Party*, by Maurice Woods.
"I found the book extremely interesting, but only because the subject of political psychology happens to be a peculiar hobby of mine. The book itself is a bad book. . . ."

C0459 FROM ALPHA TO OMEGA. *Nation & Athenaeum*, 7 June 1924, 321.
Paragraph beginning "I enjoyed 'The Nibelungs' [*sic*] now being shown at Albert Hall"; and "Things to see . . ."

C0460 PATRIOTISM AND LITERATURE. WOB. *Nation & Athenaeum*, 7 June 1924, 322.
Review of *Patriotism in Literature*, by John Drinkwater.
"Although there is any amount of patriotic literature, its quality as literature is nearly always in inverse proportion to the quantity of patriotism contained in it."

C0461 INDIA AND INDIAN POLITICS. *Nation & Athenaeum*, 7 June 1924, 326 & 328.
Unsigned review of: *Indian Politics*, by J. T. Gwynn; *India: A Bird's Eye View*, by Lord Ronaldshay; *Mahatma Gandhi*, by Romain Rolland; and *Mahatma Gandhi*, by Romain Rolland (Paris: Stock).
These three books show some of the difficulty and intricacy of the problems in India. Ronaldshay provides good background, although one may not accept his conclusions. Mr. Rolland's book, both in English and in French, is a fair sketch of the life of Gandhi, showing that the rulers must consider the country's religious nature. Mr. Gwynn took a kind of poll of "public opinion" for the *Manchester Guardian* and recorded his conversations. These show that the educated classes of India oppose the Montagu-Chelmsford reforms and Home Rule, which promised something they did not deliver.

C0462 BOOKS IN BRIEF. *Nation & Athenaeum*, 7 June 1924, 332.
Short unsigned reviews of *Memories,* by Katharine Tynan; and *Marie Elizabeth Towneley: A Memoir.*

C0463 FROM ALPHA TO OMEGA. *Nation & Athenaeum,* 14 June 1924, 353.
"Things to see or hear in the coming week."

C0464 ARCH BEYOND ARCH. WOB. *Nation & Athenaeum,* 14 June 1924, 354.
Review of *A Passage to India,* by E. M. Forster.
>Like all great books it has beneath the surface a theme or themes which give deeper meaning. In Forster's novel "Mrs. Moore, a superb character, . . . felt that 'outside the arch there seemed always an arch, beyond the remotest echo a silence.' I felt that about the book."

Reprinted in *E. M. Forster: The Critical Heritage,* ed. by Philip Gardner (1973), B80, pp. 204–06. Gardner says, "Massingham took Woolf to task for so concentrating on the aesthetic aspects of the book that he appeared to ignore totally the fact that Forster had something extremely pointed to say about India" (he cites *New Leader,* 27 June 1924, p. 10).

C0465 FROM ALPHA TO OMEGA. *Nation & Athenaeum,* 21 June 1924, 380.
First paragraph on "Tannhäuser" performed by the British National Opera Company, and "Things to see or hear . . ."

C0466 A CIVILIZED MAN. WOB. *Nation & Athenaeum,* 21 June 1924, 381.
Review of Dr. Allen's edition of Erasmus's Letters, *Erasmi Epistolae, 1522– 1524,* vol. 5; *Erasmus,* tr. by Johan Huizinga; and *Erasmus and Luther,* by R. H. Murray; with mention of Froude's *Times of Erasmus and Luther.*
>Erasmus stood up for civilization – "reason, tolerance, freedom, democracy, a kind of communal altruism and good will" –, and he opposed barbarism – "unreason, intolerance, tyranny, superstition, and a mystic belief that there is some virtue in making as many people as possible miserable."

Reprinted, minus the citations and with other minor changes, in *Essays . . .* 1927, A24, pp. 149–52.

C0467 BOOKS IN BRIEF. *Nation & Athenaeum,* 21 June 1924, 392. Short unsigned reviews of *Robert Smith Surtees (Creator of "Jorrocks"), 1803–1864,* by Himself and E. D. Cuming; The Children's Bible, & The Little Children's Bible; and *The Statesman's Year-Book 1924.*

C0468 CHARACTERS. WOB. *Nation & Athenaeum,* 28 June 1924, 413.
Review of *A Book of Characters,* by Richard Aldington.
>Theophrastus described succinctly the essential characteristics of the type of person he was delineating. Seventeenth-century English writers introduced either moral teaching or wit for its own sake into their character sketches. To see modern writing at its best one must turn to La Bruyère.

C0469 THE EMPIRE. *Nation & Athenaeum,* 28 June 1924, 418.
Unsigned review of *The Story of Empire,* by Charles Lucas; *The Resources of the Empire,* by Evans Lewin; *Health Problems of the Empire,* by Andrew Balfour and Henry H. Scott; and *Britain Overseas,* by Cumberland Clark.
>Lucas and Clark give summary treatments of a vast and complicated history from 1497 to the end of the Great War. Lewin's book is a real survey that suffers from his protectionist bias. The most interesting book, even for the layman, is by Balfour and Scott.

C0470 BOOKS IN BRIEF. *Nation & Athenaeum,* 28 June 1924, 420.
Short unsigned reviews of *Cambridge Readings in the Literature of Science,*

arranged by W. C. and M. Dampier Whetham. *The Soul of a Criminal*, by John C. Goodwin; and *Illustrated Guide to London and the British Empire Exhibitions*, 45th ed. revised

C0471 THE CLASSICS. WOB. *Nation & Athenaeum*, 5 July 1924, 442.
Notice of publication of 9 books on the classics, including 3 from the Library of Greek thought, edited by Ernest Barker: *Greek Literary Criticism*, by J. D. Denniston; *Greek Historical Thought*, by Arnold J. Toynbee; *Greek Civilization and Character*, by Arnold J. Toynbee; And 3 from the series Our Debt to Greece and Rome: *Euripides and His Influence*, by F. L. Lucas; *Language and Philology*, by Roland Kent; *Catullus and His Influence*, by K. P. Harrington. Together with: *A Lexicon of Homeric Dialect*, by Richard John Cunliffe; *M. Fabii Quintiliani Institutionis Oratoriae. Liber I*, edited by F. H. Colson.
> After reading the gloomy predictions in *The Times* of the death of the knowledge of Greek, it is good to discover these nine recently published books.

C0472 BOOKS IN BRIEF. *Nation & Athenaeum*, 5 July 1924, 454.
Short unsigned review of *Days that are Gone*, by Col. F. B. de Sales La Terriere.
> Writing of the Eton and Oxford of the past, this author thinks the English Gentleman "the finest product in the world".

C0473 FROM ALPHA TO OMEGA. *Nation & Athenaeum*, 12 July 1924, 476.
Paragraph beginning "I notice that all of the critics obviously enjoyed 'In the Snare' ... at the Savoy."

C0474 EGOISM IN PRINT. WOB. *Nation & Athenaeum*, 12 July 1924, 481.
Review of *The Life of Benjamin Franklin Written by Himself*, The World's Classics; *The Book of My Youth*, by Hermann Sudermann, tr. by Wyndham Harding; *A Russian Schoolboy*, by Serghei Aksakoff, tr. by J. Duff.
> Franklin's book is an example of the charm and vividness with which old men write about their youth.
Woolf included most of his remarks about Franklin's autobiography in "The First Person Singular", in *Essays ... 1927*, A24, pp. 108–11.

C0475 BOOKS IN BRIEF. *Nation & Athenaeum*, 12 July 1924, 490.
Short unsigned reviews of *These Things Considered*, by Margaret A. Pollock, with a Foreword by J. L. Hammond; and *John T. W. Mitchell*, by Percy Redfern.
> Mitchell, a builder of the Co-operative Movement, was chairman of the C.W.S.

C0476 MR. SHAW'S "SAINT JOAN". WOB. *Nation & Athenaeum*, 19 July 1924, 511.
Review of *Saint Joan*, by G. B. Shaw [Constable].
LW apologized 26 July, C0477, for having listed the publisher as Heinemann in this review.
> This play and *A Passage to India* by E. M. Forster may be the only books with any permanent value read in a year. Shaw is a civilizing force in his time as Erasmus was in his.

C0477 WORDS. WOB. *Nation & Athenaeum*, 26 July 1924, 538.
Review of *Four Words*, by Logan Pearsall Smith; *Michael Neo Palaeologus, His Grammar*, by Stephen N. Palaeologus; and *The Philosophy of Grammar*, by Otto Jespersen.
> Logan Pearsall Smith's work on the meaning of words as reflected in history is interesting; Palaeologus on grammar, facetious; and Jespersen's work, "immensely learned and scientific" yet "not pedantic".

C0478 BIG GAME AND THE CAMERA. *Nation & Athenaeum*, 26 July 1924, 539–40.

Unsigned review of *Stalking Big Game with a Camera in Equatorial Africa*, by Marius Maxwell (Medici Society).

> Although highly priced, the book and the photographs are magnificent. "Photographing big game is far finer sport than shooting it."

C0479 THE STRANGE HISTORY OF EDUCATION. WOB. *Nation & Athenaeum*, 2 August 1924, 566.

Review of *A Survey of the History of Education*, by Helen Wodehouse.

> "Her book has impressed one or two points upon me. One is the extraordinary conservatism of the human mind with regard to education. . . . There is one very curious feature in this educational conservatism. In all ages and among all European peoples the subject-matter of education has almost invariably been dead."

C0480 BOOKS IN BRIEF. *Nation & Athenaeum*, 2 August 1924, 572 & 574. Short unsigned reviews of *Unsolved Murder Mysteries*, by Charles E. Pearce; *The London of Charles Dickens*, by E. Beresford Chancellor; *A George Eliot Dictionary*, by Isadore G. Mudge; and *A Dictionary of the Characters and Proper Names in the Works of Shakespeare*, by Francis Griffin Stokes.

C0481 JOSEPH CONRAD. WOB. *Nation & Athenaeum*, 9 August 1924, 595. Article.

> "An artist in words . . . Conrad belonged to the school of the great self-conscious stylists."

Reprinted as the first and last parts of "Joseph Conrad" in *Essays . . .* 1927, A24, pp. 57–60 and 71. See also C0425 and C0613.

C0482 THE CONSPIRACY MANIA. WOB. *Nation & Athenaeum*, 16 August 1924, 620.

Review of *Secret Societies and Subversive Movements*, by Nesta H. Webster.

> Mrs. Webster attempts to explain the political evils of the world as a public conspiracy by Jews, Germans or Illuminists. She seems to be sane and rational, "and yet she can believe in this fantastic political nightmare of conspiracy."

C0483 PLANTS, GARDENS AND INSECTS. *Nation & Athenaeum*, 16 August 1924, 626.

Unsigned review of *The Biology of Flowering Plants*, by MacGregor Skene; *The Practical Book of Outdoor Flowers*, by Richardson Wright; and *Insect Pests*, by E. T. Ellis.

> The first book, though perhaps too scientific for those who just have a passion for gardens, is a valuable work. Mr. Wright's book is excellent for the beginner. "Mr. Ellis gives good advice upon the best methods for attacking the attackers, but he might sometimes have given a little more information to help the beginner in identifying which pest he has to deal with."

C0484 BOOKS IN BRIEF. *Nation & Athenaeum*, 16 August 1924, 626.

Short unsigned reviews of seven volumes of the Tusitala Edition of Robert Louis Stevenson; and *Book Prices Current 1923*.

C0485 NON-SECRET SOCIETIES. WOB. *Nation & Athenaeum*, 23 August 1924, 644.

Review of two books published by the English Place-Name Society: *Introduction to the Survey of English Place-Names*, and *The Chief Elements in English Place-Names*, with a discussion of facts to be learned by reading annual reports of societies.

C0486   BOOKS IN BRIEF. *Nation & Athenaeum*, 23 August 1924, 650.
Short unsigned review of *Foreign Politics of Soviet Russia*, by Alfred L. P. Dennis.

C0487   [SOCIALISTS AND THE LEAGUE]. *The Times*, 29 August 1924, p. 7.
A reporter's summary of LW's speech on the League.
> The League is doomed to failure unless politicians abandon nationalism for international co-operation.

C0488   THE MAKING OF BOOKS. WOB. *Nation & Athenaeum*, 30 August 1924, 667.
Review of *The Net Book Agreement, 1899, and the Book War, 1906–1908*, by Sir Frederick Macmillan and Edward Bell.
> Sir Frederick Macmillan tells how he substituted a fixed net publishing price for the discount system; then he and Edward Bell tell how the publishers fought the Times Book Club's bookselling methods. Over-production of books (especially worthless books) and excessive prices are the two worst problems of the book trade. They affect authors, publishers, booksellers and the reading public.

This article provoked correspondence, 13 September from Harold Forrester, 20 September from a bookseller, 27 September from Francis Birrell, and an article by J. D. Beresford entitled "The Common Sense of the Trade", 27 September.

C0489   REPRINTS. WOB. *Nation & Athenaeum*, 6 September 1924, 693.
Article praising publishers for printing worthwhile but forgotten books and recommending a few recent reprints.

C0490   BOOKS IN BRIEF. *Nation & Athenaeum*, 6 September 1924, 700 & 702.
Short unsigned reviews of *Hannibal Crosses the Alps*, by Cecil Torr. *Plato: Euthyphro, Apology and Crito*, ed. with notes by John Burnet; *Etruria and Rome*, by R. A. L. Fell; and *Conscious Auto-Suggestion*, by Emile Coué.

C0491   THE DUKE AND MISS JENKINS. WOB. *Nation & Athenaeum*, 13 September 1924, 721.
Review of *The Letters of the Duke of Wellington to Miss J., 1834–1851*, edited with extracts from the diary of the latter, by Christine Terhune Herrick.
> The Duke of Wellington countered Miss Jenkins' attempt to convert him in his old age with an attempt to seduce her.

C0492   BOOKS IN BRIEF. *Nation & Athenaeum*, 13 September 1924, 730.
Short unsigned reviews of *Philip's Handy Gazeteer of the British Isles*. Rev. & enl. edition; and *York*, by Joseph E. Morris. Little Guides.

C0493   FROM ALPHA TO OMEGA. *Nation & Athenaeum*, 20 September 1924, 749.
Last two paragraphs on a special course of lectures at the University of London. and "Things to see or hear . . ."

C0494   THE COMMON PEOPLE. WOB. *Nation & Athenaeum*, 20 September 1924, 750.
Review of *Mediaeval People*, by Eileen Power.
> The author's "accomplishment seems to me more akin to that of the biographer or the novelist than to that of the historian." She writes about the individual rather than about communal life.

Reprinted, changed, as part of "The Pageant of History" in *Essays . . . 1927*, A24, pp. 125–26 and 131–34.

C0495   BOOKS IN BRIEF. *Nation & Athenaeum*, 20 September 1924, 756.
Short unsigned review of *My Fight for British Freedom*, by Dan Breen
(Dublin: Talbot Press).
   The reader admires the courage but sees the cruel side of patriotic
   nationalism.

C0496   MUMBO JUMBO. WOB. *Nation & Athenaeum*, 27 September 1924, 776.
Review of 3 books on Napoleon: *Napoleon*, by Elie Faure, tr. by Jeffery E.
Jeffery; *The Campaign of 1812 and the Retreat from Moscow*, by Hilaire
Belloc; *Napoleon and His Court*, by C. S. Forester; *A Short History of the
World*, by H. G. Wells.
   These books illustrate the great divergence of opinion about Napoleon's
   character and achievement. Faure sees him as pure and noble; Forester, as
   mean-minded for all his achievment. "I am on the side of Wells, but then I
   must admit to a prejudice against all the great men of action who make the
   world a desert and call it a glory."

C0497   FROM ALPHA TO OMEGA. *Nation & Athenaeum*, 27 September 1924,
777.
   "Things to see or hear . . .".

C0498   OUR OWN TIMES. *Nation & Athenaeum*, 27 September 1924, 784.
Unsigned review of *These Eventful Years: The Twentieth Century in the
Making* (Encyclopaedia Britannica Co.).
   The story of the years 1900–24 is told by 84 famous men who helped
   make the events. Garvin gives a resumé of this remarkable, vivid and
   living book in 200 readable pages.

C0499   POETRY AND DREAMS. WOB. *Nation & Athenaeum*, 4 October 1924,
18.
Review of *The Meaning of Dreams*, by Robert Graves.
   "I welcome the attempt . . . to interpret poetry by using some of Freud's
   psycho-analytic theories . . . if it is honest and reasonable, even if I do not
   completely accept the explanation."

C0500   THE HARVEST OF AUTUMN BOOKS. WOB. *Nation & Athenaeum*, 11
October 1924, 54.
   "I do not believe that anyone would disagree with the statement that too
   many books are published if he had done what I have done during the last
   week or two – read carefully through all the publishers' announcement
   lists and marked those books which should be given a place in our
   Supplement."

C0501   LESSER FLEAS. WOB. *Nation & Athenaeum*, 18 October 1924, 113.
Review of 3 books of criticism: *Latitudes*, by Edwin Muir; *Contemporary
Criticism*, by Orlo Williams; and *Fritto Misto*, by E. S. P. Haynes.
   "Mr. Muir's criticism has two rare and most refreshing characteristics –
   objectivity and intelligence." The other two books are re-warmed
   journalism. Mr. Haynes' criticism revolves about himself. "Mr. Williams
   seems to fall back upon criticizing the critics [which] produces an infinite
   series of critical fleas . . .".

C0502   A FALSE STEP AT GENEVA. *Nation & Athenaeum*, 25 October 1924,
148.
Letter. Concerns "A False Step at Geneva", (October 11, pp. 42–43); and
discussion (October 18, p. 108) concerning the protocol.

C0503   TRAVELLERS' TALES. WOB. *Nation & Athenaeum*, 25 October 1924,
155.

Review of Herodotus, *History*, Book 2 tr. by George Rawlinson; *Herodotus*, by T. R. Glover; *Simplicissimus the Vagabond*, by Grimmelshausen, tr. by A. T. S. Goodrick; *Moritz's Travels in England in 1782; An Irish Peer on the Continent*, by Catherine Wilmot, ed. by Thomas U. Sadleir; and *Memories of the Foreign Legion*, by M. M., with an Introduction by D. H. Lawrence.

Herodotus is completely objective. Glover shows how complex and subtle Herodotus was. By means of imaginary and fantastic adventures Grimmelshausen "gives a picture of the appalling conditions of life in Germany in his own days during the Thirty Years' War." The German writer Moritz gives a wonderful picture of England in the eighteenth.century. The personal element which comes out in Moritz's book is more pronounced in Catherine Wilmot's. M. M. [Maurice Magnus] writes entirely about himself, but without the skill and brilliance of Lawrence.

C0504 OLD NEWS. WOB. *Nation & Athenaeum*, 1 November 1924, 187.
Review of *The Fugger News-Letters*.
"The most enjoyable book which I have come across for a very long time. To read it is, in effect, to be reading old newspapers of the sixteenth century."

C0505 GARDEN BOOKS. *Nation & Athenaeum*, 1 November 1924, 194 & 196.
Review of *The Real ABC of Gardening*, by A. J. Macself; and *Handbook of Crocus and Colchicum*, by E. A. Bowles.
The gardener can benefit from the helpful advice found in garden books. Macself gives step-by step instructions. Bowles does for the crocus what Dykes does for the Iris in the same series.

C0506 MARK TWAIN. WOB. *Nation & Athenaeum*, 8 November 1924, 217.
Review of *Mark Twain's Autobiography*. 2 vols (Harper).
The author's literary craftsmanship shows, although he dictated this book to a stenographer. The preface leads one to expect more reserve than is found in the book. Twain's humour "covers an intense seriousness and a highly intellectual interest in things and ideas."

C0507 CRIME AND CRIMINALS. WOB. *Nation & Athenaeum*, 15 November 1924, 267.
Review of *Trial of Adolf Beck (1872–1904)*, ed. by Eric R. Watson; *Problems of Modern American Crime*, by Veronica King; *Studies in Murder*, by Edmund Lester Pearson; and *The Criminal as a Human Being*, by George S. Dougherty.

C0508 PEACOCK. WOB. *Nation & Athenaeum*, 22 November 1924, 298.
Review of *Peacock's Works*, vols II-V. Halliford edition (Constable).
The volumes in this edition "are admirable". "Peacock is a great writer because he has a perfect style; it is perfectly adapted to what he wants to say."

C0509 "LOOK UP THERE WITH ME!" WOB. *Nation & Athenaeum*, 29 November 1924, 331.
Review of *To the Unknown God*, by J. Middleton Murry.
Murry's style in this book is that of Mr. Pecksniff of *Martin Chuzzlewit*, by Charles Dickens. This can be proved by intermixing quotations from the two.
Reprinted in *Essays . . . 1927*, A24.

C0510 SAMUEL BUTLER AGAIN. WOB. *Nation & Athenaeum*, 6 December 1924, 364.

Review of two volumes of the Shrewsbury edition of The Complete Works of Samuel Butler: *Luck or Cunning,* and *Alps and Sanctuaries;* and of *Samuel Butler,* by C. E. M. Joad.

Reading *Luck or Cunning* together with Butler's other books on evolution "has made me modify my opinion of Butler". Despite his good writing and use of irony "there is a littleness of mind displayed in them [stemming from] Butler's personal hostility towards those with whom he disagrees." Mr. Joad makes the absurd claim that Butler made an original contribution to nineteenth-century scientific theory. Butler did constructively criticise Darwinian theory.

Reprinted with changes as part of "Samuel Butler" in *Essays . . .* 1927, A24, pp. 44 & 52–55.

C0511 TWO AUTOBIOGRAPHIES. WOB. *Nation & Athenaeum,* 13 December 1924, 414.

Review of *Memoir of Thomas Bewick,* written by himself, with an Introduction by Selwyn Image; and *Marbacka,* by Selma Lagerlöf.

Bewick's writing has the same qualities of fresh air, solidity and naturalness as Cobbett's without the latter's prejudice. The edition includes Bewick's own delightful woodcuts. Selma Lagerlöf's reminiscences of her childhood are charming and vivid.

C0512 THE TOWER OF WALBURGA, LADY PAGET. WOB. *Nation & Athenaeum,* 20 December 1924, 444.

Article on *In My Tower,* by Walburga, Lady Paget.

"I have rarely found a book more fascinating." It "shows quite plainly" that the society of the upper classes "is incompatible with intelligence". Reprinted as part of "The Aristocratic Mind" in *Essays . . .* 1927, A24, pp. 225–30.

C0513 SWINBURNE. WOB. *Nation & Athenaeum,* 27 December 1924, 472.

Essay based on: *Creative Spirits of the Nineteenth Century,* by Georg Brandes; and *Swinburne's Collected Poetical Works.*

Brandes chose John Stuart Mill and Swinburne as the two representatives of England. "Although Swinburne may not be quite so great a poet as he seemed to be in 1900, he is a much greater poet than he seems to be to those who were born round about the year 1900." Swinburne was one of the foremost leaders in the intellectual revolt of the early twentieth century.

1925

C0514 GREEK IN ENGLISH. WOB. *Nation & Athenaeum,* 3 January 1925, 497.

Review of 4 translations from the Greek: *Aristophanes,* tr. of Benjamin Bickley Rogers; *The Pastoral Loves of Daphnis and Chloe,* English by George Moore; *The Symposium or Supper of Plato,* tr. by Francis Birrell and Shane Leslie (Nonesuch Press); and *The Antigone of Sophocles,* tr. by R. C. Trevelyan.

These are useful translations, but it is impossible to convey the original Greek in English.

C0515 THE FUTURE OF WOMAN. WOB. *Nation & Athenaeum,* 10 January 1925, 526.

Review of *Lysistrata, or Woman's Future and Future Woman,* by Anthony M. Ludovici; and *The Soul of Woman,* by Gina Lombroso.

These anti-feminist writers lack the "sense of humour and sound common sense" of Aristophanes. Both generalize too much. Gina Lombroso assumes that people can never change; Mr. Ludovici, that if man will improve his physique and throw artificial aids away he will be able to re-subject woman.

Ludovici tried to prove that LW had misrepresented what he said (letters published 31 January, 21 February and 7 March). LW replied to two letters but let the matter drop after making Ludovici lose his temper.

C0516 QUEEN VICTORIA'S UNCLE. WOB. *Nation & Athenaeum*, 17 January 1925, 553.

Review of *Letters of the King of Hanover to Viscount Strangford*. With an Historical Note by E. M. Cox and an Introduction by Charles Whibley.

The language of Ernest Augustus, Duke of Cumberland, King of Hanover, will pain the reader just as his actions hurt people. He pursued those he disliked "with the most persistent and illiterate vindictiveness". In politics he advocated foreign wars as a means of preventing revolution.

Reprinted as part of "The Aristocratic Mind" in *Essays . . .* 1927, A24, pp. 230–34.

C0517 THE NOVEL. WOB. *Nation & Athenaeum*, 24 January 1925, 584.

Comparison of Shaw's and Huxley's novels and "some inconclusive reflections upon novels generally". Based upon *An Unsocial Socialist; The Irrational Knot; Love Among the Artists;* and *Cashel Bryon's Profession,* by G. B. Shaw; and *Those Barren Leaves,* by Aldous Huxley.

"Reading them consecutively I found it difficult to see that they belonged to different ages." Shaw, whose purpose is to write a sermon, forgets it and writes a cross-section of life. Huxley, writing a cross-section of life, sometimes "gets so interested in his purpose that he forgets the story and characters."

C0518 THE FUTURE OF WOMAN. *Nation & Athenaeum*, 31 January 1925, 608.

Letter in reply to Ludovici's assertion that Woolf misrepresented his statements in the review, C0515.

C0519 CASTLEREAGH. WOB. *Nation & Athenaeum*, 31 January 1925, 613.

Review of *The Foreign Policy of Castlereagh, 1815–1822,* by C. K. Webster.

This excellent, if hard to read, book is written by an expert for experts. Like many foreign policy statesmen who play politics like chess, Castlereagh saw "very few moves ahead in the game".

Reprinted in "Statesmen and Diplomatists" in *Essays . . .* 1927, A24, pp. 172–76.

C0520 FOREIGN PARTS. WOB. *Nation & Athenaeum*, 7 February 1925, 649.

Discussion of travel books, especially, *The Coasts of Illusion,* by Clark B. Firestone; *Lady Anne Barnard at the Cape of Good Hope, 1797–1802,* by Dorothea Fairbridge; *The Shadow of the Gloomy East,* by Ferdinand Ossendowski; *The Vanished Cities of Arabia,* by Mrs. Steuart Erskine, Illustrated by Major Benton Fletcher; and *To Lhasa in Disguise,* by W. Montgomery McGovern.

The reason why people write and read travel books seems to be their romance.

C0521 THE MIND OF A CHIMPANZEE. WOB. *Nation & Athenaeum*, 14 February 1925, 681.

Review of *The Mentality of Apes,* by W. Köhler, tr. from the German; and *The Growth of the Mind,* by K. Koffka.

Köhler's experiments seem to prove that apes solve certain problems by insight rather than by instinct or by trial and error.

C0522   THE FUTURE OF WOMAN. *Nation & Athenaeum*, 21 February 1925, 712. Letter.

LW quotes from Ludovici's book (see C0515) to prove that he reported correctly what the author had said.

C0523   FROM ALPHA TO OMEGA. *Nation & Athenaeum*, 21 February 1925, 715. Paragraph beginning "The English have lost their skill with bat and ball . . .," signed Omicron. See B. J. Kirkpatrick, *Bibliography of Edmund Blunden*, C509 (Oxford University Press, 1979).

C0524   CHEKHOV'S LETTERS [*sic*]. WOB. *Nation & Athenaeum*, 21 February 1925, 717.

Review of *The Life and Letters of Anton Tchekhov* [*sic*], translated by S. S. Koteliansky and Philip Tomlinson.

The letters show Chekhov's "immense personal charm".

C0525   THE LIFE OF KEATS. WOB. *Nation & Athenaeum*, 28 February 1925, 749. Review of *John Keats*, by Amy Lowell.

The book is cluttered with details.

C0526   THE BESTSELLER. WOB. *Nation & Athenaeum*, 7 March 1925, 777. Consideration of the distinction between the real bestseller and other books being published as popular novels.

Open Confession to a Man from a Woman, by Marie Corelli, written with "passionate conviction . . . is the real thing."

C0527   THE SPRING BOOKS. WOB. *Nation & Athenaeum*, 14 March 1925, 814.

C0528   THE BIOGRAPHY OF KINGS. WOB. *Nation & Athenaeum*, 21 March 1925, 814.

Review of *King Edward VII: A Biography*, vol. I, by Sir Sidney Lee.

The importance of the world of statesmen and diplomatists seems to have unsettled the author. Perhaps it was impossible to write a good biography of Edward VII in 1925 "but I do not believe that it was necessary to make it quite so bad and so dull as Sir Sidney Lee has succeeded in doing." By reading an unreadable book backwards one can pick up some interesting facts. "No official biography of a monarch ought to be written for one hundred years after his death. . . . The less Kings and Princes are allowed to meddle with foreign politics, the better for the world."

C0529   THE LAST WORD IN CRIME. WOB. *Nation & Athenaeum*, 28 March 1925, 889.

Review of *The Crime & Trial of Leopold and Loeb*, by Maureen McKernan.

The only motive for this crime seems to have been crime itself. McKernan gives a detailed account of the proceedings of the trial which brought out the psychology of the two youths and which indicate the state of civilization of Chicago.

C0530   FROM ALPHA TO OMEGA. *Nation & Athenaeum*, 4 April 1925, 16.

3rd paragraph. Review of Irish Players production of "Persevering Pat" at Little Theatre.

C0531   ON THE EDITOR'S TABLE. *Nation & Athenaeum*, 4 April 1925, 24.

C0532   THE MODERN NATURALIST. *Nation & Athenaeum*, 11 April 1925, 53.

Unsigned review of *Waterside Creatures*, by Frances Pitt; and *The Life of the Bat*, by Charles Derennes.

Mrs. Pitt writes "in the best traditions of the classical English natural historians." M. Derennes has marred his book by sentimentality.

C0533 BOOKS IN BRIEF. *Nation & Athenaeum*, 11 April 1925, 54.
Short unsigned review of *Palgrave's Dictionary of Political Economy*,
vols I-II.
Note: There were no WORLD OF BOOKS articles 4 and 11 April 1925.

C0534 FROM ALPHA TO OMEGA. *Nation & Athenaeum*, 18 April 1925, 75.
Penultimate paragraph. "Things to see . . ."

C0535 MODERN POETRY. WOB. *Nation & Athenaeum*, 18 April 1925, 76.
Review of *The Muse in Council*, a critical work by John Drinkwater; *Troy
Park*, by Edith Sitwell; *Masks of Time*, by Edmund Blunden; *Island Blood*, by
F. R. Higgins; and *An Indian Ass*, by Harold Acton.
> Drinkwater should not insist that modern poets write in traditional forms.
> What Miss Sitwell and Mr. Acton have to say will not fit these forms, nor
> is their unintelligibility a reason for dismissing them. Poets should be
> aware that continual attempts to startle the reader can become as
> mechanical as the older poetical habit of saying the obvious.
Reprinted as part of "The Modern Nightingale: in *Essays* . . . 1927, A24, pp.
93, 95, 103–04.

C0536 FROM ALPHA TO OMEGA. *Nation & Athenaeum*, 25 April 1925, 105.
2nd paragraph on Max Beerbohm's caricatures and "Things to see and [*sic*]
hear this week."

C0537 THE RELIGION OF A —— [*sic*]. WOB. *Nation & Athenaeum*, 25 April
1925, 106.
Consideration of *What I Believe*, by Bertrand Russell; *The Religion of a
Darwinist*, by Sir Arthur Keith; and *Science and Religion*, by J. Arthur
Thomson.
> Compared to Sir Thomas Browne, whose *Religio Medici* (1635) remains
> the greatest book on the subject, these sensible, scientific men have very
> bare religious cupboards.

C0538 ON THE EDITOR'S TABLE. *Nation & Athenaeum*, 25 April 1925, 112 &
114.

C0539 FROM ALPHA TO OMEGA. *Nation & Athenaeum*, 2 May 1925, 135–36.
Review of production of G. B. Shaw's "Caesar and Cleopatra", and "Things
to see or [*sic*] hear . . ."

C0540 THE MOST DANGEROUS OF TRADES. WOB. *Nation & Athenaeum*, 2
May 1925, 137.
Review of *The Public Life*, 2 vols, by J. A. Spender.
> This description of politics since the eighteenth century is extremely
> interesting and very readable, but is presented as short disconnected
> articles. His journalistic perspective prevents Mr. Spender from consider-
> ing the underlying causes of the phenomenon he describes, the changing
> attitude of the public towards the public man.

C0541 ON THE EDITOR'S TABLE. *Nation & Athenaeum*, 2 May 1925, 146.

C0542 FROM ALPHA TO OMEGA. *Nation & Athenaeum*, 9 May 1925, 176.
Paragraph 6 praises Mr. John Randall for 50 years of skilful proof-reading at
the *Athenaeum*.
"Things to see and hear this week."

C0543 FROM FALSTAFF TO MICAWBER. WOB. *Nation & Athenaeum*, 9 May
1925, 177.
Review of *The English Comic Characters*, by J. B. Priestley.
> This is a much better book than the author's *I for One*. "Its very merits
> give it the right to be judged by higher standards . . . The Curse of

journalism is that its devotees and victims acquire the belief that to be serious, learned, analytic is to be dull and boring, and that the greatest sin which can be committed in print is not to be entertaining."

C0544   UNEDUCATED POETS. *Nation & Athenaeum*, 9 May 1925, 180–81.
Unsigned review of *Lives and Works of Uneducated Poets*, by Robert Southey.
In this collection made by Southey, his own contributions are the best.

C0545   BOOKS IN BRIEF. *Nation & Athenaeum*, 9 May 1925, 182 & 184.
Short unsigned reviews of *H.R.H. the Prince of Wales's Sport in India*, by Bernard C. Ellison; *The Elements of Chess*, by J. Du Mont; and *The History of the Fabian Society*, 2nd ed., by Edward R. Pease.

C0546   FROM ALPHA TO OMEGA. *Nation & Athenaeum*, 16 May 1925, 206.
"Things to see and hear this week."

C0547   MR. BELLOC. WOB. *Nation & Athenaeum*, 16 May 1925, 207.
Review of *The Cruise of the "Nona"*, by Hilaire Belloc.
The book "leaves one with a bitter, dusty, gritty taste in the mouth" because Belloc writes with a grievance against non Roman Catholics. He "carries stone-throwing and uncharitableness to a pitch that is almost pathological." His "false notion of 'fine writing'" leads to distorted sentences "which simply set my teeth on edge."

C0548   ON THE EDITOR'S TABLE. *Nation & Athenaeum*, 16 May 1925, 214.

C0549   BOOKS IN BRIEF. *Nation & Athenaeum*, 16 May 1925, 214.
Brief unsigned review of *Nature at the Desert's Edge*, by R. W. G. Hingston.

C0550   FROM ALPHA TO OMEGA. *Nation & Athenaeum*, 23 May 1925, 237.
"Things to see and hear this week."

C0551   THE DEATH OF MARLOWE. WOB. *Nation & Athenaeum*, 23 May 1925, 238.
Review of 2 Nonesuch Press books: The Bible. I: Genesis to Ruth. Limited ed.; and *The Death of Christopher Marlowe*, by Leslie Hotson.
Both books are beautifully printed and meant to be read. "A volume which is intended to go straight from the printers into a glass case seems to me to be, however beautiful, a typographical abortion, and I deny that a volume which nobody could or would read has a right to call itself a book. Most of the Nonesuch Press publications are as desirable for their subject-matter as they are for their appearance – a thing which can hardly be said with truth of the majority of finely printed books." Leslie Hotson's book combines "romance, scholarship, and the thrill of a good detective story."

C0552   BOOKS IN BRIEF. *Nation & Athenaeum*, 23 May 1925, 246.
Short unsigned reviews of *The Trial of Kate Webster*, ed. by Elliot O'Donell; *The Gardener's Calendar*, by T. Geoffrey W. Henslow; *Book Prices Current 1924*.

C0553   MR. BELLOC. *Nation & Athenaeum*, 30 May 1925, 264.
Letter, replying to one which called LW's review of Belloc's book "a narrow-minded attack on Catholicism."
The article was "no attack". The reader's interpretation is "amusing".

C0554   FROM ALPHA TO OMEGA. *Nation & Athenaeum*, 30 May 1925, 268.
First paragraph. Review of Russian ballet "Narcisse", and "Things to see and hear this week."

C0555   PLAYS AND THEIR CRITICS. *Nation & Athenaeum*, 30 May 1925, 269.
Ironic review of *Glamour: Essays on the Art of the Theatre*, by Stark Young; and *The Contemporary Theatre*, by James Agate, Introduction by Noel Coward.

Mr. Coward dismisses dramatic critics, except Mr. Agate, as among the most contemptible of human beings. They are really among the most unfortunate for theirs is an impossible job. When they try to use the same standards to judge mere entertainments as they use to judge dramatic works of art their readers naturally become confused and annoyed.

C0556 RUSSIAN LITERATURE. *Nation & Athenaeum*, 30 May 1925, 271.
Unsigned review of *Modern Russian Literature*, by Prince D. S. Mirsky.
A remarkably readable book of real criticism.

C0557 BOOKS IN BRIEF. *Nation & Athenaeum*, 30 May 1925, 274.
Short unsigned reviews of *A Memoir of Lord Balfour of Burleigh*, by Lady Frances Balfour; *The Gentle Art of Cookery*, by Mrs. Leyel; *Food and the Family*, by V. H. Mottram; and *Celebrated Crimes*, by George Dilnot.

C0558 FROM ALPHA TO OMEGA. *Nation & Athenaeum*, 6 June 1925, 295.
All but 1st paragraph. LW includes an obituary of J. E. C. Bodley, contributor to the *Athenaeum* and to the *Nation*.

C0559 H. W. M. WOB. *Nation & Athenaeum*, 6 June 1925, 296.
Review of *H. W. M. A Selection of the Writings of H. W. Massingham*, edited by H. J. Massingham.
Besides examples of Massingham's articles, the book contains "essays upon his personality and methods" by several writers. These give a vivid picture but fail to demonstrate Massingham's ability to stimulate his writers in his editorial interviews. [To show this LW contrasts the methods of another editor for whom he worked. He does not name the other man in this article, but repeats the characterization in *Beginning*, A41, in the section on Clifford Sharp, p. 130. Some of this essay is repeated in *Downhill*, A42, pp. 92–97.]

C0560 ON THE EDITOR'S TABLE. *Nation & Athenaeum*, 6 June 1925, 302.

C0561 BOOKS IN BRIEF. *Nation & Athenaeum*, 6 June 1925, 302–04.
Short unsigned reviews of *The Days I Knew*, by Lillie Langtry; *Round About the Sussex Downs*, by Frederick F. Wood; and *The ABC of Stocks and Shares*, by H. Parkinson.

C0562 CANNING. WOB. *Nation & Athenaeum*, 13 June 1925, 325.
Enthusiastic review of *The Foreign Policy of Canning, 1822–1827*, by Harold Temperley.
This and *The Foreign Policy of Castlereagh*, by C. K. Webster (see C0519), show that historians are paying attention to foreign policy. Canning is a more attractive subject than Castlereagh, for he "had wit, humour, and a certain vein of irony". Temperley wields a lighter, more graceful pen than Webster.

C0563 NEW KIND OF ATLAS. *Nation & Athenaeum*, 13 June 1925, 328 & 330.
Unsigned review of *The Chambers of Commerce Atlas*, ed. by George Philip.
"A systematic survey of the world's trade, economic resources, and communications."

C0564 FROM ALPHA TO OMEGA *Nation & Athenaeum*, 20 June 1925, 369.
Review of Noel Coward's "Hay Fever" and of Ashley Duke's "Man with a Load of Mischief".

C0565 ANATOLE FRANCE. WOB. *Nation & Athenaeum*, 20 June 1925, 370.
Review of *Anatole France Himself: A Boswellian Record*, by his secretary Jean-Jacques Brousson, tr. by John Pollock.
Pollock neglected to mention the original title of this amusing book, *Anatole France en Pantoufles;* he overlooked the editor's subtle malice

which fails "even to scratch" Anatole France, who "comes out of it triumphantly, a terrific pagan, witty, cynical, sensual, lovable, and infinitely wise". The reader who cannot stomach a Rabelaisian attitude will not like this book. Mr. Pollock omitted and paraphrased without telling the reader. Yet, even his translation shows the public versus the private conversation of Anatole France.

C0566 ON THE EDITOR'S TABLE. *Nation & Athenaeum,* 20 June 1925, 378.

C0567 BOOKS IN BRIEF. *Nation & Athenaeum,* 20 June 1925, 378.
Unsigned review of *The Statesman's Yearbook, 62nd year.*

C0568 FROM ALPHA TO OMEGA. *Nation & Athenaeum,* 27 June 1925, 400.
"Things to see and hear this week."

C0569 CRICKET TODAY. WOB. *Nation & Athenaeum,* 27 June 1925, 401.
Review of *Gilligan's Men,* by M. A. Noble.

C0570 A GOLF ARTIST. *Nation & Athenaeum,* 27 June 1925, 405.
Unsigned review of *The Golf Courses of Great Britain,* by Bernard Darwin, illus. by H. Rountree. Rev. ed.
This readable book is very entertaining. The author's style makes it a work of art.

C0571 ON THE EDITOR'S TABLE. *Nation & Athenaeum,* 27 June 1925, 406.

C0572 FROM ALPHA TO OMEGA. *Nation & Athenaeum,* 4 July 1925, 429.
Review of Ballet, "Les Matelots"; "Things to see . . ."

C0573 THE END OF SENSIBLE CONVERSATION. WOB. *Nation & Athenaeum,* 4 July 1925, 430.
Review recommending *Mary Hamilton,* ed. by Elizabeth G. Anson; *The Journal of Clarissa Trant, 1800–1832,* ed. by C. G. Luard; *Tom Moore's Diary,* ed. by J. B. Priestley; and *The Memoirs of Alexander Herzen,* vol. IV, tr. by Mrs. Garnett.
"I have given the books in their chronological order, for apart from their other merits, if you read them consecutively in that order, you can have the vivid experience of living vicariously in four personalities through the period from 1768–1855."

C0574 ON THE EDITOR'S TABLE. *Nation & Athenaeum,* 4 July 1925, 438.

C0575 BOOKS IN BRIEF. *Nation & Athenaeum,* 4 July 1925, 438 & 440.
Short, unsigned reviews of *Some Other Bees,* by Herbert Mace; *Illustrations of English Synonyms,* by M. Alderton Pink; and *Webster's Royal Red Book.*

C0576 FROM ALPHA TO OMEGA. *Nation & Athenaeum,* 11 July 1925, 460.
Review of play "The Rehearsal".

C0577 PLATO THE DAGO. *Nation & Athenaeum,* 11 July 1925, 461
Review of *The Greek Point of View,* by Maurice Hutton, with mention of several Loeb classics.
Professor Hutton finds the Greeks distasteful because he prefers instinct to intelligence.

C0578 FROM ALPHA TO OMEGA. *Nation & Athenaeum,* 18 July 1925, 488.
Review of Lytton Strachey's play "Son of Heaven" at the New Scala.
The play lacks both the merits of youth and the marks of maturity. The production was good, but the characters are not strong enough for tragedy.

C0579 JOHN BRIGHT. WOB. *Nation & Athenaeum,* 18 July 1925, 489.
Review of *The Life of John Bright,* new ed., by G. M. Trevelyan.
This readable biography gives the reader "all the material necessary for understanding the character, ideas, and achievements of the man who

never was, or pretended to be, a statesman." Trevelyan "allows the facts to give shape to his book". It seems curious that Bright, who almost never dealt with generalities, should have given rise to the intellectual creed of nineteenth-century liberalism.

Reprinted as "John Bright and Liberalism" in *Essays . . .* 1927, A24, pp. 218–20.

C0580   THE PRUNING OF FRUIT TREES. *Nation & Athenaeum*, 18 July 1925, 494.
Unsigned review of *The Lorette System of Pruning,* by Louis Lorette, tr. by W. R. Dykes.

    LW recommends the book and the method and describes the controversy over it.

C0581   ON THE EDITOR'S TABLE. *Nation & Athenaeum*, 18 July 1925, 494.

C0582   BOOKS IN BRIEF. *Nation & Athenaeum*, 18 July 1925, 494.
Reviews of *Kelvin the Man,* by Agnes Gardner King; and *Trial of Jessie M'Lachlan,* ed. by W. Roughead.

C0583   FROM ALPHA TO OMEGA. *Nation & Athenaeum*, 25 July 1925, 515.
Review of the Russian Ballet "House Party".

C0584   BEN JONSON WOB. *Nation & Athenaeum*, 25 July 1925, 516.
Review of *Ben Jonson,* I & II: *The Man and His Work,* ed. by C. H. Herford and Percy Simpson.

    These volumes will certainly whet the appetite for reading Jonson's own works.

Reprinted in "Ben Jonson", *Essays . . .* 1927, A24.

C0585   ON THE EDITOR'S TABLE. *Nation & Athenaeum*, 25 July 1925, 521.

C0586   BOOKS IN BRIEF. *Nation & Athenaeum*, 25 July 1925, 522.
Short unsigned reviews of *Lady Susan,* by Jane Austen; *Unpublished and Uncollected Letters of William Cowper;* and *Greek Ethical Thought,* by Hilda Oakeley.

C0587   EVERY MAN'S ONE GOOD BOOK. WOB. *Nation & Athenaeum,* 1 August 1925, 545.
Review of *My Circus Life,* by James Lloyd, with a Preface by G. K. Chesterton; and *Fifty Years of Sport,* by Lt.-Col. E. D. Miller.

    Mr. Lloyd has the good sense to know that he is not a writer. With no attempt at great literature he has told an extremely interesting story. Colonel Miller "has become aware of the existence of relative clauses and dependent sentences, and his book has, therefore, neither the brevity nor the explosive directness of the circus proprietor's. For all that it can be read with enjoyment and profit."

C0588   ON THE EDITOR'S TABLE. *Nation & Athenaeum*, 1 August 1925, 550.

C0589   A DOCTOR'S VIEW OF HISTORY. WOB. *Nation & Athenaeum*, 8 August 1925, 571.
Review of *Mere Mortals, Medico-Historical Essays,* Second Series, by Dr. C. MacLaurin.

    More people who are not professional historians should write their views on history. Dr. MacLaurin examines the results of so many monarchs having suffered from syphilis and gluttony. That their conduct was worse than that of others suffering from similar symptoms may be attributed to the power they held.

C0590   THAT PROFESSIONAL EYE. Headed WIT AND WISDOM FROM THE "WEEKLIES". *Daily Herald*, 8 August 1925, p. 4, col. 4.
Quotation from "A Doctor's View of History", C0589.

C0591   INTERNATIONAL FACTS. *Nation & Athenaeum*, 8 August 1925, 572–73.
Unsigned review of *The World After the Peace Conference* and *Survey of International Affairs*, by Arnold J. Toynbee.
> The author has the knowledge and the ability to arrange the material, plus historical imagination. A chronological list would help.

C0592   ON THE EDITOR'S TABLE. *Nation & Athenaeum*, 8 August 1925, 575.

C0593   MODERN POETRY. WOB. *Nation & Athenaeum*, 15 August 1925, 598.
Review of the first 7 pamphlets in the series *Augustan Books of Modern Poetry: Shelley; Keats; Hilaire Belloc; Rabindranath Tagore; Rupert Brooke; Edmund Blunden;* and *Robert Bridges.*
> Elaboration of the thesis that the adjective is the bane of modern poetry, with quotations to prove it.

Parts reprinted in "The Modern Nightingale", *Essays . . .* 1927, A24.

C0594   OVERWORKED   ADJECTIVES.   Headed   "WEEKLY"   WIT   AND WISDOM. *Daily Herald*, 15 August 1925, p. 4, col. 5.
Quotation from "Modern Poetry", C0593.

C0595   Sentence beginning "The White Paper on Compulsory Labour for Government Purposes [in Kenya]." In EVENTS OF THE WEEK. *Nation & Athenaeum*, 22 August 1925, 613.
> The Colonial Office has been yielding to the demand of white settlers that the government compel natives to work. [LW refers to an article published 15 August , pp. 588–90, "The Case of Mr. Cooke", about an official the settlers considered too lenient.]

C0596   FROM ALPHA TO OMEGA. *Nation & Athenaeum*, 22 August 1925, 622.
First 2 paragraphs.
> The kinds of music the various classes listen to at Brighton are related to the kinds of books they carry.

C0597   AN UNFORTUNATE MAN. WOB. *Nation & Athenaeum*, 22 August 1925, 623.
Review of *The Life of Thomas Holcroft (1745–1809)*, ed. by Elbridge Colby. 2 vols.
> This edition includes Hazlitt's muddled additions as well as Colby's notes. The autobiography is well worth republishing. It is an interesting story of the adventures of a man who seems to have striven for heights he was incapable of reaching. A limited de luxe edition is inappropriate to a story of failure.

C0598   THE PROBLEM OF THE STATE. *Nation & Athenaeum*, 22 August 1925, 625.
Unsigned review of *A Grammar of Politics*, by Harold J. Laski.
> This final volume in the author's attempt "to construct a theory of the state in the great society" is disappointing and irritating, full of misspellings and intolerable style.

C0599   BOOKS IN BRIEF. *Nation & Athenaeum*, 22 August 1925, 628.
Short unsigned review of *The Co-operative Movement in Italy*, by E. A. Lloyd (Fabian Society).

C0600   WILLIAM BLAKE. WOB. *Nation & Athenaeum*, 29 August 1925, 649.
Review of *The Writings of William Blake*, edited by Geoffrey Keynes. 3 vols (Nonesuch Press).
> "These poems owe their greatness and their strange flavour partly to the combination of extreme simplicity and elusiveness. . . . But [Blake] allowed his imagination to become his master instead of his servant, with

fatal effects upon his poetical genius and his powers as a writer." Mr.
Keynes has done a scholarly job of editing the works. "As a whole it is, in
my opinion, the most beautiful production of the Nonesuch Press. It is
only fair to mention the name of the printers, the Chiswick Press, who
must share in the credit."

C0601 FROM ALPHA TO OMEGA. *Nation & Athenaeum*, 5 September 1925,
677.
"Things to see and hear this week."

C0602 LITERATURE AND REVOLUTION. WOB. *Nation & Athenaeum*,
5 September 1925, 678.
Review of *Literature and Revolution*, by Leon Trotsky.
"One cannot help smiling at Trotsky's ferocity against the intellectuals
when one considers what a terrific intellectual he is himself." His literary
criticism and his aesthetic theories are extremely interesting and subtle.
But he has not made clear the connection he says must exist between a
living literature and the social and political system.

C0603 LIVES OF THE GREAT. WOB. *Nation & Athenaeum*, 12 September 1925,
706.
Review of *Memoirs*, 2 vols, by Sir Almeric Fitzroy; and *Courts and Countries
after the War*, by H.R.H. Infanta Eulalia of Spain.
Both books "take me into a world, physical and mental, of which I am
profoundly ignorant. . . . What is interesting in Sir Almeric's and the
Infanta's books is to see from the inside the lives and minds of the great so
perfectly fashioned and so completely dominated by breeches, buttons,
bows and the table of precedence."

C0604 BOOKS IN BRIEF. *Nation & Athenaeum*, 12 September 1925, 712.
Unsigned review of *Co-operation at Home and Abroad*, by C. R. Fay, 3rd
edition.
Such a good book should have been completely revised. The supplements
are valuable, but the text, first published in 1908 and again in 1918, is
completely out of date.

C0605 FROM ALPHA TO OMEGA. *Nation & Athenaeum*, 19 September 1925,
733.
"Things to see and hear this week."

C0606 MR. WELLS AND THE IMMORTALS. WOB. *Nation & Athenaeum*,
19 September 1925, 734.
Review of *Christina Alberta's Father*, by H. G. Wells.
"Mr. Wells has never been content to be a novelist. . . . He is passionately
interested in other things, things which he considers infinitely more
important than art and literature. There is civilization and society and
science. . . . And so in most cases, after a hundred pages or so in which he
has shown us what a novelist has been lost in him, the novel stops, the
delightful puppets are elbowed aside or put away in a box, and Mr. Wells
talks" and spoils his novel.

C0607 THE INDIAN PEASANT. *Nation & Athenaeum*, 19 September 1925, 737–38.
Unsigned review of *The Punjab Peasant in Prosperity and Debt*, by Malcolm
Lyall Darling.
This remarkable book by a member of the Indian Civil Service shows how
debt dominates existence in the East. There is always a threat of natural
disaster, but when a crop is reaped the lenders come for their heavy
interest. Darling's firsthand, sympathetic study should become a classic.

C0608 Paragraph beginning "Further information with regard to the Institute of Pacific Relations. . . ." *Nation & Athenaeum*, 26 September 1925, 753.
> Refers to a paragraph published September 5, p. 665. The results show more agreement than was expected.

C0609 FROM ALPHA TO OMEGA. *Nation & Athenaeum*, 26 September 1925, 764.
"Things to see and hear this week."

C0610 MARK TWAIN. WOB. *Nation & Athenaeum*, 26 September 1925, 765.
Review of the first 5 volumes of The Florida Edition of Mark Twain (Chatto & Windus).
> On re-reading, the bloom seems to have faded a little from the humour of *Huckleberry Finn* and *A Tramp Abroad*, and from the wings of romance of *The Prince and the Pauper*. Perhaps the American exuberance appeals more to the child than to the middle-aged man. The more restrained passages in *Huckleberry Finn* contain Twain's best writing. The edition would be improved by the addition of bibliographical information such as the first date of publication of the separate works.

C0611 PEACE AND WAR. *Nation & Athenaeum*, 26 September 1925, 767–68.
Unsigned review of *The Roots and Causes of the Wars (1914–1918)*, 2 vols, by John S. Ewart; *How the War Began: The Diary of the Russian Foreign Office*, by Major W. C. Cyprian Bridge; *The Problem of International Sanctions*, by D. Mitrany; and *Now is the Time*, by Arthur Ponsonby.
> A thoughtful article.

C0612 BOOKS IN BRIEF. *Nation & Athenaeum*, 26 September 1925, 772.
Short unsigned review of *British Flora*, by Gaston Bonnier, translated from the French by Ethel Mellor.
> The general key to identification of plants in this book is even handier than that in Bentham's handbook.

C0613 THE LAST CONRAD. WOB. *Nation & Athenaeum*, 3 October 1925, 18.
Review of *Suspense*, by Joseph Conrad.
> This last, unfinished novel may be hailed by the sentimental as the author's masterpiece, but it is really a splendid shell with nothing in it. Reprinted as "Joseph Conrad" in *Essays . . . 1927*, A24, pp. 67–70.

C0614 KNOW THYSELF. *Nation & Athenaeum*, 3 October 1925, 22 & 24.
Unsigned review of *The Galton System of Mind Training*.
> A correspondence course of 12 lessons in a system based on discoveries and theories of several different schools of modern psychology.

C0615 FROM ALPHA TO OMEGA. *Nation & Athenaeum*, 10 October 1925, 55.
Last 4 items, beginning with a review of a Greek play.

C0616 THE HARVEST OF AUTUMN BOOKS. *Nation & Athenaeum*, 10 October 1925, 56.

C0617 FROM ALPHA TO OMEGA. *Nation & Athenaeum*, 17 October 1925, 116.

C0618 BIOGRAPHIES. WOB. *Nation & Athenaeum*, 17 October 1925, 117.
Review of *Henry Montagu Butler, A Memoir*, by his son Sir James Ramsay Montagu Butler; *Monarchs and Millionaires*, by Lalla Vandervelde; *Myself Not Least; Being the Personal Reminiscences of "X"* [Herbert Vivian]; *The Life of Benito Mussolini*, by Margherita G. Sarfatti; and *Disraeli and Gladstone*, by D. C. Somervell.
> "Why is even a bad biography or autobiography nearly always a good and readable book?" The answer is "that at any moment they may give you an extremely vivid vision of some human being." Somervell "is too much

under the influence of Mr. Strachey, and, like all who suffer from this infection, he irritates the reader by continually forgetting and then remembering to be amusing or brilliant."

C0619 WHY BIOGRAPHIES SELL. *Daily Herald,* 17 October 1925, p. 4, col. 4.
Quotation from "Biographies", C0618.

C0620 ON THE EDITOR'S TABLE. *Nation & Athenaeum,* 17 October 1925, 125.

C0621 BOOKS IN BRIEF. *Nation & Athenaeum,* 17 October 1925, 126.
Short unsigned reviews: *Shelley and Keats as they Struck Their Contemporaries; The Permanent Court of International Justice,* by Alexander P. Fachiri; *Garden Craftsmanship in Yew and Box,* by Nathaniel Lloyd; *Introducing London,* by E. V. Lucas; *The Complete Jam Cupboard,* by Mrs. Leyel; and *The Second Book of the Gramophone Record,* by Percy A. Scholes.

C0622 VISCOUNT GREY. WOB. *Nation & Athenaeum,* 24 October 1925, 151.
Review of *Twenty-Five Years, 1892–1916,* by Viscount Grey of Fallodon.
Grey's attempt to explain his policy before the war is not entirely satisfactory. "Viscount Grey remains for me a psychological mystery."

C0623 ON THE EDITOR'S TABLE. WOB. *Nation & Athenaeum,* 24 October 1925, 160.

C0624 BOOKS IN BRIEF. *Nation & Athenaeum,* 24 October 1925, 160.
Short unsigned review of *The Art of the Printer,* by Stanley Morison.

C0625 FROM ALPHA TO OMEGA. *Nation & Athenaeum,* 31 October 1925, 182.
First paragraph on film society.

C0626 CRIME. WOB. *Nation & Athenaeum,* 31 October 1925, 183.
Review of *Trial of Ronald True,* ed. by Donald Carswell; *Murder, Piracy and Treason,* by Raymond Postgate; and *Tales of Bohemia, Taverns, and the Underworld,* by Stanley Scott.
Mr. Scott should remember that "a mixture of luridness and sentimentality is not really a good atmosphere for crime, and one which only the crudest writers employ." Mr. Postgate has retold the old stories in various ways; for example, he treats the affair of Edgware Road and John Thurtell from an historian's standpoint. Mr. Carswell points out the significance of the story of Ronald True to the history of English law regarding legal insanity.

C0627 ON THE EDITOR'S TABLE. *Nation & Athenaeum,* 31 October 1925, 192.

C0628 "A PAINFUL MYSTERY". WOB. *Nation & Athenaeum,* 7 November 1925, 217.
Review of 2 books about the animal world: *My Friend Toto,* by Cherry Kearton; and *Lions'n Tigers'n Everything,* by Courtney Ryley Cooper.
The title of LW's essay is from Dr. Arnold's confession that "The whole subject of the brute creation is to me one of such painful mystery that I dare not approach it." LW says that he himself considers the world "a fascinating mystery". After commenting on the merits of the books he recounts his experience of observing the elephants who refused to drink from water fouled by the victims of rinderpest. Cf. C0144.

C0629 CHARLOTTE BRONTE. WOB. *Nation & Athenaeum,* 14 November 1925, 260.
Review of *The Twelve Adventurers and Other Stories,* by Charlotte Brontë.
These fragmentary stories written between the ages of 12 and 21, though ridiculous, show glimpses of the literary work the author would later produce. She is writing here of an imaginary world. What she learned by this writing she later applied when writing about the real world. "The

woman who created Rochester also created the best male character ever drawn by a woman novelist."

C0630   BOOKS IN BRIEF. *Nation & Athenaeum*, 14 November 1925, 268.
Short unsigned reviews of *The Unpublished Diary and Political Sketches of Princess Lievan*, ed. by Harold Temperley; and *The Annals of Ennius*, ed. by E. M. Steuart.

C0631   DISRAELI. WOB. *Nation & Athenaeum*, 21 November 1925, 292.
Review and discussion of *Ixion in Heaven*, by Benjamin Disraeli; *Disraeli and Gladstone*, by D. C. Somervell (cf C0618); and *Disraeli, the Alien Patriot*, by E. T. Raymond.
> A biographer should decide whether his work is to be a record of facts or an interpretation. If the latter, he should choose those facts which are relevant to his thesis. Disraeli seems to be baffling biographers. Mr. Raymond's book has a worse fault; he tries to explain the man by his race.

C0632   ON THE EDITOR'S TABLE. *Nation & Athenaeum*, 21 November 1925, 300.

C0633   BOOKS IN BRIEF. *Nation & Athenaeum*, 21 November 1925, 300.
Short unsigned reviews of *Wynkyn de Worde and His Contemporaries; Human Factor in Business*, by B. S. Rowntree; and *The Conduct of the Kitchen*.

C0634   FROM ALPHA TO OMEGA. *Nation & Athenaeum*, 28 November 1925, 320–21.
1st paragraph on "Rima" and 2nd on "Juno and the Paycock".

C0635   THE EIGHTEENTH CENTURY. WOB. *Nation & Athenaeum*, 28 November 1925, 322.
Review of *Lyme Letters, 1660–1760*, compiled by Lady Newton. *Lord Fife and His Factor*, Letters from the second Lord Fife written between 1760 and 1800 to his factor William Rose; *The Diary of Thomas Turner of East Hoathly, Sussex (1754–1765)*; and *The Canning Wonder*, by Arthur Machen.
> The first two books picture the "intolerably pretentious dreariness" of the life of the upper classes; the second pair show glimpses of lower-class life. Thomas Turner seems to have been an unusual member of the lower class. "He had a passion for reading, and he probably read more books and had more intellectual interest than all the Leghs, Chicheleys, Duffs, and Grants of his time taken together."

Reprinted with slight change as part of "The Pageant of History" in *Essays . . . 1927*, A24, pp. 142–45.

C0636   " 'JUG JUG' TO DIRTY EARS". WOB. *Nation & Athenaeum*, 5 December 1925, 354.
Review of 3 books of poetry: *Human Shows: Far Phantasies: Songs and Trifles*, by Thomas Hardy; *English Poems*, by Edmund Blunden; and *Poems, 1909–1925*, by T. S. Eliot.
> "Personally I *like* Mr. Eliot's poems so much that I am afraid of appearing exaggerated in criticizing them. . . . My only criticism of him is that the theme he plays on these subtle strings is always the same and is very old. The splendour and romance of our desires and imaginations, the sordidness of reality. . . . The nightingale never sings anything but 'Jug jug' to dirty ears."

Much of this reprinted as part of "The Modern Nightingale" in *Essays . . . 1927*, A24, pp. 100–02.

C0637 THE NEW ART OF BIOGRAPHY. WOB. *Nation & Athenaeum,* 12 December 1925, 404.
> Review of *Essays in Biography,* by Bonamy Dobrée.
>> Dobrée has been influenced by Lytton Strachey. "He writes in a style of his own, and though, like all the modern school of biographers, he never lets an opportunity slip when a great man – or even a small one – has made a fool of himself, he is much less afraid than most of his co-experimenters of being serious and of not having a dig or a joke in every sentence." Dobrée defends the writing of biography as though it were autobiography.

C0638 ON THE EDITOR'S TABLE. *Nation & Athenaeum,* 12 December 1925, 412–14.

C0639 BOOKS IN BRIEF. *Nation & Athenaeum,* 12 December 1925, 414.
> *Shakespeare's Sonnets Reconsidered; The Odyssey Rendered into English;* 3 vols of the Shrewsbury edition of The Works of Samuel Butler; and *The Diplomatic Relations of Great Britain and the United States,* by R. B. Mowat.

C0640 ENGLISH PROSE. WOB. *Nation & Athenaeum,* 19 December 1925, 438.
> Review of *The Oxford Book of English Prose,* chosen and edited by Sir Arthur Quiller-Couch.
>> "He has tried to make his anthology 'as representatively English' as possible", although there are some curious omissions. "But even 'The Oxford Book of English Verse' never gave me the same sense of power, volume, and variety in English literature which I have got from 'The Oxford Book of English Prose.'"

C0641 ON THE EDITOR'S TABLE. *Nation & Athenaeum,* 19 December 1925, 448.

C0642 BOOKS IN BRIEF. *Nation & Athenaeum,* 19 December 1925, 448.
> Short unsigned reviews of *Bulb Gardening,* by A. J. Macself; and *The Aquarium Book,* by E. G. Boulenger.

C0643 THE OVERBURY MYSTERY. WOB. *Nation & Athenaeum,* 26 December 1925, 470.
> Review of *The Overbury Mystery,* by Judge Edward Abbott Parry.
>> This fascinating book has no footnotes and is very readable. The actors in the drama "are treated as though they had once been alive and could be made to live again for us, and their psychology and vices are frankly discussed." Judge Parry does seem a bit unfair to Overbury.

C0644 ON THE EDITOR'S TABLE. *Nation & Athenaeum,* 26 December 1925, 476.

C0645 BOOKS IN BRIEF. *Nation & Athenaeum,* 26 December 1925, 476.
> Short unsigned reviews of *Minims,* by E. X. Kapp; and *Co-operative Storekeeping,* by S. R. Elliott. Introd. by Margaret Llewelyn Davies.

C0646 OFFICIAL PAPERS. *Economic Journal,* XXXV.140 (December 1925), 649–57.
> Review of *Labour and Land in East Africa.* Report of the East Africa Commission [Cmd. 2387], 1925.

C0647 OBSCURITY. *The Chapbook* (A Yearly Miscellany), No. 40 (J. Cape, for the Poetry Bookshop, 1925), pp. 7–9.
> Essay.
>> The obscurity of modern literature stems partly from the revolt against tradition. Mr. Eliot, Mr. Joyce, Miss Sitwell and Miss Stein all deliberately suppress their transitions.

1926

C0648 FROM ALPHA TO OMEGA. *Nation & Athenaeum*, 2 January 1926, 496.
Paragraph on the *Publishers' Circular*.

C0649 THE END OF HICKEY. WOB. *Nation & Athenaeum*, 2 January 1926, 497.
Review of *Memoirs of William Hickey*, vol. IV, ed. by Alfred Spencer; and
The Diary of a Young Lady of Fashion.
> Spencer gives the history of Hickey's memoirs plus family background.
> He need not have omitted parts of the *Memoirs* for the ordinary reader.
> They include interesting historical facts. Suppressing the language encour-
> ages unhealthy pleasure in the suppressed material. The second book
> reads like a 19th-century novel.

C0650 TWO AMBASSADORS. *Nation & Athenaeum*, 2 January 1926, 500.
Unsigned review of *The Life and Letters of Walter H. Page*, 3 vols, by Burton
J. Hendrick; and *Social and Diplomatic Memories, 1902–1910*, by Sir J.
Rennell Rodd.
> Page's book includes his letters to President Wilson. Page, with the
> "enormous seriousness of the American", still has a sense of humour.
> Rodd's work is charming, old world but "anæmic".

C0651 ON THE EDITOR'S TABLE. *Nation & Athenaeum*, 2 January 1926,
504.

C0652 BOOKS IN BRIEF. *Nation & Athenaeum*, 2 January 1926, 504. Entire
column of short unsigned reviews: *Coleridge at Highgate*, by Lucy E. Watson;
The Wonderland of Big Game, by A. Radcliffe Dugmore; *The Bench and the
Dock*, by Charles Kingston; *Madame de Pompadour*, by Marcelle Tinayre;
Elizabethan Lyrics, by Norman Ault; *Canine Distemper. A Practical
Handbook*, by Louis Sewell; *English Today*, by W. T. Webb; and *A Key to
Language*, by Isabel Fry.

C0653 HANDWRITING AND CHARACTER. WOB. *Nation & Athenaeum*, 9
January 1926, 525.
Review of *The Psychology of Handwriting*, by Robert Saudek.
> Saudek has tried to make graphology a science, but has written about it in
> horrible scientific jargon. His examples do not seem to prove his theory
> that handwriting is determined by character.

C0654 A CHRONOLOGICAL SHAKESPEARE. *Nation & Athenaeum*, 9 January
1926, 530.
Unsigned review of *The Works of Shakespeare Chronologically Arranged*,
with Introduction by Charles Whibley.

C0655 BOOKS IN BRIEF. *Nation & Athenaeum* 9 January 1926, 531–32. Brief
unsigned reviews of *Rapid Calculations*, by A. H. Russell; *Beethoven*, by Paul
Bekker; and *Reminiscences*, by Marie, Princess of Battenberg.

C0656 LAURENCE STERNE. WOB. *Nation & Athenaeum*, 16 January 1926, 554.
Review of *The Life and Times of Laurence Sterne*, 2 vols., by Wilbur L. Cross.
New ed.
> This thoroughly good book is "one of those amazingly solid, sober, sound
> and detailed literary biographies, with an undercurrent of criticism, which
> are characteristic of American scholarship." The critics do not seem to
> have noticed the special kind of prose writer Sterne was: he was master of
> the "trailer", the sentence which "flows on . . .".

C0657 ON THE EDITOR'S TABLE. *Nation & Athenaeum*, 16 January 1926,
564.

C0658 BOOKS IN BRIEF. *Nation & Athenaeum,* 16 January 1926, 564. Short unsigned reviews of *Opium,* by John P. Gavitt; and *Opium as an International Problem,* by W. W. Willoughby.

C0659 ARE THERE "DISCARNATE SPIRITS"? WOB. *Nation & Athenaeum,* 23 January 1926, 585.
Review of *The Facts of Psychic Science and Philosophy,* by A. Campbell Holms.
    It seems that Mr. Holms believes all the "evidence" that comes to him. Reprinted as "Discarnate Spirits" in *Essays . . .,* A24.

C0660 ON THE EDITOR'S TABLE. *Nation & Athenaeum,* 23 January 1926, 592.

C0661 BOOKS IN BRIEF. *Nation & Athenaeum,* 23 January 1926, 592. Short unsigned reviews of *London Nights,* by Stephen Graham; and *The Rover,* by Joseph Conrad.

C0662 WHO CAUSED THE FRENCH REVOLUTION? WOB. *Nation & Athenaeum,* 30 January 1926, 615.
Review of *Pioneers of the French Revolution,* by M. Roustan, tr. by Frederic Whyte.
    This edition does not mention that it was first published in 1906 under the title "Les Philosophes et la Société Française au 18e Siècle". Roustan does not prove his thesis that the philosophers caused the French Revolution. "This raises the question of how far ideas, political and 'intellectual', determine the larger communal actions of the human race."

C0663 ON THE EDITOR'S TABLE. *Nation & Athenaeum,* 30 January 1926, 624.

C0664 BOOKS IN BRIEF. *Nation & Athenaeum,* 30 January 1926, 624.
Short unsigned reviews of the last 4 items beginning with *From Groves of Palm,* by Bella Sidney Woolf.

C0665 FROM ALPHA TO OMEGA. *Nation & Athenaeum,* 6 February 1926, 646.
"Things to see . . ." and last three items.

C0666 MR. PEPYS AND MODERNITY. WOB. *Nation & Athenaeum,* 6 February 1926, 647.
Review of *Private Correspondence and Miscellaneous Papers of Samuel Pepys, 1679–1703 . . . ,* ed. by J. R. Tanner, 2 vols.
    These well-edited letters show Pepys' insatiable curiosity and love of experience.

C0667 ON THE EDITOR'S TABLE. *Nation & Athenaeum,* 6 February 1926, 654.

C0668 BOOKS IN BRIEF. *Nation & Athenaeum,* 6 February 1926, 654.
Short unsigned reviews of The Bible, vol. II (Nonesuch Press); *Southward Ho!* by Ralph Deakin; and *Mystery Cities.* by Thomas Gann.

C0669 FROM ALPHA TO OMEGA. *Nation & Athenaeum,* 13 February 1926, 680–81.
Review of play "The Student Prince" at His Majesty's Theatre.

C0670 A MORATORIUM FOR POETRY. WOB. *Nation & Athenaem,* 13 February 1926, 682.
Notice of 9 volumes of poetry: *What's O'Clock?* by Amy Lowell; *The Bridle-Way,* by the Earl of Sandwich; *Poems,* by Mary Drinkwater; *Collected Poems,* by Teresa Hooley; *Odes and Oddities,* by A. G. Hamilton; *Fairies and Fantasy,* by A. T. Wynard-Wright; *Poems,* by Lewis W. Townsend; *The Assaying of Brabantius,* by C. S. Sherrington; and *Nature Dialogues,* by N. M. Copland.
    Poets might understand the practice of reviewing books of poetry in job lots if they could see how many arrive weekly in the newspaper office. The

only serious writers listed above are Miss Lowell and Mr. Sherrington. Miss Lowell might just as well have written her ideas in prose. If writers were to adopt a fifteen-year moratorium on poetry they might then produce something fresh.

Portion in "The Modern Nightingale", *Essays . . .*, A24.

C0671 BOOKS IN BRIEF *Nation & Athenaeum*, 13 February 1926, 690.
Short unsigned reviews of *Collected Essays*, vols I & II, by Samuel Butler; *The Town Labourer*, by J. L. and Barbara Hammond; *Soils and Fertilizers*, by A. J. Macself; and *A German-English Dictionary*, by Herman Brandt.

C0672 NEW GRAMOPHONE RECORDS *Nation & Athenaeum*, 13 February 1926, 692.

C0673 A PLENTIFUL LACK OF WIT. WOB. *Nation & Athenaeum*, 20 February 1926, 717.
Review of 6 books: *25, Being a Young Man's Candid Recollections . . .* by Beverley Nichols; *Frederic Harrison, Thoughts and Memories*, by Austin Harrison; *James Leigh Strachan-Davidson*, by J. W. Mackail; *The Memoirs of Sir David Erskine*, ed. by Mrs. Steuart Erskine; *Echoes and Memories*, by Bramwell Booth; *Reminiscences: Social and Political*, by Roma Lister.
Miss Lister's book is "the only one of these books which seems to me to contain the slightest breath of youth."
A letter to the editor published 27 February, p. 741, disputes what LW said here about Frederic Harrison.

C0674 ON THE EDITOR'S TABLE. *Nation & Athenaeum*, 20 February 1926, 722 & 724.

C0675 BOOKS IN BRIEF. *Nation & Athenaeum*, 20 February 1926, 724.
Short untitled review of *Whitaker's Cumulative Book List*.

C0676 FROM ALPHA TO OMEGA. *Nation & Athenaeum*, 27 February 1926, 745.
Paragraphs on Chekhov's "Three Sisters" and James Forlong Lectures.

C0677 QUEEN VICTORIA. WOB. *Nation & Athenaeum*, 27 February 1926, 746.
Review of the 2nd series of *The Letters of Queen Victoria*, ed. by James Earle Buckle; with mention of *Memoirs of Alexander Herzen*, vol. V.
The main interest in these letters is psychological.

C0678 ON THE EDITOR'S TABLE. *Nation & Athenaeum*, 27 February 1926, 756.

C0679 BAD DREAMS. WOB. *Nation & Athenaeum*, 6 March 1926, 778.
Review of *International Anarchy, 1904–1914*, by G. Lowes Dickinson.
In this masterly account Dickinson holds that a system of international anarchy caused World War I.
Part of "Statesmen and Diplomatists", *Essays . . .*, A24.

C0680 ON THE EDITOR'S TABLE. *Nation & Athenaeum*, 6 March 1926, 784 & 786.

C0681 NEW GRAMOPHONE RECORDS. *Nation & Athenaeum*, 6 March 1926, 788

C0682 THE PROMISE OF SPRING. WOB. *Nation & Athenaeum*, 13 March 1926, 862.

C0683 ANOTHER EMPRESS. WOB. *Nation & Athenaeum*, 20 March 1926, 862.
Review of *Catherine the Great*, by Katherine Anthony.
"On the throne a little bit of genius goes a long way."

C0684 ON THE EDITOR'S TABLE. *Nation & Athenaeum*, 20 March 1926, 868 & 870.

C0685 BOOKS IN BRIEF. *Nation & Athenaeum*, 20 March 1926, 870.
Unsigned short review of *Successful Advertising,* by Philip Smith.

C0686 NEW GRAMOPHONE RECORDS. *Nation & Athenaeum*, 20 March 1926, 872.

C0687 FROM ALPHA TO OMEGA. *Nation & Athenaeum*, 27 March 1926, 894.
Review of "Life Goes On" at The Duke of York's Theatre.

C0688 PREACHER OR ARTIST? WOB. *Nation & Athenaeum*, 27 March 1926, 896.
> Review of *The Modern Ibsen, a Reconsideration*, by Hermann J. Weigand.
> After reading a few pages one's brain buzzes with ideas. Mr. Weigand
> clearly shows that Ibsen was an artist not a preacher. Here LW refutes
> J. D. Beresford who had written to say that matter is more important than
> form. Woolf says that in literature it is form, not content, that counts.

C0689 ON THE EDITOR'S TABLE. *Nation & Athenaeum*, 27 March 1926, 906.

C0690 BOOKS IN BRIEF. *Nation & Athenaeum*, 27 March 1926, 906 & 908.
Short unsigned review of *Trial of Abraham Thornton*, ed. by John Hall.

C0691 NEW GRAMOPHONE RECORDS. *Nation & Athenaeum*, 27 March 1926, 908.

C0692 HAVELOCK ELLIS. WOB. *Nation & Athenaeum*, 3 April 1926, 17.
Review of 4 books by Ellis: *Impressions and Comments*, First and Second
Series; *Affirmations;* and *The World of Dreams.*
> Ellis "is in the line of Swift and of the writers of the simplest and most
> undecorated English, the kind of prose which, if we all spoke or wrote the
> best English, we should all naturally speak and write." He is a very good
> critic, but as an original thinker he is "something of the brilliant
> amateur . . . Olive Schreiner, I think, once complained to him that he was
> frittering himself away and becoming a mere Leslie Stephen."

C0693 LIVING VICARIOUSLY. WOB. *Nation & Athenaeum*, 10 April 1926, 45.
Review of 5 books: *Diary of a Country Parson*, by James Woodforde, ed. by
John Beresford, vol. II, 1782–1787; *Seventy Years a Showman*, by George
Sanger, Intro. by Kenneth Grahame; *Recollected in Tranquillity*, by Janet
Courtney; *Hubert Parry*, 2 vols by Charles L. Graves; and *Naphtali*, by C.
Lewis Hind.
> The first two are good books; the rest are not. A literary Puritanism which
> tends to disparage the recent interest in biography as interest in gossip is
> based on the notion that whatever is pleasant is bad. These books enable
> the reader to live different lives vicariously.

C0694 SCIENCE AND THE SCIENTISTS. WOB. *Nation & Athenaeum*, 17 April 1926, 74.
Review of *Why We Behave Like Human Beings*, by George A. Dorsey (New
York: Harper); *Science and Poetry*, by I. A. Richards; *Aphasia*, by S. A.
Kinnier Wilson; *Evolution and Creation*, by Sir Oliver Lodge.
> These books are written by scientists for the ordinary reader. Dorsey pelts
> his readers with facts; Lodge gently pours horrifying facts down his
> readers' throats; and Richards says science has destroyed poetry. When
> the scientist sticks to science he is on solid ground, but when he speculates
> about religion and metaphysics "he often talks nonsense".

C0695 MUTTON AND SHEEP. WOB. *Nation & Athenaeum*, 24 April 1926, 102.
Review of 6 volumes in Harrap's series *Essays of Today and Yesterday*,
including those by Philip Guedalla, Andrew Lang, Basil MacDonald
Hastings, James Agate, Barry Pain, and Alice Meynell.

To be good an essay must be alive, not dead like mutton. Mr. Agate alone of the above is not sheeplike, but rather canine. "His essays are tremendously alive, and what a blessing that is!"

C0696 LETTER TO THE EDITOR. *Nation & Athenaeum,* 1 May 1926, 125.
Reply to a letter from Philip Guedalla published April 24 saying that LW misunderstood his description of a bird sanctuary in Hyde Park.
An apology with a complaint.

C0697 OUT OF THE WILDERNESS. WOB. *Nation & Athenaeum,* 1 May 1926, 130.
Review of *Abraham Lincoln,* 2 vols, by Carl Sandburg.
Such a detailed book is a wilderness; it was almost impossible to get through the first volume. "The more I ploughed my way through [the] second volume, the more vivid and concrete a figure and character of Lincoln rose before me." It is hard to tell whether Sandburg's skill led to the emergence of so solid a figure or whether Lincoln really had such strength.

No *Nation and Athenaeum* was published May 8 because of the General Strike. The issue of 15 May was very short with no *Athenaeum* number. VW noted that the issue was scrapped; government intervention prevented publication of LW's article on the strike (*DVW,* III, p. 83 and *LVW* III, pp. 260–61 and notes).

C0698 THE ART OF THOUGHT. WOB. *Nation & Athenaeum,* 22 May 1926, 178.
Review of *The Art of Thought,* by Graham Wallas; and *The Language and Thought of the Child,* by Jean Piaget.
Little is known on the subject. Wallas's book promises more than it achieves. His most important section has to do with the stages of thought. Leisure is essential for the period of incubation. Our present system of education militates against leisure.

C0699 RACIAL FANTASIES. WOB. *Nation & Athenaeum,* 29 May 1926, 209.
Review of *To-day and To-morrow; The Testing Period of the White Race,* by J. H. Curle; and *Race and History, an Ethnological Introduction to History,* by Eugene Pittard.
No illusions are quite so persistent as those connected with race. Curle is racially biased. Pittard finds no scientific evidence for such bias. Racial fantasizers always find their own race superior and are horrified by the idea of miscegenation.

C0700 FROM TALLYRAND TO MR. HARRIMAN. WOB. *Nation & Athenaeum,* 5 June 1926, 250.
Review of *The Romantic Diplomat,* by M. Paléologue; and *Dollar Diplomacy,* by Scott Nearing and Joseph Freeman.
Mr. Paléologue, who sketches the lives of Talleyrand, Metternich and Chateaubriand, is a better biographer than historian. *Dollar Diplomacy* shows that financiers have replaced statesmen.
Part of "Statesmen and Diplomatists" in *Essays,* A24.

C0701 RATIONALISM AND RELIGION. WOB. *Nation & Athenaeum,* 12 June 1926, 279.
Review of *Essays on Religion,* by A. Clutton-Brock; *The Dynamics of Religion,* New ed., by J. M. Robertson; *The Religion of an Artist,* by John Collier; and *Death-Bed Visions,* by Sir William Barrett.

"Being a rationalist, I am on the side of Mr. Robertson and Mr. Collier, and the religious will therefore consider that this puts me out of court for discussing the subject. Perhaps it does, for it is a fact that I simply cannot understand the frame of mind in which the late Mr. Clutton-Brock wrote these essays. . . . Like a number of people, I think, he believed in God because he found it intolerable not to believe in God. He argued himself into a position in which he had to say that the universe is 'cold, indifferent, and meaningless to us' if there be no God; and then recoiling from the next step, from saying that the universe is cold, indifferent, and meaningless to us (as it so obviously is), he was left with the only alternative of believing in the existence of God."

C0702   GEORGE MEREDITH. WOB. *Nation & Athenaeum*, 19 June 1926, 323.
Review of *George Meredith*, by J. B. Priestley.
Except for a tone of defence or apology which leads to over-emphasis on praise, this is a good book.

C0703   "PLEASE, SIR. . . ." WOB. *Nation & Athenaeum*, 26 June 1926, 355.
Review of *The Memoirs of Raymond Poincaré*, translated and adapted by Sir George Arthur; *The Limitations of Victory*, by M. Fabre-Luce, tr. into English; and *Sarajevo*, by R. W. Seton-Watson.
These authors' attempts to place the blame for the war on someone else are simply disgusting.
Changed, forms part of "Please, Sir, it was the Other Fellow" in *Essays . . .* 1927, A24, pp. 198, and 204–07.

C0704   RATIONALISM AND RELIGION. *Nation & Athenaeum*, 3 July 1926, 381.
Letter to the Editor replying to J. Adler's criticism of his June 12 article, C0701.

C0705   "QUEERISH TALK IN THE CIRCUMSTANCES". WOB. *Nation & Athenaeum*, 3 July 1926, 386.
Review of 4 books by Walter de la Mare: *The Connoisseur; Memoirs of a Midget; Henry Brocken;* and *The Return;* and of *Modern English Fiction*, by Gerald Bullett.
The title of this article, taken from one of de la Mare's stories, is a better description of his prose than Mr. Bullett's unreserved praise.

C0706   ENGLISH HISTORY. WOB. *Nation & Athenaeum*, 10 July 1926, 418.
Review of *History of England*, by G. M. Trevelyan.
This useful history compares favourably with Green's *Short History of the English People*. The titles reflect the shift in emphasis with the "ebb in the tide of democracy, which has shown itself particularly sensitive to the malign influence of nationality and nationalism."

C0707   RATIONALISM AND RELIGION. *Nation & Athenaeum*, 17 July 1926, 440–41.
Letter replying to criticism by H. G. Wood printed in this issue.
LW admits that his opinions reflect his own experience and observations and says Wood's suggestion of a canvas of reader opinion is being considered.

C0708   IN THE CAVE. WOB. *Nation & Athenaeum*, 17 July 1926, 446.
Review of *Must Britain Travel the Moscow Road?* by Norman Angell; and *The Creed of a Tory*, by Pierse Loftus.
Angell's book is a devastating answer to Trotsky who insists that revolution is the only way to socialism. "If you want to see the delusions of conservatism at its best, you should read 'The Creed of a Tory' by Pierse

Loftus." Despite their opposing views both Trotsky and Loftus have their heads in the cave.

C0709 THE HOHENZOLLERN MIND. WOB. *Nation & Athenaeum*, 24 July 1926, 474.
Review of *I Seek the Truth: a Book on Responsibility for the War*, by ex-Crown Prince Wilhelm of Germany.
> The author has joined the chorus of voices blaming the other fellow for a war for which they were all responsible. "I do not like to see a fly struggling to extricate itself from a spider's web, even when it is the fly's fault that it is there, and even when the fly is an unpleasant fly."

Portions integrated into "Please, Sir, It was the Other Fellow" in *Essays . . .* 1927, A24. pp. 198 and 206–11. Two letters on "Rationalism and Religion" were printed in the July 24 issue of the *N & A*, p. 458.

C0710 RATIONALISM AND RELIGION. *Nation & Athenaeum*, 31 July 1926, 498.
Letter replying to several letters criticising C0701. Three letters to the editor in the *N & A*, 31 July 1926, pp. 497–98, concern articles by LW, C0701, C0703 and C0709.

C0711 FIELDING'S NOVELS. WOB. *Nation & Athenaeum*, 31 July 1926, 502.
Review of *The Life of Mr. Jonathan Wild the Great*, by Henry Fielding. Limited ed.
> This sustained satire is really more interesting than Fielding's novels, for his characters are very simple. This may be the reason that Logan Pearsall Smith did not include quotations from Fielding's work in *A Treasury of English Prose*. Critics, including Leslie Stephen, usually consider Fielding as a moralist, but Fielding saw himself as "a philosophic delineator of life in its widest sense".

C0712 SIR ROGER CASEMENT AND CHARLES PEACE. WOB. *Nation & Athenaeum*, 7 August 1926, 530.
Review of *Trial of Roger Casement*, ed. by G. H. Knott; *Scotland Yard*, by Joseph Gollomb; *Black Fame*, by J. C. Ellis; *Carlo Guesaldo, Musician and Murderer*, by Cecil Gray and Philip Heseltine; and *The Rise and Fall of Jesse James*, by Robertus Love.
> These books illustrate the interesting differences in the way men manage their affairs. The trial of Roger Casement illustrates the absurdity of applying outmoded laws. Was his treason really more heinous than the crime of Charles Peace who actually attended the trial of the innocent man convicted in his stead?

LW did not answer the criticism in a letter to the editor August 14, which holds that treason is the worst crime.

C0713 RELIGIOUS BELIEF: AN INQUIRY. *Nation & Athenaeum*, 14 August 1926, 547.
Unsigned announcement.
> There will be a canvas of religious opinions by a questionnaire inserted in the following issue.

C0714 GOTTERDAMMERUNG. WOB. *Nation & Athenaeum*, 14 August 1926, 558.
Review of *The Decline of the West*, by Oswald Spengler. Authorized translation with notes by Charles F. Atkinson, vol. I (vol. II reviewed C0915).
> Spengler's central thesis, that historical events have neither cause nor effect, is "mere moonshine, when it is not the fog of a muddled mind".

C0715 THE NATION QUESTIONNAIRE. *Nation & Athenaeum*, 21 August 1926, 575.

Unsigned announcement.

The "Questionnaire on Religious Belief," drawn up in consultation with H. G. Wood, G. Bernard Shaw, J. M. Robertson, and Augustine Birrell, will be found on a separate sheet in this issue.

C0716 QUESTIONNNAIRE ON RELIGIOUS BELIEF. Headed SUPPLEMENT TO THE NATION. *Nation & Athenaeum*, 21 August 1926.

A separate leaf or broadside, included again August 28.

C0717 QUESTIONNNAIRE ON RELIGIOUS BELIEF. *Daily News*, 21 August 1926, p. 7, cols. 1 and 2.

Worded as in the *N & A*, (C0716) with added instructions to cut out and send to the editor of *Daily News*.

In *The State of Religious Belief: an Inquiry Based on "The Nation & Athenaeum" Questionnaire* (L. & V. Woolf at the Hogarth Press, 1927), R. B. Braithwaite says that LW prepared the questionnaire. He thanks LW for assistance and suggestions in writing the book.

C0718 THE APOLLINIAN SOUL. WOB. *Nation & Athenaeum*, 21 August 1926, 586.

Review of 6 books in Heinemann's Loeb Classical Library: *Laws*, Books I-VI, by Plato; *De Corona*, and *De Falsa Legatione*, by Demosthenes; *Lives of Aratus, Artaxerxes, and Galba and Otho*, by Plutarch; *Discourses*, Books I & II, by Epictetus; *The Life*, and *Against Apion*, by Josephus; Pausanias, Books III & IV; and *Hellenic Civilization*, by Maurice Croiset (Knopf).

These books show the remarkable intellectuality of the Greeks, but it is impossible to find in them a trace of the Apollinian soul about which Spengler discourses.

C0719 THE ART OF CRICKET. WOB. *Nation & Athenaeum*, 28 August 1926, 614.

Review of *Between the Wickets*, compiled by Eric Parker.

Cricket is a genuine art. Like literature it has traditions and styles and developments. Just now cricket seems to be in its silver age, that of innovation and imitation. (LW read 3 other books on sports to help confirm this theory.)

Note: THE QUESTIONNAIRE. LETTERS TO THE EDITOR, from Julian Huxley, Walter Hill and B. Pratt, on choice of questions, Sept. 4, pp. 635–36.

C0720 POLITICAL RATIONALISM. WOB. *Nation & Athenaeum*, 4 September 1926, 642.

Review of *An Inquiry Concerning Political Justice and Its Influence on General Virtue and Happiness*, by William Godwin, ed. and abridged by R. A. Preston.

One is glad to have read it, but "it is an exasperating, an excruciating book, and only a determined reader will ever get to the end of it. . . . The hard, dry, remorseless paragraphs succeed one another, until at last one gets the feeling that one is sitting in a chair of a mental dentist."

C0721 THE QUESTIONNAIRE. *Nation & Athenaeum*, September 1926, 663.

Unsigned tabulation of the first results. To the question Do you believe in a personal God? the answers were: Yes 537; No 736; No Answer 65.

A similar tabulation headed "Their Religion" appeared in *Daily News*, September 12, p. 6, column 3.

C0722 MR. GALSWORTHY. WOB. *Nation & Athenaeum*, 11 September 1926, 674.

Review of *The Silver Spoon*, by John Galsworthy.
Even as a social document it is weak because Galsworthy's "view of Society is both superficial and unreal".

C0723 THE QUESTIONNAIRE: RESULTS TO SEPTEMBER 14. *Nation & Athenaeum*, 18 September 1926, 691.
Daily News published a similar tabulation headed "Questionnaire Figures." Final Analysis, 16 September, p. 6, columns 1 & 2.
Letter to Editor on "The Questionnaire" from G. E. Wright, Sept. 18, p. 697.

C0724 BOGEYS. WOB. *Nation & Athenaeum*, 18 September 1926, 703.
Review of *Essays on Nationalism*, by Carlton J. H. Hayes; and *The Twilight of the White Races*, by Maurice Muret, tr. by Mrs. Touzalin.
Professor Hayes of Columbia University has written an excellent book about nationalism which has become a religion and a curse. "M. Muret is bogey-ridden by nationalism" and fearful of threats to what he regards as white superiority.

C0725 MR. WELLS v. MR. BELLOC. WOB. *Nation & Athenaeum*, 25 September 1926, 735.
Review of *Mr. Belloc Objects*, by H. G. Wells.
This is Wells's reply to articles in which Belloc tried to prove Wells's ignorance of the origin of man in his *Outline of History*. The Catholic magazines in which Belloc attacked Wells refused to print Wells's replies. "I am definitely on Mr. Wells's side. . . . To Mr. Wells life in the universe is 'a steadily changing system,' and the individual life is comparatively unimportant. It is an episode which ends, though life goes on."
Note: Letter on "The Questionnaire" from A. S. Davies, p. 730.

C0726 WHITEWASH. *Nation & Athenaeum*, 2 October 1926, 766.
Review of *George IV*, by Shane Leslie.
The author's efforts to whitewash George IV by slapdash cleverness fail to hide that bad king's faults.

C0727 MR. WELLS v. MR. BELLOC. *Nation & Athenaeum*, 9 October 1926, p. 18.
Letter to the Editor in reply to Belloc's.
LW says Belloc misquoted him.
Three letters to the editor concern LW's articles of September 25, C0725. They are "The Catholic Church", "Mr. Wells v. Mr. Belloc", and "Those Purists Again". LW replied only to the one from Belloc.

C0728 THE PUBLISHING SEASON. WOB. *Nation & Athenaeum*, 9 October 1926, 24.
Estimate of the books about to be published, with listing by categories.

C0729 THE QUESTIONNAIRE: FINAL RESULTS. *Nation & Athenaeum*, 9 October 1926, 75–76.
Unsigned article.
To the results of the responses from readers of the *N & A* are added the results of responses from readers of *Daily News*.
Note: See Letter from Stanley Cook, *N & A*, 16 October 1926, p. 79 and article by H. G. Wood, "The Questionnaire", pp. 82–83.

C0730 LORD RAINGO. WOB. *Nation & Athenaeum*, 16 October 1926, 86.
Review of *Lord Raingo*, by Arnold Bennett.
The book wobbles. Mr. Bennett's method is inadequate to handle his mixture of fictional characters with real people.

C0731 THE CLASS WAR. LETTERS TO THE EDITOR. *Nation & Athenaeum*, 23 October 1926, 108.

Letter concerning a controversy already raging in the paper.

    LW explains why a number of pacifists, including himself, are members of the Labour Party. He contends that Liberals, like Conservatives, are causing the class war by trying to maintain the status quo of the capitalist system.

The Editor comments that Woolf's syllogism shows "the fallacy of the 'undistributed middle'".

C0732 THE POWER OF THE EGO. WOB. *Nation & Athenaeum,* 23 October 1926, 114.

Review of 5 autobiograpical books: *Prison Memories of an Anarchist,* by Alexander Berkman; *A Great Niece's Journals,* by Mrs. [Fanny Anne Burney] Wood; *The Days of My Life,* by H. Rider Haggard; *The Fire of Life,* by Harold Spender; and *My Reminiscences,* by Victor Sampson.

    Their authors' interest in the subjects is what makes these books interesting.

C0733 PUBLISHERS AND OLD BOOKS. WOB. *Nation & Athenaeum,* 30 October 1926, 148.

Review of *The Truth About Publishing,* by Stanley Unwin; with mention of a large number of reprints: Jane Austen's works; Noel Douglas replicas of Shakespeare's Sonnets and Blake's Poetical Sketches; *The Travels of Marco Polo,* edited by John Masefield; *The Life of Benvenuto Cellini,* tr. by Anne MacDonnell; *Moby Dick, A Selection of the Principal Navigations . . .* by Hakluyt; and *Irene Iddesleigh,* by Amanda Ros.

Article by J. M. Robertson on "That Questionnaire". *Nation & Athenaeum,* November 6, pp. 174–75.

C0734 THE ALL-HIGHEST. WOB. *Nation & Athenaeum,* 6 November 1926, 184.

Review of *Kaiser Wilhelm II,* by Emil Ludwig, tr. from the German by Ethel Mayne; with mention of *Chronicles of the Prussian Court,* by Miss Topham.

    "The System which allows a man like the Kaiser to have anything to do with government stands self-condemned."

C0735 THE SUM OF ALL VILLANIES [*sic*]. WOB. *Nation & Athenaeum,* 13 November 1926, 220.

Review of *British Slavery and Its Abolition, 1823–1838,* by William Law Mathieson.

    The move to abolish the slave trade "is one of the few instances in history of large masses of people being deeply stirred by a political principle which appeared to have no effect upon their material interests." The book throws light on the anti-slavery principle, a peculiar example of communal psychology which turned into political action.

C0736 SUGAR AND SOAP AND SALT. WOB. *Nation & Athenaeum,* 20 November 1926, 271.

Review of *My Early Life,* by William II of Germany; and *H.R.H., A Character Study of the Prince of Wales,* by Major F. E. Verney.

    To get the sugar and soap of sentimentality out of the mouth after reading these two books it was necessary to read four more books with the salt of reality.

C0737 MR. ROGER FRY. WOB. *Nation & Athenaeum,* 27 November 1926, 304.

Review of *Transformations,* by Roger Fry.

    Mr. Fry has completely overhauled his theory of form and aesthetic emotion.

C0738 FAITH AND THE SLAVE TRADE. *Nation & Athenaeum*, 4 December 1926, 333.
Letter to the editor replying to the second of 2 articles by John Lee inspired by "The Questionnaire" and "The Sum of All Villanies [*sic*]", C0735.

C0739 PALMERSTON. WOB. *Nation & Athenaeum*, 4 December 1926, 230.
Review of *Palmerston*, by Philip Guedalla.
Guedalla uses a method similar to that of Carl Sandberg in his life of Lincoln to set off the statesman against a kaleidoscope of events. All he achieves is a blur.

C0740 CARLYLE. WOB. *Nation & Athenaeum*, 11 December 1926, 388.
Review of *Thomas Carlyle*, by Mary Agnes Hamilton.
Carlyle was a prophet in the Old Testament sense. The Victorian age was one of faith, but because Carlyle demands belief he has no message for current readers.

C0741 FAITH AND THE SLAVE TRADE. *Nation & Athenaeum*, 11 December 1926, 418.
Letter concerning Mr. Lee's of December 11.

C0742 COBDEN AND COBDENISM. WOB. *Nation & Athenaem*, 18 December 1926, 424.
Review of *Richard Cobden and Foreign Policy*, by W. H. Dawson.
This is a good history and a useful book for those who want to understand foreign policy today. If Cobden were alive now he would favour a League of Nations.

C0743 THE PSYCHOLOGY OF METHODISM. WOB. *Nation & Athenaeum*, 24 December 1926, 454.
Review of *The Psychology of the Methodist Revival*, by Sydney G. Dimond; and *Up from Methodism, A Study in Religious Tolerance*, by Herbert Ashbury.
The first book is scientific and overly detailed. The second is autobiographical.

1927

C0744 LIFE THAT IS A VISION. WOB. *Nation & Athenaeum*, 1 January 1927, 482.
Review article on: *Autobiographies* . . . by William Butler Yeats; *Memoir of Jane Austen*, by James E. Austen-Leigh; *The Passionate Pilgrim*, by Francis Turner Palgrave; and *The Adventures of Johnny Walker, Tramp*, by W. H. Davies.
The authors' different visions make these books interesting.

C0745 DISRAELI THE NOVELIST. WOB. *Nation & Athenaeum*, 8 January 1927, 510.
Review of 3 of the Bradenham Edition of Disraeli's works: *Vivian Grey; The Young Duke;* and *Popanilla and other Tales* (P. Davies).
Leslie Stephen remarked on Disraeli's "faculty of gliding imperceptibly from jest to earnest", but "lamented 'the degradation of a promising novelist into a prime minister'". Disraeli was more than promising. "His satire is nearly always amusing, often brilliant, and occasionally profound." It is worth being republished in this well-printed, handsomely bound, centenary edition.

C0746 SHAKESPEARE AND MACHIAVELLI. WOB. *Nation & Athenaeum*, 15 January 1927, 539.

Review of *The Lion and the Fox, the Role of the Hero in the Plays of Shakespeare*, by Wyndham Lewis.

Mr. Lewis maintains that Shakespeare incorporated Machiavelli's two types of men, the lion-man and the fox-man, into his plays, and that the plays show that Shakespeare had a poor opinion of "the world of action and the great actors in it".

C0747 ANTHONY TROLLOPE. WOB. *Nation & Athenaeum*, 22 January 1927, 565.

Review of *Trollope, A Commentary*, by Michael Sadleir; and *The Warden*, by Anthony Trollope, a reprint (E. Matthews).

Trollope's novels were appreciated in his own day, lost popularity after his death, and are now about to be rediscovered. Mr. Sadleir has written the best biography to date. *The Warden* contains examples of the best and poorest of Trollope's characterizations.

C0748 THE APOTHEOSIS OF JOURNALISM. WOB. *Nation & Athenaeum*, 29 January 1927, 594.

Review of *The Making of Modern Journalism*, by Harold Herd.

Mr. Herd's account includes all the roses but none of the thorns of modern journalism. The syndicate is the apotheosis of journalism. Mr. Walter Lippmann has ably analyzed the problems of modern journalism and its dependence upon advertising in *Public Opinion*.

C0749 JOHN MORLEY. WOB. *Nation & Athenaeum*, 5 February 1927, 663.

Review of *Early Life and Letters of John Morley*, by F. W. Hirst.

The letters Morley wrote when he was editor of the *Fortnightly* and the *Pall Mall Gazette*, particularly those to Frederic Harrison, record his development from a journalist to a politician and the evolution of his political views into the principles of Liberalism.

C0750 BRITISH GENIUS. WOB. *Nation & Athenaeum*, 12 February 1927, 663.

Review of *A Study of British Genius*, by Havelock Ellis, revised and enlarged edition.

For the purposes of his study Mr. Ellis equates "genius" with "eminence". He chose people included in the *Dictionary of National Biography*. His most interesting chapter deals with the pathology of genius, but the evidence he presents in his attempt to correlate eminence with ill-health is not very convincing.

C0751 POLITICAL IDEAS AND POLITICAL DELUSIONS. WOB. *Nation & Athenaeum*, 19 February 1927, 698.

Review of *The Science and Method of Politics*, by G. E. G. Catlin. *Notes on Democracy*, by H. L. Mencken; and *Political Myths and Economic Realities*, by Francis Delaisi.

There are two opposing schools of political psychology: (1) political ideas cause political action; and (2) the political actions of kings, aristocrats, statesmen and intellectuals are occasionally rational, but those of the people are irrational. Mr. Delaisi's political theories are sounder than those of Mr. Catlin or Mr. Mencken, but he should not assume that all political beliefs are necessarily delusions.

C0752 DETECTIVE STORIES. WOB. *Nation & Athenaeum*, 26 February 1927, 727.

Review of *The Mystery of Belvoir Mansions*, by Ben Bolt; *The Colfax Book-plate*, by Agnes Miller; *The Big Four*, by Agatha Christie; *The Three Taps*, by Ronald A. Knox; and *The Crime at Diana's Pool*, by Victor L Whitechurch.

"A crime, a mystery, and a detective will make almost any novel, however bad it may be in other respects, readable." The best detective stories give enough information for the reader to participate actively in finding out the solution.

C0753   ITALIAN IMPERIALISM. *Labour Monthly; a Magazine of International Labour*, IX.2, February 1927, 105–11.

Article by L.W.

Motivated by a search for territory, the alleged attempt on Mussolini in 1926 was followed by a wave of terror. Besides the Fascists, only the Communist Party is able to function in Italy. [The article includes figures from the *Manchester Guardian*, 27 July, 1926.]

C0754   OLD EUROPE. WOB. *Nation & Athenaeum*, 5 March 1927, 760.

Review of 3 books: *A Diplomatist in Europe*, by Sir Arthur Hardinge; *Under Three Emperors*, by Baron von Reischach. English tr. of his reminiscences by Prince Blücher; and *Disraeli*, by D. L. Murray.

These books present a curious panorama of the world which was exploded by the First World War. "Mr. Murray's biographical study is the best that has been written in two years", but he places too much emphasis on Disraeli's Jewishness and too little on "his habit of treating politics as if it were the subject of a novel or a play."

C0755   THE PROMISE OF SPRING. WOB. *Nation & Athenaeum*, 12 March 1927, 798.

C0756   ON ADVERTISING BOOKS. *Nation & Athenaeum*, 19 March 1927, 848–49.

Feature article, third in a series entitled "Books and the Public", begun February 26 in the *N & A*.

Publishers advertise to sell books and to please authors. Advertising is probably not very effective for selling books unless there have first been good reviews.

LW and VW republished this series at the Hogarth Press in 1927 under the title *Books and the Public*, by the Editor of the *Nation* [Hubert Douglas Henderson], J. M. Keynes, Stanley Unwin... Leonard Woolf.... "On Advertising Books" is on pp. 48–52 (B16).

C0757   THE EPIC OF MODERN MAN. WOB. *Nation & Athenaeum*, 19 March 1927, 857.

Review of *Revolt in the Desert*, by T. E. Lawrence.

"The book is a minor and a modern epic." The style imitates Doughty's *Arabia Deserta*. The story has an epic quality, but the book has not the dignity or calm of the writings of Caesar or Marco Polo, for Lawrence is given to the psychological introspection of modern man.

C0758   THE MAN BEETHOVEN. WOB. *Nation & Athenaeum*, 26 March 1927, 894.

Review of 5 books: *Beethoven*, by W. J. Turner; *The Unconscious Beethoven*, by Ernest Newman; *Beethoven, the Man*, by André de Hevesy, tr. by Mr. Flint; *Beethoven*, by Harvey Grace; and *Beethoven's Pianoforte Sonatas*, by William Behrend.

The first two books are the best. In his attempt to correct the earlier adulatory biographies of Beethoven, Mr. Grace gives as wrong an impression as they do. Whether Beethoven washed himself, or spat in the drawing-room, is not relevant to his music.

C0759   THE ARMSTRONG CASE. WOB. *Nation & Athenaeum*, 2 April 1927, 927.

Review of *Herbert Rowse Armstrong,* ed. by Filson Young.

The author thinks highly of Mr. Justice Darling's handling of the case. Whether one agrees depends on what one considers a judge's duty. Should he be impartial or side with the prosecution?

C0760 THE EIGHTEENTH CENTURY. WOB. *Nation & Athenaeum,* 9 April 1927, 18.

Review of 4 books published by Routledge: *Dialogues,* by Denis Diderot, tr. by Francis Birrell; *The Sofa: a Moral Tale,* by Crébillon fils, tr. by B. Dobrée; *Letters of Voltaire and Frederick the Great,* tr. by Richard Aldington; and *Voltaire's Candide and Other Romances,* tr. by R. Aldington.

The literary art of the 18th century was never vague, but never profound.

There were no WORLD OF BOOKS articles on 16 and 23 April 1927.

C0761 GULLIVER'S TRAVELS. WOB. *Nation & Athenaeum,* 30 April 1927.

Review of *Gulliver's Travels,* by Jonathan Swift. First Edition Club reprint.

Swift achieved his effects through the plainest, simplest language. "It is probably the best and certainly the most devastating 'satire' ever written."

C0762 OLD BOOKS IN NEW COVERS. WOB. *Nation & Athenaeum,* 7 May 1927, 152.

Review of the Shakespeare Head Edition of the Writings of Laurence Sterne (B. Blackwell).

Nineteeth-century writers, including Sir Leslie Stephen and Sir Edmund Gosse, apologized for Sterne's writing because of his love affairs, obscenities, profanities and frivolities. People have only to read Sterne's writing and his biography by Wilbur Cross to see that he was a great writer.

C0763 ANCIENT BEST-SELLERS. WOB. *Nation & Athenaeum,* 14 May 1927, 186.

Review of *The Light Reading of Our Ancestors,* by Lord Ernle.

The author spoiled his book by never deciding on his subject. He did not distinguish between the 'literary novel' and the 'light reading' of ordinary people. Only someone with a passion for facts could read the book at all.

C0764 EDMUND BURKE. WOB. *Nation & Athenaeum,* 21 May 1927, 218.

Review of *Edmund Burke,* by Bertram Newman.

"Well written, well informed, sober, judicious . . . a readable and serious attempt to make us see Burke as a solid figure in the life that he lived, the thoughts that he thought, and the books that he spoke or wrote." But the author sees Burke as a great thinker. He was a great writer and orator, but not a profound philosopher.

C0765 THE GREATNESS OF GREAT MEN. WOB. *Nation & Athenaeum,* 28 May 1927, 263.

Review of 3 books: *A Great Man's Friendship,* ed. by Lady Burghclere; *Cavour.* by Maurice Paléologue. English translation; and *British Foreign Secretaries, 1807–1916,* by Algernon Cecil.

The first book contains the letters of the Duke of Wellington to Mary, Marchioness of Salisbury, 1850–52. They show that his greatness was rooted in his granitic character. M. Paléologue's spirited and readable biography shows that Cavour was a statesman who may be compared to Bismarck. In Cecil's book one sees "what different shapes and sizes the greatness of great men may assume".

C0766 CRIME AND PUNISHMENT. WOB. *Nation & Athenaeum,* 4 June 1927, 307.

Review of *Capital Punishment in the Twentieth Century,* by E. Roy Calvert; *The Convict of Today,* by Sidney A. Moseley; and *The Psychology of Murder,* by Andreas Bjerre.

Calvert's book is "sloppy, sentimental, and superficial"; Moseley's is an admirable, quiet, intelligent examination of the question. The Swedish lawyer and psychologist, Bjerre, has written "a minute analysis of the crimes and minds of three murderers", showing that fear of punishment does not deter murderers. LW includes observations he made as a civil servant in Ceylon.

C0767 NATIONALITY AND RACE. WOB. *Nation & Athenaeum,* 11 June 1927, 339.

Review of *National Character, and the Factors in Its Formation,* by Ernest Barker.

In the frightening climate of delusions about national and racial superiority it is refreshing to find a book which refers to facts and history.

C0768 MAN AND ? [*sic*] WOB. *Nation & Athenaeum,* 18 June 1927, 371.

Review of *John Sargent,* by Evan Charteris.

Charteris is an adequate biographer of Sargent as a man, but he fails to show what else Sargent was. Sargent's definition of impressionism shows that he did not know what he meant; his pictures show that he considered art to be mere representation.

C0769 SARGENT ON IMPRESSIONISM. WOB. *Nation & Athenaeum,* 25 June 1927, 410.

Letter to the Editor replying to one signed "Siela" in the same issue which said Sargent's definition is perfectly clear. LW says neither Sargent nor Siela defined impressionism. Francis Hackett objected to LW's article in a letter published 2 July 1927.

C0770 OLD BOOKS, OLD AUTHORS, AND OLD PUBLISHERS. WOB. *Nation & Athenaeum,* June 1927, 416.

Review of *Authorship in the Days of Johnson,* by A. S. Collins; and *Shadows of the Old Booksellers,* by Charles Knight. Introduction by Stanley Unwin.

Mr. Collins' book "gives the facts about authorship and the book trade during the critical years which gave birth to the modern system of publishing." On the whole the present system seems better for authors than the patronage system.

C0771 BEN JONSON. WOB. *Nation & Athenaeum,* 2 July 1927, 447.

Review of the 3rd volume of Jonson's works, *Ben Jonson,* ed. by C. H. Herford and Percy Simpson.

Ben Jonson ranks just below the greatest of English writers.

C0772 "ONE DAY . . ." WOB. *Nation & Athenaeum,* 9 July 1927, 480.

Review of 2 books and mention of others: *Memoirs of an Eighteenth Century Footman, John Macdonald: Travels, 1745–1779,* ed. by John Beresford; and *Memoirs of Mary Wollstonecraft,* by William Godwin, ed. by Clark Durant.

Beresford should be commended for the editing of a new edition of Macdonald's travels. Even the editing of Mr. Durant "cannot spoil Mary Wollstonecraft's charm and Godwin's magnificent grotesqueness."

C0773 ANIMAL LIFE. WOB. *Nation & Athenaeum,* 16 July 1927, 515.

Review of 5 books: *Moses, My Otter,* by Frances Pitt; *Tropical Aquarium Fishes . . .* by A. E. Hodge; *Bird Life at Home and Abroad,* by T. A. Coward; *How Birds Live,* by E. M. Nicholson; and *Social Life in the Animal World,* by Fr. Alverdes.

"The dog-lover yields to the primitive desire to make a friend of an animal; the cat-lover is attracted by the cold and formal beauty of animals; the bird-lover deep down has the scientific passion for classification and knowledge."

A letter to the editor signed "Felix" objects to LW's classification, *N & A*, 30 July 1927, p. 574–75.

C0774   THE NUMBER OF THE BEAST. WOB. *Nation & Athenaeum*, 23 July 1927, 549.

Review of *The Mind and Face of Bolshevism*, by René Fülöp-Miller.

This silly, prejudiced book is completely undocumented but has interesting parts.

C0775   THE DECLINE AND FALL OF MONARCHY. WOB. *Nation & Athenaeum*, 30 July 1927, 580.

Review of *The Memoirs of Catherine the Great of Russia*, ed. by Katherine Anthony; and *Franz Joseph as Revealed by His Letters*, ed. by Otto Ernst and tr. by Agnes Blake.

These books are psychologically fascinating.

C0776   THE BIG DRUMMERS. WOB. *Nation & Athenaeum*, 6 August 1927, 669.

Review of *Struggles & Triumphs, or The Life of P. T. Barnum Written by Himself*, 2 vols, ed. by George S. Bryan; and *Trumpets of Jubilee*, by Constance M. Rourke.

Barnum's book, like his circus, is at once impressive and disgusting. Miss Rourke's book about drum-beaters shows what terrific energy the Beechers, Horace Greeley, and Barnum all had. Neither book has the charm of Sanger's (see C0693).

C0777   "A FILTHY LITTLE ATHEIST". WOB. *Nation & Athenaeum*, 13 August 1927, 638.

Review of *Thomas Paine, Prophet and Martyr of Democracy*, by Mary Agnes Best.

The late President Roosevelt called Paine "a filthy little atheist". "Leslie Stephen said 'good Englishmen expressed their disgust by calling him Tom'". Stephen also commented on Paine's "vast ignorance". Miss Best shows that Paine had vast knowledge and great range of interest and thought, but her book is not well-written. No adequate biography of Paine has been written and his own books are neglected.

Charles A. Watts of the Rationalist Press Association, Ltd. takes issue with the last sentence in a letter published 2 September 1927, recommends Moncure Conway's *Life*, and says *Age of Reason* is still a best-seller.

C0778   THE REVOLT AGAINST EUROPE. WOB. *Nation & Athenaeum*, 20 August 1927, 666.

Review of *A Survey of International Affairs, 1925; vol. I: The Islamic World . . .* by Arnold J. Toynbee.

The Islamic World's revolt against western imperialism has led to the growth of nationalism, and curiously enough, to westernization of the revolters.

C0779   FROM SOCRATES TO SACCO. WOB. *Nation & Athenaeum*, 27 August 1927, 695.

Review of *Historical Trials*, by Sir John Macdonnell, ed. by R. W. Lee.

The Sacco and Vanzetti trial was judicial murder. Reading this book one gets the impression that the law is a horrible thing. Justice is never "evenhanded" in cases involving "religion, patriotism, politics, or class-interests".

Reprinted, changed, in *The Living Age*, C0793.

C0780 THE GENTLENESS OF NATURE. *Asia*, XXVII.8, August 1927, 670, 685–86.

Reprint of article first published in *New Statesman*, C0144. This printing includes a photograph of a stockade enclosing elephants captured in Ceylon.

C0781 THE HEART AND NOT THE BRAIN. WOB. *Nation & Athenaeum*, 3 September 1927, 722.

Review of *A Victorian American, Henry Wadsworth Longfellow*, by Herbert S. Gorman; and *The Golden Day, A Study in American Experience and Culture*, by Lewis Mumford.

His application of Strachey's formula for *Queen Victoria* has ruined Gorman's style and method. The book gives the reader no idea of Longfellow, who "wrote bathos in doggerel, which both he and his contemporaries genuinely mistook for poetry."

The *N & A* published numerous letters to the editor disputing LW's appraisal of Longfellow.

C0782 RHAPSODY OR DUSTY ANSWER? WOB. *Nation & Athenaeum*, 10 September 1927, 749.

Review of *Dusty Answer*, by Rosamond Lehmann; *Rhapsody*, by Dorothy Edwards; and *Faint Amorist*, by Elizabeth Sprigge.

Dorothy Edwards has written the best of these books; Miss Lehmann shows promise; but Miss Sprigge's book is stiff.

C0783 MONTAIGNE. WOB. *Nation & Athenaeum*, 17 September 1927, 778.

Review of *The Essays of Montaigne*, tr. by E. J. Trechmann, with Introduction, by J. M. Robertson.

This is a good translation, but the original French is better. To understand the irony with which Montaigne attacked the religious beliefs that made France intolerable in his day it is essential to know his exact words.

C0784 WAS LONGFELLOW A POET? *Nation & Athenaeum*, 24 September 1927, 801.

Letter replying to correspondents who attacked his article, C0780. LW asks whether they can be serious.

C0785 THE TWO JOURNALISTS. WOB. *Nation & Athenaeum*, 24 September 1927, 806.

Review of *Life, Journalism, and Politics*, by J. A. Spender; and *Lord Northcliffe, A Study*, by R. Macnair Wilson.

Mr. Spender's is a model of what an autobiography should be; Mr. Wilson's of what it should not.

C0786 WHO WON WATERLOO? *Nation & Athenaeum*, 1 October 1927, 835.

Letter to the Editor supplying additional information to an article by Mr. Postgate on Waterloo myths.

C0787 TOLSTOY'S DIARY. WOB. *Nation & Athenaeum*, 1 October 1927, 840.

Review of *The Private Diary of Leo Tolstoy, 1853–1857*, tr. by Mr. and Mrs. Maude.

Tolstoy's son is responsible for the expurgation which has destroyed much of the interest of this book. Like everything about Tolstoy, his diary both fascinates and repels.

C0788 THE AUTUMN CROP. WOB. *Nation & Athenaeum*, 8 October 1927, 22.

C0789 LANDOR. WOB. *Nation & Athenaeum*, 15 October 1927, 86.
Review of *The Complete Works of Walter Savage Landor*, vols I & II of XVI (Chapman & Hall).

> Why should so noble a monument be raised to an author so seldom read by anyone? Leslie Stephen's essay in *Hours in a Library* shows that previous generations did not find his work readable either. Landor always wrote as though he were competing for a university prize.

C0790 "TO SEE THE KINGS GO RIDING BY". WOB. *Nation & Athenaeum*, 22 October 1927, 118.
Feature article, listed in contents issue as "King Edward VII".
Review of 3 books: *King Edward VII, A Biography*, vol. II, by Sir Sidney Lee; *Queen Mary, A Life and Intimate Study*, by Kathleen Woodward; and *Speeches by H.R.H. the Prince of Wales, 1912–1926*.

> Two of these books are unreadable. Only in Miss Woodward's ecstatic praise of Queen Mary can the reader "see the kings go riding by".

C0791 "URN BURIAL" AND DONNE'S SERMONS. *Nation & Athenaeum*, 29 October 1927, 149.
Letter in answer to Hester W. Chapman prompted by LW's essay "Landor", C0789. LW admits he has never read Donne's sermons.

C0792 NOBLE LORDS. WOB. *Nation & Athenaeum*, 29 October 1927, 155.
Review of *The House of Lords in the Eighteenth Century*, by A. S. Turberville; and *The Transition from Aristocracy, 1832–1867*, by O. F. Christie.

> These books are a good basis for thoughts on the decline and fall of the British aristocracy, the causes of which were venality and corruption.

C0793 FROM SOCRATES TO SACCO. *The Living Age*, 1 November 1927, 771–73.
Reprint, with changes, from the *N & A*, 27 August 1927, C0779.

C0794 TWO PROFESSIONALS AND AN AMATEUR. WOB. *Nation & Athenaeum*, 5 November 1927, 187.
Review of *Bismarck*, by Emil Ludwig; *Disraeli, A Picture of the Victorian Age*, by André Maurois, tr. by Hamish Miles; and *Talleyrand, 1754–1838*, by Anna Bowman Dodd.

> The biography by Maurois, written in the modern style, is much like a soufflé. Miss Dodd's book is badly written and muddled. Herr Ludwig's book "allows one to see for one's self what the character and work of Bismarck really were . . . the bitterest minded and bitterest tongued man that has ever lived."

C0795 THE GREVILLE SCANDAL. WOB. *Nation & Athenaeum*, 12 November 1927, 224.
Review of *The Greville Diary*, 2 vols, ed. by Philip Whitwell Wilson.

> This badly edited book has no documentation. Wilson has arranged snippets of the diary by subject. He has "so snipped and muddled and comic-cut it as to make one of the most readable of books almost unreadable by anyone."

C0796 MRS. BARTLETT AND SOME OTHERS. WOB. *Nation & Athenaeum*, 19 November 1927, 279.
Review of *The Trial of Adelaide Bartlett*, ed. by Sir John Hall, with mention of several other books on crime.

> The psychologies of the people involved in the mystery of Adelaide Bartlett are fascinating.

C0797 THE ART OF REVIEWING BOOKS. WOB. *Nation & Athenaeum*, 26 November 1927, 320.
Review of *Book Reviewing*, by Wayne Gard (New York: Knopf).
American and English editors agree that a reviewer should state clearly the nature of the book and his opinion of its merits and defects. Assessing the book is the hardest part of writing a review, for books differ so greatly in kind and in quality. The reviewer must indicate clearly the scale of values he is using to measure the book he is discussing. The modern book review is too short to permit real essay-writing.
Francis Birrell commented on this column in his review of *Petty Papers*, 24 December 1927.

C0798 THE NOVEL OF TO-DAY. WOB. *Nation & Athenaeum*, 3 December 1927, 356.
Review of *Beauty and the Beast*, by Joseph Gordon Macleod; *The English Novel*, by J. B. Priestley; and *Scheherazade or The Future of the English Novel*, by John Carruthers.
The authors agree that the modern novel is in a bad way, but their prescriptions suggest that they do not suspect the depth of the disease. Masterpieces are written with a central idea which holds the book together from the first page to the last. Current novels lack a central idea.

C0799 EAST AND WEST. WOB. *Nation & Athenaeum*, 10 December 1927, 396.
Review of *East and West*, by Henri Massis, tr. by F. S. Flint, with preface by G. K. Chesterton; *The Pedigree of Fascism*, by Aline Lion; *Lenin and Gandhi*, by René Fülöp-Miller; and *Materialism and Empirio-Criticism*, by Lenin. English edition.
The authors of these books all try to diagnose the problems of Western civilization. They offer different panaceas.

C0800 JOHN WEBSTER. WOB. *Nation & Athenaeum*, 17 December 1927, 454.
Review of *Complete Works of John Webster*, 4 vols, ed. by F. L. Lucas.
This is an excellent edition of the works of an author worthy of immortality.

C0801 SHORT STORIES. WOB. *Nation & Athenaeum*, 24 December 1927, 487.
Review of *Great Short Stories of All Nations*, collected and ed. by Maxim Lieber and Blanche C. Williams; *Great Short Novels of the World*, collected and ed. by Barrett H. Clark; and *Select Tales of Tchechov*, tr. from the Russian by Constance Garnett.
"The short story is like a photograph where the novel is like a film."

C0802 POLITICS IN HORSHAM. WOB. *Nation & Athenaeum*, 31 December 1927, 515.
Review of *A Parliamentary History of Horsham, 1295–1885*, by William Albery, with an Introduction by Hilaire Belloc.
This very readable book throws light on the political psychology of England while giving a large number of facts.

1928

C0803 THE IMPERIALIST. WOB. *Nation & Athenaeum*, 7 January 1928, 541.
Review of *Rhodes: a Life*, by J. G. McDonald.
The biography is more satisfying as a picture of the man than as an assessment of his work. "Rhodes was an imperialist, and there is much more to be said against imperialism than would appear from Mr. McDonald's pages."

C0804 FOOLS CONTEST [*sic*]. WOB. *Nation & Athenaeum*, 14 January 1928, 569.

Review of *The Development of Political Ideas*, by F. J. C. Hearnshaw; and *Archon, or the Future of Government*, by Hamilton Fyfe.

These small books give a good idea of contemporary thought, especially its sceptical disillusionment with politics.

C0805 THOMAS HARDY. *Nation & Athenaeum*, 21 January 1928, 597–98.

Obituary article in appreciation of Hardy, with a reminiscence.

Hardy was the last to write novels "in the full English tradition, solid works built about a story. . . . Currently, none of the leading writers write novels in this pure tradition; they have other axes to grind. . . ." Hardy's novels might well be described as he described Egdon Heath, "majestic without severity . . . grand in simplicity", even "sublime".

C0806 QUEEN VICTORIA AND THE LIBERAL PARTY. WOB. *Nation & Athenaeum*, 21 January 1928, 617.

Review of *Letters of Queen Victoria, 1879–1885*, ed. by G. E. Buckle.

This may be the most interesting volume of her letters "owing to the amazing lack of discretion in the Queen at this period of her life." The letters show her virulent and treacherous opposition to her own government under Gladstone.

C0807 THE EDUCATION OF AN AMERICAN. WOB. *Nation & Athenaeum*, 28 January 1928, 652.

Review of *The Education of Henry Adams*. A reprint.

By writing in the third person singular and by using the pronoun "one" Henry Adams divides himself into actor and observer, creator and critic, pupil and teacher. This man, who never achieved as much as his background and qualifications suggest that he should have, considered his whole life to be his education.

C0808 THE NINETEENTH-CENTURY MIND. WOB. *Nation & Athenaeum*, 4 February 1928, 687.

Review of *Politicians and Moralists of the Nineteenth Century*, by Emile Faguet. English translation by Dorothy Galton, vol. III.

The curious mixture of scepticism and idealism included in this volume is characteristic of the nineteenth-century French mind.

C0809 THE OTHER SIDE. WOB. *Nation & Athenaeum*, 11 February 1928, 718.

Review of *The Great Problem, and Evidence of Its Solution*, by George Lindsay Johnson, with a Foreword by Sir Arthur Conan Doyle.

Doyle's observation, that Johnson's evidence about life after death is informative and consoling, "is almost more amazing than Dr. Johnson's book". It includes nothing that substantiates his claims.

C0810 WHO ARE THE CRIMINALS? WOB. *Nation & Athenaeum*, 18 February 1928, 751.

Review of *Trial of the Duchess of Kingston*, ed. by Lewis Melville; *Elizabeth Cudleigh, Duchess of Kingston*, by Beatrice Curtis Brown; and 4 volumes in the British Trials Series: *The Thaw Case*, by F. A. MacKenzie; *The Peltzer Case*, by Gérard Harry; *The Trial of Patrick Mahon*, with Introduction by Edgar Wallace; and *The Trial of Professor Webster*, by George Dilnot.

The Duchess of Kingston claimed "the benefit of the peerage" to avoid punishment for bigamy. Harry Thaw, millionaire, escaped punishment for a murder to which there were numerous witnesses, first by claiming insanity, then by attempting to prove the return of sanity after the murder.

When this failed, his family hired a gang to rescue him from prison. After rearrest a jury declared him sane. Contrast this with what happened to Sacco and Vanzetti whose guilt was never proven. The question of who are the criminals is even more puzzling in the Peltzer case.

C0811 TRIAL BY WHITEHALL. WOB. *Nation & Athenaeum*, 25 February 1928, 782.

Review of *Justice and Administrative Law*, by William A. Robson.

A valuable book for the expert. The ordinary man should be made aware of some of the implications of "administrative law" which has to a large extent abolished the separation of the executive from the judiciary. What began as a means of saving money and speeding the regulation of social welfare could lead to the denial of the rights of the individual.

C0812 PHANTASMAGORIC LIFE. WOB. *Nation & Athenaeum*, 3 March 1928, 815.

Review of *The Pilgrimage of Henry James*, by Van Wyck Brooks.

People writing about Henry James seem to fall into a habit of parodying him. Mr. Brooks's analysis brings out the relation between matter and form in James's novels. James first tried writing realistic novels, but he abandoned that when "he discovered or invented [the] strange phantas-magoric life of personal relations and psychological subtleties over which his own literary style and form miraculously fitted like a glove."

C0813 THE PROMISE OF SPRING. WOB. *Nation & Athenaeum*, 10 March 1928, 849.

C0814 NAPOLEON AT ST. HELENA. WOB. *Nation & Athenaeum*, 17 March 1928, 907.

Review of *Napoleon in Captivity*, selections from the reports of Count Alexander Antonovich de Balmain, the Russian commissioner appointed to ascertain Napoleon's continued presence on St. Helena, tr. into English by Julian Park.

The mania for dignity which possessed the inhabitants of St. Helena prevented Count Balmain from actually seeing Napoleon during the four years he was there.

C0815 NATHANIEL HAWTHORNE. WOB. *Nation & Athenaeum*, 24 March 1928, 939.

Review of *The Rebellious Puritan: Portrait of Mr. Hawthorne*, by Lloyd Morris.

Mr. Morris is only partially successful in his admirable attempt to supply a critical biography of Hawthorne. The latter was such a good novelist that it would have taken little more to make him one of the greatest. In psychological analysis he is superior to Dickens; his creation of atmos-phere ranks with that in *Wuthering Heights*. He is a real story-teller and a technical artist. But he analyzed character to the point of obliterating it. Even worse, everything he wrote is low-key.

C0816 SIR THOMAS BROWNE. WOB. *Nation & Athenaeum*, 31 March 1928, 971.

Review of the first 6 volumes of *The Works of Sir Thomas Browne*, ed. by Geoffrey Keynes; and *Sir Thomas Browne's Christian Morals*, 2nd ed. with the Life of the Author by Samuel Johnson, ed. with Introduction and Notes by S. C. Roberts.

Keynes's editing is excellent, but considering the high price of the slim volume one wishes there were more editorial comment and bibliographical detail. Comparison of what Johnson wrote with the comments of 20th-century writers shows that the 18th century was interested in what Browne said; the 20th, with how he said it. De Quincey is the best critic of Browne.

C0817 Untitled review of *The Olives of Endless Age,* by Henry Noel Brailsford (New York; London: Harper). *Labour Magazine,* VI.11, March 1928, p. [520].

In this consideration of the urgent problem of the need for international union the author is too impatient with the progress of the League of Nations.

There were no WORLD OF BOOKS articles 7 and 14 April 1928.

C0818 BOOKS IN BRIEF. *Nation & Athenaeum,* 7 April 1928.

Short unsigned review of *A Poor Man's House,* by Stephen Reynolds.

C0819 EVENTS OF THE WEEK. *Nation & Athenaeum,* 21 April 1928, 65.

Third paragraph. Obituary of Miss Jane Harrison.

She had the curiosity of the Greeks, was "a pioneer in the spirit of adventure", and an "inspiring teacher".

C0820 SIR ROBERT PEEL. *Nation & Athenaeum,* 21 April 1928, 79.

Review of *Sir Robert Peel,* by Miss A. A. W. Ramsay.

To defend Peel the author attacks his opponents.

C0821 FOREIGN AFFAIRS. *Nation & Athenaeum,* 21 April 1928, 84.

Unsigned review of 4 books: *Survey of International Affairs, 1925,* vol. II, by C. A. Macartney; *Survey of International Affairs, 1925, Supplementary Chronology of Events and Treaties; Recent Revelations of European Diplomacy,* by G. P. Gooch, 3rd imp.; and *Lord Grey and the World War,* by Hermann Lutz, tr. by E. W. Dickes.

All reflect the renewed interest in foreign affairs since the war.

C0822 COLUMBIA RECORDS. *Nation & Athenaeum,* 21 April 1928, 88.

C0823 EVENTS OF THE WEEK. *Nation & Athenaeum,* 28 April 1928, 95–96. Last paragraph begins: "The American proposals for outlawing wars and the Briand-Kellogg. . . ."

C0824 GELD IS DER MANN. WOB. *Nation & Athenaeum,* 28 April 1928, 110.

Review of *The Rise of the House of Rothschild,* by Count Corti, tr. from the German by Brian and Beatrix Lunn.

If wealth could give a sense of humour the Rothschilds might have taken the motto "Geld is der Mann". Count Corti's book, based on official documents, memoirs and letters, seems unbiased and intelligent. It shows what others thought of the Rothschilds but not what they thought of those with whom they dealt.

C0825 ON THE EDITOR'S TABLE. *Nation & Athenaeum,* 28 April 1928, 120.

C0826 BOOKS IN BRIEF. *Nation & Athenaeum,* 28 April 1928, 120.

Short unsigned review of *The Story of the Hive,* by Canning Williams.

C0827 THE ANATOMY OF NATIONS. WOB. *Nation & Athenaeum,* 5 May 1928, 143.

Review of *Englishmen, Frenchmen, Spaniards,* by Salvador de Madariaga.

Unlike most books on nationalities this book is written by an intelligent man. Even he does not escape the pitfalls of generalizations risked by authors writing on the subject.

C0828 BOOKS IN BRIEF. *Nation & Athenaeum,* 5 May 1928, 152 & 154.

Short unsigned review of *Select Bibliography of Principal Modern Presses . . . in Great Britain and Ireland,* by G. S. Tomkinson.

C0829 EMILY BRONTE. WOB. *Nation & Athenaeum*, 12 May 1928, 178.
Review of 4 books: *The Brontë Sisters*, by Ernest Dimnet; *Haworth Parsonage* . . . by Isabel C. Clarke; *Wuthering Heights*, with an Introduction by Valentine Dobrée; *All Alone, the Life and Private History of Emily Jane Brontë*, by Romer Wilson.
> It is surprising that M. Dimnet, a Frenchman, should give such high marks to the disorderly English genius. Miss Clarke treats her own hypotheses as facts; Mrs. Dobrée's crticism is sympathetic and subtle; but Miss Wilson attributes experiences in her own life to the life of Emily Brontë.

C0830 ON THE EDITOR'S TABLE. *Nation & Athenaeum*, 12 May 1928, 186.

C0831 BOOKS IN BRIEF. *Nation & Athenaeum*, 12 May 1928, 186.
Short unsigned review of *Human Migration and the Future*, by W. Gregory.

C0832 "I REMEMBER" AND OTHER MOTIVES. WOB. *Nation & Athenaeum*, 19 May 1928, 210.
Review of 3 autobiographies and 3 biographies: *My Life*, by Isadora Duncan; *A Diplomat Off Duty*, by Sir Francis Lindley; *Diplomacy and Foreign Courts*, by Meriel Buchanan; *James the Second*, by Hilaire Belloc; *Letizia Bonaparte (Madame Mère)*, by Clement Shaw; and *Charles Baudelaire*, by François Porché.
> Probably the best reason for writing autobiography is to share one's memories. Mr. Belloc's book is not biography but anti-Protestant propaganda.

C0833 ON THE EDITOR'S TABLE. *Nation & Athenaeum*, 19 May 1928, 218.

C0834 BOOKS IN BRIEF. *Nation & Athenaeum*, 19 May 1928, 218 & 220. Short unsigned reviews of *The Public Schools Yearbook, 1928;* and *The Short Stories of Thomas Hardy*.

C0835 NEW GRAMOPHONE RECORDS. *Nation & Athenaeum*, 19 May 1928, 220.

C0836 SO THIS IS HISTORY. WOB. *Nation & Athenaeum*, 26 May 1928, 255.
Review of *The Diaries of Sylvester Douglas (Lord Glenbervie)*, ed. by Francis Bickley. 2 vols.
> This place-seeker who thought marriage to Lord North's daughter was his claim to political advancement shows his antipathy towards Pitt for failing to recognize it.

C0837 THE CORPSE FACTORY. *Nation & Athenaeum*, 26 May 1928, 259–60.
Unsigned review of Arthur Ponsonby's *Falsehood in Wartime*.
> Discussion of propaganda surrounding World War I.

C0838 ON THE EDITOR'S TABLE. *Nation & Athenaeum*, 26 May 1928, 260.

C0839 PLAYS AND PICTURES. *Nation & Athenaeum*, 2 June 1928, 297.
Paragraph 5: report that some libraries are making it hard for readers to get *My Life*, by Isadora Duncan.

C0840 WHO GOES HOME? WOB. *Nation & Athenaeum*, 2 June 1928, 299.
Review of *How Animals Find Their Way About*, by Etienne Rabaud, tr. into English by I. H. Myers.
> The author rejects the notions of special senses and assumes that animals find their way by using ordinary senses and sensory memory. He leaves a lot unexplained. LW describes an experience he had in Ceylon as illustration of some amazing phenomena.

C0841 ON THE EDITOR'S TABLE. *Nation & Athenaeum*, 2 June 1928, 306.

C0842 BOOKS IN BRIEF. *Nation & Athenaeum*, 2 June 1928, 306. Short unsigned reviews of *Tales of Hearsay*, by Joseph Conrad; and *The Libraries, Museums, and Art Galleries of the British Isles*.

C0843 NEW GRAMOPHONE RECORDS. *Nation & Athenaeum*, 2 June 1928, 308.

C0844 NABOTH'S VINEYARD. *Nation & Athenaeum*, 9 June 1928, 319–20.
Article on a proposal by Sir Edward Grigg concerning Native Reserves in Kenya.
> The consequences for the natives will be grave if this bill is passed.
Letter to the editor, June 16, from John H. Harris welcomes this article and adds information.

C0845 CIVILIZATION. WOB. *Nation & Athenaeum*, 9 June 1928, 331.
Review of *Civilization*, by Clive Bell, with mention of *The Case of Jean Calas*, by F. H. Maugham.
> Mr. Bell starts numerous hares but makes some erroneous assumptions, for example, that a civilized society cannot have any of the elements of a barbarous one. In fact, most societies have elements of both civilization and barbarism. The proportions of these opposing characteristics determine the degree of civilization.

C0846 ON THE EDITOR'S TABLE. *Nation & Athenaeum*, 9 June 1928, 338.

C0847 BOOKS IN BRIEF. *Nation & Athenaeum*, 9 June 1928, 338. Short unsigned review of *The Statesman's Yearbook, 1928*.

C0848 WOMEN IN THE EIGHTEENTH CENTURY. WOB. *Nation & Athenaeum*, 16 June 1928, 363.
Review of *The Woman of the Eighteenth Century*, by Edmond and Jules Goncourt, tr. by Jacques le Clerq and Ralph Roeder.
> This is a bad translation of a muddled book. All that interested the Goncourts about women is the question of chastity which was not so much a concern in the 18th as in the 19th century. After chastity the Goncourts seem to prize feeblemindedness in women. They give a clear picture of women in high society, a terrible picture of the "enlightened" woman, and no idea at all of the ordinary woman.

C0849 SOME BOOKS ON MUSIC. *Nation & Athenaeum*, 16 June 1928, 368.
Unsigned review of *William Byrd*, by Frank Howes; *Henry Purcell*, by Dennis Arundell; *Tchaikovsky*, by Eric Blom; and *Musical Meanderings*, by W. J. Turner.

C0850 ON THE EDITOR'S TABLE. *Nation & Athenaeum*, 16 June 1928, 370.

C0851 NEW GRAMOPHONE NOTES *Nation & Athenaeum*, 16 June 1928, 372.

C0852 ENGLISH PROSE. WOB. *Nation & Athenaeum*, 23 June 1928, 395.
Review of *English Prose Style*, by Herbert Read.
> "One of the most fascinating things in Mr. Read's book is the quotations with which he has the good sense and courage always to test and illustrate his theories and judgments." His analysis and classification of prose styles is a bit too subtle.

C0853 ON THE EDITOR'S TABLE. *Nation & Athenaeum*, 23 June 1928, 402.

C0854 IS SHAKESPEARE A GREAT POET? WOB. *Nation & Athenaeum*, 30 June 1928, 427.
Review of *Question of Taste*, by John Bailey; and *Shakespeare in the Eighteenth Century*, by D. Nichol Smith.
> Neither author makes a thorough analysis of Shakespeare's reputation. The taste for Shakespeare changes from age to age. Mr. Smith quotes isolated passages from the works of 18th-century critics. The amount of agreement of 18th- and 20th-century critics is amazing when one considers the different basis on which judgment is made.

A letter to the editor published 7 July, p. 457 praises LW's article as "a valuable service to clear thinking."

C0855 BOOKS IN BRIEF. *Nation & Athenaeum*, 30 June 1928, 438. Short unsigned review of *The Oxford Book of Mediæval Latin Verse*, chosen by Stephen Gaselee.

C0856 ON THE EDITOR'S TABLE. *Nation & Athenaeum*, 30 June 1928, 438.

C0857 NEW GRAMOPHONE RECORDS. *Nation & Athenaeum*, 30 June 1928, 438 & 440.

C0858 GRANVILLE SHARP. WOB. *Nation & Athenaeum*, 7 July 1928, 463.
Review of *Granville Sharp*, by E. C. P. Lascelles.
Mr. Lascelles has used the modern method of biography, ransacking history to find comedy. "The Anti-Slavery Movement is one of the strangest examples of communal psychology in history . . . a rare instance of popular altruism. . . . The initiation of the movement was due to the solitary action of an obscure Civil Servant, Granville Sharp." He was able to make the judges concede that slavery was illegal.

C0859 BEFORE AND AFTER THE DELUGE. *Nation & Athenaeum*, 7 July 1928, 472.
Review of 7 books on international questions: *Memoirs of Raymond Poincaré*, vol. II, tr. by Sir George Arthur; *Tragedy of Trianon*, by Sir Robert Donald; *Justice for Hungary*, by Albert Apponyi; *Law of Nations*, by J. L. Brierly; *Learning and Leadership*, by Alfred Zimmern; *League of Nations*, by John Spencer Barrett; and *The New Democratic Constitutions of Europe*, by Agnes Headlam-Morley.

C0860 MUSIC AND CIVILIZATION. *Nation & Athenaeum*, 7 July 1928, 474.
Unsigned review of *History of Music*, by Cecil Gray.

C0861 ON THE EDITOR'S TABLE. *Nation & Athenaeum*, 7 July 1928, 474.

C0862 LIVES OF THE SAINTS. WOB. *Nation & Athenaeum*, 14 July 1928, 498.
Review of *Saints and Leaders*, by the Rev. H. F. B. Mackay.
Despite the differences in their outlook, Mr. Mackay must be counted as one of Mr. Strachey's disciples. His up-to-date style is sometimes flippant. As a corrective to Mr. Mackay's adulation of St. Athanasius one should read Mr. E. M. Forster's comments in *Pharos and Pharillon*.

C0863 ON THE EDITOR'S TABLE. *Nation & Athenaeum*, 14 July 1928, 506.

C0864 BOOKS IN BRIEF. *Nation & Athenaeum*, 14 July 1928, 506. Short unsigned reviews of *Buying a Car? The Carbuyer's Annual*, by Leonard Henslowe; and *The Gardener's Year Book, 1928*, ed. by D. H. M. Read.

C0865 BORROW'S "CELEBRATED TRIALS". WOB. *Nation & Athenaeum*, 21 July 1928, 531.
Review of *Celebrated Trials*, first compiled and ed. by George Borrow, now newly rev. and ed. by Edward Hale Bierstadt. 2 vols.
There is some question as to whether Borrow did more than use scissors for the original edition of 1825. Most of the text is taken verbatim from reports of the trials. They are a pretty sorry record of British justice, especially the judicial murders.

C0866 ON THE EDITOR'S TABLE. *Nation & Athenaeum*, 21 July 1928, 538.

C0867 GRAMOPHONE RECORDS. *Nation & Athenaeum*, 21 July 1928, 538.

C0868 WHY WE LAUGH. WOB. *Nation & Athenaeum*, 28 July 1928, 563.
Review of *Springs of Laughter*, by C. W. Kimmins.
From the accounts by Mr. Kimmins of the theories of Hobbes, Descartes,

Hazlitt, Spencer, Darwin, Bergson, Freud, and Chesterfield it is apparent that the subject of laughter has a distinguished history.

C0869 BOOKS IN BRIEF. *Nation & Athenaeum*, 28 July 1928, 570. Short unsigned reviews of *A Wayfarer in French Vine-yards*, by E. I. Robson; *Printing of Today*, by Oliver Simon..., Introduction by Julian Huxley; and *The Advertiser's A.B.C. 1928*.

C0870 ON THE EDITOR'S TABLE. *Nation & Athenaeum*, 28 July 1928, 570.

C0871 NEW GRAMOPHONE RECORDS. *Nation & Athenaeum*, 28 July 1928, 570.

C0872 THE WELL OF LONELINESS. WOB. *Nation & Athenaeum*, 4 August 1928, 593.
Review of *The Well of Loneliness*, by Radclyffe Hall.
The book, though interesting as a psychological study of the difficulties encountered by a woman who is physically attracted to women rather than to men, is a complete failure as a work of art because it lacks emotion. It is an intellectual tract not a novel.

C0873 EXPORTING DEMOCRACY. *Nation & Athenaeum*, 11 August 1928, 612–13.
Unsigned article. Mentions Donoughmore's report on the workings of the Ceylon Constitution.
Ceylon has no political parties corresponding to the British. The emergence of such parties is inhibited by racial and religious separations. The Donoughmore Commission suggests that a new constitution be tried.

C0874 THE STUARTS. WOB. *Nation & Athenaeum*, 11 August 1928, 623.
Review of *English Constitutional Conflicts of the Seventeenth Century, 1603–1689*, by J. R. Tanner.
Mr. Tanner presents the facts and interprets them with a passion for truth. It is hard to believe he is writing about the same events and people as Mr. Belloc in his recent book of religious propaganda. The Stuarts were more intelligent than most royal families, but they failed to understand their English subjects and tried to impose absolute monarchy on men who already wanted parliamentary government.

C0875 NEW GRAMOPHONE RECORDS. *Nation & Athenaeum*, 11 August 1928, 629.

C0876 RUSKIN'S LITERARY CRITICISM. WOB. *Nation & Athenaeum*, 18 August 1928, 650.
Review of *Ruskin as Literary Critic*, ed. by A. H. R. Ball.
"I am afraid that after reading Mr. Ball's selections I find myself in entire agreement with Professor Saintsbury and those who think Ruskin's theories and opinions largely nonsense ... delightful and very interesting nonsense."

C0877 JONAH IN DIPLOMACY. *Nation & Athenaeum*, 25 August 1928, 683.
Unsigned review of *Heading for the Abyss*, by Prince Lichnowsky. English translation.
The author recounts his own diplomatic activities as Ambassador to London, 1912–14, and gives his view of Bismarck's policy towards Austria and Russia.

C0878 THE MAKING OF ENGLISH. WOB. *Nation & Athenaeum*, 25 August 1928, 679.
Review of *Shakespeare's English*, by George Gordon. S.P.E. Tract.

This short pamphlet contains an amazing amount of information about changes occurring in the language during an age of linguistic freedom. By contrast present-day English is stagnant.

C0879   THE ANTI-BABELISTS. WOB. *Nation & Athenaeum*, 1 September 1928, 706.

Review of *An International Language*, by Otto Jespersen.

An international language is needed for such things as conferences of the League of Nations. Because of the difficulty of getting the various nationalities to agree on which language, Professor Jespersen and others propose an artificial language. How can people be induced to learn an artificial language if they will not even learn a foreign one?

C0880   THE YOUNG SWINBURNE. WOB. *Nation & Athenaeum*, 8 September 1928, 734.

Review of 2 books by Georges Lafourcade: *Swinburne's Hyperion and Other Poems, with an Essay on Swinburne and Keats*; and *La Jeunesse de Swinburne, 1837–1867*.

M. Lafourcade thinks Swinburne imitates Keats. But the poem "Hyperion" is an imitation of Milton and it has no value as poetry. One suspects Lafourcade would like it less if it were in his own language. He has spent more time on his 2-volume work than the poet's juvenilia is worth.

C0881   A LIFE OF BACH. *Nation & Athenaeum*, 8 September 1928, 738.

Unsigned review of *J. S. Bach: A Biography*, by Charles Sanford Terry.

This strictly biographical work is valuable for its facts.

C0882   ADMIRAL BYNG. WOB. *Nation & Athenaeum*, 15 September 1928, 762.

Review of *Admiral Byng and the Loss of Minorca*, by Brian Tunstall.

This is a well-written story of the barbarous affair of the only British admiral ever tried by court-martial and executed.

C0883   NEW GRAMOPHONE RECORDS. *Nation & Athenaeum*, 15 September 1928, 772.

C0884   TRUTH AND FICTION. WOB. *Nation & Athenaeum*, 22 September 1928, 794.

Review of *This Side Idolatry, A Novel*, by Ephesian [C. E. Bechhofer Roberts]; and *Charles Dickens*, by Ralph Straus.

The first book is a biography of Dickens containing the same facts as Mr. Straus's more straightforward biography, but with invented conversations. Neither writer has shown the complexity of Dickens who was both "mean and insensitive" and "violently generous and acutely sensitive" and whose chief characteristic was "demonic energy".

C0885   THROUGH GERMAN EYES. WOB. *Nation & Athenaeum*, 29 September 1928, 823.

Review of *The Tragedy of Edward VII*, by Dr. W. H. Edwards; and *The Memoirs of Prince Max of Baden*, 2 vols.

Prince Max has written what may be the best of the war memoirs. It concerns the tragedy of Kaiser Wilhelm II. Dr. Edwards has the curious "thesis that King Edward VII was a political genius and a great orator".

C0886   THE LAW AND PRACTICE OF NATIONS. *Nation & Athenaeum*, 29 September 1928, 830 & 832.

Unsigned review of *British Documents on the Origins of the War, 1898–1914*. vol. III. *Testing of the Entente, 1904–6*, ed. by G. P. Gooch; *The Development of International Law*, by Sir Geoffrey Butler and Simon

Maccoby; *The British Year Book of International Law, 1928* and *Studies in International Law and Relations*, by A. Pearce Higgins.

C0887 NEW GRAMOPHONE RECORDS. *Nation & Athenaeum*, 29 September 1928, 832.

C0888 THE COLONIAL PROBLEM. *Bulletin of the Labour and Socialist International*, Series 2, no. 3. English ed. Zurich, September 1928, 10–17.
Resolutions of the Congress of the L.S.I. Brussels, 5–11 August 1928, Item 3 of Agenda.

By LW and Morel or Buxton? Cf. B6, B15, B23, C1562.

Reprinted almost verbatim as "XI. The Resolution on the Colonial Problem Adopted by the Congress of the Labour and Socialist International in Brussels, 9th August 1928" in *The Colonial Problem. Material Submitted to the IIIrd Congress of the Labour and Socialist International Brussels, August 1928*. Special ed., with Appendix including the Proceedings and the Resolution of the Congress. Zurich: L.S.I.; London: Labour Party, 1928, pp. 190–96 [Reports and Proceedings Section V].

C0889 DOROTHY OSBORNE. WOB. *Nation & Athenaeum*, 6 October 1928, 18.
Review of *The Letters of Dorothy Osborne to William Temple*, ed. by G. C. Moore Smith.

Careful editing has turned these letters by an obscure person into a classic. They preserve the vitality of 17th-century English language and portray a psychologically interesting person.

C0890 THE NEW CROP. WOB. *Nation & Athenaeum*, 13 October 1928, 50.

C0891 FROM MOSES TO WELLINGTON. WOB. *Nation & Athenaeum*, 20 October 1928, 110.
Review of 5 biographies: *Charles James Fox*, by John Drinkwater; *Wellington*, by Oliver Brett; *Mary Queen of Scots*, by Margaret Kurlbaum-Siebert, tr. from the German by Mary Agnes Hamilton; *John Law, a Fantastic Financier, 1671–1729*, by George Oudard, tr. from the French by G. C. E. Massé; and *The Life of Moses*, by Edmond Fleg, tr. from the French by Stephen Haden Guest.

The first two are serious books; the others have fictional imaginary conversations added to the facts. The proportion of fiction to fact is greater in the book on Moses because so little is known of him.

C0892 THE EXISTENCE OF MOSES. *Nation & Athenaeum*, 27 October 1928, 136–37.
Letter to the Editor, replying to a correspondent who objected to his remark in the review, C0891, that Moses was "a man who probably never existed and about whom we can know nothing with certainty."

C0893 SLAPDASHDOM. WOB. *Nation & Athenaeum*, 27 October 1928, 144.
Review of *The Victorian Illusion*, by E. H. Dance.

Mr. Dance knows his subject well, but his style is abominable – pretentious, clever, clumsy, irritating. "Any dunce can rewrite history by ignoring a sufficient number of historical facts."

C0894 MEMORIES OF THE WAR. WOB. *Nation & Athenaeum*, 3 November 1928, 178.
Review of 3 books: *My War Memories*, by Dr. Benes; *The Intimate Papers of Colonel House*, arranged by Charles Seymour, vols III & IV; and *Versailles*, by Karl Friederich Nowak.

Colonel House's papers are the most interesting of these books. The first book will interest the expert, and the last is not entirely reliable.

C0895   THE LIFE OF THE ARTIST. WOB. *Nation & Athenaeum*, 10 November 1928, 211.
Review of *Dante Gabriel Rossetti*, by R. L Mégroz; and *The Life of Charles M. Doughty*, by D. G. Hogarth.
> Few people appreciated the work of either Rossetti or Doughty during their lifetimes. Why is it that so many biographies are written about people who lead dull lives – writers, artists and musicians?

C0896   THE FREEDOM OF THE PRESS. WOB. *Nation & Athenaeum*, 17 November 1928, 258.
Review of *The Struggle for the Freedom of the Press, 1819–1832*, by William H. Wickwar.
> This factual book about the persecutions and prosecutions resulting from suppression of books has real historical value.

C0897   "OBSCENE" BOOKS. THE BOW STREET DECISION. *Manchester Guardian*, 22 November 1928, p. 20, col. 2.
Letter to the Editor, signed by 45 people including Leonard and Virginia Woolf and the Editor of the *Nation*, H. D. Henderson. G. B. Shaw drafted the letter and Desmond MacCarthy edited it. Cf. Dan Laurence *Bernard Shaw: A Bibliography*, C2755a.
> The charge of obscenity brought against *The Well of Loneliness* because of "the tendency to deprave those whose minds are open to immoral influences" could equally well be made against "many masterpieces of English literature".

C0898   BOOK BAN DENOUNCED: EMINENT PEOPLE DEFEND *"WELL OF LONELINESS"*. *Daily Herald*, 22 November 1928, p. 5, col. 4.
Same letter as C0897.

C0899   BANNED BOOK. *Daily News*, 22 November 1928, p. 5, col. 5.
Same letter as C0897.

C0900   "A FLY IS STRUGGLING IN THE WEB." WOB. *Nation & Athenaeum*, 24 November 1928, 294.
Review of *The Diary of Tolstoy's Wife, 1860–1891*, tr. by Alexander Werth; and *The Diary of Dostoyevsky's Wife*, tr. from the German by Madge Pemberton.
> Both women were married to impossible men. Countess Tolstoy never learned to deal with the spider she had married, but the shorthand typist knew exactly how to treat her more human spider – she laughed at him.

C0901   CRIME AND CRIMINALS. WOB. *Nation & Athenaeum*, 1 December 1928, 326.
Review of *More Famous Trials*, by the Earl of Birkenhead; *Landru*, by F. A. Mackenzie; *Trial of Charles the First*, ed. by J. G. Muddiman; *The Newgate Calendar*, Reprint with Intro. by Henry Savage; *The Case of Constance Kent*, by John Rhode; *A Handbook on Hanging*, by Charles Duff; and *A New Way with Crime*, by A. Fenner Brockway.
> Books in which a single crime is discussed at length seem more interesting than the modern anthologies of several crimes.

C0902   HEALY AND O'BRIEN. WOB. *Nation & Athenaeum*, 8 December 1928, 359.
Review of *Letters and Leaders of My Day*, by Tim Healy; and *The Life of William O'Brien*, by Michael MacDonagh.
> In these books we read "the tragic history of England and Ireland from 1880–1922". MacDonagh's book is better written than Healy's.

C0903 WHAT WE MAY BE COMING TO. WOB. *Nation & Athenaeum,* 15 December 1928, 415.
> Review of *Anthony Comstock,* by Heywood Broun and Margaret Leech.
>> Magistrates should read this book. Anthony Comstock devoted his life to hunting pornography. The book shows a fascinating side of American society in the seventies.

C0904 YOUTH AMONG THE RUINS. WOB. *Nation & Athenaeum,* 22 December 1928, 446.
> Review of *Alma Mater, or the Future of Oxford and Cambridge,* by Julian Hall; and *The New Universities, an External Examination,* by H. G. Herklots.
>> Both books characterize the current University generation as apathetic. "It seems probable that civilizations perish when one generation behaves in such a way that the next sees nothing but shams and ruins."

C0905 JUST FOR THE RIBAND TO STICK IN THEIR COATS. WOB. *Nation & Athenaeum,* 29 December 1928, 468.
> Review of *The Great Betrayal,* by Julien Benda, tr. from the French *La Trahison des Clercs,* by Mr. Aldington.
>> The thesis of the book is that the "clercs", i.e., the thinkers, artists and writers of the present, are "lost leaders" who no longer pursue the truth, but pursue comforts and money. M. Benda has not proved that this is only a modern phenomenon.

1929

C0906 NOVELS AND DECENCY. *Nation & Athenaeum,* 5 January 1929, 488.
Letter to the Editor replying to one from F. E. Pollard (22 December, p. 440), about LW's article, C0903.
> Question about censorship versus individual responsibility of novelists. Pollard replied to this in the 12 January issue.

C0907 BUTTERFLIES. WOB. *Nation & Athenaeum,* 5 January 1929, 495.
Review of *Collected Works of Ronald Firbank,* with an Introduction by Arthur Waley, and a Memoir by Osbert Sitwell, 5 vols; and *The Dreadful Dragon of Hay Hill,* by Max Beerbohm.
> Firbank's butterfly type of writing does not compare with Beerbohm's really beautiful prose.

C0908 THE FIRST RADICALS. WOB. *Nation & Athenaeum,* 12 January 1929, 526.
Review of *The Growth of Philosophic Radicalism,* by Elie Halévy, tr. from the French by Mary Morris.
> In this difficult but valuable book Halévy has dug deeply into the social, political and economic beliefs of the past. LW talks of Bentham's influence.

C0909 NOVELS AND DECENCY. *Nation & Athenaeum,* 19 January 1929, 549.
Letter to the Editor.
> Novelists probably write with as much sense of responsibility as other writers. One's views on moral questions are not necessarily wrong because they do not agree with someone else's.

C0910 "WHIGS" AND "TORIES". WOB. *Nation & Athenaeum,* 19 January 1929, 555.
Review of *The Structure of Politics at the Accession of George III,* 2 vols, by L. B. Namier.

Mr. Namier's "learning is immense, and he has highly developed that strange respect for a fact . . . which will send the historian tunnelling and burrowing like some sublimely inspired mole or marmot, down through the dusty MSS in Museums and Record Offices merely to satisfy himself. . . ." "No book that I know gives one so deep an insight into the politics of England in the eighteenth century as this."

C0911 1778–1878 WOB. *Nation & Athenaeum*, 26 January 1929, 585.

Review of *Barnard Letters*, ed. by Anthony Powell; *The Farington Diary*, by Joseph Farington, vol. VIII, ed. by James Greig; and *The Paris Embassy During the Second Empire*, [correspondence of Lord Cowley], ed. by F. A. Wellesley.

These not very exciting books do show the changes in feelings and attitudes reflected in the language during the 100-year period.

C0912 THE POPULARITY OF DEAN INGE. WOB. *Nation & Athenaeum*, 2 February 1929, 619.

Review of *Assessments and Anticipations*, by William Ralph Inge, Dean of St. Paul's Cathedral.

Dean Inge is an accomplished amateur journalist who in his opinions and thoughts "is always to be found walking in the middle of the road." Only when he meets a socialist or a Bolshevik does he take a stand, a violently "anti" stand.

This article sparked a heated controversy which began the following week with letters from Edwyn Bevan and Charles Wright.

C0913 RUSSIAN NOVELISTS. WOB. *Nation & Athenaeum*, 9 February 1929, 654.

Review of Volumes 3 and 19 of the Centenary edition of Tolstoy's Works; *Childhood, Boyhood and Youth;* and *Resurrection*; and *Adepts in Self-Portraiture*, by Stephan Zweig, in English translation.

The print in this edition of Tolstoy is too small to be easily read. H. G. Wells's Introduction to *Resurrection* "is short, wrong-headed, and very interesting". It is true that in this book the preacher in Tolstoy drove out the artist. But Wells thinks Russian novelists are over-rated. Stephan Zweig is right in saying that Tolstoy described realities. Russian novelists from Gogol to Chekhov had this ability.

C0914 "FORCE IS NO REMEDY". WOB. *Nation & Athenaeum*, 16 February 1929, 689.

Article replying to a Letter to the Editor from Edwyn Bevan, 9 February, p. 650, about C0912. Bevan said LW left the maxim quoted in the title in a fog.

LW's attempt to clarify what he had said about Dean Inge's position on force takes precedence over the review scheduled on Spengler's *Decline of the West*, but is related to it, for Spengler thought force the only remedy. LW quips, "Like most pacifists, I cannot resist a quarrel."

Two more letters from Charles Wright and Arnold Lupton were published in the *N & A*, 23 February, and one from W. M. Crook, 2 March.

C0915 SPENGLER. WOB. *Nation & Athenaeum*, 23 February 1929, 722.

Review of *The Decline of the West*, vol. II: *Perspectives of World-History*, tr. from the German by Charles Francis Atkinson. (LW reviewed vol. I, C0714.)

Spengler is typical of the prophet and sage of the twilight of civilization. He has immense learning but does not play fair intellectually, does not stick to his own definitions, and mixes mysticism with fact. He fails to prove his assertions.

A Letter to the Editor from E. M. Wishart, published 2 March, p. 748, says that Woolf does not prove his own assertions about Spengler, but tries to hide "his lack of undertanding under a pitiful mask of superiority. . . . It is the intuition, not the intellect that must judge. Either you grasp the whole of the philosopher's meaning or you miss it altogether."

C0916   "THE PILGRIM'S PROGRESS". WOB. *Nation & Athenaeum,* 2 March 1929, 753.

Review of *The Pilgrim's Progress,* by John Bunyan, ed. by James Blanton Wharey.

This attempt to establish an authentic text for the scholar was a difficult task. Childhood memories of a book used as a kind of child's Bible make it hard even for adults to judge it. Bunyan was an unsophisticated author who wrote vividly and concretely. His work is as entertaining as it is pious.

C0917   SPENGLER. *Nation & Athenaeum,* 9 March 1929, 781.

Letter to the Editor replying to Mr. Wishart, C0915.

"I cannot see by intuition a philosophy of history which requires two volumes of 1,000 large pages for its explanation and I admit that I find it absolutely impossible to read 1,000 pages of argument without using my intellect. Mr. Wishart is apparently more fortunate."

C0918   THE SPRING LISTS. WOB. *Nation & Athenaeum,* 9 March 1929, 786.

C0919   LIFE AND LIVES. WOB. *Nation & Athenaeum,* 16 March 1929, 842.

Review of *The Tempestuous Prince,* by E. M. Butler; *The Life of Sir Charles Hanbury-Williams,* by the Earl of Ilchester and Mrs. Langford-Brooke; and *The Letters of the Tsar to the Tsaritsa, 1914–1917,* tr. by A. L. Haynes, with an Introduction by Dr. Hagberg Wright.

The Tempestuous Prince is the best biography read so far this season; the second book is "rather flat"; and the third is a psychological study revealed by letters from which the Tsar emerges as a most unpleasant character.

C0920   THE SCIENCE AND ART OF BIOGRAPHY. WOB. *Nation & Athenaeum,* 23 March 1929, 882.

Review of *Aspects of Biography,* by André Maurois, tr. from the French by S. C. Roberts; and mention of *Alexander the Great,* by E. Iliff Robson.

This excellent book would be better if Maurois had dealt only with "the relation between biography as a science and biography as an art". Because all that is known of Alexander the Great is his place in history Mr. Robson has not been able to recreate his character. Even Mr. Strachey cannot get over this difficulty.

C0921   OBSCENITY IN LITERATURE. *Nation & Athenaeum,* 30 March 1929, 908.

Letter to the Editor in reply to one from Gilbert Murray published 23 March, p. 876.

Murray says that all great literature, except for comedy, is free from obscenity which destroys the higher imaginative values. He would have been just as convincing if he had said that all great literature, except for tragedy, is full of obscenity which heightens the imaginative values.

Now began a large correspondence concerning this topic.

C0922   THE ROMANCE OF JOURNALISM. WOB. *Nation & Athenaeum,* 30 March 1929, 914.

Review of *The Autobiography of a Journalist,* [ed. by Michael Joseph];

Secrets of Your Daily Paper: The Veil Off Fleet Street, by Frederick W. Carter; and *The Truth Behind The News, 1918–1928,* by George Seldes.

The last book is the best – readable and exciting, full of good stories. Seldes tells particularly about censorship of foreign correspondents. The other two books paint a romantic picture of journalism.

C0923 RETICENCE. WOB. *Nation & Athenaeum,* 6 April 1929, 17

Review of 2 volumes of the Centenary Edition of Tolstoy's Works. I. *Life of Tolstoy: First Fifty Years,* by Aylmer Maude; and XVIII. *What is Art? and Essays on Art;* and of *The Letters of Tolstoy and His Cousin, Countess Alexandra Tolstoy, 1857–1903,* tr. by Leo Islavin; and *The Autobiography of Lord Alfred Douglas.*

Mr. Maude's use of Tolstoy's letters, diaries and works makes this work as much an autobiography as a biography. Tolstoy threw off any reticence he had in his letters. Lord Alfred Douglas has produced a second-rate book in spite of his irreticence in telling how he forced Robert Ross to prosecute him for libel.

C0924 THE CANONIZATION OF GENERAL DYER. *Nation & Athenaeum,* 6 April 1929, 21.

Unsigned review of *General Dyer,* by Ian Colvin.

This biography says that General Dyer, the man responsible for the shooting at Amritsar, in Punjab, 13 April 1919, "was entirely in the right".

C0925 THE TEXT OF SHAKESPEARE. *Nation & Athenaeum,* 6 April 1929, 22.

Review of *The Works of Shakespeare,* ed. by Herbert Farjeon, vol. I (Nonesuch Press); *Antony and Cleopatra: Julius Caesar; As You Like It; The Winter's Tale.* Facsimiles of the First Folio Text, Introduction by J. Dover Wilson (Faber & Gwyer).

The first is worthy of the Nonesuch Press. The second, affordable group will be invaluable to the student.

C0926 THE DRAMA. WOB. *Nation & Athenaeum,* 13 April 1929, 45.

Review of several books of plays: *Great Modern British Plays,* selected by J. M. Marriott; *The Oil Islands* and *Warren Hastings,* by Lion Feuchtwanger, tr. by Willa and Edwin Muir; and *Easter, and Other Plays,* by August Strindberg.

It is too bad that Marriott could not include the greatest British playwright [LW means G. B. Shaw who would not permit his plays to be anthologized]. Modern plays seem to lack depth. None of the plays in these books is great, though Strindberg approaches greatness except in his failures, *Easter* and *A Dream Play.*

Eskil Sundström wrote to the editor to protest against LW's valuation of *A Dream Play,* saying many plays must be judged as played, not as read (10 April, p. 73).

C0927 NEW GRAMOPHONE RECORDS. *Nation & Athenaeum,* 13 April 1929, 56.

C0928 OBSCENITY AND THE CENSOR. WOB. *Nation & Athenaeum,* 20 April 1929, 77.

Review of *To the Pure . . . A Study in Obscenity and the Censor,* by Morris L. Ernst and William Seagle.

The book shows that there is no agreement about what constitutes obscenity or about the effect that books have upon people's lives or thoughts. "Mr. Murray missed the point of a little letter which I wrote. . . .

The topic does not make a book great or prevent its being great." [Murray had stated that *Village in the Jungle* shows that LW's practice differs from his professed theory of literature (letter to the Editor, 13 April, p. 40)].

C0929   ON THE EDITOR'S TABLE. *Nation & Athenaeum,* 20 April 1929, 86.

C0930   LORD ALFRED DOUGLAS AND ST. ANTHONY. *Nation & Athenaeum,* 27 April 1929, 105.
Letter to the Editor. Response to Lord Alfred Douglas who complained that Woolf sneered at him in his review of April 6, C0923.

C0931   THE TORY MIND. WOB. *Nation & Athenaeum,* 27 April 1929, 111.
Review of *Peel and the Conservative Party,* by George Kitson Clark; *Toryism and the People, 1832–1846,* by Richard Hill; *Seven Nineteenth-Century Statesmen,* by G. R. Stirling Taylor; and *Daniel O'Connell and the History of Catholic Emancipation,* by Michael MacDonagh.
"To judge from these books neither the Tory mind nor the founder of the Conservative Party are inspiring subjects for writers.... The reason is that Peel had the Tory mind and that fog is an element...".
Charles Sturge, in a Letter to the Editor, denies this, and says Peel was becoming a Liberal (11 May, p. 199).

C0932   ON THE EDITOR'S TABLE. *Nation & Athenaeum,* 27 April 1929, 122.

C0933   THROUGH FRENCH EYES. WOB. *Nation & Athenaeum,* 4 May 1929, 162.
Review of *A History of the English People; Epilogue, Vol. I, 1895–1905,* by Elie Halévy, a translation of his book published in 1926 with the sub-title *Les Impérialistes au Pouvoir.*
A foreign writer may have an advantage of distance and detachment. The book shows great knowledge and historical perspective.

C0934   ON THE EDITOR'S TABLE. *Nation & Athenaeum,* 4 May 1929, 172 & 174.

C0935   BOOKS IN BRIEF. *Nation & Athenaeum,* 4 May 1929, 174. Short unsigned reviews of *The Gardener's Year-Book, 1929,* ed. by D. H. Moutray Read; and *The Subject Index to Periodicals 1927.*

C0936   JUDGE JEFFREYS IN THE WEST COUNTRY. WOB. *Nation & Athenaeum,* 11 May 1929, 204.
Review of *The Bloody Assize,* by Sir Edward Parry.
Judge Parry writes history as drama while sticking strictly to historical facts.
In a letter headed "Titus Oates", Frank MacDermott says that LW "gives a misleading impression of Oates's last years" (*N & A,* 25 May, p. 271).

C0937   ON THE EDITOR'S TABLE. *Nation & Athenaeum,* 11 May 1929, 214.

C0938   NEW GRAMOPHONE RECORDS. *Nation & Athenaeum,* 11 May 1929, 216.

C0939   OBSCENITY IN LITERATURE. *Nation & Athenaeum,* 18 May 1929, 235.
Letter to the Editor.
The controversy on this subject is so out of hand that nobody understands what the others are saying.

C0940   QUEENS AND KINGS. WOB. *Nation & Athenaeum,* 18 May 1929, 240.
Review of several books about monarchs: *Louis XI,* by Pierre Champion, tr. by Winifred S. Whale; *Queen Louise of Prussia,* by Gertrude Aretz, tr. by Ruth Putnam; *William the First,* by Paul Wiegler, tr. by Constance Vesey; *Ludwig II, of Bavaria,* by Guy de Portalés; *Napoleon III,* by Edmund B. D'Auvergne; and *The English King,* by Michael Macdonagh.

C0941 BOOKS ON MUSIC. *Nation & Athenaeum*, 18 May 1929, 244.
Unsigned review of *The Oxford Book of Music*, ed. by Percy C. Buck, New ed., vol. I: *The Theories of Claude Debussy*, by Léon Vallas, tr. by Maire O'Brien; *Beethoven the Creator*, by Romain Rolland; and *Moussorgsky*, by Oscar von Reisemann, tr. by Paul England.

C0942 ON THE EDITOR'S TABLE. *Nation & Athenaeum*, 18 May 1929, 250.

C0943 NEW GRAMOPHONE RECORDS. *Nation & Athenaeum*, 18 May 1929, 252.

C0944 ANOTHER SON OF HILKIAH. WOB. *Nation & Athenaeum*, 25 May 1929, 275.
Review of *Paleface: The Philosophy of the Melting Pot*, by Wyndham Lewis.
Mr. Lewis pelts his reader with so many ideas that he confuses him. His book is mostly a jeremiad about the attitude of white people towards black people. He offers few suggestions for reform.

C0945 INTERNATIONALISM AND NATIONALISM. *Nation & Athenaeum*, 25 May 1929, 280.
Unsigned review of *The Memoirs of Raymond Poincaré*, vol. III, tr. and adapted by Sir George Arthur; *The Origins of the World War*, by Sidney Bradshaw Fay, 2 vols; *Survey of American Foreign Relations, 1928*, by Charles P. Howland; *War as an Instrument of National Policy*, by James T. Shotwell, with an Introduction by Gilbert Murray; and *The International Community and the Right of War*, by Don Luigi Sturzo.
Useful books for the student of international affairs. Poincaré's suffers from the translation; Fay's is an historical analysis; the third book includes post-war limitation of armaments. Shotwell's is the most important and interesting. It and Sturzo's book concern the Kellogg proposals.

C0946 BOOKS IN BRIEF. *Nation & Athenaeum*, 25 May 1929, 282 & 284. Short unsigned reviews of *Trial of James Blomfield Rush*, ed. by W. Teignmouth Shore; and *Remembered Yesterdays*, by Sir Solomon Dias Bandaranaike.

C0947 JACK THE RIPPER, AND OTHERS. WOB. *Nation & Athenaeum*, 1 June 1929, 307.
Review of several books on crime: *The Mystery of Jack the Ripper*, by Leonard Matters; *The Trial of T. H. Allaway*, ed. by W. Lloyd Woodland; *Trial of John Donald Merrett*, ed. by William Roughead; *Guilty or Not Guilty?* by Guy B. H. Logan; and *Curious Trials and Criminal Cases*, by Edward Hale Bierstadt.

C0948 ON THE EDITOR'S TABLE. *Nation & Athenaeum*, 1 June 1929, 314.

C0949 NEW GRAMOPHONE RECORDS. *Nation & Athenaeum*, 1 June 1929, 314.

C0950 THE VICTORIAN WOMAN. WOB. *Nation & Athenaeum*, 8 June 1929, 338.
Review of *Victorian Working Women*, by Wanda Fraiken Neff.
"An extraordinarily detailed account of the social, economic, and intellectual condition of 5 groups of women between 1832 and 1850: the textile worker, the non-textile worker, the dressmaker, the governess, and the middle- or upper-class woman who did no work at all. . . . It is one of the best documented historical studies that I have ever read."

C0951 THE HOURS PRESS. *Nation & Athenaeum*, 8 June 1929, 344.
Unsigned review of 3 books published by Nancy Cunard at the Hours Press: *La Chasse au Snark*, by Lewis Carroll, tr. by Aragon; *St. George at Silene*, by Alvaro Guevara, and *The Eaten Heart*, by Richard Aldington.

C0952 BOOKS IN BRIEF. *Nation & Athenaeum*, 8 June 1929, 346.
Short unsigned reviews of *The Truth About Publishing*, by Stanley Unwin, 3rd ed.; and *Etchings of To-day*, by C. Geoffrey Holme.

C0953 NEW GRAMOPHONE RECORDS. *Nation & Athenaeum*, 8 June 1929, 348.

No WORLD OF BOOKS articles were published 15 or 22 June.

C0954 NEW GRAMOPHONE RECORDS. *Nation & Athenaeum*, 22 June 1929, 410.

C0955 THE FOUNDERS OF LIBERALISM. WOB. *Nation & Athenaeum*, 29 June 1929, 434.
Review of *French Liberal Thought in the Eighteenth Century*, by Kingsley Martin, ed. by Harold Laski.
This "really masterful book" shows its author's encyclopedic knowledge.

C0956 MORE DOCUMENTS. *Nation & Athenaeum*, 29 June 1929, 440.
Unsigned review of *British Documents on the Origins of the War, 1898– 1914*, by G. P. Gooch and Harold Temperley.

C0957 LADY BYRON. WOB. *Nation & Athenaeum*, 6 July 1929, 478.
Review of *The Life & Letters of Anne Isabella, Lady Noël Byron*, by Ethel Colburn Mayne.
This is a sympathetic account.

C0958 ON THE EDITOR'S TABLE. *Nation & Athenaeum*, 6 July 1929, 486.

C0959 HARRIETTE WILSON. WOB. *Nation & Athenaeum*, 13 July 1929, 509.
Review of *Harriette Wilson's Memoirs of Herself and Others*, with a Preface by James Laver.
A welcome reprint. Despite the author's profession of courtesan and the fact that she wrote the book to blackmail her former customers, she gives a lively and interesting account of 18th-century high society.

C0960 BOOKS IN BRIEF. WOB. *Nation & Athenaeum*, 13 July 1929, 514. Short unsigned reviews of *The Annual Register 1928*; and *The Book of the Tulip*, by Sir Daniel Hall.

C0961 HOW NOT TO READ POETRY. WOB. *Nation & Athenaeum*, 20 July 1929, 538.
Review of *Practical Criticism: A Study of Literary Judgment*, by I. A. Richards.
Mr. Richards bases his study of the misreading of poetry on a kind of poll. The respondents seem to have been incredibly stupid.

C0962 NEW GRAMOPHONE RECORDS. *Nation & Athenaeum*, 20 July 1929, 543.

C0963 FROM MOZART TO MISS STEIN. WOB. *Nation & Athenaeum*, 27 July 1929, 566.
Review of *Memoirs of Lorenzo da Ponte*, tr. by L. A. Sheppard; *The Diary of the Revd. William Jones, 1777–1821*, ed. by O. F. Christie; *Pomp and Circumstance*, by Elizabeth de Gramont; *Relations and Complications*, by H.H. the Dayang Muda of Sarawak [née Gladys Brooke]; and *Harlequinade*, by Constance Collier.

C0964 FRENCH IN THE ORIGINAL AND IN TRANSLATION. *Nation & Athenaeum*, 27 July 1929, 569.
Unsigned review of *Introduction to the Method of Leonardo da Vinci*, by Paul Valéry, tr. by Thomas McGreevy. Limited ed.; *Adolphe*, by Benjamin Constant; and *Oeuvres de Molière*, Publiées avec des notes par B. Guegan. t.5.

C0965 NOVELS IN BRIEF. *Nation & Athenaeum*, 27 July 1929, 574. Short unsigned reviews of 3 books under an erroneous title (these are not novels): *The Listener's History of Music*, vols II & III, by Percy A. Scholes; *The Works of Sir Thomas Browne*, ed. by Geoffrey Keynes, vol. IV; and *Survey of International Affairs, 1927*, by Arnold J. Toynbee.

C0966 NEW GRAMOPHONE RECORDS. *Nation & Athenaeum*, 27 July 1929, 576.

C0967 MODERN ART. WOB. *Nation & Athenaeum*, 3 August 1929, 597.
Review of *The New Interior Decoration*, by Dorothy Todd and Raymond Mortimer.
> In this book on art the letterpress is as interesting as the illustrations. The authors include examples of exterior architecture with those of the furnishings. The examples by Bloomsbury artists are "ornate, decorative, romantic".

C0968 COUNT HERMANN KEYSERLING. WOB. *Nation & Athenaeum*, 10 August 1929, 626.
Review of two books by Keyserling: *Creative Understanding* and *The Recovery of Truth*.
> Like Spengler and Steiner the author offers a cosmic panacea, "significance", but he fails to explain what it means.

C0969 THE OLD FOX. WOB. *Nation & Athenaeum*, 17 August 1929, 654.
Review of *Henry VIII*, by Francis Hackett.
> A fascinating book.

C0970 THE ART OF THOUGHT. WOB. *Nation & Athenaeum*, 24 August 1929, 682.
Review of *The Art of Thinking*, by Ernest Dimnet.
> M. Dimnet does not even consider one of the most important aspects of thought which Mr. Graham Wallas dealt with admirably: that for any creative thought one must have periods of idleness.

C0971 BOOKS IN BRIEF. *Nation & Athenaeum*, XLV.21, 24 August 1929, 688.
Brief unsigned review of *A Greek-English Lexicon*, by Henry George Liddell and Robert Scott.

C0972 NEW GRAMOPHONE RECORDS. *Nation & Athenaeum*, 24 August 1929, 688.

C0973 VARIETIES OF CRIME. WOB. *Nation & Athenaeum*, 31 August 1929, 709.
Review of *Trial of Jean Pierre Vaquier*, ed. by R. H. Blundell and R. E. Seaton; *The Trial of Norman Thorne*, by Helena Normanton; *The Milligan Case*, ed. by Samuel Klaus; and *Indian Village Crimes*, by Sir Cecil Walsh.
> Authors of books about foreign countries should not forget that the occasion of clearing up a crime is as out of the ordinary in a native village as in England.

C0974 BOOKS IN BRIEF. *Nation & Athenaeum*, 31 August 1929, 714.
Short unsigned review of *The Ponsonby Family*, by Sir John Ponsonby.

C0975 NEW GRAMOPHONE RECORDS. *Nation & Athenaeum*, 31 August 1929, 714 & 716.

C0976 INTERNATIONAL THOUGHT. WOB. *Nation & Athenaeum*, 7 September 1929, 737.
Review of *The Growth of International Thought*, by F. Melian Stawell.
> Miss Stawell "provokes thought" but totally ignores the growth of international organizations.

C0977 THE COMPLEAT WALTON. WOB. *Nation & Athenaeum*, 14 September 1929, 765.

Review of *The Compleat Walton*, ed. by Geoffrey Keynes (Nonesuch Press). The excellent editing enhances one of the most beautiful books produced by the Nonesuch Press. Walton himself is rather a bore. He looks at everything through rose-coloured glasses, but he appeals to many readers. "He was a middle-witted man of very limited psychological insight." Harold Nicolson called him "our first deliberate biographer".

C0978 BOOKS IN BRIEF. *Nation & Athenaeum*, 14 September 1929, 714. Short unsigned review of *A Guide to the Best Historical Novels and Tales*, by Jonathan Nield, 5th ed.

C0979 BORN WRITERS. WOB. *Nation & Athenaeum*, 21 September 1929, 798.

Review of *Alice Meynell, A Memoir*, by Viola Meynell; and *A Book About Myself*, by Theodore Dreiser.

Mrs. Meynell was able to write literature despite her involvement in journalism. If Mr. Dreiser had her gift of language his might be a great book, for it is full of life and has the raw material of great art. [LW admits he has not read Dreiser's novels.]

C0980 EMPIRES AND IMPERIALISMS. *Nation & Athenaeum*, 21 September 1929, 800 & 802.

Unsigned review of *History of French Colonial Policy, 1870–1925*, by Stephen Roberts, 2 vols; *Empire to Commonwealth*, by Walter Phelps Hall; *British Colonial Policy and the South African Republics, 1848–1872*, by C. W. de Kiewiet; *Bantu, Boer, and Briton, the Making of the South African Native Problem*, by W. M. Macmillan; *The History of Nigeria*, by A. C. Burns; *East Africa in Transition . . . Hilton Young Commission; The Future of the Negro*, by Sir Gordon Guggisberg and A. G. Fraser; and *Black Democracy; the Story of Haiti*, by H. P. Davies.

The first one by Stephen Roberts is the most important, but one is inclined to recommend them all.

C0981 NEW GRAMOPHONE RECORDS. *Nation & Athenaeum*, 21 September 1929, 808.

C0982 AD ASTRA? WOB. *Nation & Athenaeum*, 28 September 1929, 829.

Review of *The Ascent of Humanity*, by Gerald Heard; and *The Universe Around Us*, by Sir James Jeans.

The curious twisted style of Mr. Heard's prose is sometimes beautiful, but it makes this book hard to read. Sir James Jeans makes even the most difficult facts of physics and astronomy intelligible.

C0983 INTERNATIONAL LAW. *Nation & Athenaeum*, 28 September 1929, 836. Unsigned review of *Annual Digest of Public International Law Cases, Years 1925 and 1926*, ed. by Arnold D. McNair and H. Lauterpacht.

This edition of this valuable book is excellent. The most complete work of its kind, the book shows how much international law already exists.

C0984 NEW GRAMOPHONE NOTES. *Nation & Athenaeum*, 28 September 1929, 840.

C0985 THE LETTERS OF DISRAELI. WOB. *Nation & Athenaeum*, 5 October 1929, 17.

Review of *The Letters of Disraeli to Lady Bradford and Lady Chesterfield*, ed. by the Marquis of Zetland, 2 vols.; *and The Life of Disraeli*, by Monypenny and Buckle. New ed., 2 vols.

Disraeli was a born writer. His letters hold great interest both personally and politically.

C0986 AUTUMN BOOKS. WOB. *Nation & Athenaeum*, 12 October 1929, 51.

C0987 "A GREAT MAN". WOB. *Nation & Athenaeum*, 19 October 1929, 109.

Review of *Lord Fisher, Admiral of the Fleet*, by Admiral Sir R. H. Bacon. "The author ... has about as much idea of how to write a book as an experienced author has of how to navigate a battleship." He is also partisan. Fisher is a good subject. In competent hands his would be an interesting biography. Despite Bacon's attempt to whitewash Fisher, his book shows Fisher's faults.

Ernest Fayle wrote to the editor to comment that Woolf must have enjoyed writing this article, for it is fun to despise "one's fellow creatures in whole categories at one time" (*N & A*, October 26, p. 137).

C0988 PASSIONATE PILGRIMS. WOB. *Nation & Athenaeum*, 26 October 1929, 141.

Review of 6 biographies: *Diaries of William Johnston Temple, 1780–1796; Livingstone*, by the Rev. R. J. Campbell; *The Life and Letters of Sir Harry Johnston*, by his brother Alex Johnston; *Mrs. Eddy*, by Edwin Franden Dakin; *Isadora Duncan's End*, by Mary Desti; and *The Career of Sir Basil Zaharoff*, by Richard Lewinsohn.

Sir Willam Temple is the only one of these people who had no passion.

C0989 ADMIRALS AND SCHOOLBOYS. *Nation & Athenaeum*, 2 November 1929, 168.

Letter to the Editor. Reply to Mr. C. Ernst Fayle (see C0987).

C0990 THE GRAMOPHONE. WOB. *Nation & Athenaeum*, 2 November 1929, 173.

Review of *Modern Gramophones and Electrical Producers*, by P. Wilson and G. W. Webb with a Foreword by Compton Mackenzie.

This book is written for the expert, but parts of it are interesting to the layman. It tells how telephone engineers improved the instruments for playing records. Proper care of records and needles also helps.

C0991 "THE HOLY STRIFE OF DISPUTATIOUS MEN". WOB. *Nation & Athenaeum*, 9 November 1929, 205.

Review of *A History of Freethought in the Nineteenth Century*, by J. M. Robertson, 2 vols.

The author's thorough knowledge of the facts makes him seem omniscient. Unfortunately he accords the same importance to every fact.

C0992 THE GERMAN TRIBES. WOB. *Nation & Athenaeum*, 16 November 1929, 254.

Review of *Lord D'Abernon's Diary*, vol. II: *The Years of Crisis; Walter Rathenau, His Life and Work*, by Count Harry Kessler; *July, 1914*, by Emil Ludwig; and *War Diaries and Other Papers*, by Major-General Max Hoffman.

Lord D'Abernon was a good writer and a good ambassador. Count Kessler's book shows Walter Rathenau's character as so complex that tragedy was almost inevitable, especially as he was a Jew in anti-Semitic Germany.

C0993 PURITANS AND IMPURITANS. WOB. *Nation & Athenaeum*, 23 November 1929, 286.

Review of *After Puritanism*, by Hugh Kingsmill (Duckworth); and *The Impuritans*, by Harvey Wickham.

Neither book is entirely successful, but compared to Mr. Wickham's, Mr. Kingsmill's is a masterpiece.

C0994 RUSSIAN LITERATURE. WOB. *Nation & Athenaeum*, 20 November 1929, 318.

Review of *The Countess Tolstoy's Later Diary; New Dostoevsky Letters*, tr. by S. S. Koteliansky; and *Oblomov*, by Ivan Goncharov, tr. by Natalie Duddington.

The diaries of Countess Tolstoy make one sympathize with her husband. He was a man who was able "to impress himself upon things, events, persons; but it was things, events, persons which impressed themselves upon Dostoevsky." Even with no plot and no very good characters *Oblomov* is a masterpiece. "Sentence by sentence, it is built up into a form of amazing sweep and vastness, a great epic, a terrible comedy, into one of those great works of art in which no one can say exactly where the tragedy begins and the comedy ends."

C0995 THE EAST GOES WEST. WOB. *Nation & Athenaeum*, 7 December 1929, 351.

Review of *A History of Nationalism in the East*, by Hans Kohn, tr. from the German by Miss M. M. Green.

"Whatever its limitations, it is a book which deserves to be read." Will the nationalism of the East be as great a curse as the nationalism of the West?

C0996 THE BOLSHIES ON PARNASSUS. WOB. *Nation & Athenaeum*, 14 December 1929, 402.

Review of *Tradition and Experiment in Present-Day Literature*.

The ten authors of the ten essays which make up this disappointing book seem to conclude that "successful experiment becomes tradition."

C0997 MONTAIGNE. WOB. *Nation & Athenaeum*, 21 December 1929, 578.

Review of *Montaigne, An Essay in Two Parts*, by André Gide, tr. by S. H. Guest and T. F. Blewitt (Blackamore Press).

Gide misses the deepest and truest interpretations of Montaigne's complex character in this expensive book intended for the collector.

C0998 ON THE BENCH AND IN THE DOCK. WOB. *Nation & Athenaeum*, 28 December 1929, 460.

Review of *The 'Young Person's' Complete Guide to Crime*, by C. G. L. du Cann; and *Chief Justice Coke, His Family and Descendants at Holkham*, by Charles Warburton Jones; with mention of *The Bloody Assizes*, ed. by J. G. Muddiman.

Mr. du Cann tries to be funny all of the time; Mr. Jones, to whitewash Coke; and Mr. Muddiman, to whitewash Jeffreys.

1930

C0999 MR. CHESTERTON AND MR. BELLOC. WOB. *Nation & Athenaeum*, 4 January 1930, 486.

Review of *A Companion to Mr. Wells's "Outline of History"*, by Hilaire Belloc, 2nd ed.; *The Thing*, by G. K. Chesterton; *G. K. C. as M. C., Being a Collection of 37 Introductions by G. K. Chesterton*, ed. by J. P. Fonseka; and *The Philosophy of St. Thomas Aquinas*, by Etienne Gilson, tr. by E. Bullough, 2nd ed.

These books are Catholic propaganda. Mr. Belloc suffers from narrow parochialism.

Two letters to the editor comment on LW's remark about Belloc in the January 11 issue.

C1000   THE NATURAL HISTORY OF A POLITICAL ANIMAL. WOB. *Nation & Athenaeum*, 11 January 1930, 512.

Review of *Democracy, Its Defects and Advantages*, by C. Delisle Burns; *Studies in the English Social and Political Thinkers of the Nineteenth Century*, by R. H. Murray; and *Edmund Burke and the Revolt against the Eighteenth Century*, by Alfred Cobban.

Political science often disintegrates into political propaganda because writers fail to distinguish between political ideas and political actions, that is, between what ought to be and what is.

C1001   A PREMIUM ON SAFE DRIVING. *Nation & Athenaeum*, 18 January 1930, 533–34.

Signed article.

Competent but reckless drivers cause most accidents by speeding. All drivers should therefore be compelled to buy liability insurance, but no one should be allowed to buy insurance which covers the costs of damaging his own car by collision or overturning.

Three letters to the editor concerning this article were published January 25, p. 573.

C1002   BROWSING IN THE PAST. WOB. *Nation & Athenaeum*, 18 January 1930, 573.

Review of *The Hardman Papers*, [3rd instalment], ed. by S. M. Ellis; *The Diary of a Country Parson, the Rev. James Woodforde*, ed. by John Beresford. vol. IV [1793–1796]; with mention of *The Life of Napoleon*, by Dmitri Merezhkovsky; and *The Autobiography of Calvin Coolidge*.

Reliving his life with Hardman can be pleasurable. Mr. Ellis provides helpful historical background. Volume IV of *The Diary of a Country Parson* is as charming as the earlier volumes. The book on Napoleon is hero worship. "I thoroughly enjoyed President Coolidge."

C1003   MEDITATIONS ON RELIGION. WOB. *Nation & Athenaeum*, 25 January 1930, 578.

Review of *The Present and Future of Religion*, by C. E. M. Joad.

In this puzzling book Mr. Joad first shows that religious belief has declined markedly; then he announces that religion has a great future; and that "the political impulse" is "essentially religious".

C1004   MOTORING AND INSURANCE. *Nation & Athenaeum*, 1 February 1930, 604.

Letter to the Editor.

Reply to criticisms of his January 10 article, C1001. Another letter appears on the same page.

C1005   THE COUNT OF MONTE CRISTO. WOB. *Nation & Athenaeum*, 1 February 1930, 610.

Review of *Dumas, the Incredible Marquis*, by Herbert S. Gorman.

"The biography is too long and too wordy; the story and the style both have a tendency to flop." The author gives many facts and lets them speak for themselves.

C1006   A CENSORSHIP AT WORK. WOB. *Nation & Athenaeum*, 8 February 1930, 642.

Review of *Cato, or the Future of Censorship*, by William Seagle; and *The Index of Prohibited Books*, New ed.

Mr. Seagle's book would be more interesting if he had considered the working of Papal censorship by the Index. LW recommends the Index to anyone wanting some amusement from the inconsistencies.

Letters to the Editor the following two weeks show that Roman Catholic correspondents disagreed about the effect of the Index.

C1007 THE IDEALS OF JOURNALISM. WOB. *Nation & Athenaeum,* 15 February 1930, 674.

Review of *The Newspaper of To-morrow,* by Harold Herd; and *Deucalion,* by Geoffrey West.

Mr. Herd wears rosy spectacles; Mr. West takes a gloomier view. But West is wrong in his assumption that reviewers lack critical background and that all they do is praise or pan a book. "In the last seven years it has been my fate to read attentively thousands of different reviews by hundreds of different reviewers. These reviewers practically never said that a book was a masterpiece or an abomination. . . ."

This is the last of Leonard Woolf's WORLD OF BOOKS articles.

C1008 ENGLAND AND THE WORLD. *Nation & Athenaeum,* 8 March 1930, 770 & 772.

Review of *England,* by Wilhelm Dibelius, tr. from the German by Mary Agnes Hamilton; and *England's Voice of Freedom: An Anthology of Liberty,* selected with an Introduction by Henry W. Nevinson.

Both books deal with English conceptions of liberty. Mr. Dibelius is thorough and misunderstands little, though he does show his national bias.

Charles Wright objected that LW made mis-statements in this review (letters published 15 and 29 March).

C1009 DIBELIUS'S "ENGLAND". *Nation & Athenaeum,* 22 March 1930, 858.

Letter to the Editor objecting to the fact that Charles Wright signed only his initials (C1008).

C1010 VOLTAIRE AND CASANOVA. *Nation & Athenaeum,* 29 March 1930, 896–97.

Review of *Voltaire, raconté par ceux qui l'ont vu,* ed. by J. G. Prod'homme; and *Giocomo Casanova, His Life and Memoirs,* tr. from the French by Arthur Machen. Selected and ed. by G. D. Gribble, 2 vols.

Prod'homme gives the reader a glimpse of the contradictory elements combined in Voltaire's character. His icy surface covered a volcanic spirit which made itself known in a wit that made him enemies. Casanova records meeting Voltaire after Prod'homme went to Geneva in 1754. The translation is so abridged that it may not give the quality of the original.

C1011 DIBELIUS. *Nation & Athenaeum,* 5 April 1930, 12.

Letter to the Editor.

Charles Wright attributes mis-statements to Dibelius (C1008).

C1012 "TIGER OR TOM CAT". *Nation & Athenaeum,* 19 April 1930, 85–86.

Review of *Grandeur and Misery of Victory,* by Georges Clemenceau.

The book shows that M. Clemenceau's nickname "the Tiger" was a misnomer. He had none of the grandeur of the tiger, but was little and stupid. He had been a journalist and had a bitter tongue and pen.

C1013 FROM SARAJEVO TO GENEVA. *Political Quarterly,* I.2 (April 1930), 186–206.

First signed article by LW in this periodical.

Sarajevo is symbolic of nationalism; Geneva, of internationalism.

Abstract of this printed in *Social Science Abstracts* II.15312, p. 1814, signed L. B. Pearson.

C1014 BOOKS IN BRIEF. *Nation & Athenaeum*, 3 May 1930.
Short unsigned review of *Herbs, Salads and Seasonings*, by X. M. Boulestin and Jason Hill.

A book for gardeners and cooks.

C1015 THE FEMALE AT HOME AND ABROAD. *Nation & Athenaeum*, 10 May 1930, 178 & 180.
Review of *Mary Gladstone; Diary and Letters*, ed. by Lucy Masterman; and *The Letters of Gertrude Bell*, ed. by Lady Bell. New ed.

To judge a book from another time it helps to measure it against another book from the same period. Gertrude Bell moved in the wake of adventure, but Mary Gladstone moved in the wake of Mr. Gladstone and Mr. Drew. She could have had an exciting life, for she knew all the great men of her time, but she seems to have been bogged down in "frantically busy aimlessness".

C1016 TOLSTOY AGAIN. *Nation & Athenaeum*, 17 May 1930, 219–20.
Review of *The Life of Tolstoy; Later Years*, by Aylmer Maude, vol. II, Tolstoy Centenary ed.; *Childhood, Boyhood and Youth; What is Art?* and *Essays on Art*, by Leo Tolstoy, tr. by Aylmer Maude.

Maude's rewritten second volume of Tolstoy's biography is interesting, but the print of this edition is hard to read. Tolstoy's character, his powerful and pungent individuality, is what makes this life fascinating. In this "he stands with Socrates, possibly Christ, and certainly Montaigne."

C1017 THE PROBLEM OF AFRICA. *Nation & Athenaeum*, 24 May 1930, 254.
Review of *Africa and Some World Problems*, by J. C. Smuts; and *White and Black in Africa. A Critical Examination of the Rhodes Lectures of General Smuts*, by J. H. Oldham, signed L.W.

The argument of General Smuts that all British Africa should be arranged by segregation has no foundation. His book is dangerous because he has authority on his side. Luckily, Mr. Oldham subjects the book to devastating and just criticism. LW mentions the problem in Kenya.

C1018 A EUROPEAN SENSATION. *Nation & Athenaeum*, 7 June 1930, 322–23.
Review of *A Cultural History of the Modern Age, from the Black Death to the World War*, vol. I. *Introduction: Renaissance and Reformation*, by Egon Friedell; tr. from the German by Charles Francis Atkinson (New York: Knopf), signed L.W.

The publisher compares the sensation of this book to that of Spengler's. Herr Friedell is one of the modern quacks who have a contempt for facts and ignore reason. Still, he is intelligent and well-informed.

C1019 THE SCHOLAR'S LIFE. *Nation & Athenaeum*, 21 June 1930, 381–82.
Review of *My Recollections, 1848–1914*, by Ulrich von Wilamowitz-Moellendorff, tr. by G. C. Richards, signed L.W.

The author is a classical scholar and an aristocrat. The book "is tightly packed with material", and the English translation is bad. Reading it causes mental fatigue.

C1020 MARRIAGE AND THE FAMILY. *Nation & Athenaeum*, 28 June 1930, 412.
Review of *Marriage, Past, Present, and Future*, by Ralph de Pomerai; and *Chronos, or the Future of the Family*, by Eden Paul.

Both books deserve wide reading. "The consciousness of individuality and the claims of the individual to equality of opportunity, which in the late eighteenth and early nineteenth centuries caused the political revolutions, were extended in the late nineteenth and early twentieth century to every sphere of social life."

C1021   THE WORD OF ELIJAH. *Nation & Athenaeum*, 5 July 1930, 431–32.
Unsigned article which refers to White Papers on East Africa.

White settlers in Kenya have been taking the natives' lands and then making the natives work it for hire, a reenactment of the tragedy of Naboth's vineyard. To prevent this it is important that the British Government retain the power and not let the white settlers govern East Africa. LW refers to his article, C1017.

C1022   A REVOLUTIONARY. *Nation & Athenaeum*, 12 July 1930, 474.
Review of *My Life*, by Leon Trotsky.

"This is one of the best books of reminiscences which has come my way in a long time." Trotsky is a born writer who can describe people and places vividly. He does not measure history by his personal fate. Although interesting politically and historically, the book is polemical.

C1023   A TRAVELLER IN THE EAST. *Nation & Athenaeum*, 26 July 1930, 535.
Review of *Oriental Memories of a German Diplomatist*, by Friedrich Rosen; and *The Quatrains of Omar Khayyam*, newly translated with an Introduction by Friedrich Rosen.

Dr. Rosen's ability to write English and his love and understanding of Eastern peoples make his reminiscences charming. He was in the German Consular service in Syria, Persia, Bagdad, and Jerusalem, but had the leisure to travel and to study oriental languages and literature. Besides a leisurely, meditative manner, he has a sense of humour which adds flavour to his book.

C1024   THE IRRITABLE AND ERRATIC EGO. *Nation & Athenaeum*, 2 August 1930, 569.
Review of *Bengal Lancer*, by F. Yeats-Brown; *Misfit*, by Captain F. R. White; and *Some Personal Reminiscences*, by Sir Bampfylde Fuller.

These three members of the ruling class went to India and all were infected by some sort of mysticism.

C1025   SIR EDWARD GRIGG. *Nation & Athenaeum*, 23 August 1930, 641–42.
Article signed "From a Correspondent". Refers to C1021.

Sir Edward Grigg holds that the White Papers are a reversal of earlier policy. He opposes native interests. Sir Charles Eliot, Secretary of State, has resigned in protest.

Norman Leys, in a letter to the Editor published August 30, commends this article, but asks for action. Lord Lothian, in a letter published September 6, calls the article a vicious anonymous attack on Grigg's speech.

C1026   STATES AND CHURCHES. *Nation & Athenaeum*, 23 August 1930, 651.
Review of *Church, State, and Study*, by Ernest Barker.

C1027   SIR EDWARD GRIGG. *Nation & Athenaeum*, 13 September 1930, 727–28.
Letter to the Editor, signed Your Correspondent.

"It is an amusing fact that whenever anyone raises his voice in favour of 'native policy' in East Africa and and against the 'settlers' policy' of Lord Delamere and his party, some respectable person rises up in England and lectures him in approved schoolmasterly manner on being bitter, intemperate, and prejudiced."

C1028 DREAMS AND REALITIES. *Nation & Athenaeum*, 13 September 1930, 735.

Review of *The Problem of the Twentieth Century*, by David Davies.

International sanctions is a difficult subject to discuss, and the book is a hard one to review for a reviewer who believes in internationalism. It is an honest book which tries to face the problems of the use of force in the world, but it is not entirely realistic.

In a letter to the Editor ("International Sanctions", September 27, p. 787) "Lex" says LW is not quite just in this review.

C1029 MODERN WITCHCRAFT. *Nation & Athenaeum*, 27 September 1930, 795.

Review of *The Story of Psychic Science*, by Hereward Carrington; *Rudi Schneider: A Scientific Examination of his Mediumship*, by Harry Price; and *Some Modern Mediums*, by Theodore Besterman.

These three books will entertain the cynic.

C1030 LORD D'ABERNON AND LOCARNO. *Nation & Athenaeum*, 4 October 1930, 18.

Review of *An Ambassador of Peace: Lord D'Abernon's Diary*, vol. III: *The Years of Recovery, January 1924-October 1926*.

The modest, self-effacing day by day account reveals the important part Lord D'Abernon played behind the scenes. "He is a skilful etcher of character; his comments are shrewd and have a kindly acidity which is often refreshing."

C1031 SOVIET FOREIGN POLICY. *Nation & Athenaeum*, 18 October 1930, 109.

Review of *The Soviets in World Affairs*, by Louis Fischer, 2 vols.

The author is a pro-Bolshevik American journalist who was given access to documents and other information by the Soviet government. His is a history of foreign relations through Soviet eyes.

C1032 THREE SIDES OF A PICTURE. *Nation & Athenaeum*, 25 October 1930, 139.

Review of *The Age of the Chartists, 1832–1854*, by J. L. and Barbara Hammond; *Lord John Russell*, by A. Wyatt Tilby; and *British Colonial Policy in the Age of Peel & Russell*, by W. P. Morrell.

These three books present different aspects of society in the same historical period. The Hammonds study the idea which animated the urban population, the desire to 'get on' and the resulting disillusionment. Mr. Tilby's political biography shows the period through the eyes of the governing classes; and Mr. Morrell's book studies the colonial policy during the same period.

C1033 GREAT FUN. *Nation & Athenaeum*, 8 November 1930, 197–98.

Review of *My Early Life*, by the Rt Hon. Winston Churchill; *John, Lord Montagu of Beaulieu*, by Lady Troubridge and Archibald Marshall; and *Makers of Modern Europe*, by Count Sforza.

Winston Churchill seems to treat every aspect of life as a game. The biography of Lord Montagu reads like a newspaper report of a wedding or a funeral, except when he determined "to show the natives in the boat how a 'sahib' would die" after it had been torpedoed. "The sublime insolence of this remark about natives and sahibs is only equalled by its sublime ignorance." Lord Curzon seems to have baffled Count Sforza.

A Letter to the Editor published November 22 says Montagu wanted only to show that an Englishman could die as decently as a native.

C1034 THE LATE LORD MONTAGU OF BEAULIEU. *Nation & Athenaeum,* 29 November 1930, 293.
> Letter to the Editor.
>> LW questions the statement of the anonymous friend of Montagu, C1033.

C1035 COBBETT. *Nation & Athenaeum,* 29 November 1930, 298.
> Review of *Cobbett's Rural Rides,* ed. by G. D. H. and Margaret Cole, 3 vols.
>> An excellent library edition – the printing, the binding, the paper are all excellent, as is the editing. Cobbett has many prejudices but he strikes a poetic chord when he discusses what he likes.

C1036 THE ANTEDILUVIANS. *Nation & Athenaeum,* 13 December 1930, 379.
> Review of *The Diaries of John Bright,* with a Foreword by Philip Bright; ed. by R. A. J. Walling.
>> One wondered, on beginning to read, what relevance the life of Bright had for a world in which all that he had done was dead and rotten. Then from his diary emerged his daily thoughts and "the contemporary aroma of antediluvian England. . . . He was a man of real intelligence, who yet remained human and humane; a man of quick and easy emotion who kept his brain clear and active; a man of high principles who never allowed them to fuddle or warp his mind or his sense of humour. He seems to me to have had in him the seeds of a type of democratic civilization which, if the course of history had oscillated ever so slightly, might have developed and established itself in Europe during the nineteenth century."
> Woolf's irony in lamenting the passing of Democracy was so heavy that some readers thought he was belittling Bright's achievements. Correspondence appeared in the *Nation & Athenaeum,* 3, 10, 24, and 31 January and 7 February 1931, pp. 455, 479, 538, 569, and 597.

C1037 DEMOCRACY LISTENS-IN. *The Spectator,* 13 December 1930, 931–32.
> Letter to the Editor.
>> The recent article in *The Spectator* by Sir John Reith, "Broadcasting and a Better World", raised an interesting question. Free discussion of all subjects should be permitted on the B.B.C.

1931

C1038 MUCH ADO ABOUT NOTHING. *Nation & Athenaeum,* 3 January 1931, 461–62.
> Review of *In Defence of Sensuality,* by John Cowper Powys.
>> The book contains "an enormous bulk of words for so small a kernel of matter." It is an attack on humour. Powys has a mystic's contempt for reason.

C1039 THE DIARIES OF JOHN BRIGHT. *Nation & Athenaeum,* 10 January 1931, 479.
> Letter written in response to one published the previous week from F. E. Pollard, who spelled out Bright's achievements.
>> Pollard misread the review (C1036) if he thinks LW is ignorant of the facts because he wrote ironically.

C1040 THE ADAMS FAMILY. *Nation & Athenaeum,* 17 January 1931, 514 & 516.
> Review of *The Adams Family,* by James Truslow Adams; and *Letters of Henry Adams (1858–1891),* ed. by Worthington Chauncey Ford.

The first book is worth reading, but Adams's letters are dull and boring. His *Education* shows that Adams "was always psychologically surrounded by a slight aura of depression."

C1041 JOHN BRIGHT. *Nation & Athenaeum*, 31 January 1931, 569.
Letter in reply to one from P. B. Roth published the previous week.
LW explains that his review (C1036) was meant to praise Bright.

C1042 THE LAW. *Nation & Athenaeum*, 31 January 1931, 575–76.
Review of *Essays in Jurisprudence and the Common Law*, by Arthur L. Goodhart; and *In Quest of Justice*, by Claud Mullins.
These extremely interesting books should be read by both lawyers and laymen.

C1043 THE WORLD, 1929. *Nation & Athenaeum*, 7 February 1931, 604.
Review of *Survey of International Affairs, 1929*, by Arnold J. Toynbee; and *Documents on International Affairs, 1929*, ed. by John W. Wheeler-Bennett.

C1044 ECONOMIC EQUALITY. *Nation & Athenaeum*, 21 February 1931, 669.
Review of *Equality*, by R. H. Tawney.
The matter is as entertaining as, and more important than, the vigorous style. It is a realistic account of economic inequality.

C1045 RUSSIA AND THE RUSSIANS. *New Statesman and Nation*, n.s. I.1. Amalgamation number, 28 February 1931, 22 & 24.
Review of *Russia: A Social History*, by D. S. Mirsky.
The author fails to piece together the disparate facts about Russia.

C1046 THE TRAGIC COMEDIAN. *New Statesman and Nation*, 6 June 1931, 547–48.
Review of *Lassalle*, by Arno Shirokauer, tr. from the German by Eden and Cedar Paul.
Lassalle negotiated for a time on an equal footing with Bismarck and had claims to having founded the Social Democratic Party. His biography should be interesting, but this is a lamentable production. The author "is so much occupied with being clever and brilliant that he has no time to attempt to understand his victim."

C1047 THE FUTURE OF BRITISH BROADCASTING. *Political Quarterly*, II.2 (April-June 1931), 172–85.
Article on the potentialities of broadcasting and the role of the B.B.C., founded in 1927, in developing public opinion. LW mentions *Public Opinion*, by Walter Lippmann.
Abstract by H. McD. Clokie. *Social Science Abstracts* 4.1210, p. 102.

C1048 Review of *England in the Age of the American Revolution*, vol. I, by L. B. Namier. *Political Quarterly*, II.2 (April-June 1931), 288–92.
"Namier interprets historical events as a kind of kaleidoscopic confusion."

C1049 BRITISH JUSTICE AND THE ROUSE CASE. *New Statesman and Nation*, 1 August 1931, 143.
Review of *Trial of Alfred Arthur Rouse*, ed. by Helena Normanton.
Mrs. Normanton does not fully appreciate that this was not a fair trial. No motive for the murder was established in court, but the newspapers had prejudiced the jury.

C1050 EDUCATING THE LISTENER-IN. *New Statesman and Nation*, 5 September 1931, 274–75.
Unsigned article, listed in the index as by Leonard Woolf.

The B.B.C. has great potential both for adult education and for propaganda. So far the topics and the speakers have been well chosen. But "why should the B.B.C. muzzle the sceptic and agnostic?"

C1051 Reviews. *Political Quarterly*, II.3 (July-Sept 1931), 440–44.
Democracy on Trial, by Lord Eustace Percy; and *A Realist Looks at Democracy*, by Alderton Pink. Introduction by Aldous Huxley.
Percy wants government by an elite. Pink despairs of democracy; he does not believe the average person can be educated to take part.

C1052 IS DEMOCRACY FAILING? Headed THE MODERN STATE – I. *Listener*, 7 October 1931, 571–72.
The first of six articles based on talks by LW broadcast by the B.B.C. entitled "The Modern State".
Democracy "rests on a new idea about happiness and particularly the happiness of ordinary people," that it is the duty of government to see that all people get an equal right to it. "A democratic system treats everyone politically merely as an individual and as an equal political unit", ignoring class, birth or political affiliation.

C1053 HAVE WE THE RIGHT TO BE HAPPY? Headed CAN DEMOCRACY SURVIVE? – II. *Listener*, 21 October 1931, 666 & 669.
[THE MODERN STATE II]. Includes picture of London's Lido.
Democratic legislation includes social reforms such as regulation of the conditions of labour, and provides social services such as recreational facilities, free libraries and universal education. Education determines one's social and economic position as well as what one is able to enjoy, for the ability to read is the source of much happiness. Everyone should have leisure time and the possibility of enjoying it. "The difference between a civilised and an uncivilised person consists largely in the different way in which they spend their free hours. . . . One of the chief problems before democracy is to provide people with means to employ their leisure well and to teach them to use them."

C1054 DEMOCRACY AND EQUALITY. THE MODERN STATE – III. *Listener*, 21 October 1931, 666 & 669.
The democrat holds that "for the purposes of government and the organisation of society . . . people ought not to be treated as members of particular classes but simply as individuals." In order for democracy to work everyone "should be sufficiently educated to understand the larger questions and to use his vote intelligently."

C1055 BERNARD SHAW SURVEYS THE CRISIS. *Everyman*, 22 October 1931, 402.
Extracts from the symposium on constitutional crisis in the Oct-Dec *Political Quarterly*, C1063.

C1056 SHOULD WE DO WHAT WE WANT? THE MODERN STATE – IV. *Listener*, 28 October 1931, [711], 712 & 745.
The democrat must realise the necessity for compromise between authority and liberty if there is not to be anarchy. It is not just absolute government that threatens democracy, but also a disease which grows out of democracy itself, standardisation.

C1057 GODS OR BEES? THE MODERN STATE – V. *Listener*, 4 November 1931, 766–67.
Pericles' description of the Athenian constitution "is the ideal of a democratic society". It is based on liberty and equality. By contrast, the

members of the modern non-democratic state must perform set functions like bees in a hive. Their individuality is suppressed in the interest of efficiency.

C1058 DEMOCRACY AND EQUALITY. *Listener*, 4 November 1931, 789.
Letter replying to one from Mr. Lever.
> "All I am doing in these talks (C1052–54, C1056–57, C1060) is to try to elucidate what that ideal reality [Democracy] is, in other words what the kind of government, society, civilisation is at which the democrat is aiming."

C1059 FRENCH POLITICAL THOUGHT. *New Statesman and Nation*, 7 November 1931, 582.
Review of *French Political Thought in the Nineteenth Century*, by Roger Soltau.
> The book forms an excellent companion and continuation to Kingsley Martin's *French Liberal Thought in the Nineteenth Century*. It is a brave, but only partially successful, attempt to deal with a really complex subject. Perhaps Soltau's chronological arrangement added to his difficulties.

C1060 CITIZENS OF THE WORLD. THE MODERN STATE – VI. *Listener*, 11 November 1931, 817.
> Nationalism and imperialism are forces hostile to democracy.

This concludes LW's talks. Lord Eustace Percy continued the series the following week. Publication of correspondence concerning LW's statements continued for several weeks. The series was republished as *The Modern State*, B20, in 1933.

C1061 ROSEBERY. *New Statesman and Nation*, 21 November 1931, 645–46.
Review of *Lord Rosebery*, by the Marquess of Crewe.
> "If the reputation of an ex-Prime Minister has to be biographically buried in two volumes, Lord Crewe performs the operation admirably." Lord Rosebery's son-in-law has written "in the style of the Albert Memorial and a *Times* obituary." By contrast Antonina Vallentin has written a truly remarkable book in the life of Gustav Stresemann (see C1068).

C1062 KEYNESSANDRA. *New Statesman and Nation*, 19 December 1931, 788.
Review of *Essays in Persuasion*, by John Maynard Keynes.
> Mr. Keynes is more successful as a prophet than as a persuader. His long-term prophecies are more convincing than his short-term. It is clear from the book that he is more intelligent than the people who have failed to take his advice. His gloomy predictions about economics and politics make melancholy reading.

C1063 ON A CONSTITUTIONAL REVOLUTION. *Political Quarterly*, II.4 (Oct-to Dec 1931), 475–77.
Part of "Reflections on the Crisis: A Symposium", by G. B. Shaw, J. A. Hobson, H. J. Laski, G. Lowes Dickinson, Alfred Zimmern, Leonard Woolf, Kingsley Martin, and William A. Robson, pp. 457–84 (see C1055).
> The handling of the economic crisis by Ramsay MacDonald and the King are a threat to democratic government.

1932

C1064 AN ANGEL OF PEACE. *New Statesman and Nation*, 9 January 1932, 43.
Review of *The Unseen Assassins*, by Sir Norman Angell.

The author tries in this book to find the psychological causes of war. He considers most people too poorly educated to see the implications of policies such as nationalism and protectionism.

C1065 LYTTON STRACHEY. Headed MISCELLANY. *New Statesman and Nation*, 30 January 1932, 118–19.
Obituary article.

Appreciation and discussion of Strachey's character in relation to his writing. LW says Strachey's character was made up of "a whole series of contradictory qualities. . . . He was a realist and a cynic and yet he was a romantic who loved the pageantry of life and history." He set high standards for himself and others, yet "he would display, on occasions, an almost contemptuous, if not unscrupulous, disregard of accuracy in detail."

C1066 MR. WELLS'S WORK AND DAYS. *New Statesman and Nation*, 27 February 1932, 266.

Review of *The Work, Wealth and Happiness of Mankind*, by H. G. Wells. This third volume of the trilogy, which began with *The Outline of History* and continued with *Science of Life*, traces the evolution of man. Despite its length it is interesting and easy to read. "The other day one of the younger generation . . . dismissed Mr. Wells as a thinker who could not think. . . . Mr. Wells thinks imaginatively rather than intellectually. . . ." He never loses sight of the enormous picture he draws, and he makes his reader think.

Wells broke with LW over this review (*Beginning Again*, A41, pp. 194–97).

C1067 Review of *Politics and the Younger Generation*, by A. L. Rowse. *Political Quarterly*, III.1 (Jan-March 1932), 136–38.

Mr. Rowse may be too optimistic about socialism. He over-emphasises the psychological effect of economics and is too dependent upon universal causes and remedies.

C1068 Review of *A Political Biography: Stresemann*, by Antonina Vallentin, tr. by Eric Sutton. Foreword by Albert Einstein. *Political Quarterly*, III.1, (Jan–March 1932), 143–44.

This very good political biography gives a brilliant picture of a remarkable man and helps to explain the history of Germany since the war.

C1069 Review of *England in Palestine*, by Norman Bentwich. *Political Quarterly*, III.2 (April-June 1932), 298–300.

This is a factual, complete, authoritative account of the administration.

C1070 BEHIND THE BARS. *New Statesman and Nation*, 9 July 1932, 44.
Review of *Twenty Thousand Years in Sing Sing*, by Warden Lewis E. Lawes. The author shows that wardens are sometimes more understanding than justices. LW quotes from Shakespeare's "King Lear".

C1071 Review of *Studies in Politics*, by Harold Laski. *Political Quarterly*, III.3 (July-Sept 1932), 443–44.

The author's vision gives unity to this collection of journalistic articles on different subjects.

C1072 LORD OXFORD. *New Statesman and Nation*, 22 October 1932, 485–86.
Review of *The Life of Henry Herbert Asquith, Lord Oxford and Asquith*, 2 vols, by J. A. Spender and Cyril Asquith.

The authors have done fairly well with the personal picture and less well with the political picture of Asquith. The usual excuse of writers that it is too soon to judge objectively the effectiveness of a politician or statesman does apply in this case, for his decisions affected everyone.

1933

C1073 GENERAL GORDON. *New Statesman and Nation,* 28 January 1933, 105–06.
Review of *Gordon: An Intimate Portrait,* by H. E. Wortham; and *Gordon: The Sudan and Slavery,* by Pierre Crabitès.
> Both books owe a lot to Bernard Allen's *Gordon and the Sudan.* Mr. Crabitès favours his hero too much; Mr. Wortham is more impartial.

C1074 ROUSSEAU: A MODERN MAN IN THE ANCIENT WORLD. Headed SOME MAKERS OF THE MODERN SPIRIT. *Listener,* 22 February 1933, 276–78.
Article.
> Rousseau taught that one should develop one's capacities and think for oneself. For this reason he was viewed as a threat by the aristocrats and dogmatists who held power in his time.

Reprinted, 1933, as "Rousseau" in *Some Makers of the Modern Spirit,* B22, pp. 98–110; and again in *Readings in the History of Civilization,* eds. Harry H. Kimber and Stebelton H. Nulle, 1948, Michigan State College Press, pp. 533–44.

C1075 INTELLECTUAL CRIME. *New Statesman and Nation,* 25 February 1933, 227–28.
Review of *Intellectual Crime,* by Janet Chance; and *Is Christianity True? A Discussion between Arnold Lunn and C. E. M. Joad.*
> Mrs. Chance maintains that religious creeds are intellectual crimes against the young. Neither Mr. Lunn nor Mr. Joad manages to influence the other in his beliefs. Their dispute is like a good dogfight or rugger match. It shows only that there are no "intellectual standards of truth in our minds today".

C1076 FROM GENEVA TO THE NEXT WAR. *Political Quarterly,* IV.1 (Jan-March 1933), 30–43.
Article.
> The League of Nations is a start toward international government and away from nationalism and militarism. Negative factors include statesmen regarding the League as an instrument of national policy, and lack of an informed public to lend weight to the pacifist side. Nationalism became more popular between 1930 and 1932, and support for the League declined. Hitlerism, the League's failure to effect disarmament, the League's failure to cope with Japanese aggression, and the government's foreign policy and attitude towards the League will contribute to another war.

C1077 Review of *The Life of Joseph Chamberlain,* vol. I: *1836–1885,* by J. L. Garvin. *Political Quarterly,* IV.1 (Jan-March 1933), 130.
> The book gives previously unknown details of Chamberlain's political development.

C1078 *Political Quarterly,* IV.1 (Jan-March 1933), 298–300.
Review of *Survey of International Affairs, 1931; Documents on International Affairs, 1931; Denmark's Right to Greenland,* by Knud Berlin; *Essays on the Manchurian Problem,* by Shushi Hsü; *The League on Trial,* by Max Beer, tr. by C. K. Webster; and *The Religious Foundations of Internationalism,* by Norman Bentwich.

C1079 ETHERIAL PROBLEMS [*sic*]. *New Statesman and Nation,* 22 July 1933, 99–100.

Review of *Shall I Listen?* by Filson Young; with reference to *Wireless over 30 Years,* by R. N. Vyvyan.

> The tone of the B.B.C. is that of cheerful uplift in the manner of Dickens's Mr. Pecksniff. The other danger is that the B.B.C. might become an aesthetic, a political and a moral dictatorship.

C1080 SOCIALISM IN OUR TIME. *New Statesman and Nation,* 9 September 1933, 302 & 304.

Review of *Problems of a Socialist Government,* by Sir Stafford Cripps and others.

> This is a concrete and practial contribution towards the foundation of a socialist state.

C1081 Review of *The Life of Joseph Chamberlain,* vol. II: *1885–1895,* by J. L. Garvin. *Political Quarterly,* IV.3 (July-Sept 1933), 452–55.

> What happened to Liberal Government may be compared to the tragedy of Oedipus. The party failed to concede economic equality when it conflicted with the economic interests of the ruling class.

C1082 BIOGRAPHY "IN EXTREMIS". *New Statesman and Nation,* 7 October 1933, 418.

Review of *The Post Victorians.* Introduction by W. R. Inge.

> The choice of people to include in the category Post Victorians makes no sense. The forty biographies by forty writers read like obituary notices.

C1083 THE LIFE OF A MILLIONAIRE. *Listener,* 11 October 1933, Book Supplement, p. iv.

Review of *The Life of Andrew Carnegie,* by Burton J. Hendrick.

> Carnegie is interesting not because he made money, but because he had a tough enquiring mind and a sense of social responsibility.

C1084 WE PREFER CATHAY. *New Statesman and Nation,* 14 October 1933, 448.

Review of *Fifty Years of Europe. A Study in Pre-War Documents,* by J. A. Spender.

> Spender is better at analysing incidents than at drawing conclusions about them. The book is objective and fair. The terrible waste brought about by the stupidities and ineptitudes of the rulers and statesmen is disgusting.

C1085 "A HAPPY ANNIVERSARY" BEING AN EDITORIAL FROM OUR LEADING NATIONAL DAILY, JAN. 1, 1939 [*sic*]. *New Statesman and Nation,* 4 November 1933, 541–42.

Unsigned, fictitious account of the first year of the Fascist regime of Lord Benito Hustler.

> ["Leonard Woolf wrote a scathing parody of a *Times* leading article which the printers refused to publish until I had altered *Times* into 'Britain's Leading Newspaper' . . . Leonard was furious with me for giving way to the printer" (Kingsley Martin, *Editor . . . Autobiography, 1931–61,* 1968, p. 12).]

Reprinted in *Essays of the Year,* 1934, B26, pp. 85–91.

C1086 MR. MONKHOUSE AND MOSCOW. *New Statesman and Nation,* 11 November 1933, 606.

Review of *Moscow, 1911–1933,* by Allan Monkhouse.

C1087 EDOUARD VII. *Listener,* 29 November 1933. Book Supplement, p. xv.

Review of *King Edward and His Times,* by André Maurois, with English translation by Hamish Miles.

The French lightweight book, meant to be read and thrown away, was more appropriate for this work than the English translation which is too heavy to hold and meant to be kept for posterity.

C1088   QUACK, QUACK! OR HAVING IT BOTH WAYS. *New Statesman and Nation*, 2 December 1933, 702 & 704.

Review of *Counter Attack from the East, the Philosophy of Radhakrishnan*, by C. E. M. Joad.

Mr. Joad, using the methods of the mystic, again attempts to reason about the unreasonable and explain the inexplicable.

Joad replied that LW attributed mysticism to him because he writes about it (*NS & N*, 16 Dec 1933, 807).

C1089   EGYPT. *New Statesman and Nation*, 30 December 1933, 873.

Review of *Ismail, the Maligned Khedive*, by Pierre Crabitès; and *The Suez Canal; Its Past, Present, and Future*, by Lt.-Col. Sir Arnold T. Wilson.

C1090   LABOUR'S FOREIGN POLICY. *Political Quarterly*, IV.4 (Oct-Dec 1933), 504–23.

Article.

The British government must support the League of Nations and take a hard line against the Fascist powers. LW refers to *Labour's Foreign Policy*, by Arthur Henderson.

C1091   THE BLOODY TRAFFIC. *Political Quarterly*, IV.4, (Oct-Dec 1933), 607–609.

Review of *The Bloody Traffic*, by A. Fenner Brockway; *Air Power and War Rights*, by J. M. Spaight. 2nd ed.; and *War, Sadism & Pacifism: Three Essays*, by Edward Glover.

Dr. Glover's book is about "communal psychology and behaviour".

1934

C1092   THE COOPERATIVE COMMONWEALTH. *Cooperation*, San Francisco: Cooperative League of the U.S.A., XX (January 1934), 9.

Excerpt from *Cooperation and the Future of Industry*, A12, which forms part of an ad offering to sell the work at $1.65.

C1093   HOW WE WON THE WAR. *New Statesman and Nation*, 3 February 1934, 157–58.

Review of *Four and a Half Years*, by Christopher Addison, vol. I, signed L. Woolf.

In this personal diary from June 1914 to January 1919, the author does not omit his own mistakes or attempt to blame others.

C1094   MUDDLE, MUDDLE, TOIL AND TROUBLE. *New Statesman and Nation*, 10 March 1934, 332–33.

Unsigned leader article.

The English government's muddled disarmament proposals, made while budgeting huge sums for military purposes, have contributed to failure of the Disarmament Conference.

C1095   THE MODERN PRISON. *New Statesman and Nation*, 10 March 1934, 362.

Review of *The Modern English Prison*, by L. W. Fox.

This is an informative, well-arranged manual by a humane and enlightened prison authority.

C1096   THE B.B.C. AND ITS CRITICS. *New Statesman and Nation*, 31 March 1934, 476–77.

Unsigned article.

> The directors of the B.B.C. should ignore the recent "natural, healthy and undeserved criticism". To help defend democracy they should be less cautious, broadcast opposing controversial views, and eliminate their class bias.

C1097 BRITISH IN INDIA. *New Statesman and Nation*, 30 June 1934, 997–98.
Review of *Rise and Fulfilment of British Rule in India*, by Edward Thompson and G. T. Garratt.

> It is remarkable that the authors have made a readable book of such a dreary story. Despite the muddle the British made of ruling India, children are still taught that empire-builders are heroes.

C1098 Review of *Government in Transition*, by Lord Eustace Percy. *Political Quarterly*, V.2 (April-June 1934), 300–02.

> Percy assumes that the object of industry must be to earn a profit, not to produce what we need to consume. This leads him to the absurd conclusion that decreasing populations mean shrinking profits.

C1099 CIVILISATIONS. *New Statesman and Nation*, 18 August 1934, 213–14.
Review of *A Study of History*, by Arnold J. Toynbee, vols I-III.

> "The book is really an investigation into the nature of civilisation and into the causes of the genesis, growth, breakdown, and disintegration of civilisations." The author relates his speculations to contemporary problems.

C1100 TOO TRUE TO BE GOOD. *New Statesman and Nation*, 8 September 1934, 298.
Review of *Prefaces*, by Bernard Shaw.

> Shaw's journey in pursuit of honesty, decency, humanity might have succeeded had not the war destroyed civilisation. He thinks he can civilise even dictators. "Well, perhaps Mr. Shaw is right and his indomitable optimism justified, for, as Montaigne and many of the other civilised men with whom he stands have remarked, it is the journey, not the arrival, which matters."

C1101 Review of *Curzon: The Last Phase, 1919–1925*, by Harold Nicolson. *Political Quarterly*, V.3 (July-Sept 1934), 430–32.

> Nicolson's sketch of Curzon in *Some People* is his masterpiece. This new book is neither a repetition nor an anti-climax.

C1102 Unsigned review of books on political and economic problems. *Political Quarterly*, V.3 (July-Sept 1934), 554–57.
Germany's Third Empire, by Moeller van der Bruck; *The Hour of Decision*, by Oswald Spengler; *The Bloodless Pogrom*, by Fritz Seidler; *Socialism's New Start*, by Miles [pseud.], tr. from the German *Neu Beginnen*, Preface by H. N. Brailsford; *Democracy*, by J. A. Hobson; and *Democracy and Dictatorship*, by Hugh Sellon.

C1103 FROM VIENNA TO VERSAILLES. *Listener*, 10 October 1934, Book Supplement, p. viii.
Review of *Freedom and Organisation, 1814–1914*, by Bertrand Russell.

> This attempt to trace the chief causes of political change during the hundred years is exhilarating and amusing. The title is too narrow for the contents; the analysis is not carried far enough.

C1104 THE LAST HALF CENTURY. Headed NEW LITERATURE. *London Mercury*, October 1934, 551–52.
Review of *A Short History of Our Times*, by J. A. Spender.

The book suffers from the author's political bias for the Liberal Party and from his oversimplified and rosy view of history.

C1105   *Political Quarterly*, V.4 (Oct-Dec 1934), 595–97.
Reviews: *A History of National Socialism*, by Conrad Heiden; *Germany Unmasked*, by Robert Dell; *Fascism and Social Revolution*, by R. Palme Dutt; and *Hitler's Official Programme*, by Gottfried Feder.

1935

C1106   HOW WE HAVE DONE IT. *New Statesman and Nation*, 12 January 1935, 49–50.
Review of *Our Own Times, 1913–1934*, vol. I, by Stephen King-Hall.
The author has attempted to tell both what happened and why. His narrative is honest and impartial. This is a greater achievement than clarity in a political and economic survey of "our own times".

C1107   THE ANIMAL WORLD. *The Monologue*, ed. by Lyn Irvine [Newman], No. 23, 15 January 1935, 8–10.
Letter.
About the souls of animals.

C1108   LORD ESHER. Headed NEW LITERATURE. *London Mercury*, January 1935, 290–91.
Review of *Journals and Letters of Reginald Viscount Esher*, vol. II, *1903– 1910*, ed. by Maurice V. Brett.
Lord Esher moved up and down the backstairs "among the Lords . . . and . . . the Cabinet Ministers". His is a fascinating account of upper-class life, political intrigue and human nature.

C1109   WAR AND CAPITALISM. *New Statesman and Nation*, 16 February 1935, 210.
Letter to the Editor, Kingsley Martin, concerning his comments on Norman Angell's thesis ("A London Diary", *NS & N*, 2 February, p. 134), and subsequent correspondence between Angell and Brailsford.
Reprinted 1935 in *Does Capitalism Cause War?* See B28.

C1110   A HISTORY OF EUROPE. *New Statesman and Nation*, 2 March 1935, 285– 86.
Review of *A History of Europe*, by H. A. L. Fisher, vol. I. *Ancient and Mediaeval*.
Written on a huge scale the book has "a considerable amount of wobble", but even so it "can be read with profit and pleasure".

C1111   THE MODERN TORY. *New Statesman and Nation*, 9 March 1935, 330– 31.
Review of *Frederick Edwin Earl of Birkenhead; The Last Phase*, by his son Lord Birkenhead.
"The common idea that any fool can write a book – and particularly a biography – is a delusion. Authorship is just as skilled a trade as bricklaying, the law, or the army." The general impression given by this book is "a blur".

C1112   IF I WERE DICTATOR. *New Statesman and Nation*, 30 March 1935, 457.
Review of *If I Were Dictator*, by James Maxton; and *If I Were Dictator*, by H. R. L. Sheppard.
Having agreed to write 20,000 words on the subject, these men were in trouble. Maxton wittily resigns on the last page. Canon Sheppard is

terribly worried by the effort. Realising that dictatorship can do nothing for the Church he discusses instead reforms he would like to make.

C1113   *Political Quarterly*, VI.1 (Jan-March 1935), 137–42.
Discussion of (1) 8 books on internationalism: *Survey of International Relations, 1933; A Short History of International Affairs, 1920–1934; Peace with Honour*, by A. A. Milne; *Labour and War*, by Bjarne Braatoy, Preface by Harold Laski; *A Better League of Nations*, by F. N. Keen; *Nationality and the Peace Treaties*, by W. O'Sullivan Molony; *International Narcotics Control*, by L. E. S. Eisenlohr; and *The Saar and the Franco-German Problem*, by B. T. Reynolds; and (2) 6 biographies: *The Life of Joseph Chamberlain*, vol. III, *1895–1900*, by J. L. Garvin; *The Life of Lord Carson*, vol. II, by Ian Colvin; *The Rise of Gladstone to the Leadership of the Liberal Party, 1859–1868.* by W. E. Williams; *Mr. Gladstone and the Board of Trade*, by Francis E. Hyde; *George Tierney.* by H. K. Olphin; and *Fox*, by Christopher Hobhouse.

C1114   A GREAT QUEEN. *Listener*, 8 May 1935, Late Spring Supplement, p. vii.
Review of *Queen Victoria*, by E. F. Benson.
The queen's personal biases, especially her treatment of Gladstone, embarrass the reader.

C1115   UP AND UP OR DOWN AND DOWN. *New Statesman and Nation*, 29 June 1935, 957–58.
Article, signed A.C., but listed in the index as by Leonard Woolf.
Reflections on the psychological interdependence of ruler and ruled in Fascist countries and on the fluctuations of the barometer of enthusiasm, based on observations during trips in Italy in May 1933 and in Germany and Italy in May 1935.

C1116   LABOUR HONOURS. *New Statesman and Nation*, 29 June 1935, 959.
Letter in response to one from Professor R. H. Tawney published the previous week, p. 922.
Tawney had objected to the acceptance of a knighthood by the chief party whip. LW agrees: "I have never understood why the Party and the Labour Peers should play the Tories' game by treating the House of Lords seriously and taking part in its farcical debates."

C1117   Review of *The State in Theory and Practice*, by H. J. Laski. *Political Quarterly*, VI.2 (April-June 1935), 290–93.
The author of this exceptionally good analysis is pessimistic about the future. He is wrong in saying that the state is both the supreme authority which holds a society together and the way in which that society is organised and in calling both by the same name. This personifies the state, which is composed of, and governed by, individuals.

C1118   Review of *Political Power*, by Charles E. Merriam (New York: McGraw Hill), signed L.W. *Political Quarterly* VI.2, April-June 1935, 302–03.
The author fails to consider the relation of political power to control of the armed forces or to analyse the relationship between political power and magical properties.

C1119   WHAT IS CALLED A LIBERAL. *New Statesman and Nation*, 6 July 1935, 24–25.
Review of *Condorcet and the Rise of Liberalism*, by Salwyn Schapiro.
In this sober, honest work Schapiro apologises for Condorcet's Liberalism and absurdity. He was not a Liberal but "a philosophe of eighteenth-century France, a humane and civilised man of great intellectual integrity and political foresight. . . . He stood for justice and humanity at a moment

when other people stood for cutting off other people's heads." He had no sense of humour and could not disguise what people considered absurdity.

C1120 THE FAILURE OF FASCISM. *New Statesman and Nation*, 27 July 1935, 130–31.

Review of *Mussolini's Italy*, by Herman Finer; and *Mussolini Red and Black*, by Armando Borghi.

> Dr. Finer has written the best book so far about Mussolini. He admires him, but he analyses his failures fairly and humorously. Borghi is so obviously partisan that he defeats his purpose.

C1121 AT EUROPE'S BEDSIDE. *New Statesman and Nation*, 10 August 1935, 130–31.

Review of *Europe's Crisis*, by André Siegfried.

> Siegfried diagnoses Europe's problems and prescribes a dreadful remedy, that we should either reduce the standard of living and become Nazis or Americanise Europe.

C1122 Review of three books on the history and influence of the Newspaper. *Political Quarterly*, VI.3 (July-Sept 1935), 450–51.

History of the Times. "The Thunderer" in the Making, 1785–1841; *The Press in England*, by Kurt von Stutterheim; and *Newspaper Headlines*, by Heinrich Straumann.

C1123 BAD CONSCIENCES. *New Statesman and Nation*, 12 October 1935, 498.

Review of *The Eve of 1914*, by Theodor Wolff.

> The editor of the *Berliner Tageblatt* for 27 years tries to justify himself and most of the German government in the question of guilt for the Great War. He fails in this, but he writes an interesting book based on wide reading and an ability to write history.

C1124 THE GREAT DIVIDE. *New Statesman and Nation*, 23 November 1935, 778–79.

Review of *The Dreyfus Case*, by Armand Charpentier, tr. by J. Lewis May.

> Reading this detailed, straightforward, chronological account of the events helps one to see "the *Affaire* was an important part of that great divide between modern civilisation and modern barbarism." After it was clear that Dreyfus "had been wrongfully found guilty . . . the machinery of judicial murder was set in motion . . . to preserve the honour of the French Army."

C1125 THE B.B.C. AND MUSIC. *Political Quarterly*, VI.4, Oct-Dec 1935, 519–29.

Article, signed A Listener.

> There is no basis for the claim of the B.B.C. that what people want to hear is only second-best music or worse, and that one who demands the best is a highbrow. Germany and other European countries provide better programming than the B.B.C. "There are standards of value in music and art generally." The B.B.C. pays only lip service to them.

William Robson says LW wrote this ("The Problems of the 1930's." *Political Quarterly*, XLI.1 (1970), 32).

C1126 Review of *The Defence of Freedom*, by M. Alderton Pink. *Political Quarterly*, VI.4 (Oct-Dec 1935), 605–06.

> Hitler and Mussolini are making the author rally to democracy.

1936

C1127 ROBESPIERRE. *New Statesman and Nation*, 4 January 1936, 19.
Review of *Robespierre*, by J. M. Thompson. 2 vols.
This is the best history and biography of Robespierre, but even Thompson cannot explain his psychology.

C1128 MR. BELLOC ON THE HOLY LAND. *New Statesman and Nation*, 22 February 1936, 276 & 278.
Review of *The Battle Ground*, by Hilaire Belloc.
Mr. Belloc could write well if he would stop nagging the people he does not like.

C1129 THE MASK OF JOHN GALSWORTHY. Headed NEW LITERATURE. *London Mercury*, February 1936, 438–39.
Review of *The Life and Letters of John Galsworthy*, by H. V. Marrot.
This is "one of the worst constructed biographies we have read." Galsworthy's letters reveal nothing of his personality; his novels are social documents.

C1130 MEDITATION ON ABYSSINIA. *Political Quarterly*, VII.1 (Jan-March 1936), 16–32.
Article.
The invasion of Abyssinia by Fascist troops will be a test of whether the League of Nations will live up to the Covenant. The British policy of ignoring the Covenant and its government's repudiation of the League by its actions is wrong. Whether or not the League survives, nations must choose between violence and civilised methods of settling disputes.
Reprinted B78.

C1131 Review. *Political Quarterly*, VII.1 (Jan-March 1936), 137–39.
Dwight Morrow, by Harold Nicolson. *Gustav Stresemann; His Diaries, Letters and Papers*, vol. 1, ed. by Eric Sutton; and *The Eve of 1914*, by Theodor Wolff.

C1132 A HISTORY OF RECENT TIMES. *London Mercury*, April 1936, 647–48.
Review of *England, 1870–1914*, by R. C. K. Ensor.
Ensor is too close to his subject and knows too much about it. He had "made the best of a bad job".

C1133 THE FUTURE OF MARRIAGE. Headed NEW LITERATURE. *London Mercury*, May 1936, 64–65.
Review of *The Future of Marriage in Western Civilisation*, by Edward Westermarck.
The author starts a lot of hares but gives few conclusions.

C1134 'LORD PUMICESTONE'. *Listener*, 6 May 1936, Supplement, pp. iii-iv.
Includes a cartoon from *Punch* 1862, reproduced in the book.
Review of *Lord Palmerston*, by Herbert C. F. Bell, 2 vols.
This is an exceptionally thorough history of Palmerston's foreign policy. "We wish to pay Professor Bell the compliment of disagreeing with him." He has adopted Palmerston's views and has failed to give an adequate account of the views of his opponents. He admires the bullying methods Palmerston adopted for the good of his country.

C1135 FREEDOM OF THE PRESS IN THE EIGHTEENTH CENTURY. *Listener*, 17 June 1936, 1176.
Review of *Government and the Press, 1695–1763*, by Laurence Hanson.

"The government's chief weapon against the political writer in the eighteenth century was, as it still remains in this country, prosecution, not only of the writer, but also of the publisher and printer, for seditious libel."

C1136 HITLER. *New Statesman and Nation,* 20 June 1936, 984 & 986.
Review of *Hitler the Pawn,* by Rudolph Olden.
This is a long-winded, disorderly cross between a biography of Hitler and a history of the rise of the National Socialist Party.

C1137 Review of 4 books on internationalism. *Political Quarterly,* VII.2 (April-June 1936), 289–91.
Survey of International Affairs, 1934; The League of Nations and the Rule of Law, 1918–1935, by Alfred Zimmern; *International Law,* 5th ed., vol. II: *Disputes, War and Neutrality,* by L. Oppenheim; and *The Anti-Drug Campaign,* by S. H. Bailey.

C1138 ENGLISH HOTELS. *New Statesman and Nation,* 15 August 1936, 220–21.
Letter criticising "French Journey" by Raymond Mortimer (*New Statesman and Nation,* 1 August 1936, 157–58).
English hotels have improved in the last 20 years. If people like English cooking they can get good food in England.

C1139 MEDITATIONS ON LIFE AND DEATH. *New Statesman and Nation,* 15 August 1936, 230–31.
Review of *Euthanasia and Other Aspects of Life and Death,* by Harry Roberts.
Dr. Roberts writes in support of individual liberties. It is ironic that the right to choose suicide is perhaps the only individual right that the authoritarian state will leave to its citizens.

C1140 TO THE EDITOR OF THE TIMES. *The Times,* 19 August 1936, p. 6, col. 3.
Letter signed by 30 people including LW and VW.
The press is misrepresenting the nature of the present government of Spain in reporting its struggle against the Fascists. The British government should give sympathetic support to the Spanish government.

C1141 BRITAIN AND THE SPANISH WAR. *New Statesman and Nation,* 22 August 1936, 250–51.
Letter to the editor signed by 33 people including LW and VW. Same as C1140 except for 3 more signatures.

C1142 ENGLISH HOTELS. *New Statesman and Nation,* 22 August 1936, 254.
Letter to the editor in answer to one from Mr. Mortimer, see C1138. In the August 29 issue E. M. Forster and Clive Bell joined the controversy over English vs. French accommodations.

C1143 TO THE EDITOR OF THE TIMES. *The Times* (London), 24 August 1936, p. 6, column 4.
Letter. Attempt to explain what the writers of the letter, C1140, meant to convey.

C1144 ENGLISH HOTELS. *New Statesman and Nation,* 5 September 1936, 317.
Letter to the Editor.
Concerns Forster's and Bell's letters, see C1138 and C1142.
The controversy continued. George Richards in a letter published September 12 called LW "an intellectual defending the uneatable".

C1145 ONE DAMN THING AFTER ANOTHER. *New Statesman and Nation,* 19 September 1936, 400.
Review of *Great Britain, Empire and Commonwealth, 1886–1935,* by J. A. Spender.

Mr. Spender contents himself with presenting facts without questioning why things happened.

C1146 THE IDEAL OF THE LEAGUE REMAINS. *Political Quarterly*, VII.3 (July-Sept 1936), 330–45.
Article.
There are moments in history when the suicidal impulse pervades. Such a period could be studied in *The Times* leaders and correspondence "Communal Suicide" during May 1936. The idea that a nation can defend itself by building up armaments is a suicidal delusion.

C1147 Review of *The Rise of European Liberalism*, by Harold Laski. *Political Quarterly*, VII.3 (July-Sept 1936), 455–56.

C1148 HISTORY OF SOUTH AFRICA. *Listener*, 14 October 1936, Supplement, p. xv.
Review of *The Cambridge History of the British Empire*, vol. VIII: *South Africa*.
This elephantine book by 24 authors and 3 editors is good for reference, but it is not a history.

C1149 LABOUR'S CHOICE. Headed CORRESPONDENCE. *New Statesman and Nation*, 24 October 1936, 623.
Mr. Cole calmly reports that the Labour Party Conference at Edinburgh returned a deliberately ambiguous answer on the question of armaments and collective security. This is political suicide.

C1150 SHINING ARMOUR. *New Statesman and Nation*, 24 October 1936, 634 & 636.
Review of *The Kaiser and English Relations*, by E. F. Benson.
This readable book is of general interest but of little importance as serious historical biography. The author's judgments are wrong.

C1151 GOTTERDAMMERUNG. *New Statesman and Nation*, 14 November 1936, 784 & 786.
Review of *Arthur James Balfour, First Earl of Balfour*, by Blanche E. C. Dugdale, vol. II.
This "rather vague and disappointing" biography reflects on the role of Balfour's obtuseness in the collapse of Democracy and the rise of Fascism.

C1152 NEW FABIAN RESEARCH BUREAU. *New Statesman and Nation*, 21 November 1936, 808.
Letter to the Editor recommending the organisation signed by 20 people including LW.

C1153 A LONDON DIARY. *New Statesman and Nation*, 19 December 1936, 1017–18.
Signed article.
The crisis of the royal marriage illustrates the communal psychology of the country. The opposition to the King stems not from Puritanism but from reaction to the breakdown of the myth of royalty.

C1154 A LONDON DIARY. *New Statesman and Nation*, 26 December 1936, 1054–55.
Signed article.
The outcry against the Archbishop's commination broadcast is exaggerated. Surely he is the one to tell the King. In an article the Dean of Durham deplores lady novelists' disregard of morality. Two new books and an article on family life in Soviet Russia, about to appear in the *Political Quarterly*, show that modern witch-hunting is political not religious.

C1155 LABOUR AND WAR RESISTANCE. FOREWORD. *Fabian Quarterly* (New Fabian Research Bureau), 22, Autumn 1936, 30.

"As Chairman of the International Section of the Bureau, I have been asked to write a brief foreword explaining the origin of the following symposium on war resistance." Doubts have been expressed about whether the Bureau should have published the pamphlet by Covenanter [Zilliacus], NFRB Research Series #29, May 1936. The purpose of the Bureau is research and its only policy is to encourage socialists to engage in research.

C1156 THE DANGERS OF BEING HUMAN. *Political Quarterly*, VII.4 (Oct-Dec 1936), 588–97.

Review of *Retreat from Reason*, by Lancelot Hogben.

This exploration of the "relation of science and scientists to politics" is disappointing and depressing.

1937

C1157 A LONDON DIARY. *New Statesman and Nation*, 2 January 1937, 6–7. Signed article.

Comments on: Hitler's speech delivered by Hess on Christmas Eve; Depressed classes in India changing religion; Pleasure of hearing Desmond MacCarthy read Swinburne's poetry on the B.B.C.; A reader who said he disliked what Kingsley Martin signed in the *New Statesman and Nation* but took the paper for "A London Diary" by Critic. LW quips, "Would everyone agree that 'Critic' is Jekyll and the editor Hyde?"

C1158 VICTORIAN ENGLAND: PORTRAIT OF AN AGE. *London Mercury*, February 1937, 419–421.

Review of *Victorian England: Portrait of an Age*, by G. M. Young.

Packed with facts, generalisations and references, this book is not easy to read although it is clearly and wittily written. It is not so much a portrait as a map. The author explores education and religion thoroughly, but not politics. The book needs an index.

C1159 LORD GREY. *Listener*, 10 March 1937. Early Spring Supplement, p. viii.

Review of *Grey of Fallodon*, by G. M. Trevelyan.

Mr. Trevelyan tells the story of Grey's private life so well that it is too bad to have to disagree with his assessment of Grey as a statesman.

1160 TALLEYRAND. *New Statesman and Nation*, 13 March 1937, 420 & 422.

Review of two books: *Talleyrand*, by Comte de Saint-Aulaire, tr. by George Frederic Lees and Frederick J. Stephens; and *The Lives of Talleyrand*, by Crane Brinton.

Neither book provides a new interpretation of the psychology of Talleyrand or an analysis of his most important years. The translation of Saint-Aulaire's book is almost unreadable.

C1161 LENIN THE MAN. *London Mercury*, March 1937, 513–14.

Review of *The Letters of Lenin*, tr. by Elizabeth Hill and Doris Mudie.

"One learns more about the human than the political Lenin from these letters." He was a strange mixture of opposites. There is "a bleakness about his humanity" but an "extraordinary tenacity and clarity [in his] political mind."

C1162 ARMS AND PEACE. *Political Quarterly*, VIII.1 (Jan-March 1937), 21–35.

Signed article. Refers to *Which Way to Peace?* by Bertrand Russell; *Alternative to Rearmament*, by Jonathan Griffin; *The Struggle for Peace*, by

Sir Stafford Cripps; *The Alternative to War*, by Charles Roden Buxton; and *The Private Manufacture of Armaments*, vol. I, by Philip Noel-Baker.

> Vacillation of the government has led to destruction of the League of Nations.

C1163 Unsigned review of *The Story of Dictatorships*, by E. E. Kellett. Headed SHORTER NOTICES. *New Statesman and Nation*, 8 May 1937, 784.

> A useful, readable book which shows the sameness of dictatorships.

C1164 NAPOLEON. *New Statesman and Nation*, 15 May 1937, 817.

> Review of *Bonaparte*, by Eugene Tarlé, tr. from the Russian by John Cournos. This "sensible, straight-forward, readable (psychological) biography" does not include the new material promised on the jacket.

C1165 THE FUTURE OF THE CO-OPERATIVE MOVEMENT. *New Statesman and Nation*, 26 June 1937, 1068 & 1070.

> Review of *England Cradle of Co-operation*, by Sydney R. Elliott. Despite too rosy optimism, this is one of the best recently published books on the subject.

C1166 Review of *Survey of International Affairs 1935*, by Arnold J. Toynbee. *Political Quarterly*, VIII.2 (April-June 1937), 300–01.

C1167 SOVIET TRIALS. *New Statesman and Nation*, 31 July 1937, 181–82.

> Letter to the Editor concerning Palme Dutt's comments on Brailsford's letter. Dutt "sees everything as either pure white or pure black (except that for him white is red and black white)."

C1168 THE DEFEAT OF PACIFISM. *New Statesman and Nation*, 18 September 1937, 410 & 412.

> Review of *Collective Insecurity*, by H. M. Swanwick. Mrs. Swanwick thinks the human race hopeless. She misunderstands the League of Nations system.

A letter published September 18, p. 440, signed H.C.D., attributes some of what LW says about the book to LW. A letter to him from Mrs. Swanwick objects to his criticism (in LW Papers Sussex).

C1169 THE RESURRECTION OF THE LEAGUE. *Political Quarterly*, VIII.3 (July-Sept 1937), 337–52.

> Article. Fascism and the breakdown of the League are the two threats to peace. A peace front must take the initiative from the Fascists.

C1170 PORTRAIT OF A GREAT MAN. *New Statesman and Nation*, 16 October 1937, 616.

> Review of *Great Contemporaries*, by Winston Churchill. The essays are all worth reading, even if one doubts that the men were all great.

C1171 LISTENER'S BOOK CHRONICLE. *Listener*, 3 November 1937, 976.

> Unsigned review of *Haldane 1856–1915*, by Sir Frederick Maurice; and *Moments of Memory*, by the Hon. Herbert Asquith. Both books show that Haldane was a good person and statesman. He was unpopular for not being a good party man as a Liberal and for writing about German philosophy. Although the soldiers knew it was Haldane who made it possible to win the war, the politicians destroyed him.

C1172 YOU WANT FREEDOM – YES, BUT WHAT SORT? *Daily Herald*, Friday, 5 November 1937, p. 12.

> Review of *Soviet Communism: A New Civilisation*, by Sidney and Beatrice Webb.

The Webbs excuse Soviet dictatorship, but it is not necessary to Socialism. Political freedom does not exist in the Soviet Union.

C1173 UNHEARD OF ADVENTURES. *New Statesman and Nation*, 4 December 1937, 971–72.

Review of *Michael Bakunin*, by E. H. Carr; and *History of Anarchism in Russia*, by E. Yaroslavsky.

C1174 DOES EDUCATION NEUTRALISE THOUGHT? *Listener*, 22 December 1937, 1366–68.

An essay on clear thinking.

Graham Wallas has explained how clear thinking is a preliminary to creativity in *The Art of Thought*. Our educational system teaches us not to think.

1938

C1175 ANATOMY OF EMPIRE. *New Statesman and Nation*, 12 March 1938, 444.

Review of *Trials in Burma*, by Maurice Collis.

Collis tells how he tried to be fair and just to both Europeans and Burmese. Readers of travel books, adventure books and autobiographies will enjoy it.

C1176 *Political Quarterly*, IX.1 (Jan-March 1938), 123–24.

Reviews of *The House that Hitler Built*, by S. H. Roberts; *The Spirit and Structure of German Fascism*, by Robert A. Brady; *Government in the Third Reich*, by Morstein Marx, Rev. ed.; and *What Next, O Duce?* by Beatrice Baskerville.

C1177 THE RELIGION OF THE STAKE. *New Statesman and Nation*, 9 April 1938, 624.

Review of *Inquisition and Liberty*, by G. G. Coulton.

Coulton's book would have shocked his readers if he had written it before the modern totalitarians got under way.

C1178 WORDS AND THINGS. *New Statesman and Nation*, 7 May 1938, 778 & 780.

Review of *The Tyranny of Words*, by Stuart Chase.

A book about semantics, or the study of the relation of the words we use to the things they represent.

C1179 THE SECOND VISCOUNT ESHER. *London Mercury*, June 1938, 173–74.

Review of *Letters and Journals of Reginald Viscount Esher*, vol. III: *1910–1915*, ed. by Oliver Viscount Esher.

Esher emerges as "a patchwork of contradictions".

C1180 Review of *Gustav Stresemann: His Diaries, Letters and Papers*, ed. & tr. by Eric Sutton, vol. II.

Political Quarterly, IX.2 (April-June 1938), 295–97.

The editor should have given the German title.

C1181 Review of *International Sanctions: A Report by a Group of Members of the Royal Institute of International Affairs. NFRB Quarterly* (formerly *Fabian Quarterly*), no. 18, Summer 1938, 36, signed L.W.

C1182 THE PROPHET. *New Statesman and Nation*, 3 September 1938, 352–53.

Review of *Mohammed*, by Essad Bey, tr. by Helmut L. Ripperger.

The author brings out some important aspects of the psychology of the Prophet.

C1183 Review of *Victorian Critics of Democracy*, by B. E. Lippincott (Univ. of Minnesota Press). *Political Quarterly*, IX,3 (July-Sept 1938), 444–45.

C1184 MODERN HISTORY. *New Statesman and Nation,* 1 October 1938, 502.
Review of *The Modern Historian,* by C. H. Williams; and *Aspects of History,*
by E. E. Kellett.
Both show the validity of different approaches and methods of writing
history.

C1185 WHITELEY. *New Statesman and Nation,* 22 October 1938, 624 & 626.
Review of *The Universal Provider: A Study of William Whiteley and the Rise
of the London Department Store,* by Richard S. Lambert.
An interesting and amusing, still serious, work.

C1186 THE CONSTITUTION UNDER STRAIN. *New Statesman and Nation,* 12
November 1938, 782 & 784.
Review of *The British Constitution,* by H. R. G. Greaves; and *Parliamentary
Government in England,* by Harold Laski.
The opinions and subject matter of these men who both teach at the
London School of Economics are almost identical. [LW disagrees with
them about the place of capitalism in the functioning of the constitution.]

C1187 FORCE AND POWER. *London Mercury,* November 1938, 74–76.
Review of *Power: A New Social Analysis,* by Bertrand Russell.
The author may not have carried his analysis far enough.

C1188 CANONIZATION OF THE NORTH. *New Statesman and Nation,* 10
December 1938, 1014 & 1016.
Review of *Lord North,* by W. Baring Pemberton.
By writing denigratory biography imitators of Lytton Strachey "have
misinterpreted his object and travestied his method." Strachey told facts
about people which Victorians would not allow, juxtaposing "littleness
and greatness" to get "a legitimate artistic effect". His imitators sling mud
and debunk the truth. In reaction Mr. Pemberton returns to a Victorian
method, white-washing the man who lost America.

C1189 A GIANT AMONG PIGMIES. *London Mercury,* December 1938, 228–29.
Review of *Gladstone and the Irish Nation,* by J. L. Hammond.
It is the most detailed and searching study of Gladstone's statesmanship
which has appeared.

C1190 Short review of *The Government of the Island of Ceylon and the Case for
Reform of Its Constitution,* by the Padikara Mudaliyar of Ceylon. *NFRB
Quarterly,* no. 20, Winter 1938–39, p. 31.

1939

C1191 CHATHAM. *New Statesman and Nation,* 18 February 1939, 256–57.
Review of *William Pitt, Earl of Chatham,* by Brian Tunstall.
LW reviews Chatham's career and praises the book.
Letter to the editor from Basil Williams, *Nation & Athenaeum,* 25 February,
p. 285, criticises review.

C1192 POLITICAL IDEAS. *London Mercury,* February 1939, 456–57.
Review of *Political Thought: The European Tradition,* by J. P. Mayer and
others.
Crossman has written the best part of this.

C1193 THE DEFEAT OF DEMOCRACY. *New Statesman and Nation,* 11 March
1939, 392 & 394.
Review of *Pursuit of Happiness, The Story of American Democracy,* by
Herbert Agar.

This distinguished book has the wrong title. It contains nothing about happiness. It tells about the American plutocracy which prevents democracy.

C1194   DEMOCRACIES, UNITE! *New Statesman and Nation*, 18 March 1939, 434 & 436.

Review of *Union Now,* by Clarence Streit.

The author argues powerfully and intelligently for an international union or federation of 12 to 20 leading democracies, but fails to recognise the snag of state sovereignty.

C1195   Review of *Gladstone,* by Erich Eych, tr. by Bernard Miall. *Political Quarterly,* XI.1 (Jan-March 1939), 147.

The author admires Gladstone, but gives his own views.

C1196   THE PERFECT AMERICAN. *New Statesman and Nation,* 1 April 1939, 510.

Review of *Benjamin Franklin,* by Carl van Doren.

The entire book is interesting.

C1197   LORD BROUGHAM. *New Statesman and Nation,* 6 May 1939, 702 & 704.

Review of *Lord Brougham and the Whig Party,* by Arthur Aspinall (Manchester University Press).

"Evidence that Brougham was even more destitute of principles than one had supposed him to be."

C1198   PEACE AND WAR AIMS. *New Statesman and Nation,* 12 August 1939, 246.

Letter to the Editor concerning "Peace Aims" published August 5, 203–04.

The Empire must be dismantled and the nations must submit to an international authority.

Reprinted in the *Left Forum,* C1201.

C1199   IDEALS IN WAR. *New Statesman and Nation,* 2 September 1939, 334.

Letter to the Editor concerning Critic's (Kingsley Martin's) "London Diary" of the previous week on abstract causes of war.

C1200   MORIBUND CIVILISATIONS. *New Statesman and Nation,* 23 September 1939, 433–34.

Review of *A Study of History,* vols IV-VI, by Arnold J. Toynbee.

In this fascinating, stimulating book of great scope Mr. Toynbee reaches his conclusions through faulty logic.

C1201   PEACE AND WAR AIMS. *Left Forum (Controversy),* No. 36, September 1939, 239.

Reprinted from a discussion, *NS and N,* C1198.

C1202   Reviews. *Political Quarterly,* X.3 (July-Sept 1939), 453–56.

Fascism: Who Benefits? by Max Ascoli and Arthur Feiler; *When There Is No Peace,* by Hamilton Fish Armstrong; *Men Must Act,* by Lewis Mumford; and *Security: Can We Retrieve It?* by Sir Arthur Salter.

C1203   EUROPEAN CIVILISATION. *New Statesman and Nation,* 21 October 1939, 586 & 588.

Review of *The Rise of European Civilisation,* by Charles Seignobos, tr. by Catherine A. Philips.

The author did not show how and why European civilisation arose.

C1204   RIGHT REPLY TO HITLER. *New Statesman and Nation,* 28 October 1939, 610.

Letter to the Editor about "Uncommon Sense About the War", by G. B. Shaw published 7 October, pp. 483–84, and other letters.

Shaw seems blind to what dictators and totalitarianism are doing to Europe.

C1205 TWO REVOLUTIONARIES. *New Statesman and Nation*, 11 November 1939, 686.

Review of *Lafayette*, by W. E. Woodward; and *Saint Just*, by J. B. Morton.

C1206 Short review of *Dictatorship in Newfoundland*, by T. Lodge, signed L.W. *Fabian Quarterly* (Successor to *NFRB Quarterly*), no. 23, Autumn 1939, 36.

C1207 WAR AND PEACE. *Round Table: A Quarterly Review of the Politics of the British Commonwealth*, XXX.117 (December 1939), 5–26.

Unsigned article.

The only way to ensure lasting peace is to establish international government. This can succeed only if nations will relinquish sovereignty and co-operate.

C1208 DE PROFUNDIS. *Political Quarterly*, X.4 (Oct-Dec 1939), 463–76.

Article.

Hitler is a result of an insane system of independent states with power held by the few.

Reprinted in *Political Quarterly in the Thirties*, by William A. Robson, 1971, B78, pp. 239–50.

C1209 Review of *Capital Investment in Africa*, by S. Herbert Frankel. *Political Quarterly*, X.4 (Oct-Dec 1939), 617–18.

1940

C1210 *Political Quarterly*, XI.1 (Jan-March 1940), 120–23.

Reviews of *The Smaller Democracies*, by E. D. Simon; *Democracy Up-to-Date*, by Stafford Cripps; *The Defence of Democracy*, by John Middleton Murry; *Democracy and Socialism*, by A. Rosenberg; and *Personality in Politics*, by David Thomson.

Everyone who writes about democracy should read Sir E. D. Simon's book *The Smaller Democracies*.

C1211 RICHELIEU. *New Statesman and Nation*, 13 April 1940, 508.

Review of *Richelieu, His Rise to Power*, by Carl J. Burckhardt, tr. and abridged by Edwin and Willa Muir.

It is too bad that the translation of this remarkable historical biography was abridged.

C1212 THE NATIONAL ASSEMBLY. *New Statesman and Nation*, 18 May 1940, 646–47.

Review of *The Beginning of the Third Republic in France. A History of the National Assembly*, by Rev. F. H. Brabant.

C1213 THE JEWS AND THEIR FUTURE. *New Statesman and Nation*, 1 June 1940, 706–07.

Review of *The Jewish Fate and Future*, by Arthur Ruppin.

This book by a professor of Jewish Sociology at the Hebrew University of Jerusalem is factual, but it is not easy to read.

C1214 PRINCIPIA SOCIOLOGICA. *New Statesman and Nation*, 29 June 1940, 807.

Review of *Man and Society in an Age of Reconstruction*, by Karl Mannheim.

This is a very difficult book with some good ideas if one can just put them into plain English.

C1215 UTOPIA AND REALITY. *Political Quarterly*, XI.2 (April-June 1940), 167–82.

Article on two books by E. H. Carr: *Twenty Years Crisis, 1919–1939;* and *The Foreign Policy of Britain from 1819 to September 1939.*

C1216   Review of *The Politics of Democratic Socialism,* by E. F. M. Durbin. *Political Quarterly,* XI.2 (April-June 1940), 271–73.

C1217   THE POLITICIAN AND THE INTELLECTUAL. *New Statesman and Nation,* 20 July 1940, 56–57.

Article. Mentions *Life and Letters of Austen Chamberlain.*

LW quotes Chamberlain as saying "I profoundly distrust logic when applied to politics."

C1218   GOLDEN BRANCH AMID THE SHADOWS. *New Statesman and Nation,* 3 August 1940, 120 & 122.

Review of *James George Frazer,* by R. Angus Downie.

Downie was so enthusiastic about *The Golden Bough* that he became Frazer's assistant. Ruth Benedict takes exception to the Frazer school of mental evolution, but there is really room for both schools.

C1219   SAHIBS OR SOCIALISTS? *New Statesman and Nation,* 17 August 1940, 164.

Review of *Barbarians and Philistines: Democracy and the Public Schools,* by T. C. Worsley.

Worsley's book shows a link between British public-school education and Nazi education.

Correspondence followed about differences in educational practices in Britain and in Germany and on the significance of the swastika as emblem. L. B. Pekin, in a letter published August 31, p. 206, comments on this article. Brailsford wrote an article on the swastika, published September 28, pp. 305–06.

C1220   THE WAR AND THE U.D.C. *New Statesman and Nation,* 31 August 1940, 208.

Letter signed by 28 people, including LW.

C1221   FUHRERPRINZIP. *New Statesman and Nation,* 7 September 1940, 232.

Letter replying to one from I. B. Inman published August 24 re C1219.

Experience has not shown those educated at public schools to be more disinterested than others.

C1222   THE SWASTIKA. *New Statesman and Nation,* 14 September 1940, 261.

Letter to the Editor answering one from Sir Philip Hartog.

Another correspondent, Alex. M. Thompson, says Clemenceau explained the symbol, see C1219.

C1223   MEN AND IDEAS; ESSAYS BY GRAHAM WALLAS. *Political Quarterly,* X.3 (July-Sept 1940), 301–03.

Review of *Men and Ideas; Essays,* by Graham Wallas, with an Introduction by Gilbert Murray.

Professor Murray draws attention to Mr. Wallas's fresh thought and observation.

C1224   WHY NOT? *New Statesman and Nation,* 2 November 1940, 445.

Letter to the Editor proposing that Mr. Gandhi be made viceroy of India.

C1225   LISTENER'S BOOK CHRONICLE. *Listener,* 12 December 1940, 851.

Unsigned review of *The Irish Free State and Its Senate,* by Donal O'Sullivan; and *The Age of Reform and Revolution,* by Nicholas Mansergh.

It is almost impossible to write an impartial history of Anglo-Irish relations. Mr. O'Sullivan has written a first-rate book on the subject. Mr. Mansergh's commentary is interesting.

C1226 EDITORIAL NOTE. *Political Quarterly,* XI.4 (Oct-Dec 1940), 313. Unsigned.

> Notice that Dr. Robson has entered government service; the paper shortage means the issues will be reduced to 120 pages; air raid damage to the London offices means correspondence should be addressed to Leonard Woolf at Monks House, Rodmell, Sussex.

C1227 DEMOCRACY AT BAY. *Political Quarterly,* XI.4 (October to December 1940), 335–40.

> Article on the fall of France.

C1228 Reviews. *Political Quarterly,* XI.4 (Oct-Dec 1940), 419–21.

> *Recent Revelations of European Diplomacy,* by G. P. Gooch, 4th ed.; *The War Crisis in Berlin, July-August, 1914,* by Sir Horace Rumbold; *Life and Letters of the Rt Hon. Sir Austen Chamberlain,* vol. II, by Sir Charles Petrie; *Gustav Stresemann; His Diaries, Letters and Papers,* vol. III, ed. by Eric Sutton; and *The Causes of the War,* by A. Berriedale Keith.

1941

C1229 RENASCENT DEMOCRACY. *New Statesman and Nation,* 4 January 1941, 16 and 18.

> Review of *Marxism and Democracy,* by Lucien Laurat.
> Laurat holds that true Marxism can only be democracy.

C1230 THE FUTURE OF IMPERIALISM. *New Statesman and Nation,* 25 January 1941, 76–77.

> Article. Mentions *Survey of British Commonwealth Affairs,* vol. II: *Problems of Economic Policy, 1918–1939.* Part I, by W. K. Hancock.
> Discussion of the relationship of imperialism to peace.
> Reprinted as "Survival of the British Empire" in *Living Age,* C1242.

C1231 INQUEST ON GENEVA. *New Statesman and Nation,* 15 February 1941, 162–64.

> Review of *A Great Experiment: An Autobiography,* by Viscount Robert Cecil.
> Cecil's book about the failure of the League is more valuable than most. He knows more about it than anyone else, for he spent his whole life working for it.

C1232 CULTURAL CHAOS. *New Statesman and Nation,* 8 March 1941, 253–54.

> Review of *The Culture of Cities,* by Lewis Mumford.

C1233 ENGLISH SOCIALISM. *New Statesman and Nation,* 22 March 1941, 304–05.

> Review of *British Working Class Politics, 1832–1914,* by G. D. H. Cole.
> Cole's useful book is full of hard facts.

C1234 AN ANNOUNCEMENT. *Political Quarterly,* XII.1 (Jan-March 1941), half-title page [verso names Leonard Woolf as editor].

> Editorial explanation of the purpose of continuing publication even in war-time. This announcement was repeated in subsequent issues.

C1235 Review of *Stalin's Russia and the Crisis in Socialism,* by Max Eastman. *Political Quarterly,* XII.1 (Jan-March 1941), 108–11.

C1236 *Political Quarterly,* XII.1 (Jan-March 1941), 118–19.

> Review of *A History of the Gambia,* by J. M. Gray; *Portrait of a Colony,* by Alan H. Hattersley; and *A History of South Africa,* 2nd ed., by Eric A. Walker.

C1237 EDITORIAL NOTE. *Political Quarterly,* XII.1 (Jan-March 1941), p. [120].
Paragraph of apology for postal delays is added to the note on publishing
changes necessary in war-time first published at the end of 1940, p. 313.
Unsigned.

C1238 THE NEW DEMOCRATIC ORDER. *Listener,* 10 April 1941, 535.
Review of a series, "The Democratic Order", ed. by Francis Williams; *What
We Are Waiting For,* by Francis Williams; *Make Fruitful the Land,* by Sir
George Stapledon; *Freedom is Our Weapon,* by Tom Wintringham; *Start
Planning Britain Now,* by Ritchie Calder; *To Hell with Culture,* by Herbert
Read; and *Democratise the Empire,* by William Miller Macmillan.

C1239 WHAT IS HISTORY? *New Statesman and Nation,* 12 April 1941, 390 &
392.
Review of *History as the Story of Liberty,* by Benedetto Croce.
Croce's mystical approach makes this book difficult.

C1240 Letter to the Editor. *Sunday Times,* 4 May 1941, p. 4, col. 6.
Attempt to correct newspaper reports of the wording of VW's suicide letter.

C1241 THE TRADITION OF LIBERTY. *New Statesman and Nation,* 24 May
1941, 36.
Review of *Political Liberty: A History of the Conception in the Middle Ages
and Modern Times,* by A. J. Carlyle.
The author gives valuable facts about the ideas of various authors but fails
to show that there was any difference in the theories through the centuries.

C1242 SURVIVAL OF THE BRITISH EMPIRE. *Living Age,* May 1941, [222]-225.
Reprint with changed title and other minor changes of "The Future of
Imperialism", *New Statesman and Nation,* C1230.

C1243 WORLD SETTLEMENT AFTER THE WAR. *Headway,* No. 20, May 1941,
pp.1–2.
Article on a statement issued by the Executive of the League of Nations
Union.
There must be immediate consideration of what world organisation to
form after the war.

C1244 Review of *The Cambridge History of the British Empire.* Vol. II: *The New
Empire, 1783–1870. Political Quarterly,* XII.2 (April-June 1941), 229–30.
A reference book for the historian with 20 contributions by writers of
varying merit, written mostly from the imperialist point of view.

C1245 BACK TO SAMUEL SMILES. *New Statesman and Nation,* 26 July 1941, 86.
Review of *The Recovery of the West,* by Michael Roberts.
This book is full of half-truths and sloppy generalisations. The con-
clusions are simplistic.

C1246 THE FOUR NOTES OF FATE. *New Statesman and Nation,* 16 August 1941,
159.
Letter to the Editor.
The four notes of Beethoven's Fifth Symphony echo the "binding song" in
the *Eumenides* of Aeschylus. It is hoped that [a quotation from Verrall's
translation] is "prophetic of the fate of the Nazis".

C1247 LENIN TURNS THE KEY. *New Statesman and Nation,* 6 September 1941,
234.
Review of *To the Finland Station,* by Edmond Wilson.
Edmond Wilson is a better psychological than world historian.

C1248 Unsigned review of *Out of the People,* by J. B. Priestley. *Listener,* 18
September 1941, 413.

Priestley argues that as the people and democracy checked Hitlerism so they will win the war and peace.

C1249 Review of *The British Constitution*, by Ivor Jennings. *Political Quarterly*, XII.3 (July-Sept 1941), 350–51.

Written by an expert as an explanation to the ordinary reader, the book could not be better.

C1250 Review of *The Ideas and Ideals of the British Empire*, by Ernest Barker. *Political Quarterly*, XII.3 (July-Sept 1941), 351–52.

The book has merits, but Barker forgets that progress towards self-rule is not all rosy.

C1251 THE INDIAN RIDDLE. *New Statesman and Nation*, 4 October 1941, 333. Review of *Modern India and the West*, by L. S. S. O'Malley; *India and Democracy*, by George Schuster and Guy Wint; and *The Choice Before India*, by J. Chinna Durai.

To solving the riddle of what should be done in India Durai is no help; O'Malley is disappointing; Schuster and Wint are "intelligent and imaginative".

In a letter published 25 October, pp. 376–77, Schuster takes issue with some points LW made in this review.

C1252 THE SECOND RISORGIMENTO. *New Statesman and Nation*, 8 November 1941, 413.

Review of *The Remaking of Italy*, by Pentad [5 anonymous writers].

C1253 DODGING REALITY. *New Statesman and Nation*, 27 December 1941, 528–29.

Review of *The Pool of Memory*, by E. Phillips Oppenheim.

This autobiography is insincere and irrelevant. [LW gives reasons for the popularity of thrillers and best-sellers.]

C1254 HOW TO MAKE THE PEACE. *Political Quarterly*, XII.4 (Oct-Dec 1941), 367–79.

Article. Recommends *The Reconstruction of World Trade*, by J. B. Condliffe.

C1255 Review. *Political Quarterly*, XII.4 (Oct-Dec 1941), 457–59.

The Roots of National Socialism, 1783–1933, by Rohan Butler; *Thus Spake Germany*, ed. by W. W. Coole and M. F. Potter, With an Introduction by Lord Vansittart; *German Versus Hun*, by Carl Brinitzer and Berthe Grossbard. With a Foreword by Duff Cooper; and *What To Do With Germany*, by Colonel T. H. Minshall.

1942

C1256 THE WAY THEY HAVE IN THE ARMY. *New Statesman & Nation*, 31 January 1942, 80.

Review of *Khaki and Gown*, An Autobiography by Field-Marshal Lord Birdwood; *The Life of General Sir Charles Warren*, by Watkin Williams; and *Tinned Soldier*, by Alec Dixon.

The third book is the only lively one.

C1257 Review of *Survey of International Relations, 1938*, by A. J. Toynbee. *Political Quarterly*, XIII.1 (Jan-March 1942), 115–16.

C1258 THE TANGLE IN PALESTINE. *New Statesman and Nation*, 18 April 1942, 260–61.

Review of *Palestine: A Policy*, by Albert M. Hyamson, with a Foreword by Sir Ronald Storrs.

The author is scrupulously impartial. [LW speculates on the success of the bi-national state.]

C1259 SOCIETY AND THE WORK OF ART. Headed ART AND DEMOCRACY. *Kingdom Come*, III.10, Spring 1942, [8]-13.

Part 3 of a series of articles, "Art and Democracy".

Part 1, by Herbert Read, and part 2, by Kingsley Martin appeared Nov-Dec 1941; part 4, by Eric Newton follows LW's part in this issue; parts 5 and 6 by Norman Demuth and Paul Bloomfield were published in the Winter 1942 issue.

> It is hard to say anything worthwhile about either democracy or art. Democratic freedom is generally more helpful to artists, especially writers, than the strictures of authoritarian governments.

Reprinted in *Wartime Harvest*, 1943, B43, pp. 13–18).

C1260 Review of *Treitsche's Origins of Prussianism*, tr. by Eden and Cedar Paul; and of *The Prussian Spirit; A Survey of German Literature and Politics, 1914–1940*, by D. S. Stirk. *Political Quarterly*, XIII.2, April-June 1942, 219–21.

C1261 Review of *The Lost Peace*, by Harold Butler; and *The Impulse to Dominate*, by D. W. Harding. *Political Quarterly*, XIII.2 (April-June 1942), 223–25.

C1262 THE CANDID FRIEND. *New Statesman and Nation*, 11 July 1942, 29.

Review of *And Hell Followed*, by Odette Keun.

> The author says that she predicted the war long before it began but that no one heeded her. She blames the British, especially Chamberlain.

C1263 THE ECONOMIC DETERMINATION OF JANE AUSTEN. *New Statesman and Nation*, 18 July 1942, 39–41.

Article.

> Jane Austen lived in the setting of the 18th-century gentleman and died before the industrial revolution. It is surprising that her attitudes to work, professions, money and social class are those we associate with a capitalist bourgeoisie.

Reprinted (1948) in *Turnstile One*, B53, pp. 54–59 and in part in *Critics on Jane Austen*, ed. by J. O'Neill (G. Allen and Unwin, 1970).

C1264 U.S.S.R. *New Statesman and Nation*, 29 August 1942, 146.

Review of *Russia and Her Western Neighbours*, by George W. Keeton and Rudolph Schlesinger.

> The book is concise and clear, but the exposition and arrangement are confusing. The authors recognise the need for co-operation with the Russians.

C1265 Review of *Plan for Africa*, by Dr. Rita Hinden, signed L.W. *Fabian Quarterly*, no. 34 (Summer 1942), 36.

> An admirable report.

C1266 HITLER SPEAKS. *New Statesman and Nation*, 26 September 1942, 208–09.

Review of *The Speeches of Adolph Hitler, 1922–1939*, an English translation, ed. by Norman Baynes (cf C1271).

> The speeches reveal Hitler's personality, his will-power, patience, persistence and obsessions, his meanness, hatred and cunning.

C1267 Review of *Conditions of Peace*, by E. H. Carr; *The New Freedom of the Seas*, by W. Arnold-Forster; and *Versailles Twenty Years After*, by Paul Birdsall. *Political Quarterly*, XIII.3 (July-Sept 1942), 328–32.

> Carr is one author who makes the reader think.

C1268 Review of *The Life and Times of Sir Robert Peel,* by Sir Tresham Lever. *Political Quarterly,* XIII.3 (July-Sept 1942), 341–43.

> By specious arguments the author defends Peel's opposition to Parliamentary Reform.

C1269 BERNARD SHAW. *New Statesman and Nation,* 5 December 1942, 375–76. Review of *Bernard Shaw: His Life and Personality,* by Hesketh Pearson.

> Shaw helped the author with this amusing biography. He said of himself that the clown in him tripped up the tragedian. Shaw can destroy but not build.

C1270 A NOTE ON VIRGINIA WOOLF'S *NIGHT AND DAY. Southerly,* Sydney, Australia, III.3, December 1942, 10–11.

C1271 HITLER'S PSYCHOLOGY. *Political Quarterly,* XIII.4 (Oct-Dec 1942), 373–84.

> Article based on *The Speeches of Adolph Hitler . . .* (See C1266).
> LW compares Hitler to Jack the Ripper.

1943

C1272 BACK TO MUMBO-JUMBO. *New Statesman and Nation,* 9 January 1943, 28–29. Review of *Man the Master,* by Gerald Heard.

> Generalisations and false analogies are mixed with "half-baked psychoanalysis".

C1273 PLAYING WITH FIGURES. *New Statesman and Nation,* 23 January 1943, 64–65. Review of *A Short History of Labour Conditions Under Industrial Capitalism,* vol. I. *Great Britain and the Empire, 1750 to the Present Day,* by Jurgen Kuczynski.

> The author's lack of objectivity is a disservice to the socialism he advocates.

C1274 LORD OLIVIER. *New Statesman and Nation,* 27 February 1943, 138–39. Obituary and personal tribute, with reminiscences.

> A socialist from 1880 on, Lord Olivier held his own views, expected and was willing that others should do the same.

C1275 Review of *Diary of a Diplomatic Correspondent,* by George Bilainkin. *Political Quarterly,* XIV.1 (Jan-March 1943), 113–14.

> Correspondent of the Allied Newspapers in 1940, the author throws light on the psychology of the time in Anglo-Soviet relations but fails to distinguish between the trivial and the important.

C1276 INDIAN NATIONALISM. *Tribune,* April 1943, p. 14.

> Letter commenting on one from George Orwell published in *Tribune,* 19 March 1943, p. 15.
> LW denies that he is "angry" in his introductory letter to *Letters on India,* B40.

C1277 HIPPY AND HITLER. *New Statesman and Nation,* 1 May 1943, 294. Review of *Hippy: In Memoriam. The Story of a Dog,* by Nevile Henderson [*sic*].

> The British ambassador in Berlin and his dog Hippy shared a passion for game-hunting. The dog would have been better able to deal with Hitler and his gang, for he spoke their language.

C1278 Review of *Science and Ethics,* by C. H. Waddington and others. *Political Quarterly,* XIV.2 (April-June 1943), 202.

C1279 Review of *The Russian Peasant*, by Sir John Maynard; and *Soviet Planning and Labour in Peace and War*, by Maurice Dobb. *Political Quarterly*, XIV.2 (April-June 1943), 205–06.

C1280 ASIA AFTER THE WAR. *New Statesman and Nation*, 31 July 1943, 78–79. Review of *The Future of South-East Asia*, by K. M. Panikkar.

The author, an intelligent, well-educated Indian, and a practical politician, has written a concrete, realistic book. He recognises the need for organizing the security of the region and for its people to become autonomous.

C1281 A CHALLENGE TO ALL OF US. Two views on the RESPONSIBILITIES OF COLONIAL EMPIRE. Part I. by Leonard Woolf. *Listener*, 12 August 1943, 179–80. Part II, by Elspeth Huxley, pp. 180–81.

B.B.C. Home Service talk.

LW: To talk about this complex subject it is necessary to qualify what one says. As to self-government in the colonies, different parts of the empire with differing stages of development in terms of education and experience will have to be treated differently. Ceylon should have self-government right away, but most Africans will need education and training in self-government before they assume responsibility.

E. Huxley: Leonard Woolf's comments are about 20 years out of date. The Africans have for some time been participating in their own government. Democracy is not the right type of government for Africans.

C1282 BEATRICE WEBB (1858–1943). *Economic Journal*, LIII.201–02 (June-Sept 1943), 284–90.

Obituary and appreciation with personal reminiscence.

Beatrice and Sidney Webb were "a composite personality". Below their surface intellectuality they were humane. In the course of their work of social investigation they greatly influenced young people of promise.

C1283 THE FUTURE OF THE SMALL STATE. *Political Quarterly*, XIV.3 (July-Sept 1943), 209–24.

Article.

The insistence of each nation upon sovereign rights contributed largely to the failure of the League of Nations. Provisions should be made for minority groups. Great powers must not override or ignore the national feelings of the small states.

C1284 Review of *The Spanish Labyrinth; An Account of the Social and Political Background of the Civil War*, by Gerald Brenan. *Political Quarterly*, XIV.3 (July-Sept 1943), 289.

A remarkable book. The author his intimate knowledge of the subject, is intelligent and impartial.

C1285 THE ITALIAN COLONIES. *Fabian Quarterly*, 39, October 1943, pp. 30–32.

Article.

After the war there should be international supervision of those Italian colonies which are unfit for independent status.

1944

C1286 BABEL. *New Statesman and Nation*, 26 February 1944, 144. Review of *The Loom of Language*, by Frederick Bodmer, ed. by Lancelot Hogben; and *Interglossa*, by L. Hogben.

Bodmer's guide to learning foreign languages is thorough but disorderly. Hogben has produced the best international language to date.

C1287 THE FUTURE OF INTERNATIONAL LABOUR ORGANISATION. *Political Quarterly*, XV.I (Jan-March 1944), 66–76.
Article, signed An Observer.
Suggestions of possible trends under the U.N. based on history from the Treaty of Versailles.

C1288 Review of *Constructive Democracy*, by John McMurray; and *Business as a System of Power*, by Robert A. Brady. *Political Quarterly*, XI.1 (Jan-March 1944), 90–92.

C1289 A LIBERAL. *New Statesman and Nation*, 8 April 1944, 246.
Review of *Ramsay Muir. An Autobiography and Some Essays*, ed. by Stuart Hodgson.
Muir lacks strong passion; his writing is arid.

C1290 BOOKS IN GENERAL. *New Statesman and Nation*, 29 April 1944. 291.
Review of *Tolstoy: His Life and Work*, by Derrick Leon.
Leon is too solemn.

C1291 CHOPPY SEAS FOR THE I.L.O. *New Statesman and Nation*, 20 May 1944, 331.
Unsigned report of the Philadelphia Conference plus forecasts.

C1292 CHIMPANZEE. *New Statesman and Nation*, 27 May 1944, 358.
Review of *Chimpanzees: A Laboratory Colony*, by Robert M. Yerkes.
The amount of intelligence accorded to apes seems to reflect the degree of intelligence of the investigator.

C1293 TROUBLE ABOUT KENYA. *New Statesman and Nation*, 4 June 1944, 372.
Review of *Race and Politics in Kenya. A Correspondence Between Elspeth Huxley and Margery Perham*. With an Introduction by Lord Lugard; and *Soviet Light on the Colonies*, by Leonard Barnes.
Mrs. Huxley sides with the white settlers and Margery Perham with the Africans. Mr. Barnes's conversations with a Soviet observer point up the failures of the British colonial system.

C1294 Review of *Great Britain, France and the German Problem, 1918–1939*, by W. M. Jordan. *Political Quarterly*, XV.2 (April-June 1944), 176–77.

C1295 Reviews. *Political Quarterly*, XV.2 (April-June 1944), 183-[84].
Transition from War to Peace. Report of the Delegation on Economic Depressions, Part I (League of Nations); *The Displacement of Population in Europe*, by Eugene M. Kulisher (International Labour Office); and *The United States in the World Economy*. Department of Commerce, U.S.A. (H.M.S.O.).

C1296 G. B. S. *New Statesman and Nation*, 16 September 1944, 188.
Review of *Everybody's Political What's What*, by Bernard Shaw.
Shaw repeats here much of what he has said better before in his plays and prefaces. He explains his success and his failure, admitting his habit of overstating his case.

C1297 Review of *How It Can Be Done*, by Sir Richard Acland; and *The New Age*, by Edward Hulton. *Political Quarterly*, XV.3 (July-Sept 1944), 268–69.
Had these books proposing social reform been written in 1918 their authors would have been called utopians or reds. Currently criticism of society is stronger and deeper than it was then.

C1298 THE FUTURE OF MANDATES: A SYMPOSIUM. *African Affairs*, XLIII.172, October 1944, 159–71 (LW's portion, p. 168).

The mandate system is at least better than what preceded it and it may be better than what is being proposed to replace it.

C1299 TWICE REMOVED FROM DOUGHTY. *New Statesman and Nation*, 23 December 1944, 425.

Review of *The Golden Carpet*, by Somerset de Chair.

An affordable edition of a lively, interesting account of the conquest of Bagdad in 1941.

1945

C1300 AN ENGLISH KNIGHT ERRANT. *New Statesman and Nation*, 10 February 1945, 96–97.

Review of *Visions and Memories*, by H. W. Nevinson.

Nevinson, quixotic, eccentric and adventurous, was at once a pacifist and a war correspondent.

C1301 THE UNITED NATIONS. *Political Quarterly*, XVI.1 (Jan-March 1945), 12–20.

Article.

An attempt to explain to the ordinary person the tentative proposals of the Dumbarton Oaks Conference for the United Nations and their relationship to the League of Nations.

C1302 NATIONALISM AND SELF-DETERMINATION. *New Statesman and Nation*, 14 April 1945, 242–44.

Review of *National Self-Determination*, by Alfred Cobban; and *Nationalism and After*, by Edward Hallett Carr.

The authors of these books erroneously assume that powerful states must inevitably subdue or regulate less powerful ones.

C1303 DISILLUSION. *New Statesman and Nation*, 19 May 1945, 324.

Review of *The Yogi and the Commissar*, by Arthur Koestler.

Koestler is a brilliant writer, but his personal bitterness defeats his purpose.

C1304 THE VIRTUES OF DEMOCRACY. *New Statesman and Nation*, 26 May 1945, 340–41.

Review of *The Free State*, by D. W. Brogan.

The author writes to persuade Germans to adopt a democratic form of government. He makes a convincing case while admitting the difficulties.

C1305 Book reviews. *Political Quarterly*, XVI.2 (April-June 1945), 177–78.

The Peace Conference of 1919, by F. S. Marston; and *Public Opinion and the Last Peace*, by R. B. McCallum.

Mr. McCallum's book has a jaunty smartness. It is easier to read than Mr. Marston's but is not so accurate or objective.

C1306 THE CENTENARY OF THE CO-OP. *New Statesman and Nation*, 4 August 1945, 81–82.

Review of *A Century of Co-operation*, by G. D. H. Cole.

"It is the best history of co-operation in Britain so far written."

C1307 TRUTH AND PUBLIC OPINION. *New Statesman and Nation*, 3 November 1945, 303–304.

Review of *Truth and the Public*, by Kingsley Martin.

An historical and philosophical consideration of "the relation between truth, reason, and politics."

C1308 MEMOIRS OF AN ELDERLY MAN: SEDDON AND MISS THOMAS. *Orion: A Miscellany*, I (Nicholson & Watson, 1945), 76–87.

Short story.

Account of a personal experience with changed names and place. LW repeated this in his Autobiography with actual names.

1946

C1309   PATHS TO PEACE. *New Statesman and Nation*, 5 January 1946, 12–13.
Review of *Patterns of Peacemaking*, by David Thomson, E. Meyer and A. Briggs; and *The Path to Peace*. A Debate, ed. by George W. Keeton.

In a letter to John Lehmann, 3 Feb. '46 (at University of Texas) LW says he will edit the *New Statesman* for the week beginning February 11. Nothing signed by him appears Feb. 16.

C1310   BUS SERVICES. *New Statesman and Nation*, 23 February 1946, 139.
Letter.
   LW compares a bus which moved through London refusing to pick up passengers to heavenly bodies moving in mysterious ways.

C1311   THE UNREPENTENT LIBERAL. *New Statesman and Nation*, 30 March 1946, 234–35.
Review of *Victors Beware*, by Salvador de Madariaga.
   The author identifies liberalism with democracy and attacks authoritarianism.

C1312   BRITAIN IN THE ATOMIC AGE. *Political Quarterly*, XVII.1 (Jan-March 1946), 12–24.
Article.
   The British Isles are most vulnerable to atomic attack. The government should insist upon international control of all offensive weapons.

C1313   EMINENT RESPECTABILITY. *New Statesman and Nation*, 11 May 1946, 344–45.
Review of *J. A. Spender*, by Wilson Harris.
   When too sympathetic a friend or colleague writes a biography it tends to become "an Albert Memorial".

C1314   THE REPETITIONS OF HISTORY. *New Statesman and Nation*, 27 July 1946, 68.
Review of *The Congress of Vienna: A Study in Allied Unity*, by Harold Nicolson.
   This is an informative and entertaining book.

C1315   TWO AMBASSADORS. *New Statesman and Nation*, 31 August 1946, 156.
Review of *Ambassador on Special Mission*, by Sir Samuel Hoare, Viscount Templewood; and *An Ambassador in Bonds*, by Sir Lancelot Oliphant.
   Both give insights into the diplomatic service. Sir Lancelot, although typical of those who enter it, cannot compete with Sir Nevile [*sic*] Henderson as "an amiable simpleton". Sir Samuel Hoare has what is necessary for difficult diplomatic missions – intelligence, patience and foresight.

C1316   WINSTON CHURCHILL. *Political Quarterly*, XVII.3 (July to September 1946), 275 & 277.
Review of *Winston Churchill*, by Lewis Broad, New ed.
   To his first edition the author has added the period 1941–45. The added part is not so much a biography as a history of the war with long quotations from speeches by Churchill.

With this issue William Robson resumed co-editing the *Political Quarterly*.

C1317 VIRGINIA WOOLF. *Times Literary Supplement*, 5 October 1946, 479.
Letter commenting on a review of *Prater Violet*.
> The reviewer states "that Virginia Woolf did not produce her best work and was 'almost silent' during the thirties." The list of her publications during that time shows that this is not so.

C1318 BLUM. *New Statesman and Nation*, 12 October 1946, 270.
Review of *For All Mankind*, by Léon Blum. Translation of *A l'Echelle Humaine* by W. Pickles.
> Blum is optimistic about the future of democracy, but his analysis is not complete enough for the reader to share his optimism.

LW discussed this book in *Political Quarterly*, C1322.

C1319 BOOKS IN GENERAL. *New Statesman and Nation*, 19 October 1946, 285–86.
Review and discussion of *The Truth About Publishing*, 4th ed., by Sir Stanley Unwin.
> This technical classic has stood the test of time. The author's portraits of authors, publishers and literary agents is not flattering. Each group is out for itself, obeying the economic laws of the capitalist system, run like a dogfight.

C1320 HITLER AT WORK. *New Statesman & Nation*, 7 December 1946, 425.
Review of *The Nuremburg Documents: Some Aspects of German War Policy, 1939–45*, by Peter de Mendelssohn.
> There is more analysis in this book than in the author's previous one.

C1321 PATTERN IN HISTORY. *New Statesman & Nation*, 14 December 1946, 446.
Review of *History Has Tongues*, by Wilfred Wolfendale. The author fails to prove that history repeats itself.

C1322 Reviews. *Political Quarterly*, XVII.4 (Oct-Dec 1946), 359–60.
Our Threatened Values, by Victor Gollancz; *A l'Echelle Humaine*, by Léon Blum (Gallimard); and *For All Mankind*, by Léon Blum (Gollancz).

1947

C1323 BRITISH FOREIGN POLICY. *New Statesman and Nation*, 8 March 1947, 158–59.
Review of *Documents on British Foreign Policy, 1919–1939*, ed. by E. L. Woodward & Rohan Butler, 2nd series, vol. I (H.M.S.O.).
> The most interesting part deals with naval disarmament in the 30s.

C1324 I KNOW EVERYTHING. *New Statesman and Nation*, 5 April 1947, 239.
Review of *Secretary of Europe, The Life of Friedrich Gentz*, by Golo Mann, tr. by W. H. Woglom.
> Gentz emerges as a more complex person than the shadowy figure behind Metternich of history. A kind of Boswell, with an admixture of Pitt and Burke, his superior knowledge of affairs disillusioned him about the fate of Europe.

C1325 TOO MUCH KNOWLEDGE. *New Statesman and Nation*, 14 June 1947, 439–40.
Review of *Machiavelli*, by J. H. Whitfield.
> "The book has almost every fault with which learning can load the printed page." The attempt to prove all other commentators wrong seems to be an attempt to prove that Machiavelli was not machiavellian.

C1326 THE MAN OF MUNICH. *Political Quarterly*, XVIII.3 (July-Sept 1947), 199–205.
Article based on *The Life of Neville Chamberlain*, by Keith Feiling.
The author has attempted to praise Chamberlain, but no one can prevent his condemnation. Rather than praise he should pity him.

C1327 Reviews. *Political Quarterly*, XVIII.3 (July-Sept 1947), 244–66.
The Anatomy of Peace, by Emery Reves; *War, Sadism and Pacifism. Further Essays*, by Edward Glover; and *Peace & the Public: A Study in Mass Observation*.
These books are based on untenable theories.

C1328 THE LAST DAYS OF HITLER. *Political Quarterly*, XVIII.3 (July-Sept 1947), 270–71.
Review of *The Last Days of Hitler*, by H. R. Trevor-Roper.
It seems incredible that the "machine" continued to work even after decent people knew that Hitler was mad and his court of Nazis a gang of thugs.

C1329 SENSE OR SENSIBILITY IN POLITICS. *New Statesman and Nation*, 18 October 1947, 314.
Review of *Reason and Unreason in Society*, by Morris Ginsberg; and *The Comforts of Unreason*, by Rupert Crawshay-Williams.
Ginsberg's book is about sociology, not about reason and unreason in society. Crawshay-Williams holds that the unpleasantness of social facts makes us resort to unreason. Such comfort is illusory.

C1330 THE GREAT DEBATE. *New Statesman and Nation*, 13 December 1947, 469–70.
Letter. Reply to the attack on LW's *Foreign Policy*, A36, by K. Zilliacus in comments on Richard Crossman's article and Ewer's response, 15 and 22 November (*NS and N*, 6 December 1947, pp. 450–51).
Zilliacus is being jinxed by spider-fly promises.

C1331 PALESTINE MISSION. *Political Quarterly*, XVIII.4 (Oct-Dec 1947), 367.
Review of *Palestine Mission*, by Richard Crossman.
An unusually impartial book on the subject.

1948

C1332 THE CONCERT OF EUROPE. *New Statesman and Nation*, 17 January 1948, 55–56.
Review of *The Aftermath of the Napoleonic Wars*, by H. G. Schenk.
The reader is apt to confuse the authorities quoted with the facts.

C1333 Review of *Philosophy and Politics*, by Bertrand Russell; and *Ethical and Political Thinking*, by E. F. Carritt. *Political Quarterly*, XIX.1 (Jan-March 1948), 77–78.
LW stresses the authors' recognition of the dangers of absolutism to civilisation and the importance of scepticism and agnosticism as antidotes.

C1334 Review of *Personality in Politics. Studies of Contemporary Statesmen*, by Sir Arthur Salter. *Political Quarterly*, XIX.1 (Jan-March 1948), 78.
Sir Arthur is too kind to the actors he portrays. His final chapter is a study of the relationship of the shapers of history to the actual events.

C1335 HISTORY AND MR. BRAINBALLA. *New Statesman and Nation*, 10 April 1948, 300–01.

Review of *Documents on British Foreign Policy, 1919–1939,* First and
Second Series.
    The valuable facts in these collections are buried in a vast amount of
    useless material.

C1336   FRENCH REVOLUTION. *New Statesman and Nation,* 24 April 1948, 339.
Review of *The Coming of the French Revolution,* by Georges Lefebvre, tr. by
R. R. Palmer.
    This book was published in 1939 as *Quatre-vingt-neuf.* Written from the
    Republican point of view, it is still a moderate and objective study of class
    structure and psychology.

C1337   Review of *The History of The Times.* vol. III. *The Twentieth Century, 1884–
1912. Political Quarterly,* XIX.2 (April-June 1948), 184.
    This volume is more interesting than the earlier ones despite the bad
    writing. One must re-read to get the meaning. It concerns the Parnell
    letters, the relation of *The Times* to foreign affairs, and Lord Northcliffe's
    purchase of the paper.

C1338   Review of *India Called Them,* by Lord Beveridge. *Political Quarterly,* XIX.2
(April-June 1948), 192.
    The author tells his parents' biography largely through the letters they
    wrote to each other.

C1339   MR. REED'S NIGHTMARES. *New Statesman and Nation,* 24 July 1948,
80–81.
Review of *From Smoke to Smother,* by Douglas Reed.
    Mr. Reed, though a brilliant journalist, is paranoid in his denunciation of
    Jews and Communists.

C1340   THE DANGER OF WORDS. *New Statesman and Nation,* 23 October 1948,
355–56.
Review of *The Pattern of Imperialism,* by E. M. Winslow.
    In the attempt to define his terms the author gets "lost in a jungle of
    words".

C1341   Review of *Our Partnership,* by Beatrice Webb, ed. by Barbara Drake and
Margaret I. Cole. *Political Quarterly,* XIX.3 (July-Oct 1948), 277–78.
    This autobiography for the years 1892–1911 is a frank account of how
    Beatrice and Sidney Webb influenced history by manipulating and
    permeating the ruling classes. Beatrice Webb revealed her thoughts,
    feelings, motives and actions in her diary and transferred them to her
    book.

C1342   Review of *Sydney Olivier. Letters and Writings,* ed. by Margaret Olivier, with
Some Impressions by Bernard Shaw; and *Charles Roden Buxton. A Memoir,*
by Victoria de Bunsen. *Political Quarterly,* XIX.4 (Oct-Dec 1948), 376–77.
    Each of these books gives a living picture of the man himself. Both men
    were socialists and members of the Labour Party. Olivier worked for
    internationalism and peace and a better status for colonial people;
    Charles Buxton as member of Parliament and in his books worked for the
    Labour Party's colonial policy.

1949

C1343   Short review of *A History of the Labour Party from 1914,* by G. D. H. Cole.
Fabian News, LX.1, January 1949, 21.
    "A straightforward, chronological record."

C1344 SOCIETY. *New Statesman and Nation*, 26 February 1949, 213–14.
Review of *The State and the Citizen*, by J. D. Mabbott.
> Mr. Mabbott thinks and writes clearly, honestly and intelligently about ¾ of the time. It is too bad he did not decide what topic he was discussing.

C1345 THE HABSBURGS. *New Statesman and Nation*, 5 March 1949, 235–36.
Review of *The Habsburg Monarchy 1809–1918*, by A. J. P. Taylor.
> In this completely rewritten version of the book published in 1941, Taylor has managed better than most writers to explain the fantastic and impossible situation, but by exaggerating the stupidity of the principal actors he has oversimplified.

C1346 BETWEEN TWO WORLDS. *New Statesman and Nation*, 14 May 1949, 510.
Review of *Edwardian Heritage. A Study in British History, 1901–1906*, by William Scovell Adams.
> The author derives the brightness and some of the method of his account of the reign of Edward VII from Lytton Strachey. It is a good record of events but gives no idea of cause and effect.

C1347 A LIFE OF TOLSTOY. *New Statesman and Nation*, 21 May 1949, 534–35.
Review of *Leo Tolstoy*, by Ernest J. Simmons.
> The book is too long and has no documentation. Tolstoy's character, a remarkable combination of the ridiculous and the sublime, is so interesting that he has saved even Mr. Simmons with his lamentable style.

C1348 THE BELIEFS OF KEYNES. *Listener*, 9 June 1949, 993.
Review of *Two Memoirs. Dr. Melchior: A Defeated Enemy* and *My Early Beliefs*, by John Maynard Keynes.
> The first paper recalls Keynes as a Cambridge undergraduate; the second, Keynes as a famous man. They are private papers read to a circle of close friends in the "Memoir Club" which probably do not convey as much to people who do not have the key to understand them. "In one important point he is, I think, wrong. It is true that he and his generation believed in the efficacy of reason, but it is not true that any of us believed in the rationality of human nature."

C1349 Review of *The White House Papers of Harry L. Hopkins, An Intimate History*, by Robert E. Sherwood, vol. I; and *Ciano's Diplomatic Papers*, ed. by Malcolm Muggeridge. *Political Quarterly*, XX.2 (April-June 1949), 182–83.
> Sherwood's book shows that most Americans and British have "a higher standard of human decency and public morality" (even in foreign diplomacy) than the Italians or Germans. One can only feel shame reading Ciano's account of Neville Chamberlain.

C1350 THE STALIN MYSTERY. *New Statesman and Nation*, 9 July 1949, 46.
Review of *Stalin*, by I. Deutscher.
> This very readable political biography shows how a powerful machine can advance even a stupid man. Stalin sat at the centre of a great web in which he entangled abler men. Without any long range vision he managed to change an 18th-century agricultural country into an industrialized modern state in two decades.

C1351 MUSIC IN MOSCOW. *Political Quarterly*, XX.3 (July-Sept 1949), 210–18.
Article discussing the steps taken by the Soviet State to control music with reference to two books: *Musical Uproar in Moscow*, by Alexander Werth; and *Realist Music*, by Rena Moisenko.

Letter from Mrs. Pike, Central Office of Information, Overseas Office, asks permission to include this article in their international review *British Ally* (LW Papers, Sussex) [not found].

C1352 Review of *Trial and Error. The Autobiography of Chaim Weizmann; Mahatma Gandhi*, by H. S. L. Polak, H. N. Brailsford, and Lord Pethick-Lawrence; and *The Story of My Experiments with Truth*, by M. K. Gandhi. *Political Quarterly*, XX.3 (July-Sept 1949), 284–85.

From high idealism both of these men pursued freedom and nationalism regardless of the consequences of slaughter and misery.

C1353 THE PROMISED LAND. *New Statesman and Nation*, 29 October 1949, 490–92.

Review of *Promise and Fulfilment: Palestine, 1917–1949*, by Arthur Koestler.

"A moving and brilliant" book whose author is objective about the need for reconciliation of the Arabs and the Jews.

C1354 THE UTOPIANS. *New Statesman and Nation*, 26 November 1949, 624.

Review of *Paths in Utopia*, by Martin Buber, tr. by R. F. C. Hull.

Professor Buber considers theoretical utopianism and its practical application in the organisation of society.

C1355 Review of *Economic Survey of Europe in 1948;* and *Yearbook on Human Rights for 1947* (both United Nations and H.M.S.O.). *Political Quarterly*, XX.4 (Oct-Dec 1949), 388.

1950

C1356 ... IN OTHER WORDS. *Saturday Review of Literature*, New York, XXX.10, 5 February 1950, 10.

Reprint, with changed title, of LW's "Note" to *Reviewing*, by Virginia Woolf also reprinted here under the title "Books Starred and Daggered" (pp. 9, 11, 31–33). The *Saturday Review* editor states that the essay will be included in *The Captain's Death Bed*, B56.

C1357 WHAT IS POLITICS? *Current Affairs*, No. 99 (London Bureau of Current Affairs), 4 February 1950, pp. 3–14 of a 16-page issue which includes a description of the series, discussion notes, a note "For the Teachers", and cartoons by Nicolas Bentley.

C1358 THE MODERN SCHOLASTICISM. *New Statesman and Nation*, 25 March 1950, 345.

Review of *Marx, His Time and Ours*, by Rudolf Schlesinger.

Dr. Schlesinger is to Marxism what the ancient schoolmen were to theology.

C1359 NOTES AND COMMENTS. *Political Quarterly*, XXI.1 (Jan-March 1950), 1–8.

Unsigned editorial on hostile camps: U.S.A. vs. Soviets; facts vs. ideology.

C1360 Review of 7 books on Socialism. *Political Quarterly*, XXI.1 (Jan-March 1950), 96–97.

Socialism: A Short History, by Norman MacKenzie; *The Socialist Tragedy*, by Ivor Thomas; *Fifty Years' March. The Rise of the Labour Party*, by Francis Williams; *Can Parliament Survive?* by Christopher Hollis; *Parliamentary Government in Britain. A Symposium* (Hansard Society); *Marxism and Contemporary Science*, by Jack Lindsay; and *Dialectical Materialism and Science*, by M. Cornforth.

The difference between German and English thought. is the thread holding these 7 books together. MacKenzie's book has permanent value.

C1361 Unsigned review of *Political Thought in France from the Revolution to the Fourth Republic*, by J. P. Mayer. *Political Quarterly*, XXI.1 (Jan-March 1950), 108.

The extracts from the thinkers' works are too short to give their ideas, and Mayer has not provided sufficient connecting material.

C1362 Letter to the Editor. *Venture*, II.3, April 1950, 8.

Dr. Rita Hinden is wrong in saying Charles Buxton and Sir John Maynard were utopians who wished merely to liquidate the empire (February issue).

C1363 THE BRIGHTER SIDE OF HISTORY. *New Statesman and Nation*, 3 June 1950, 636 & 638.

Review of *From Napoleon to Stalin: Comments on History and Politics*, by A. J. P. Taylor.

The author's essays about people are better than those about events. In using the clever epigram he sometimes oversimplifies.

C1364 NOTES AND COMMENTS. *Political Quarterly*, XXI.2 (April-June 1950), 109–13. Unsigned editorial introduction to this issue devoted to the subject of nationalisation.

C1365 NOTES AND COMMENTS. *Political Quarterly*, XXI.3 (July-Sept 1950), 133–38.

Unsigned comments on the United Nations Organisation.

C1366 LIFE WITH TOLSTOY. *New Statesman and Nation*, 18 November 1950, 462.

Review of *The Tolstoy Home: The Diaries of Tatiana Sukhotin-Tolstoy*, tr. by Alec Brown.

Tolstoy's daughter gives no new information but provides insights to, and sympathy for, her strange tortured family.

C1367 NOTES AND COMMENTS. *Political Quarterly*, XXI.4 (Oct-Dec 1950), 333–37.

Unsigned comments on *Labour and the New Society* (Labour Party).

1951

C1368 Unsigned review of *The Life of John Maynard Keynes*, by R. F. Harrod. *Listener*, 25 January 1951, 151.

In this unsatisfactory biography the author makes inappropriately intimate comments and asks strings of rhetorical questions.

C1369 NOTES AND COMMENTS. *Political Quarterly*, XXII.1 (Jan-March 1951), 1–6.

Unsigned summary and synthesis of a symposium on the Cold War included in this issue. Cites *A Defence of the Cold War*, by a Study Group of the Royal Institute of International Affairs.

C1370 Review of *The State of Europe*, by Howard K. Smith. *Political Quarterly*, XXIII.1 (Jan-March 1951), 108 & 110.

A brilliant survey.

C1371 A TWENTIETH CENTURY MYSHKIN. *Listener*, 26 April 1951, 670.

Review of *World Within World*, by Stephen Spender.

The author shares his experiences of these troubled times with a simplicity befitting the poet.

C1372 NOTES AND COMMENTS. *Political Quarterly*, XXII.2 (April-June 1951), 117–20.
Unsigned editorial on the B.B.C. Broadcasting Committee report.

C1373 Review of *Testament for Social Service: An Essay in the Application of Scientific Method to Human Problems,* by Barbara Wootton. *Political Quarterly,* XXII.2 (April-June 1951), 205–06.
The difficult subject of this admirable book makes it hard to read.

C1374 Review of *The Bolshevik Revolution, 1917–1923,* Vol. I, by Edward Hallett Carr. *Political Quarterly,* XXII.2 (April-June 1951), 209–10.
Professor Carr seems to regard power as the only important cause of history and its successful use as its justification for whatever happens.

C1375 WEST AFRICAN TRADE UNIONS. *Venture,* III.6, July 1951, 8–9.
Report of a congress held at Doula under the auspices of the International Conference of Free Trade Unions, signed W.H. and L.W.

C1376 THE FUTURE OF BOOKS. *Fabian Journal,* IV, July 1951, 22–24.
Article.
The rising cost of publishing – more expensive paper, printing and binding – is seriously affecting the future of "serious books". Simultaneous publication of cloth-bound and paper-bound editions of the same book and the demand of public libraries may help.

C1377 NOTES AND COMMENTS. *Political Quarterly,* XXII.3 (July-Sept 1951), 217–20.
On the dismissal of General MacArthur; civil vs. military authority. Unsigned.

C1378 "A POLITICAL QUARTERLY". In "Bernard Shaw and the Political Quarterly", *Political Quarterly,* XXII.3 (July-Sept 1951), 221–39.
Reprint of a prospectus [*c.* 1927] signed by several people including Leonard Woolf, pp. 222–25.

C1379 Review: *Freedom and Catholic Power,* by Paul Blanshard; *Roman Catholicism,* by Thomas Corbishley, S.J. *Political Quarterly,* XXII.3 (July-Sept 1951), 302–04.
The American Mr. Blanshard says the Catholic Church uses its power dangerously against a free society. Father Corbishley mentions none of this and presents an opposite picture.

C1380 THE NATURE OF POLITICS. *New Statesman and Nation,* 6 October 1951, 384 & 386.
Review of *Dominations and Powers,* by George Santayana; and *Civitatas Dei,* by Lionel Curtis.
Mr. Curtis applies common sense to history and politics; Mr. Santayana "follows the well-trodden path of mysticism and muddle."

C1381 Letter to the Editor. *The Observer,* 14 October 1951, p. 8, col. 1.
A profile of C. Day-Lewis stated that early Hogarth Press poetry did not sell well. LW refutes this, saying he and VW published poetry by Eliot, Graves, Aiken and others which sold well by standards of the time.

C1382 POLITICS OF A MATHEMATICIAN. *New Statesman and Nation,* 10 November 1951, 540.
Review of *New Hopes for a Changing World,* by Bertrand Russell.
Discussion of the conflicts in society by "one of the few thinkers who have become progressively less reactionary with age."

C1383 SPLENDOURS AND MISERIES OF REASON. *New Statesman and Nation,* 15 December 1951, 712.

Review of *After All*. Autobiography, by Norman Angell.

LW quotes from his comments on *The Great Illusion* (1908), "In the Cave", C0708, which Angell quoted in this autobiography. He says readers misunderstood the book, though it was based on reason.

C1384 NOTES AND COMMENTS. *Political Quarterly*, XXII.4 (Oct-Dec 1951), 317–22.

Unsigned editorial on Labour and secondary education.

C1385 Review of *The Life of Joseph Chamberlain*, vol. IV: *1901–1903*, by Julian Amery (continuation of a work begun by J. L. Garvin); and *With Milner in South Africa*, by Lionel Curtis. *Political Quarterly*, XXII.4 (Oct-Dec 1951), 396–97.

Mr. Amery has to use the plan Garvin adopted and write at greater length and in more detail than necessary. Mr. Curtis throws light on the careers of Chamberlain and Milner.

1952

C1386 THE LEAGUE OF NATIONS. *New Statesman and Nation*, 29 March 1952, 377.

Review of *A History of the League of Nations*, by F. P. Walters.

Mr. Walters presents the facts but does not speculate upon the causes of failure of the League of Nations. Because the nations are unwilling to use the machinery established by the League and adopted by the United Nations to prevent war the United Nations is "a still-born abortion".

Stephen W. Pollak took exception to LW's "sweeping and frivolous metaphors" in the April 12 issue. For the reply see C1390.

C1387 NOTES AND COMMENTS. *Political Quarterly*, XXIII.1 (Jan-March 1952), 1–4.

Unsigned introduction to special number on the Soviet Union.

C1388 REVIEWS. *Political Quarterly*, XXIII.1 (Jan-March 1952), 99–101.

The Inhuman Land, by Joseph Czapski; *It Happens in Russia*, by Vladimir Petrov; *Russian Purge and the Extraction of Confession*, by F. Beck and W. Godin; *The Katyn Wood Murders*, by Joseph Mackiewicz; and *Stalin's Slave Camps*.

These books should be read in sorrow rather than in anger in order to grasp the cause of the terrible epidemic of barbarism in Europe and attempt a cure.

C1389 REVIEWS. *Political Quarterly*, XXIII.1 (Jan-March 1952), 102 & 104.

Freedom, Power and Democratic Planning, by Karl Mannheim, ed. by Hans Gerth, E. K. Bramstedt and Julia Mannheim; and *The Logic of Liberty*, by M. Polanyi.

The book edited from manuscripts by Dr. Mannheim sets forth the contradiction between individual liberty and social order and analyses it with imagination. Beside it Professor Polyani's book seems superficial.

C1390 IS U.N. STILL-BORN? *New Statesman and Nation*, 19 April 1952), 465.

Letter in response to Pollak.about LW's review, C1386.

"Mr. Pollak's letter . . . shows me that I cannot make myself intelligible about anything to anyone."

C1391 NOTES AND COMMENTS. *Political Quarterly*, XXIII.2 (April-June 1952), 117–21.

Unsigned reflections on the Middle East, and secondary education.

C1392   Review of *Leslie Stephen. His Thought and Character in Relation to his Time*, by Noel Annan. *Political Quarterly*, XXIII.2 (April-June 1952), 196–97.
Mr. Annan presents Leslie Stephen to his readers as a living man.

C1393   CHINESE EXECUTIONS. *New Statesman and Nation*, 6 September 1952, 265.
Letter to the Editor.
Comment on Kingsley Martin's statement the previous week about whether some executions were "really necessary".

C1394   SCIENCE AND HUMANITY. *The Times*, 12 September 1952, p. 7, col. 7.
Letter to the Editor.
LW recommends that A. L. Rowse, who said all ills result from over-population, emigrate.

C1395   NOTES AND COMMENTS. BROADCASTING; & THE TIMES (*History of The Times*, vol.IV). *Political Quarterly*, XXIII.3 (July-Sept 1952), 217–21.

C1396   Review of *Noel Buxton, A Life*, by Mosa Anderson. Foreword by G. P. Gooch. *Political Quarterly*, XXIII.3 (July-Sept 1952), 315.

C1397   FATHER WORSHIP. *New Statesman and Nation*, 20 December 1952, 761–62.
Review of *Jan Christian Smuts*, by J. C. Smuts.
For a son who admires his father to write a good biography of him is almost impossible. Smuts is also ignorant of history and a poor writer.

C1398   SOMETHING NEW OUT OF AFRICA. *Political Quarterly*, XXII.4 (Oct-Dec 1952), 322–31.
Article. Cites several government publications or Command Papers: *The Dilemma of South Africa*, by John Hatch; *Report on South Africa*, by Basil Davidson; and *The Choice Before South Africa*, by E. S. Sachs.
It is only the white minority who desire federation of three British territories in central and southern Africa. It would lead to the same kind of situation as obtains in South Africa.

1953

C1399   CHRISTIAN NAMES. *New Statesman and Nation*, 31 January 1953, 122.
Letter to the editor on the use of Christian names by strangers.

C1400   A GREAT RACONTEUR. *Listener*, 26 March 1953, 531.
Review of *Memories*, by Desmond MacCarthy.
The best of talkers, Desmond MacCarthy was a born writer who never fulfilled his promise. He admitted a repugnance to doing what he knew he should do.
LW repeats much of this in his autobiography.

C1401   NOTES AND COMMENTS. *Political Quarterly*, XXIV.1 (Jan-March 1953), 1–4.
Unsigned editorial about the survey of the Labour Party appearing in this issue.

C1402   Reviews. *Political Quarterly*, XXIV.1 (Jan-March 1953), 116–17.
Hitler: A Study in Tyranny, by Alan Bullock; *Ernest Bevin: Portrait of a Great Englishman*, by Francis Williams, Foreword by Clement Attlee; *The Forsaken Idea: A Study of Viscount Milner*, by Edward Crankshaw.
These biographies of very different men illuminate one another.

C1403   THE GENIUS OF HITLER. *New Statesman and Nation*, 16 May 1953, 586 & 588.

Review of *Hitler's Table Talk, 1941–1944*. Introductory essay by H. R. Trevor-Roper.

> Hitler's monologues, recorded by Martin Bormann, are boring; they show his conceit, ignorance, stupidity and brutality. Trevor-Roper says Hitler was a systematic thinker, a claim often made for men who have held power. But it is a disruption in society which allows such a charlatan to seize power.

C1404 NOTES AND COMMENTS. *Political Quarterly*, XXIV.2 (April-June 1953), 125–28.

Unsigned editorial on the Conservative Party.

C1405 *Political Quarterly*, XXIV.2 (April-June 1953), 210–12.

Reviews of *Harold Laski*, by Kingsley Martin; *The Dilemma of Our Times*, by Harold J. Laski; and *The Attack*, by R. H. Tawney.

> The reviews of Mr. Martin's biography show that many of Mr. Laski's opponents still misrepresent him. His only real failing was a childish vanity. He is attacked mostly because he was an intellectual. He was a great teacher, but because he tried to do too many things, he wrote too much and thought too little. Mr. Tawney writes with intellectual imagination.

C1406 LUCUS A NON LUCENDO. *New Statesman and Nation*, 8 August 1953, 160–61.

Review of *Malenkov*, by Martin Ebon; and *Russia after Stalin*, by Isaac Deutscher.

> These books point up our ignorance of Russia. Deutscher's is the better book, but even he is trying "to make bricks without straw".

C1407 G. E. MOORE AND THE "PRINCIPIA ETHICA". *TLS*, Special Autumn Number, 28 August 1953. Insert entitled "Thoughts and Second Thoughts upon Some Outstanding Books of the Half-Century 1900–1950", p. iv.
Review article.

> Moore's book was not reviewed in the *TLS* when first published in 1903. The Cambridge University Press is bringing out a new edition. Although he wrote only three books and a few articles, Moore influenced many different people. For the first 50 pages the *Principia Ethica* seems to be "a bare and bleak book . . . but as one goes on the cumulative effect becomes tremendous." Moore's simple, direct writing and common sense are the reason a man like Keynes could say he is better than Plato. He should really be compared to Socrates.

Letters between LW and Alan Pryce-Jones, 10–14 July 1953, show that the latter requested a 2000-word article and that LW had to borrow a copy of the book from him (LW Papers, Sussex).

C1408 WORDS AND POLITICS. *New Statesman and Nation*, 26 September 1953, 352.

Review of *The Vocabulary of Politics*, by T. D. Weldon.

> Weldon's thought is confused; his use of words slipshod. He should have been more careful when criticising the use of words by political writers.

C1409 NOTES AND COMMENTS. *Political Quarterly*, XXIV.3 (July-Sept 1953), 233–35.

Unsigned editorial on antagonism between Russia and the U.S.A., and McCarthyism.

C1410 Review of *Socialist Thought. The Forerunners, 1789–1850*, by G. D. H. Cole. *Political Quarterly*, XXIV.3 (July-Sept 1953), 325.

Cole has encyclopedic knowledge of his subject, yet treats each socialist thinker separately and fails to relate one to another.

C1411   VOCABULARY OF POLITICS. *New Statesman and Nation,* 10 October 1953, 423.

Letter. Response to two letters in the previous issue which attacked his review of Weldon's book, C1408.

C1412   VOCABULARY OF POLITICS. *New Statesman and Nation,* 24 October 1953, 489.

Letter responding to one from Jack Parsons published 17 October, p. 456.

C1413   [PAGES FROM A DIARY BY VIRGINIA WOOLF]. *Encounter,* I.1, October 1953, 5–11.

Pre-publication printing from *A Writer's Diary,* ed. by Leonard Woolf, B59.

C1414   SHAW AND THE FABIANS. *New Statesman and Nation,* 14 November 1953, 601.

Letter to the Editor objecting to Mr. Brailsford's interpretation of LW's contribution to *Shaw and Society,* B58, in his review, 31 October 1953, p. 532.

C1415   NOTES AND COMMENTS. *Political Quarterly,* XXIV.4 (Oct-Dec 1953), 333–37.

Unsigned editorial on the future of television and the B.B.C., and governmental sponsorship of commercial TV.

1954

C1416   GIBT ES POLITISCHE NEUROSEN? Eine Diskussion um Arthur Koestlers Aufsatz [in Heft 63]. *Der Monat,* 6 Jahrgang, Heft 65, February 1954, 469–73.

Comments by Leonard Woolf, Michael Freund, Jules Monnerot, Alexander Mitscherlich, and Theodor W. Adorno, pp. 464–82.

Reprinted in English in *Encounter,* March 1954, C1418.

Correspondence relating to this article is in the LW Papers, Sussex. Melvin J. Laski requested it in time to have it translated into German.

C1417   THE BRITISH POODLE. *Listener,* 11 March 1954, 439.

Review of *Mr. Balfour's Poodle,* by Roy Jenkins; and *The Future of the House of Lords. A Symposium,* ed. by Sydney D. Bailey.

C1418   REASON IN POLITICS. *Encounter,* II.3, March 1954, 54–56.

Letter to the Editor concerning Koestler's article, "A Guide to Political Neuroses", in the November issue. Except that it is in Engiish and has a different title this letter is almost exactly the same as the article in *Der Monat,* C1416.

Koestler has oversimplified Freud's theories, especially with regard to political rationality.

Koestler replied, "After gently chiding me through five columns, Mr. Woolf ends up repeating, in an admirably concise form, exactly what I said" (p. 56).

C1419   NOTES AND COMMENTS. THE COLONIAL EMPIRE. *Political Quarterly,* XXV.1 (Jan-March 1954), 1–4.

Unsigned editorial citing *The New West Africa,* by F. Le Gros Clark and others; and *Kenya,* by Norman Leys.

Note Barbara Wootton's review of *Principia Politica,* A37, in this number of *Political Quarterly,* pp. 88–90.

C1420   THE MEANING OF 1789. *Encounter*, II.4, April 1954, 78–80.
Review of *The French Revolution, 1788–1792*, by Gaetano Salvameni; and *The French Revolution*, by A. Goodwin.
> Goodwin has managed to give changing interpretations of the subject as he intended. Both books contribute to the history of the period. Both authors see that revolution was already in the minds of men before it actually happened.

C1421   THE DISUNITED UNITED NATIONS. *Fabian International Review*, No. 5, May 1954, pp. 10–12.
Article.
> The UNO has not achieved its promise because the Soviets have used it as an instrument of hostility. The real achievements of the UNO have gone unnoticed because only sensational events are reported in the news.

C1422   NOTES AND COMMENTS. THE BERLIN CONFERENCE AND AFTER. *Political Quarterly*, XXV.2 (April-June 1954), 101–04.
Unsigned editorial.
> Nothing good will come of refusing to allow Germany to rearm and help with European defence.

C1423   Review of *The Prophet Armed. Trotsky: 1879–1921*, by I. Deutscher. *Political Quarterly*, XXV.2 (April-June 1954), 179–80.
> This is even better than the author's biography of Stalin, partly because Trotsky was one of the few Bolshevik leaders who had some humanity and civilisation in his make-up.

C1424   Review of *Report on the Atom*, by Gordon Dean. *Political Quarterly*, XXV.2 (April-June 1954), 191.
> The chairman of the Atomic Energy Commission in the U.S.A., 1950–53, has written this book to explain the story of atomic energy to the ordinary man. "It is a sober, serious book, well worth reading."

C1425   WHAT IS BLOOMSBURY? *Encounter*, III.3, September 1954, 78 & 80.
Review of *The Bloomsbury Group, A Study of E. M. Forster, Virginia Woolf and Their Circle*, by J. K. Johnstone.
> "The Bloomsbury group was a circle of friends each of whom was an extreme individualist, doing his or her work in his or her way, unconscious of a common purpose theory, or philosophy." Mr. Johnstone fails in his attempt to force these very different writers into the same Procrustean bed, but he does include some sensible literary criticism.

Much of what LW says here about Bloomsbury is also in his autobiography.

C1426   NOTE ON A NOTE. *Literature and Psychology*, New York, IV.4, September 1954, 64.
Letter to Dr. Erwin Steinberg. Steinberg quoted it in his letter to the Editor. Having been asked to rebut an article on the use of symbols in the novel by Dr. Wyatt, Steinberg had questioned LW about his wife's knowledge of Freudian psychology when she wrote *Mrs. Dalloway*. LW replied:
> Virginia Woolf never read much Freud, and she had read very little before she wrote Mrs. Dalloway. "I very much doubt whether my wife ever used symbols in quite the way you think she used them in relation to the knife."

C1427   NOTES AND COMMENTS. *Political Quarterly*, XXV.3 (July-Sept 1954), 201–04.
Unsigned editorial on the state of the Labour Party.

C1428   Reviews. *Political Quarterly*, XXV.3 (July-Sept 1954), 280–82.
Pio Nono: A Study in European Politics and Religion in the XIX Century, by

E. E. Y. Hales; *The Quaker Approach to Contemporary Problems,* ed. by John Kavanagh; and *Communism and Christ,* by Charles W. Lowry.
These books point up the relation between religion and politics.

C1429 Reviews. *Political Quarterly,* XXV.4 (Oct-Dec 1954), 400–02.
German Marxism and Russian Communism, by John Plamenatz; *Socialist Thought: Marxism and Anarchism, 1850–1890,* by G. D. H. Cole; and *The Challenge of Socialism,* ed. by Henry Pelling.
These writers do not seem to agree on a definition of socialist thought.

1955

C1430 KOT. *New Statesman and Nation,* 5 February 1955, 170 & 172.
Obituary article.
S. S. Koteliansky, translator from the Russian, worked with L and VW and others. "His English was indeed strange, but also so vivid and individual that I was often tempted to leave it untouched."
LW repeats his portrait in his autobiography.

C1431 NOTES AND COMMENTS. LIBERALISM AND SOCIALISM. *Political Quarterly,* XXVI.1 (Jan-March 1955), 1–3.
The Liberals did their best to kill liberalism, but it rises in such unlikely places as Africa in relation to British Government and Empire.

C1432 Reviews. *Political Quarterly,* XXVI.1 (Jan-March 1955), 85–86.
Gladstone: A Biography, by Philip Magnus; and *Tempestuous Journey: Lloyd George, His Life and Times,* by Frank Owen.
From these books and Garvin's *Life of Chamberlain* one could write a work on the decline and fall of liberalism, for Gladstone, Lloyd George and Chamberlain wrecked the Liberal Party.

C1433 Review of *The Spy Web: A Study in Communist Espionage,* by Francis Noel-Baker. *Political Quarterly,* XXVI.1 (Jan-March 1955), 93–94.
The Russian spy system differs from those of other nations. It is more highly organised; it is active, not passive, in gathering information, assuming a permanent state of war; and, though it sometimes relies on paid traitors, these traitor spies work not so much for pay as because they are fanatical communists fighting for Russia against their own countries.

C1434 SHORTER NOTICES. *Political Quarterly,* XXVI.1 (Jan-March 1955), 98.
Unsigned reviews of *Yearbook of the United Nations;* and *The Constitution of Ceylon,* 3rd ed., by Sir Ivor Jennings.

C1435 MR. APOLLINAX. *New Statesman and Nation,* 18 June 1955, 836–37.
Unsigned article about Bertrand Russell, accompanied by a cartoon of Russell signed Vicky. The title is from T. S. Eliot's "The Love Song of J. Alfred Prufrock". (Clipping in LW Papers, Sussex)
In spite of being fined and imprisoned for pacifism in World War I, and of being an intellectual, Russell had received the Order of Merit by 1950, perhaps because he had become a popular broadcaster. His mind is quicker even than that of Maynard Keynes.

C1436 SHORTER NOTICES. *Political Quarterly,* XXVI.2 (April-June 1955), 206.
The British Constitution, 3rd ed., by H. R. G. Greaves; and *Organizing for Peace,* by Daniel S. Cheever and H. Field Haviland, Jr.

C1437 NOTES AND COMMENTS. IS THERE A REVOLT AGAINST REASON? *Political Quarterly,* XXVI.3 (July-Sept 1955), 207–10.
The articles in this issue lead to the conclusion that man must continue to use his reason.

C1438 WHAT IS HISTORY? *Political Quarterly*, XXVI.3 (July-Sept 1955), 220–26.
Article based on *A Study of History*, by Arnold Toynbee; and *Historical Inevitablity*, by Isaiah Berlin.

> Herodotus and Thucydides interpreted history as cause and effect. Some 19th- and 20th-century historians have treated it as a mystery. Among those who have tried to discover the universal cause of all events are Marx, Spengler, Acton, Schopenhauer, Dilthey and Toynbee. Berlin is sceptical.

Summary of this in *International Political Science Abstracts*, vol. IV, p. 469 (1955).

C1439 Reviews. *Political Quarterly*, XXVI.3 (July-Sept 1955), 297–98.
The Origin of Communist Autocracy, by Leonard Schapiro; *The Russian Revolution 1917*, by N. N. Sukhanov; *The Illusion of an Epoch. Marxism-Leninism . . .*, by H. B. Acton; and *Heretics and Renegades*, by Isaac Deutscher.

> The best of these books is by Leonard Schapiro. The eye-witness account by Sukhanov, of which the English translation is an abridgment, is nearly as important. Mr. Acton deals with the system of thought of Communism. Mr. Deutscher has collected together reviews, articles and essays.

C1440 COMING TO LONDON – II. *London Magazine*, II.10, October 1955, 49–54.
Article on the author's first impressions of the London literary world.
Reprinted as "Coming to London: 2" in *Coming to London*, B62.
Much of this is repeated in the autobiography.

C1441 THOU SHALT NOT KILL. *New Statesman and Nation*, 12 November 1955, 608 & 610.
Article about Victor Gollancz and his pamphlet *Capital Punishment, the Heart of the Matter*.

> Gollancz wants to eliminate capital punishment but he gives the wrong reasons; his sympathy is with the criminal. Judicial murder harms those who carry it out and the whole of society more than it does the criminal. Besides, there is no evidence that capital punishment is a deterrent to crime.

Reprinted in *Looking at Life*, an anthology for Australian Schools (Longmans) Not seen; this appears to be a *New Statesman* periodical published in Melbourne. Correspondence, LW Papers, Sussex.

C1442 NOTES AND COMMENTS. AFTER GENEVA. *Political Quarterly*, XXVI.4 (Oct-Dec 1955), 319–22.
Unsigned editorial on conferences in July and August on war and peace.

> The immense destructive power of the atomic bomb makes it impossible to settle anything by war. If peace is to be maintained there must be a revolution in political psycholgy and organization.

C1443 SHORTER NOTICES. *Political Quarterly*, XXVI.4, (Oct-Dec 1955), 418.
Review of *Personalities and Powers*, by Sir Lewis Namier.

1956

C1444 NOTES AND COMMENTS: TRADE UNIONS IN A CHANGING WORLD. *Political Quarterly*, XXVII.1 (Jan-March 1956), 1–5.
Unsigned editorial.

C1445 Review of *The Unknown Prime Minister: The Life and Times of Andrew Bonar Law, 1858–1923*, by Robert Blake. *Political Quarterly*, XXVII.1 (Jan-March 1956), 120–21.

This well-written book points up Law's strange character and the important part he played at a critical time in history.

C1446 NOTES AND COMMENTS. WASHINGTON AND MOSCOW. *Political Quarterly*, XXVII.2 (April-June 1956), 125–28.

Unsigned editorial.

There is little to choose between the stated policy of Eisenhower and Eden toward the Soviet Union and Krushchev's stated policy towards the West.

C1447 ESPIONAGE, SECURITY, AND LIBERTY. *Political Quarterly*, XXVII.2 (April-June 1956), 152–62.

Article which cites two official U.S. Documents: *Transcript of Hearing before the Personnel Security Board*, and *Texts of Principal Documents and Letters;* and several books: *A Nation's Security: The Case of Dr. J. Robert Oppenheimer, ed. from official transcript of evidence; Report of the Royal Commission on Espionage* (Government of Australia); and *Soviet Espionage,* by David J. Dalin.

Spying done for "ideological reasons" corrupts the good, and poses a danger to the very fabric of society, damages liberty and social decency, and leads to witch-hunts. To minimise spying governments should strive to have few secrets.

Abstract in *International Political Abstracts*, VI.3, 1956, p. 337 (Blackwell).

C1448 SHORTER NOTICES. *Political Quarterly*, XXVII.2 (April-June 1956), 232.

Unsigned reviews of *The International Who's Who*, 1955; and *Geoffrey Dawson and Our Times*, by John Evelyn Wrench.

C1449 NOTES AND COMMENTS: EMPLOYERS AND LABOUR PROBLEMS. *Political Quarterly*, XXVII.3 (July-Sept 1956), 233–36.

Unsigned editorial.

C1450 Review of *Beatrice Webb's Diaries, 1924–1932*, ed. with an Introduction by Margaret Cole. *Political Quarterly*, XXVII.3 (July-Sept 1956), 342–43.

An intelligent woman's picture of the drama of half a century of history in which she played an important part, this diary is a work of art which includes vivid pictures of people that compare with the best vignettes. Her self-portrait is an honest, penetrating revelation of her personality.

C1451 KNOWLEDGE AND OPINION. *Listener*, 11 October 1956, 583.

Review of *The New Outline of Modern Knowledge*, ed. with a Preface by Alan Pryce-Jones.

It is hard to tell how much of this outline by 26 experts is knowledge and how much is opinion.

C1452 LUGARD: THE YEARS OF ADVENTURE 1858–1898. *Venture*, VIII.7, December 1956, 11.

Review of a book of this title by Margery Perham.

Miss Perham gives the facts from which the reader should be able to decide what part Lugard played in the scramble for Africa. "Miss Perham quotes me as having written in 1920 that Lugard worked for an evil policy for noble motives because he was muddle-headed. I do not think that Miss Perham agrees with this judgment. . . ."

C1453 NOTES AND COMMENTS: THE SUEZ CANAL CRISIS. *Political Quarterly*, XXXVII.4 (Oct-Dec 1956), 361–65.
Unsigned editorial.
All international waterways should be subject to international control.

1957

C1454 NOTES AND COMMENTS: THE MIDDLE EAST AFLAME. *Political Quarterly*, XXVIII.1 (Jan-March 1957), 1–4.
Unsigned editorial.

C1455 Review of *Governments of Greater European Powers: A Comparative Study*, by Herman Finer. *Political Quarterly*, XXVIII.1 (Jan-March 1957), 81–82.
Written with knowledge and imagination, the book is lively for a survey. It should have been divided into volumes for comfortable reading.

C1456 Review of *Men and Power, 1917–18*, by Lord Beaverbrook. *Political Quarterly*, XXVIII.1 (Jan-March 1957), 98–99.
The editor of the *Daily Express* who controls the fate of many authors is a poor writer himself. His contacts enable him to see history from the inside, but his view is limited to "a personal struggle for place and power".

C1457 VIRGINIA WOOLF AND 'THE WAVES'. *Radio Times*, London, 28 June 1957, 25.
Signed article about VW's writing habits and her plan for *The Waves*. Illustrated with her photo.

C1458 NOTES AND COMMENTS: THE STORM CENTRE. *Political Quarterly*, XXVIII.2 (April-June 1957), 101–06.
Unsigned editorial.
The only way for Britain and the United States to stem the present crisis in the Middle East is to act through the United Nations.

C1459 Reviews. *Political Quarterly*, XXVIII.2 (April-June 1957), 190–92.
Essays in Sociology and Social Philosophy, 2 vols, by Morris Ginsberg; and *German Sociology*, by Raymond Aron, tr. by Mary and Thomas Bottomore. These two books show what social science is.

C1460 MEN AND MYTH IN ISRAEL. *The Nation*, New York, CLXXXV, 3 August 1957, 55–56.
Review of *Bridgehead, the Drama of Israel*, by Waldo Frank.
Mr. Frank has expanded into a book a series he wrote on the return of the Jews to the Promised Land. He has obscured everything in meaningless mysticism.

C1461 NOTES AND COMMENTS: ISRAEL AND THE MIDDLE EAST. *Political Quarterly*, XXVIII.3 (July-Sept 1957), 209–13.
Unsigned editorial based on personal impression from a visit to Israel.
The Jews in Israel seem not to be angry, bitter, or resentful against their enemies. The U.S. and G.B. must stop playing power politics in the Middle East. Unless deterred, the Russians will continue to fish in troubled waters.

C1462 TO THE EDITOR OF *THE TIMES*. *The Times*, 7 October 1957, p. 9, col. 5.
Letter dated October 4, Rodmell, commenting on one published the day before in which Mrs. Lee suggested that all fat old dogs about whom nobody cares be exterminated.
LW facetiously supports the proposal and suggests that it be carried to its logical conclusion of exterminating all fat old persons. He adds that he himself is thin [cf. Swift's *Modest Proposal*].

C1463 Review. *Political Quarterly*, XXVIII.4 (Oct-Dec 1957), 405–06.
  The Opium of the Intellectuals, by Raymond Aron, tr. by Terence Kilmartin.
    The author writes brilliantly about the effect of Marxist theory on the
    minds of Frenchmen, but he pursues some ideas so relentlessly that he
    forgets their relationship to his argument.

1958

C1464 NEMESIS OF BEING TOO LATE. *New Statesman: The Week-End Review*,
  LV, 4 January 1958, 5–6.
  Signed article.
    What positive actions could the British Government take to prevent
    nuclear war? Steps towards disarmament are essential.
  "Britain's Suicide Pact," a letter published 11 January, p. 45, seems to be a
  response to this article.
C1465 PRESSURE GROUPS IN BRITAIN. *Political Quarterly*, XXIX.1 (Jan-March
  1958), 1–4.
  Unsigned editorial.
C1466 Reviews. *Political Quarterly*, XXIX.1 (Jan-March 1958), 87–89.
  The New Cambridge Modern History, vols I & VII; and *Europe Since
  Napoleon*, by David Thomson.
C1467 NOT SO UTOPIAN. *New Statesman*, 24 May 1958, 670.
  Review of *World Peace through World Law*, by Grenville Clark and Louis B.
  Sohn.
    "A blue-print for perpetual peace."
  LW discussed this again, *Political Quarterly*, C1475.
C1468 NOTES AND COMMENTS: TOWARDS THE SUMMIT CONFERENCE.
  Political Quarterly, XXIX.2, April-June 1958, 101–04.
  Unsigned editorial.
C1469 Review of *Sovereignty: An Inquiry into the Political Good*, by Bertrand de
  Jouvenel, tr. by J. F. Huntingdon. *Political Quarterly*, XXIX.2 (April-June
  1958), 186–87.
    This book is hard to read and hard to understand. Reviewers give it a good
    press but shy away from real discussion of it. The author professes to be
    discussing political science but mixes metaphysics and theology into his
    argument.
C1470 SHAKESPEARE ON RECORDS. *New Statesman: The Week-end Review*,
  LVI, 2 August 1958, 143.
  Review of 3 plays by Shakespeare on records, a joint venture of the British
  Council, Cambridge University Press, the Marlowe Society of Cambridge and
  Mr. George Rylands.
    On the whole Mr. Rylands' troupe has followed Hamlet's strictures on the
    way words in a play should be spoken. But some other conventions of the
    stage have carried over into these recordings.
C1471 THE FUTURE OF THE SERIOUS WRITER. *TLS*, 15 August 1958. Section
  "Books in a Changing World," p. xviii.
  Article of personal reminiscences about publishing at the Hogarth Press, and
  reflections on the future of serious books.
    It may be harder for the serious writer to gain recognition in an age when
    reading has so much competition from other kinds of entertainment.
  Much of this is restated in the autobiography.

C1472 ALL OUR WOE? *New Statesman*, 13 September 1958, 358.
Review of *The Decision to Intervene*, by George Kennan.
> The book is as exciting as a first-rate detective novel. Kennan shows that the facts are different from the story presented by the Russians. He is skillful in portraying character and motives. His picture of Raymond Robins, American knight errant, is masterly.

C1473 "THE TWICE BORN". *TLS*, 26 September 1958, 545.
Letter protesting against the September 5 review of a Hogarth Press publication, *The Twice Born*, by G. Morris Carstairs.
> The reviewer does not tell what the book is about or any of the author's qualifications.

C1474 THE SPLENDOURS AND MISERIES OF COLONIALISM. *Political Quarterly*, XXIX.3 (July-Sept 1958), 209–14.
Unsigned editorial.
> From colonialism subject peoples learned the very principles of liberty and equality that inspire their revolt against it. The pretence of the U.S.S.R. to champion the victims of imperialism is frightening.

C1475 BOOK REVIEWS. *Political Quarterly*, XXIX.3 (July-Sept 1958), 301–02.
Defence in a Nuclear Age, by Stephen King-Hall; *Defence and the English-Speaking Role*, by Norman Angell; *Russia, the Atom, and the West*, by George F. Kennan; *Will the Atom Unite the World?* by Angelos Angelopoulos; and *World Peace through World Law*, by Grenville Clark and Louis B. Sohn.

C1476 LABOUR'S PLAN FOR PROGRESS. *Political Quarterly*, XXIX.4 (Oct-Dec 1958), 317–22.
Unsigned editorial.

C1477 Review of *The Arms Race*, by Philip Noel-Baker. *Political Quarterly*, XXIX.4 (Oct-Dec 1958), 399.
> The author effectively argues the case for disarmament. He has experience in the House of Commons, the League of Nations, and the United Nations.

1959

C1478 G. E. MOORE. Headed NOTES & TOPICS. *Encounter*, January 1959, 68–9.
Obituary article and tribute.
> Moore was a great man with a Socratic mind.

Reprinted as part of a Symposium in *Listener*, see C1483; repeated in LW's autobiography.

C1479 THE LISTENER'S BOOK CHRONICLE. *Listener*, 19 February 1959, 341.
Review of *The Imperial Idea and Its Enemies*, by A. P. Thornton.

C1480 THE LISTENER'S BOOK CHRONICLE. *Listener*, 5 March 1959, 423.
Review of *Ethel Smyth. A Biography*, by Christopher St John.
> The author presents a kaleidoscope, but Ethel Smyth was not a kaleidoscopic character. She did everything, composed music, wrote books, played golf and pursued friendships, with enormous energy. She had talent and drive but not the sensitivity needed to produce great art.

C1481 BACKGROUND TO CONFLICT. AFRICANS' PLACE IN FEDERATION. *The Times*, 6 March 1959, p. 11, col. 5.
Letter from Victoria Square address.
> In the March 3 issue Lord Robins says Africans have not developed the qualities needed to govern themselves. The same issue reports that white settlers jeered Mr. Stonehouse when he visited Northern Rhodesia.

C1482   Review of *Conviction*, ed. by Norman McKenzie. *Political Quarterly*, XXX.1 (Jan-March 1959), 90–91.
> The 12 contributors are disappointed in the achievement of the Labour Government since 1945.

C1483   THE INFLUENCE AND THOUGHT OF G. E. MOORE. A SYMPOSIUM BY FOUR OF HIS FRIENDS. *Listener*, 30 April 1959, 755–59 & 762. LW's contribution, pp. 756–57.
Reprint with slight change from January *Encounter*, C1478.

C1484   MY PARENTS AND GRANDPARENTS. *Listener*, 25 June 1959, 1103–04.
Text of an autobiographical talk on B.B.C. radio.
Repeated in the autobiography.

C1485   Review of *The Charm of Politics*, by R. H. S. Crossman; and *Distinguished for Talent*, by Woodrow Wyatt. *Political Quarterly*, XXX.2 (April-June 1959), 197–98.

C1486   HENRY JAMES AND THE YOUNG MEN. *Listener*, 9 July 1959, 53–54.
The second of two autobiographical talks.
E. M. Forster commented on this article in a letter published 16 July, p. 103.
LW repeated this in his autobiography.

C1487   THE COLOUR OF OUR MAMMIES. *Encounter*, July 1959, 3–8.
Letter.
> Commenting on Anglo-Saxon attitudes, LW includes incidents from his experiences in Ceylon.
Letters objected to his use of the term "mammy".

C1488   THE SPIDERS AND THE NURSE. *Listener*, 17 September 1959, 434–35.
Article.
Reprinted in the autobiography.

C1489   Review of *The Seat of Pilate; An Account of the Palestine Mandate*, by John Marlowe. *Political Quarterly*, XXX.3 (July-Sept 1959), 309–11.

C1490   Review of *The Dictionary of National Biography*. *Political Quarterly*, XXX.4 (Oct-Dec 1959), 430.
> This work is generally of the same high calibre as the original edition.

C1491   Review of *Primitive Rebels*, by E. J. Hobsbawn. *Political Quarterly*, XXX.4 (Oct-Dec 1959), 430–31.
> The author breaks new ground in his discussion of the agrarian revolutionary movement.

1960

C1492   Reviews. *Political Quarterly*, XXXI.1 (Jan-March 1960), 89–90.
Trotsky's Diary in Exile 1935, tr. by Elena Zarudnaya; and *The Prophet Unarmed. Trotsky: 1921–1929*, by Isaac Deutscher.
> Trotsky's diary shows him as more humane than the usual Bolshevik.
> Deutscher based his book on thorough scholarship, but he lacks judgment.

C1493   AFTER FIFTY YEARS. *New Statesman*, 23 April 1960, 579–80 & 582.
Article about the changes in Ceylon LW noticed during his visit in February 1960.
Reprinted in the *Ceylon Daily News*, See C1497.
Note: "Diaries in Ceylon" was scheduled to be published in April 1960 but did not actually appear until February 1962, see C1514.

C1494   MME. DOROTHY BUSSY. AUTHOR OF "OLIVIA". *The Times*, 13 May 1960, p. 17, col. 3.
An obituary tribute, signed L.W.

C1495   MR. OLIVER STRACHEY. CHARM AND ABILITY. *The Times*, 15 May
1960, p. 16, col. 4.
Unsigned obituary tribute.

C1496   HISTORY AND COMMON SENSE. *New Statesman*, 8 May 1960, 798.
Reviews of *The New Cambridge Modern History*, vol. XII, ed. by David
Thomson; and *The First World War*, by Cyril Falls.

C1497   TWO PROFOUND CHANGES IN CEYLON. 50 YEARS AFTER. *Ceylon
Daily News*, Thurs. 19 May 1960, p. 6, cols. 3–6.
This and the following item are reprinted from the *New Statesman*, see
C1493.

C1498   THE CIVIL SERVICE HAS CHANGED. AFTER FIFTY YEARS – 2. *Ceylon
Daily News*, Fri, 20 May 1960, p. 6, cols. 3–6.

C1499   Reviews. *Political Quarterly*, XXXI.2 (April-June 1960), 204–06.
Common Sense About Africa, by Anthony Sampson; and *African Nationalism*, by Ndabaningi Sithole.
These books explain the origins and importance of the liberation
movement in Africa.

C1500   Review of *Journey to America*, by Alexis de Tocqueville, tr. by George
Lawrence, ed. by J. P. Mayer. *Political Quarterly*, XXXI.2 (April-June 1960),
226–27.
In these notebooks the author shows intelligence, power of observation,
imaginative understanding and sensitivity.

C1501   THE PROFESSIONAL PESSIMIST. *New Statesman*, 16 July 1960, 96.
Review of *Dean Inge*, by Adam Fox.
Dean Inge made a handsome living from journalism. Canon Fox has
shown that he was a fairly happy man and not so gloomy as he seemed.

C1502   Review of *The Observer and J. L. Garvin, 1908–1914*, by Alfred M. Gollin.
Political Quarterly, XXXI.3 (July-Sept 1960), 394–95.
Garvin's influence through his editorship of *The Observer* is shocking.
This book shows that he was not merely stupid and politically wrong-
headed but also dishonest.

C1503   Review of *Doctor Goebbels*, by Roger Manvell and Heinrich Fraenkel.
Political Quarterly, XXXI.3 (July-Sept 1960), 403–04.
The authors swallow some of the propaganda of Hitler and Goebbels.
Their book is cinematographic and superficial but worth reading.

C1504   Unsigned review of *Essays in Labour History. In Memory of G. D. H. Cole*.
Political Quarterly, XXXI.3 (July-Sept 1960), 414–16.
LW describes the book and assesses Cole's work.

C1505   THE LISTENER'S BOOK CHRONICLE. *Listener*, 20 October 1960,
699.
Review of *Sir George Goldie and the Making of Nigeria*, by John E. Flint.
The book is much better than the one by the Duchess of Wellington. Mr.
Flint's story of Goldie's acquisition of Nigeria is more detailed than earlier
accounts. Goldie was more unscrupulous than most empire builders.

C1506   SENTENCED TO DEATH. *The Times*, 1 November 1960, p. 13, col. 6.
Letter. Request for stay of execution for a man named Forsyth, signed by 30
people including LW.

C1507   Review of *Neither War Nor Peace; The Struggle for Power in the Post-War
World*, by Hugh Seton Watson. *Political Quarterly*, XXXI.4 (Oct-Dec 1960),
511.
A detailed and accurate book by an intelligent and objective writer.

1961

C1508 ECONOMIC IMPERIALISM – TRANSLATION INTO JAPANESE, by Tadashi Kawata. *Proceedings of the Department of Social Science, College of General Education, University of Tokyo,* X, March 1961, 207–63.
At least part of this was reprinted: the Woolf Library, WSU, has a copy that belonged to LW.

C1509 ARRESTS IN PORTUGAL. *The Times,* 31 August 1961, p. 174.
Letter signed by 8 people calling themselves the Council for Freedom in Portugal and the colonies, including LW.

Note: *Growing* was being published serially by the *Daily Mirror* according to Shelton C. Fernando in a letter to LW, 2 Oct. 1961 (LW Papers, Sussex). This is not found in Sept-Oct in the London edition – it may be in a Ceylon publication.

C1510 Review of *Jomo Kenyatta,* by George Delf. *Political Quarterly,* XXXII.3 (July-Sept 1961), 196–99.
LW relates his attempts to persuade the Labour Government to reform its policy towards Kenya in 1929. He deplores the failure.

C1511 Review of *Administrators in Action. British Case Studies,* vol. I, by F. M. G. Willson. *Political Quarterly,* XXXII.4 (Oct-Dec 1961), 401–02.
Actual cases of national and local public administration are admirably presented.

1962

C1512 THE DEATH PENALTY. *The Times,* 2 January 1962, p. 9, col. 5.
Letter signed by 37 people calling themselves the National Campaign for the Abolition of Capital Punishment, including LW.

C1513 Letter to the Editor. *Ceylon Observer,* 25 February 1962, p. 7.
Not seen. Information from Frederic Spotts.

C1514 DIARIES IN CEYLON 1908–1911. *Ceylon Historical Journal,* July 1959-April 1960, vol. IX, nos. 1–4, pp. 1–244 and Preface, pp. lxxv-lxxx. First edition February 1962.
Shelton C. Fernando in letters to LW described the many delays of publication (LW Papers, Sussex).
Reissued by the Hogarth Press, April 1963, as a book which was also printed in Columbo, Ceylon, and is identical except for the title page and publishing information, see A40.

C1515 STORIES FROM THE EAST. *Ceylon Historical Journal,* vol. IX, as above, C1514, pp. [253]-286.
Reprint with modified title of the stories first published as a separate book at the Hogarth Press in 1921, A18.

C1516 Book reviews. *Political Quarterly,* XXXIII.1 (Jan-March 1962), 93–94.
Hanged by the Neck, by Arthur Koestler and C. H. Rolph; and *Hanged in Error,* by Leslie Hale.
These two books contain all the relevant facts about capital punishment in Britain and all the pros and cons.

C1517 J. T. SHEPPARD. *TLS,* 29 June 1962, 477.
Letter.
LW disputes reviewer who said G. E. Moore's circle included Dick Sheppard and David Garnett.

C1518   Review of *The Story of Fabian Socialism,* by Margaret Cole. *Political Quarterly,* XXXIII 2 (April-June 1962), 228–29.
>   Secretary to the Fabian Society for 20 years, Mrs. Cole knows her subject, but her lack of objectivity, her prejudice against the Webbs and Shaw, and her slovenly writing spoil the book.

C1519   THE DJILAS CASE. *Encounter,* July 1962, 94.
>   Letter, protesting against re-arrest of Milovan Djilas in Yugoslavia for "theoretical and historical remarks" and petitioning his release, signed by a large number of people including LW.

C1520   MR. SAXON SYDNEY-TURNER. THE BLOOMSBURY GROUP. *The Times,* 13 November 1962, p. 14, col. 5.
>   Obituary.
>   A character sketch of his friend. Repetition of what he said in *Sowing,* A38.

Reprinted by S. P. Rosenbaum in *The Bloomsbury Group,* B81.

C1521   THE POTATO FAMINE. *New Statesman,* 30 November 1962, 776.
>   Letter. Objects to review by A. J. P. Taylor of *The Great Hunger,* by C. Woodham-Smith, entitled "Genocide", 23 November, pp. 741–42.
>>   Mr. Taylor makes no distinction between a famine for which the British were not responsible and the deliberate actions of the Nazis.
>   Mr. Taylor replied that LW had not read the book.

C1522   THE POTATO FAMINE. *New Statesman,* 7 December 1962, 825.
>   Letter.
>>   LW says he did not refer to the book but to Taylor's article. He deplores Taylor's attitude.

C1523   THE POTATO FAMINE. *New Statesman,* 21 December 1962, 900.
>   Letter replying to Miss Robinson, who tried to defend Taylor in a letter published December 14.
>>   "It is precisely because [Taylor] is humane and sympathetic and a serious historian that it is so distressing that he should write as he does about the events of 1933 and 1945."

C1524   "GOING INTO EUROPE": A SYMPOSIUM. *Encounter,* December 1962, 55–56.
>>   "On the whole it would probably be advisable for us to enter the Common Market."

1963

C1525   MUZZLING THE PRESS. *New Statesman,* 22 March 1963, 422.
>   Letter concerning misuse of Freedom of the Press in Vassall case. Reference to article by Francis Williams published March 15, pp. 366 & 368.
>   Williams replied to his critics, 29 March, pp. 450 & 452. B. W. Levy sided with LW, 5 April.

C1526   LEONARD WOOLF REFUTES SENEX. *Sunday Times of Ceylon,* 31 March 1963, p. 8.
>   Letter, with photo of LW.
>>   The letters the *Sunday Times* has been publishing contain "lies and libels. The writer cannot even spell my name correctly."

Sunday Times of Ceylon also published a rebuttal of Senex by S. C. Fernando.

C1527   Review of *John Anderson, Viscount Waverley,* by John W. Wheeler-Bennett. *Political Quarterly,* XXXIV.1 (Jan-March 1963), 110–11.
>   A success story unsuccessfully written.

C1528 [Second of] TWO SHARP REJOINDERS . . . A REPLY TO SENEX. *Sunday Times of Ceylon,* 14 April 1963, p. 1, col. 1.
> The continued attacks by Senex are amusing.

C1529 'THE VILLAGE IN THE JUNGLE'. *TLS,* 24 May 1963, 373.
> Letter. Response to reviewer of *Diaries in Ceylon* who said *The Village in the Jungle* should be reissued.
>> The book is in print and has been since its publication in 1913.

C1530 THE PAPAL REVOLUTION. *New Statesman,* 14 June 1963, 899.
> Letter about Paul Johnson's article on the reforms of Pope John XXIII, *New Statesman,* 7 June, 854 & 856.
>> None of the changes Mr. Johnson reports the Pope has made are revolutionary.
>
> Johnson replied that reactionary Roman prelates and Protestants are both trying to minimize the changes. "I think Mr. Woolf cuts a poor figure in such company."

C1531 THE PAPAL REVOLUTION. *New Statesman,* 21 June 1963, 932.
> Letter.
>> Mr. Johnson's evidence, C1530, did not prove real change. "His answer now is to call me names. . . ."
>
> Johnson said he would leave the reader to judge.

C1532 THE REAL VIRGINIA WOOLF. *Show, the Magazine of the Arts,* New York, September 1963, 80–83, 108, 110, 112. With her portrait by Man Ray.
> Excerpts from *Beginning Again,* A41.

1964

C1533 WRITERS, EDITORS, POLITICIANS. SOME PORTRAITS. Headed PRESS. *Encounter,* January 1964, 75–82.
> Excerpts from *Beginning Again,* A41, including journalism and journalists: Desmond MacCarthy, the Webbs, Shaw, Wells, Ramsay MacDonald and Rupert Brooke.

C1534 MAX AND VIRGINIA WOOLF. *Encounter,* March 1964, 92.
> Letter about Edmund Wilson's statement that Max Beerbohm did not like VW's work (December issue).
>> LW quotes from a letter Beerbohm wrote to VW in 1927 saying he did like her work.

C1535 Review of *Ernest Simon of Manchester,* by Mary Stocks. *Political Quarterly,* XXXV.1 (Jan-March 1964), 116–17.
>> Lord Simon was at once a very simple and a very complex man. His friend has over-emphasized the wrinkles. Her account of his career and achievements in "industry, education, politics, the B.B.C. and journalism" is excellent.

C1536 HOW THE HOGARTH PRESS BEGAN. *The Bookseller,* 11 April 1964, 1586–88 & 1590.
> Extracts from *Beginning Again,* A41.

C1537 HOW THE HOGARTH PRESS BEGAN. *The Bookseller,* 18 April 1964, 1664 & 1666.

C1538 DULWICH MADE ME. *New Statesman,* 25 September 1964, 458.
> Review of *The Voyage Home,* by Richard Church.
>> The author of this civilised, honest autobiography may be too generous in some of his portraits.

1965

C1539 VIRGINIA WOOLF: WRITER AND PERSONALITY. *Listener,* 4 March 1965, 326 & 328.

Article based on a broadcast interview of LW by Joanna Richardson. Includes portrait of VW by F. Dodd.

Repetition of some stories included in *Beginning Again,* A41.

C1540 Review of *The Eichmann Trial,* by Peter [i.e. Petros Achilleos] Papadatos. *Political Quarterly,* XXXVI.1 (Jan-March 1965), 106–07.

Mr. Papadatos was official observer of the International Commission at the trial. His book is short and concise, but the subject is depressing. The author's flat English makes it more so.

C1541 GENIE ET FOLIE DE VIRGINIA WOOLF, tr. by Hélène de Wendel. *Revue de Paris,* LXXII, July-Aug 1965, 91–111.

Excerpt from *Beginning Again,* A41.

C1542 LABOUR'S FIRST YEAR: A REVIEW OF THE GOVERNMENT'S RECORD. RADICALS COMMENT ON THE ANNIVERSARY. *New Statesman,* 15 October 1965, 556–57.

"It is easier to be progressive in opposition than in power."

1966

C1543 Review of *Plough My Own Furrow; the Story of Lord Allen of Hurtwood,* by Martin Gilbert. *Political Quarterly,* XXXVII.1 (Jan-March 1966), 96–97.

The most interesting thing about Lord Allen was his character. He undertook a number of causes: conscientous objection, work with Ramsay MacDonald in the I.L.P. and the *Daily Citizen,* work with Harold Macmillan, work to convince Ribbentrop and Hitler to behave in a civilised manner. Eventually he quarrelled with all his associates. He was a high-minded political Pecksniff.

1967

C1544 "THE GODS ARE NOT GLUTTONS". *TLS,* 5 January 1967, 9.

Letter to the Editor.

Objection to review of books on Greek literature, 24 November 1966, which declared literary criticism written before 1916 out of date.

C1545 A CIVILIZED WOMAN. *New Statesman,* 10 March 1967, 332.

Review of *In a World I Never Made,* by Barbara Wootton.

This completely frank autobiography shows a sense of humour. The author, a classical scholar, university professor, Governor of the B.B.C., Deputy Speaker of the House of Lords, etc, does not take herself too seriously.

C1546 Book reviews of 2 books by Harold Macmillan: *The Winds of Change, 1914–1939;* and *The Middle Way. Political Quarterly,* XXXVIII.1 (Jan-March 1967), 96–97.

Clichés, adjectives and mechanical metaphors deaden the sense in *The Winds of Change.* "No one ought to write like this; that a scholar of Eton and Balliol and an ex-Prime Minister should do so is shocking. . . . The style is the man. . . ." He and other leading British politicians never asked the questions vital to preventing the war with Hitler.

C1547 LITERARY REPUTATIONS AND EARNINGS. *The Bookseller*, 8 April 1967, 1841–44.
> Excerpt from *Downhill All the Way*, A42.

C1548 MR. JAMES STRACHEY. *The Times*, 3 May 1967, p. 12, col. 8.
> Obituary article.
>> James Strachey and his wife Alex translated the complete works of Freud as "a work of art as well as of meticulous scholarship."

C1549 Review of *The Autobiography of Bertrand Russell, 1872–1914*, vol. 1. *Political Quarterly*, XXXVIII.3 (July-Sept 1967), 315–16.
>> Russell is "a mixture of Socrates, Don Quixote, and Puck" whose "books are illuminated by his wit, the brilliance of his mind, and his astringent individuality." He was violently prejudiced against Lytton Strachey and Maynard Keynes.

C1550 DYING OF LOVE. *New Statesman*, 6 October 1967, 438.
> Review of *Lytton Strachey*, by Michael Holroyd, vol. I: *The Unknown Years, 1880–1910*.
>> Holroyd is "a heavy-handed and heavy-minded writer who covers the simplest fact with . . . pomposity" and has no sense of humour. He misreads the character of Lytton Strachey who liked to dramatise himself but did not really have strong passions. He does show some of the contradictions in Strachey's character.

C1551 "AUNT BO". *New Statesman*, 10 November 1967, 642.
> Review of *Beatrice Webb, A Life, 1858–1943*, by Kitty Muggeridge and Ruth Adams.
>> This is an extraordinarily good biography. The authors have given the right proportion of the book to Sidney, though perhaps not enough sympathy; he and Beatrice were like Siamese twins. The authors may not have shown the extent to which the Webbs influenced the British Labour Movement.
> LW had an advance copy inscribed with the authors' thanks for help with the book.

1968

C1552 MENAGE A CINQ. *New Statesman*, 23 February 1968, 241.
> Review of *Lytton Strachey*, vol. II: *The Years of Achievement, 1910–1932*. by Michael Holroyd.
>> The author has given a detailed account of Strachey's life; he assessed his works well, but took Lytton too seriously and misjudged Carrington. He does bring Lytton and the people around him to life.

C1553 A JUST FIGHT. *The Times*, 28 March 1968, p. 11, col. 3.
> Letter about Lady Fisher's statement that the Arabs attacking Israelis are heroes and brave men, not terrorists.
>> All violence is bad regardless of who makes it.

C1554 EVERYTHING LOVELY. *Listener*, 25 April 1968, 540–42.
> Review of *Diaries 1915–1918*, by Lady Cynthia Asquith.
>> In his foreword Mr. L. P. Hartley says the author "is the most brilliant and entrancing character". The diaries do not confirm this. Rather, they show a dying aristocratic society whose members "seem to have no sense of social duty".
> Mr. Hartley attacked LW for criticizing the morals of others and counterattacked the morals of Bloomsbury (*Listener*, 30 May 1968, pp. 703–04).

C1555 THUGS AND BEETLES. *New Statesman*, 31 May 1968, 728–29.
Review of *Bloomsbury*, by Quentin Bell.
Bell's hostility to Bloomsbury, shown with humour and detachment, is perhaps the reason for including his book in this series on ferocious types. He goes wrong only in not holding the line against the false assumption that the people known as the Bloomsbury Group shared common goals and ideals.

C1556 "A CASE FOR TREATMENT". *Encounter*, May 1968, 91.
Letter. Reply to Goronwy Rees who in the March issue of *Encounter* asked why LW never mentioned Lytton Strachey's homosexuality.
LW says the subject is irrelevant to his autobiography and to his relationship with his friends. Further, subjects which may cause pain to the living should be avoided.

C1557 IN DEFENCE OF LADY CYNTHIA. *Listener*, 6 June 1968, 733.
Letter.
Mr. Hartley's letter published 30 May is amusing. His preference of Lady Cynthia's writing to Virginia Woolf's is a matter of taste.
Hartley would not let the number drop. LW wrote privately to him asking that he halt a public correspondence that could only be painful to the Asquith family (LW Papers, Sussex).

C1558 LABYRINTHINE WAYS. *The Times*, 25 September 1968, p. 11, cols. 6–8.
Letter.
Higher costs and less efficiency in the Post Office are a result of complication of the system.

C1559 Review of *The Autobiography of Bertrand Russell, 1914–1944*, vol II. *Political Quarterly*, XXXIX.3 (July-Sept 1968), 343, 345, & 347.

C1560 STROKE OF THE PEN. *The Times*, 16 October 1968, p. 11, col. 4.
Letter.
"The Postmaster General by a stroke of the pen has converted what was among the most efficient postal services in the world into what is now among the most inefficient."

1969

C1561 "JACK SQUIRE". *TLS*, 2 January 1969, 12.
Letter.
Objection to Alan Pryce-Jones's statement that Bloomsbury and the Sitwells disliked Squire (19 December 1968).

C1562 LABOUR AND IMPERIALISM. *New Statesman*, 10 Jan. 1969, 48. Letter about review by John Hatch of *Critics of Empire*, by Bernard Porter, 3 January, pp. 22–23.
Hobson and Morel did not really influence the official policy of the Labour Party between 1919 and 1939. Charles Buxton and LW wrote the pamphlets *Empire in Africa: Labour's Policy* (1920), and *The Colonial Empire* (1933). They were approved by the Advisory Committee on Imperial Questions and adopted by the Annual Conference. A long memorandum to the 3rd Congress of the Labour and Socialist International at Brussels, 1928, "The Colonial Problem", states the official party policy in much the same words (quotes). [Cf C0888. See also B6, B15, B23.]

C1563 KIPLING. *Sunday Times*. [Not found].
Christopher Ricks asked LW for an article, Letter 14 March '69. LW accepts,

letter dated 19 March '69; submits article 25 March '69. Ricks thanks him 27 March (LW Papers, Sussex).

C1564 Letter to the Editor. *Fabian News*, June 1969, 4.

"Margaret Cole's account of Kingsley Martin's appointment as editor of the *New Statesman* is . . . fluffy." LW offers corrections. M. Cole replies.

C1565 WHY THE GOOD SMALL PUBLISHER WILL SURVIVE. *Bookseller*, 21 August 1969, pp. 1458 & 1460–61.

Excerpt from *The Journey Not the Arrival Matters*, A43.

C1566 KINGSLEY MARTIN. *Political Quarterly*, XL.3 (July-Sept 1969), 241–45. Obituary tribute. Leonard Woolf's last article.

As editor Kingsley Martin permeated the *New Statesman* and the *Political Quarterly* even more than Massingham did *The Nation*. He was more egotistic, exuberant and stimulating, and he made more changes in what his contributors wrote.

D Manuscript collections

No list of Woolf's manuscripts could be entirely complete. Given the diversity of his political, publishing, editorial, literary and other activities, records of his life were inevitably scattered widely. His letters were sent to literally hundreds of correspondents; their editor (*Letters of Leonard Woolf*, 1989, Harcourt, Brace; 1990, Weidenfeld & Nicolson), Frederic Spotts, estimated that they number more than 40,000, and lists the locations of some of those still in private hands on p. xviii.

This section lists British and North American libraries and archives that contain Woolf's manuscripts or letters. It is based on a survey of likely institutions conducted in 1991, and on published guides to manuscript collections such as the *Location Register of Twentieth-Century English Literary Manuscripts and Letters: A Union List...* (Boston, MA: G. K. Hall, 1988). Collections in private hands or in repositories not easily accessible to the general public have not been traced. Nevertheless, we hope that researchers trying to locate primary source materials will find it useful.

British repositories

Brighton

D1   University of Sussex
When LW died in 1969, he left all the manuscripts, records and papers in his possession to Mrs Ian Parsons, who transferred them to the University of Sussex later that year. Most of the papers relating particularly to Virginia Woolf had already been segregated, arranged and catalogued prior to 1969, when Quentin Bell was preparing his biography of Virginia Woolf. These records were kept together and are known as the "Monks House Papers". The remaining records were designated the "Leonard Woolf Papers, 1885–1969" and cataloguing of them was completed in 1977. Some materials have been added since that date as well. Papers relating to LW can be found in both collections.

LW was a meticulous, perhaps compulsive, record-keeper, and the documents he preserved in these two collections number more than 60,000 items. They include incoming and outgoing correspondence, business papers, literary manuscripts, political documents, medical records, personal diaries, and seemingly trivial ephemera. Fortunately, the University of Sussex has prepared two detailed handlists to provide access to this great mass of material, and researchers should consult copies of those for full information about the papers. What follows is a very brief synopsis intended only as a convenient overview for researchers interested primarily in LW.

The Monks House Papers contain copies of more than 200 letters from LW. Correspondents include: Janet Case, 5 items, 1913–1914; Robert Cecil, 1 item, no date; Margaret Llewelyn Davies, 57 items, 1913–1942; Edward Arnold, unspecified number of items relating to *The Village in the Jungle*; Lytton Strachey, 97 items, 1904–1911; H. G. Wells, 7 items, 1932; Virginia Woolf, 44 items to her and 49 from her; Kingsley Martin, 19 items, 1929–63.

They also contain LW's letters to owners of Virginia Woolf's letters regarding their possible publication.

The Leonard Woolf Papers are divided into three parts, each of which is subdivided by topic.

Part One: Work Life
Sections A–C: government service, including Ceylon
Sections D–G: political organizations, including the Labour Party, Fabian Society, and WWI peace organizations
Sections H–K: work for journals, including the *New Statesman, Nation, International Review* and *Political Quarterly.*
Sections L–P: literary career, including complete manuscripts or other papers relating to the following books: *After the Deluge* (and *Principia Politica*), *Barbarians At the Gate, Co-operation and the Future of Industry, Diaries in Ceylon and Stories from the East, Empire and Commerce In Africa, Future of Constantinople, The Hotel, International Government, Quack, Quack!, Village in the Jungle, War for Peace, Wise Virgins, Sowing, Growing, Beginning Again, Downhill All the Way, Journey Not the Arrival Matters*; as well as to LW's journalism.
Sections Q–S: other work, including the Hogarth Press and broadcasting.

Part Two: Personal life
Papers documenting LW's education, family, marriage, relationship with Virginia, philanthropy, pets, real estate and personal property, health, travel and other topics.

Part Three: General correspondence
Letters LW received from approximately 500 individuals, a veritable "who's who" of British literary and political life during the 20th century; about 260 copies of his replies are also present.

Cambridge

D2   King's College
J. T. Sheppard Papers: letter to J. T. Sheppard, 1941.
J. M. Keynes Papers: 11 letters to John Maynard Keynes and 4 letters to Lydia Lopokova Keynes, 1922–45.
Charleston Papers: letters to Clive Bell, 1906–63; 17 letters to Julian Bell, 1929–37; letter to Thoby Stephen, 1904.
E. M. Forster Papers: letter to E.M. Forster, 1966.
W. J. H. Sprott Papers: 3 letters and a postcard to Sprott, 1933–41.
John Hayward Papers: 3 letters to John Hayward, 1926–30; letter to T. S. Eliot, 1948.
Fry Papers: letter to Pamela Diamond Fry, 1956.

D3   Clare College: Forbes Collection: letter to Mansfield Forbes, 1931.

D4   Cambridge University Library
Geoffrey Keynes Collection: letter to Keynes, 1942.
Centre of South Asian Studies: 1 box relating to Ceylon Civil Service, 1904–11.
Add. 8330: 6 letters to G. E. Moore, 1925–51.
Stanley Morison Papers: letter to Curwen Press, 1922.

D5   Fitzwilliam Museum: Letter to L. C. G. Clarke, 1942.

D6   Trinity College: RCT 17–19, and 21–22: letters to R. C. Trevelyan, 1905–1950.

Coventry

D7   University of Warwick: Anglo-Soviet Public Relations Comm.: records relating to LW's participation, 1941–42.

Dorchester

D8   Dorset County Museum: Hardy Memorial Collection: letter to Thomas Hardy, 1927.

Durham

D9   University of Durham: William Plomer Collection: 48 letters to William Plomer.

Edinburgh

D10   National Library of Scotland: MS.19673: letter to Edwin Muir, 1941.

Hatfield

D11   Hatfield House: Marquess of Salisbury Papers: letters, 1916–1957.

Leeds

D12   Brotherton Library: Smallwood Correspondence: letters to Norah Smallwood, of the Hogarth Press/Chatto & Windus, 1952–68.

London

D13   Record Office, House of Lords: Lloyd George Papers: letter, 193-?

D14   Royal Society of Literature: 5 letters to the Royal Society, 1963–66.

D15   Labour Party Archives: William Gillies Papers: letters, 1919–41.

D16   City of London Polytechnic
A.L. vol. XXVIIF: letter to Phillippa Strachey, 1951.
Fawcett Library: 3 letters to Vera Douie, 1956–66; letter to Mrs Horton, 1966.

D17   British Library of Political and Economic Science
Beveridge Papers: letter to Sir William Beveridge, 1960.
Dalton Papers: letter to Hugh Dalton, 1947.
Passfield Papers: 3 letters to Sidney & Beatrice Webb, 1942–43.

D18   British Library
Add. Mss. 48974: letter to S. S. Koteliansky, 1946.
Add. Mss. 52553: letter to H. G. Wells, 1941.
Add. Mss. 56234: 3 letters to John Lehmann, 1941.
Add. Mss. 60734: letters to James and Lytton Strachey.

D19   India Office Library: MSS.Eur.F.127: letter to Lady Strachey, 1908.

Manchester

D20   John Rylands University Library, Manchester University. Richard Church Collection: letter to Richard Church, 1968; Manchester Guardian Archive: letters, 1923–46.

Oxford

D21   Rhodes House Library

MSS.Brit.Emp.s.285: 2 letters to Charles Greenidge, 1945- 49.

MSS.Brit.Emp.s.365: correspondence with Fabian Colonial Bureau, 1947–51; reply
to Fabian Colonial Bureau's questionnaire on foreign policy, 1954; correspondence with Hilda Selwyn Clarke, 1956; letter to Rita Hinden, 1943.

MSS.Brit.Emp.s.332: letter to Arthur Creech-Jones, 1955.

D22   The Library, Nuffield College: Fabian Society Papers: Many manuscript items
by or about LW are scattered throughout the Fabian Society Papers; at least 36
locations are indexed under his name in the unpublished handlist. These include
records of the Fabian Research Dept., New Fabian Research Bureau, minutes of
meetings, plans for conferences, and correspondence of various Fabian Society
sections.

D23   Bodleian Library

MS.Eng.lett.c.: letters to Eric Walter White, 1928–29; letter to W. H. Dickinson,
1918; letters to Frank Hardie, 1933–49.

Gilbert Murray Papers: letters to Murray, 1918–55.

Mavrogordato Coll.: letter, ca. 1951.

MSS. Curtis 66.67: letter, 1951.

MS.Eng.hist.c.: letters, 1918 and 1958.

Walter de le Mare Papers: letter to de la Mare, 1938.

MSS. Hammond: letters to J. L. L. Hammond, 1928–29.

MSS. Sidgwick & Jackson: letters, 1928–46.

Reading

D24   University of Reading

Hogarth Press Archives: contain much LW material dating from the 1920s through
the 1950s.

MS1979/68: 2 letters to R. L. Mégroz, 1926.

Chatto & Windus Archives: letters, 1928–39.

MS1640 (George Bell & Sons Archives): 5 letters, 1930–66.

D25   BBC Written Archives Centre: Radio Contributors. Talks & Copyright Files:
Correspondence, 1940–1962.

North American Repositories

British Columbia

D26   McPherson Library, University of Victoria

Herbert Read Archive: 2 letters to Sir Herbert Read, 1935; 2 letters to Freedom
Defence Committee, 1945.

John Betjeman Archive: letter to Sir John Betjeman, 1947.

California

D27   Huntington Library, San Marino

HM42120–42183: 64 letters to Saxon Sydney-Turner, 1900–18.

Wallace Stevens Papers (WAS366): printed form completed by LW and addressed to
Wallace Stevens, 1927?

HM 53102: letter to Elizabeth Bowen, 1946.
RB 444603: notes on revisions to be made in Conrad Aiken's *Senlin*, 1925.
HM 42119: "Chronological List of Mystics . . .", by LW, 1901.
HM 42120–42183: 2 poems (1901, 1910) in letters to Saxon Sydney-Turner.

Connecticut

D28   Beinecke Library, Yale University, New Haven
Yale Review Collection: letter to Helen McAfee re V. Woolf, 1929.
Gertrude Stein Papers: 11 letters to Stein, 1925–34.
David Low Papers: letter to David Low, 1937.
Enid Bagnold Papers: letter to Enid Bagnold, 1962.

Illinois

D29   University of Illinois Library, Urbana: H. G. Wells Papers: 23 letters to H. G. Wells and family, 1919–42.

D30   Northwestern University Library, Evanston: 184 pieces, 1956–64, relating to sale of Virginia Woolf manuscripts to the Berg Collection, New York Public Library.

Indiana

D31   Lilly Library, Indiana University, Bloomington: Eng. Lit. MSS: preliminary scheme for a partnership between LW and John Lehmann to take over the Hogarth Press, 1938.

Massachusetts

D32   Special Collections, Mugar Memorial Library, Boston University, Boston
Allan Knight Chalmers Papers: letter to Chalmers, 1957.
Robert Speaight Papers: letter to Speaight, 1966.
Alec Waugh Papers: letter to Waugh, 1962.
Terence de Vere White Papers: letter to White, n.d.
Robert and Sylvia Lynd Collection: letter to Sylvia Lynd ca. 1923.

D33   Houghton Library, Harvard University, Cambridge: bMS Am1432: 3 letters to T. S. Eliot, 1922–27; bMS Eng854: 1 letter to Henry Goddard Leach, 1925.

New Jersey

D34   Princeton University Library: Robert H. Taylor Collection: 2 letters to Lytton Strachey; 4 to T. S. Eliot, 1911–22; 2 letters to Raymond Mortimer, 1930–49.

New York

D35   Butler Library, Columbia University
Collections:
Colles: 1 letter to Mr or Ms Wilson, 1928.
W. W. Norton: 36 letters to the publishing firm, 1929–65; 1 letter to Roy Lamson.
Naomi Mitchison: 3 letters to Naomi Mitchison, 1931–41.
Random House: 2 letters to the publishing firm, 1935 and 1938.
A. Watkins: 2 letters to Nancy Brettner, 1942.
Clifford: letter to James L. Clifford, 1960.

Trilling: letter to Lionel Trilling, 1959.
Salisbury: 3 letters to Leah Salisbury, 1959- 61.

D36   Berg Collection, New York Public Library
(A) "m.b." collection
  (1) 2pp. typescript of foreword to Mitchell Leaska's *Virginia Woolf's Lighthouse*, 1969?
  (2) ms. corrections to VW's obituary notice of Lady Ottoline Morrell, 1938.
  (3) preliminary materials from which VW's collection *The Moment* was prepared, including clippings of articles from which the type was set, typescripts of 6 of the essays, and printer's dummy; with LW's editorial notes and ms. corrections. 1947?
  (4) letter to Barbara Bagenal, 1917.
  (5) 15 letters to Violet Dickinson, 1912–21.
  (6) 55 letters to Harcourt Brace, 1924–44.
  (7) 5 letters to Sir Edward Marsh, 1913–30.
  (8) 18 letters to Vanessa Bell, 1918–38.
  (9) postcard to Francis Birrell and David Garnett, 1920.
  (10) letter to Walter de la Mare, 1927.
  (11) letter to John Waller Hills re: VW, 1915.
  (12) letter to Dan H. Laurence, 1967.
  (13) letter to Claire Luce, 1963.
  (14) letter to G. E. Moore, 1904.
  (15) letters to Vita Sackville-West, 1925.
  (16) 6 notes to May Sarton, 1941–63.
  (17) note to Jacob Schwarts, 1961.
  (18) letter to Dame Ethel Smyth, 1930.
  (19) 2 notes to Lola Szladits, 1966.
  (20) letter to V. Woolf, 1912.
  (21) 4 letters to J. B. Pinker & Son, 1923–24.
  (22) 4 letters to Edward Sackville-West, 1941–55
  (23) correspondence with Cecil Woolf and John Bagguley concerning their book, *Authors Take Sides on Vietnam*, 1967.

(B) [collection not specified]
  (1) two typescripts of *Beginning Again*, the first (167pp.) dated Jan. 14–Sept. 21, 1962, and the second (301pp.) undated.
  (2) editorial corrections and instructions to the printer of VW's *Between the Acts*, 1941

D37   Herrick Memorial Library, Alfred University, Alfred, N.Y.
[collection unspecified] 7 letters to Jane Bussy, Ursula Roberts, C. K. Ogden, the Folio Society, and a Mr Greene, 1935–54.

Ontario

D38   Mills Memorial Library, McMaster University, Hamilton: Bertrand Russell Archives: 2 letters to Russell, 1917 and 1962.

Pennsylvania

D39   Canaday Library, Bryn Mawr College, Bryn Mawr: Note to D. B. Green, of the Bryn Mawr English Dept., 1956.

Texas

D40   Harry Ransome Humanities Research Center, University of Texas, Austin
Collections:
H. E. Palmer: letter, on Hogarth Press letterhead, 1928.
John Lehmann: 122 letters, 1930–60; 84 memos, 1942–45.
Katherine Mansfield: letter to Ruth Elvish Mantz, 1930.
Lady Ottoline Morrell: 1 letter, n.d.
Edward Garnett: 3 letters to Edward Garnett, 1923–26; letter to Liam O'Flaherty,
    1923.
Glenn Arthur Hughes: 1 letter, 1928.
Edmund Blunden: 5 items, 1924–41.
Robert Guy Howarth: 2 pp. note on VW's *Night and Day*, 1942.
Mary Hutchinson: 10 letters to Hutchinson, 1923–60.
Rupert Croft-Cooke: letter to Curtis Brown, 1920.
D. H. Lawrence: 20 letters to Robert Mountsier, 1922–23.
Ernst Toller: 2 letters to Toller, 1934.
Nancy Cunard: 2 letters to Nancy Cunard, 1951.
T. S. Eliot: letter to T. S. Eliot, 1930.
Robinson Jeffers: 2 letters to Jeffers, 1929- 30.
Richard Church: 5 items to Richard or Catherine Church, 1963–65.
Lytton Strachey: 84 letters, 1900–04.
London Magazine: 2 letters, 1964.
Robert Guy Howarth: letter to Howarth, 1950.
Richard Aldington: single item, on *Nation & Athenaeum* letterhead, 1924.
PEN: letter to J. B. Priestley, 1937.
Leonidas Warren Payne: letter to Payne, 1938.
Virginia Woolf: letter to Angelica Bell Garnett, 1941; 4 letters to Francis Hackett,
    1923–34.
Hugh Walpole: 5 letters to Walpole, 1924–41.

Washington (State)

D41   Manuscripts, Archives & Special Collections, Washington State University
    Library, Pullman
2 letters to Dorothy Bussy, 1955.
1 letter to D. A. Heath & Co., 1953.
2 letters to "Mr. Howard", 1969.
27 letters to William and Dorothy Humphrey, 1962–69.
1 letter to Stanley Unwin, 1931.
1 letter to J. Wendell, of Bernard Quaritch Ltd., 1968.
copy of 1 letter to R. R. Crossette Thambiah, 1960.
4 documents concerning the Estate of Roger Fry.
1 essay entitled "Empedocles", in English and Greek.

Appendix 1
Writings for the co-operative movement

The decade following Woolf's return from Ceylon was arguably the most productive of his career. Between 1912 and 1922 he wrote two novels, an influential book on international government, an investigation of European imperialism in Africa, and several shorter works on political subjects. During those years Woolf also wrote dozens of reviews and articles, helped establish the Hogarth Press, and became active in several different political organizations.

Much of his work in that decade was done for the consumers' co-operative movement. Woolf published two books, seven pamphlets, and more than 40 articles on co-operative topics during those years, and became recognized as a leading theoretician and propagandist for the movement. Many of us have had contact with a neighbourhood food co-op or independent retail co-operative society, but most people are unfamiliar with the British co-operative movement and its place in British politics early in this century. Such familiarity is essential to understanding Woolf's political development and activism, and the purpose of this appendix is to provide a context for his writings on this subject.

The co-operative movement began in 1844 with a single co-op at Rochdale in Lancashire. By Woolf's time there were more than 1300 co-ops united in the Co-operative Wholesale Societies of Great Britain, which served over four million people and had retail sales of nearly £200m. [Bonner, pp. 160–62].

The object of the co-operative movement was to produce commodities for use rather than for profit. As the foregoing figures reveal, it did not operate on a small scale. For example, wheat was grown on co-operative farms in Canada, ground in co-op mills, baked in co-op bakeries, and sold as bread in co-op stores throughout Britain. Other movement products included soap, jam, eggs, milk, boots, tea, household cleaners, insurance and groceries; in 1920 the first co-op motor car rolled off the production line.

All profit was eliminated by returning any surplus to the consumers through regularly paid dividends. The administrative hierarchy that supervised production, distribution, and prices was democratically elected by local co-op members. Co-operative employees were unionized and paid competitive wages.

Although the movement was nominally open to all consumers, in practice it was overwhelmingly working-class and in fact drew heavily from the most prosperous class of workers. The reason for this is obvious: families living on a few shillings a week had a stronger motive than the more affluent for saving a penny here and there at the co-op stores, or for receiving the small dividend.

This helps to explain the movement's general conservatism – what one writer called its "bovine complacency". While all around them co-operators saw the expansion of working-class organizations, trade unions, and various socialist parties, co-op managers concentrated on producing quality goods at the lowest cost and the members remained primarily concerned about the size of their dividends. Until the First World War the movement maintained staunch political neutrality, fearing that involvement in party politics might alienate potential recruits, or taint the image of impartial democracy which was central to its ideology.

Woolf was a gadfly in the co-operative movement, trying in his articles and pamphlets to awaken the membership to its revolutionary potential as a form of economic democracy. He became active in the movement through its most politically sophisticated branch, the Women's Co-operative Guild, which was run by his and Virginia's friends, Margaret Llewelyn Davies and Lillian Harris. While the movement's weekly newspaper, *Co-operative News*, printed bland editorials, personal interest stories, and light fiction, its regular "Women's Corner" ran articles on unions for housewives, communal kitchens, sex education, and a minimum wage for mothers. While the front pages of the *News* gently criticized capitalists and "private traders", the "Women's Corner" defended the Russian Revolution, protested against the Allied blockade of Germany after the war, and urged total disarmament. In an article for the Independent Labour Party's weekly journal on the Women's Guild's 1916 conference, Woolf praised them as "an object lesson in efficient organization, combined with a natural genius for politics, and the finest working-class spirit . . . the Guild . . . has firmly grasped the necessary elements in a constructive working-class social and political programme." [*Labour Leader*, v. 13, no. 27; 6 July 1916: 5].

In his articles for *Co-operative News* and his pamphlets published by the Guild, Woolf tried to educate the membership on issues affecting the movement. He explained the new system of scientific management, or "Taylorism", then being introduced from America, and sketched the history and goals of the syndicalist movement which was causing an uproar in France. He preached active co-operative participation in the labour movement as a whole, urging closer ties between the Trades Union Congress, the Labour Party and the CWS, and pushed for the establishment of a co-operative college for workers.

Woolf also explained specific political events or policies and their potential effect on the co-operative movement. For instance, early in the First World War he outlined the likely effect of wartime shortages on co-operative production and pricing, and opposed conscription as "a new weapon in the hands of the employing classes." When the government raised a furore by trying to tax co-op dividends, Woolf gave a series of lectures on the subject of taxation in general. He also dissected and criticized the official government plan for industrial reconstruction after the war.

Woolf also propagandized for the co-operative movement in the mainstream press. Important essays and articles on the movement by him appeared in *Daily News, Manchester Guardian, New Statesman*, and *Encyclopedia Britannica*.

Several of Woolf's articles and reviews were reprinted or expanded into pamphlet form and published by the Women's Co-operative Guild. He also wrote a series of theoretical works on co-operation as a democratic means of organizing the economy. His most detailed analysis of the political importance of co-operation appeared in the two books *Co-operation and the Future of Industry* (1919; A12) and *Socialism and Co-operation* (1921; A17). The former relates the history and structure of the movement and explains how it could be expanded as a system of democratic socialism; the latter juxtaposes co-operation against capitalism, state socialism, and guild socialism, and contains Woolf's most eloquent arguments against the capitalist system.

By the early 'twenties Woolf's energies were largely committed to other ends (see appendix 2). Though he never repudiated his arguments for co-operation as the best method of establishing democratic socialism, his expertise in colonial and international affairs led him to work more energetically on foreign policy than on industrial organization. The co-operative movement continued to thrive, but never reached what Woolf considered its true potential as a socialist system. Preoccupied with its parochial concerns, the movement failed to participate fully in the Labour Party. Though it has always remained sympathetic to co-operation, when the Party came to real power after WWII, co-operation occupied a very small place in its vision of the welfare state.

Appendix 2
Writings for the Labour Party and Fabian Society

When at the end of the First World War it became clear that the fledgling Labour Party might soon be called upon to form a government, the Party's leaders formed several "advisory committees". These were intended to educate the Party's national executive and Members of Parliament and advise them on political events and legislation from a socialist point of view.

From 1919 until after the Second World War, Woolf was the secretary of two of these committees: the Advisory Committee on International Questions and the Advisory Committee on Imperial Questions. The first considered matters of foreign policy in general while the second confined itself to colonial administration and relations within the British Empire.

These committees amassed vast amounts of information, reduced it to brief memoranda or pamphlets, and recommended specific courses of action to the leadership. The annual reports of the Labour Party between the wars show that the two committees on which Woolf served submitted as many as two hundred memoranda *per year* to the Executive Committee. It was the kind of work at which Woolf excelled, and for nearly three decades he was one of the principal architects of Labour's foreign and imperial policies.

The Committee on Imperial Questions concerned itself primarily with Indian independence and the administration of Britain's African colonies. At a time when most British citizens cherished the Empire, Woolf and his colleagues recommended that it be dismantled as quickly as possible. Their plans called for "substituting a system based on the common economic interests of the inhabitant for the existing system based upon the economic exploitation of the native by the white man." As a first step they recommended dramatic expansion of native education, which they saw as the prerequisite for "substituting a political system of responsible and representative government for the existing autocracy."

Although those quotations are from a pamphlet published in 1920, they remained for three decades the central themes of Labour's colonial policy. The committee urged that the League of Nations mandate system, which claimed "the well-being and development of [colonized] peoples form a sacred trust of civilization", be expanded and conscientiously applied as the mechanism for ending imperialism.

Nothing of the sort happened, of course. Under the mandate system the victorious Allies increased their exploitation of the Third World, and in the mid-thirties, Germany – having been stripped of her colonies under the Versailles Treaty – demanded a share of the spoils. When in the autumn of 1935 members of the British government suggested giving Germany colonial territories to appease Hitler, Woolf's committee forcefully restated Labour's policy: "we must abandon the whole idea of exploitation, not merely hand over the right to exploit." But between the wars Labour had only brief opportunities to attempt implementation of these policies, and not until the middle of the Second World War did the irresistible nationalist movements in the colonies and severe economic hardship at home compel the British government to relinquish its Empire; even then it was done haphazardly and reluctantly. "It has been a process of slow torture to millions of ignorant and innocent human beings," Woolf wrote in his autobiography, which "would have been avoided if the imperialist powers had not blindly and doggedly resisted the demands of the subject peoples, but had carried out their own principles and promises by educating them and leading them to independence." [*Downhill All the Way*, p. 235]

The Advisory Committee on International Questions devoted itself initially to "the various developments arising out of the Peace Treaties, the Russian War and other matters connected with the resettlement of Europe." [1920 Labour Party Annual Conference Report, p. 39] Naturally it urged strong support for the League of Nations and opposition to the Allied invasion of the Soviet Union, urging instead that the new Soviet government receive full diplomatic recognition. In the early 'twenties it strongly opposed French demands for reparations and her occupation of the Ruhr.

Throughout the next decade, the committee focused on questions of international trade and specific issues facing the League. It opposed collective military response by the League against aggression, mistrusting collective security agreements as the same sort of diplomatic entanglements that had produced the First World War. Hitler's rise to power and Germany's threat to world peace split the committee (and the Labour Party) on this issue. As Woolf recalled, "There was a majority in favour of the League system of collective security and armaments adequate for resisting aggression. But there was a minority of some who . . . with their eyes open, opposed rearmament and of some who shut their eyes . . ., inconsistently combining support of resistance to aggression with opposition to rearmament." [*Downhill All the Way*, pp. 243–45] With the outbreak of war in 1939, Woolf and the committee produced a speculative pamphlet on the future of international government, but when hostilities actually commenced in 1940 the committee was suspended for the duration of the war [1944 Labour Party Annual Conference Report, p. 22].

During the war Woolf shifted his foreign policy activities from the Labour Party to the newly rejuvenated Fabian Society. Though he had been a member for 25 years, as the Fabian Society became moribund during the 'twenties, he had been more active in the Labour Party. In 1931 a group led by G. D. H. Cole formed the New Fabian Research Bureau; Woolf became a member of its Executive Committee and chaired its International Section. When the NFRB merged with its parent organization in 1939, he became a member of the Fabian Executive and its Colonial Bureau, and chaired its International Bureau from 1943 to 1953 [*Downhill All the Way*, p. 221].

In December 1942 Woolf participated in a Fabian seminar on the problems of post-war economic reconstruction and wrote a foreword to its proceedings when they were published the following year as *When Hostilities Cease*. In the summer of 1944, under the auspices of the Fabian International Bureau, he produced a scheme for "the international post-war settlement", urging a truly democratic united nations organization. At the close of the war, the foreign policy dilemma that faced the British Left was whether to align with the socialist Soviet Union despite its authoritarian government, or with the democratic United States despite its capitalist economy. In *Foreign Policy: The Labour Party's Dilemma*, Woolf outlined the options, insisted that world peace must be Britain's ultimate goal, and recommended a pragmatic policy of technical impartiality, supporting each camp whenever possible.

Woolf resigned from both Labour Party advisory committees in 1945, receiving the "deep appreciation of your great services to the Party by enthusiastic and persistent hard work, through many years and over periods of great discouragement" [1946 Labour Party Annual Conference Report, p. 25], and stepped down from the Fabian International Bureau in 1953. In his 35 years of committee work for the two organizations, Woolf wrote seven books and pamphlets, contributed to thirteen others, and, given his leadership roles on committees, undoubtedly helped to prepare many more.

Appendix 3
Leonard Woolf and the book review
by Leila Luedeking

From 1912, when he abandoned his career as a colonial administrator in Ceylon to marry Virginia Stephen, the book review played an important role in the life of Leonard Woolf. Adopting journalism, he pursued it with the energy and zest he brought to all his activities. His confidence in this means of making a living may have been bolstered by the fact that Virginia had been earning money by reviewing books since 1904, as well as by the fact that her father, Sir Leslie Stephen, had been a successful journalist. Virginia's association with editors, including Bruce Richmond of the *Times Literary Supplement*, and with publishers, helped Leonard get books to review. Virginia also introduced Leonard to people involved in political reform, including Margaret Llewelyn Davies of the Co-operative Movement. His writing for this organisation led to work for the Fabian Society and the British Labour Party.

Free-lance writing enabled LW to review books which interested him. He used the information gleaned from this reading in his longer works. Moreover, free-lancing permitted him to organise his time so that he could be with Virginia and also engage in other activities. By writing reviews each of the Woolfs earned a modest income. Meantime, Leonard's success as a reviewer and writer of articles led to editorial positions on some of the periodicals for which he wrote: *War and Peace* for part of 1917 and 1918, the *International Review* December 1918-December 1919, the *Contemporary Review* 1920–1922, the *Nation & Athenaeum* 1923–1930, the *Political Quarterly* 1930–1962, and the *New Statesman and Nation* occasionally.

Virginia's diary reveals her changing and ambivalent attitudes to reviewing. Her record of LW's progress in journalism shows that she was pleased with his success but concerned that this editorial work might interfere with their private lives. Neither she nor Leonard wanted him tied to an office. She recognised that his journalism gave her more time to write novels and criticism. She writes to Violet Dickinson, "It seems idiotic to put Leonard into an office for the sake of a bigger income" (*LVW*, I, p. 505).

LW's description of his work habits shows that he took his review writing for granted. He reminisced in his autobiography, "If we were in in the evening, I would usually read a book for review or in connection with what I was writing" (*Journey*, A43, p. 130). He appears to have meant that he read an entire book. He wasted no time when describing what he had read. VW marvelled at how easily he wrote reviews. In 1916 she reported that he had "trained himself to compose straight on to a typewriter, without making a mistake in sense or spelling" (*LVW*, II, p.83).

By contrast, while grudging the time it took, VW wrote and rewrote her reviews, but admitted that she did not give reviews by others the serious attention she paid to other forms of writing. She wondered whether it might not be easier in the long run for LW to earn their living at newspaper work than for her to agonise at writing reviews. In 1920 she wrote:

> To have broken free at the age of 38 seems a great piece of good fortune – coming at the nick of time, & due of course to L. without whose journalism I couldn't quit mine. But I quiet my conscience with the belief that a foreign article once a week is of greater worth, less labour, & better paid than my work; & with luck if I can get my books done, we shall profit in moneymaking eventually. And, when one faces it, the

book public is more of an ordeal than the newspaper public, so that I'm not shirking responsibility. (*DVW*, II, p. 66 and *passim*).

Events proved this was the right decision.

Both Leonard and Virginia Woolf paid close attention to reviews of their original writing. VW's record of her trepidations arising from reviews of her writing suggests that she was more ambivalent about her husband's success as a creative writer than about his journalism. Her diary shows that she sought Leonard's opinion about her works before she published and consulted him when her works were unfavourably reviewed. She valued his opinion as the ultimate critic and final editor of her work, but she was jealous when his works were praised and hers were dismissed as negligible. (In his "Editorial Note" to *The Death of the Moth* (B39) LW says he published the essays "as they stand, except that I have punctuated them and corrected obvious verbal mistakes. I have not hesitated to do this, since I always revised the MSS of her books and articles in this way before they were published.") VW could not understand why unfavourable reviews of his works did not upset LW. Leonard was aware of VW's extreme sensitivity to reviews of her works. In his autobiography he suggested that the anxieties caused by the process of completing her books may have contributed to her breakdowns.

Early reviews by LW concern books on topics including industrial management, problems faced by workers, and the Co-operative Movement, as well as literary works. He used first-hand knowledge gained while working in Ceylon as a basis for judging books about that colony. In some of his early reviews he employed a narrative style. He frequently used animal imagery to illustrate and reinforce the points he made.

LW wrote many reviews, articles and books in an effort to remedy social problems, abolish the colonial system, and ease international tensions. When the Webbs enlisted him to write for the Fabian Society in 1915, he had for some time been using the book review as a forum for discussing issues and ideas which interested him. He says that Jack Squire, Literary Editor of the *New Statesman*, "used to send me enormous parcels . . . of books and leave it to me to decide whether to review them or not . . . and in a year or two I was reviewing for him practically all the books published on the war, foreign affairs, and international questions" (*Beginning Again*, A41, pp. 128–29).

After they established the Hogarth Press in 1917, the Woolfs depended to some extent upon book reviews to help sell the books they published. They used quotes from reviews of Hogarth Press books in the advertisements they placed in journals and newspapers, on the dust wrappers of books, and in Hogarth Press catalogues and leaflets. An example of their advertising can be seen in the press opinions, good and bad, bound in at the end of the first Hogarth Press edition of *Jacob's Room*, by Virginia Woolf.

The Woolfs collaborated at least once in writing a review of books they themselves had published. VW confided in two letters that John Middleton Murry had insisted that she review his book, *The Critic in Judgment*, and T. S. Eliot's *Poems*. She wrote the part of the review dealing with Murry's book but got Leonard to review Eliot's. To introduce their non-committal review entitled "Is This Poetry?" the Woolfs wrote in the person "this reviewer". But in their discussions of the individual works each Woolf used the first person plural "we". In a letter asking T. S. Eliot to let Leonard review *The Sacred Wood*, Virginia begs Eliot not to tell Murry about the collaboration. LW added a note saying that he almost never reviewed books of literature or criticism and wondering whether he should review this one (*LVW*, II, #1065, pp. 373–74 & #1138, pp. 437–38; C0195).

His reviews of Eliot's works are evidence that LW was an able literary critic. While avoiding explicit praise of Eliot in his anonymous review, he quoted from the work to illustrate the points he made about it. He said that Eliot was building a new form of poetry different from the poetry which had preceded it, and that he was doing this by an interesting juxtaposition both of ideas and of words. By comparing Eliot's method of criticism to that of Aristotle in the second review (C0297), LW gave high commendation to *The Sacred Wood*.

Virginia hoped that Leonard's opportunity to edit the *International Review* would mean that he would no longer have to write so many reviews. That he owned and annotated copies of most of the books for which unsigned reviews appeared in the *International Review* during the thirteen months of its existence suggests that he may have written many of the unsigned reviews included in this paper. He also wrote the lead article, "An International Diary" (C0165, C0166, C0167, C0170, C0174, C0183, C0191, C0201, C0210, C0215, C0225, C0228, and C0234). LW and Miss Louise Matthaei chose excerpts from government documents and newspapers both at home and abroad for the feature, "The World of Nations: Facts and Documents" (C0168, C0172, C0175, C0184, C0192, C0197, C0205, C0213, C0220, C0226, C0232, C0236). Probably Miss Matthaei did most of the translations for these, and LW wrote the introductory matter. The reviews complimented these features. According to Duncan Wilson, LW invented documentary journalism when he edited the *International Review*. LW continued his "World of Nations" for the *Contemporary Review*. When, in 1922, its owners shortened the space allotted to his contribution, he was distressed, but the experience gained from having to summarise his findings in his signed article, "Foreign Affairs", was probably good training for later writing.

For many of his reviews LW seems to have followed the instructions from the *Athenaeum* found in his copy of *A History of the Chartist Movement*, by Julius West (1920). It instructs the reviewer to write a critical essay on the subject rather than just summarise the book, but also to expose the faults of the book if it is inaccurate.

The years 1923–30 were good for the Woolfs. The war was behind them. Leonard could relax his efforts to mould public opinion on political issues. When John Maynard Keynes offered him the post of Literary Editor of the *Nation & Athenaeum* he accepted without hesitation. Virginia was enthusiastic, even though she foresaw some loss of freedom. She regarded LW's editorship as an opportunity to gain influence and she began to try to find reviewers for him just as she urged people to submit their manuscripts to the Hogarth Press. Furthermore, she welcomed the chance to earn more money. She appears not to have minded having Leonard edit her work so much as she minded having others edit it. B. J. Kirkpatrick's *Bibliography of Virginia Woolf* shows that Virginia increased her writing for periodicals while LW was Literary Editor of the *Nation & Athenaeum*. Virginia's diary entries for this period suggest that she did not at this time consider reviewing to be so burdensome as she had earlier. Apparently she had found her stride. Having decided with the publication of *Jacob's Room* that she would write without regard to her critics, she discovered that she could alternate between creative and critical or review writing and also spend hours doing Hogarth Press work. Both she and Leonard continued to write reviews after the success of her novels and of the Hogarth Press had removed the necessity for doing so.

LW's own reviews during this period were more varied in subject matter and in style than at any other time during his writing career. It was then that he wrote the majority of his literary reviews. He also reviewed books on many other subjects, including history, politics, the law, social theory, psychology, economics, travel, games, animals, and gardening. His preference for biographical works is evident both in the books he chose to review and in the comments he made. By the early 1920s he was skilled at comparing several books on a topic or of a similar genre in one review article. He frequently did this in his weekly column, "The World of Books". In these articles he was as apt to discuss republications of old books or classics as new publications. Both the Woolfs depended heavily upon their own growing library. It contained books which had belonged to Sir Leslie Stephen, books from Leonard's school years, books he and Virginia had themselves collected, and books they were given to review.

LW prepared seasonal lists of coming publications by category. To make these lists interesting, as well as informative, he interspersed entries with comments about which books seemed promising or with comparisons of the current publishing season with previous ones. In later reviews he described some of the books included in these lists in greater detail. Newly published books were often dealt with in yet another review by one of the other contributors to the periodical. His role as editor gave LW the opportunity to provide some of his budding Hogarth Press authors with work as reviewers. As editor he had "to read attentively thousands of different reviews by hundreds of different reviewers" (C1007).

Included in the reviews LW wrote while editor of the *Nation & Athenaeum* are statements about the qualities he thought necessary for a good book as well as about the elements he thought detracted from books. He frequently showed his preference for a simple writing style. For example, in his review (C0415) of *Early Memories: Some Chapters of Autobiography*, by John Butler Yeats, he says the author is a born writer who plays with words "as if they were little live creatures". Not being a professional writer, he "did not have to unlearn anything in order to write naturally" and his writing is simple and vivid. In a review of a book of essays by Bonamy Dobrée (C0637) he says, "A golden rule for a clever writer is to try every now and then to be as simple and unliterary as possible."

It must be admitted that LW frequently attacked the style of an author whose theories or beliefs he rejected. This is particularly true of books on religious or political mysticism. His attack on *Essays on Religion*, by Arthur Clutton-Brock in "Rationalism and Religion" (C0701) had repercussions for months. He contrasted the author's religious views with what he called the "rational" view presented in *The Dynamics of Religion*, by J. M. Robertson, and *The Religion of an Artist*, by John Collier. Clutton-Brock, said LW, was a skilled journalist who "was attacked by an infectious disease which is endemic and epidemic in Fleet Street and Printing House Square, the *morbus verbosus*. In this disease the words multiply themselves indefinitely with little or no reference to meaning. . . . He argued himself into a position in which he had to say that the universe is 'cold, indifferent, meaningless to us' if there be no God; and then recoiling from the next step, from saying that the universe is cold, indifferent and meaningless to us (as it so obviously is), he was left with the only alternative of believing in the existence of God."

A flurry of outraged letters to the editor protested against Woolf's assertion that "the universe is cold, indifferent, and meaningless to us." His reply that this was a quotation from Clutton-Brock failed to satisfy the correspondents. After much discussion, LW designed a "Questionnaire on Religious Belief". It was first published in the *Nation & Athenaeum* (C0715) and simultaneously in the *Daily News* (C0717).

Possibly emboldened by the first results in answer to the question, "Do you believe in a personal God?" published 11 September, which showed 537 respondents answering "yes"; 736, "no"; and 65, "no answer", LW asserted in his review "Mr. Wells v. Mr. Belloc" (C0725) that he agreed with Wells that individual life "is an episode which ends, though life goes on." Belloc wrote a letter accusing Woolf of not reading his work and of being "irresponsible, aggressive and hysterical in language." LW replied (C0727) that Belloc had not quoted his full sentence. Meantime, the correspondence on "Rationalism and Religion" continued. One writer made a charming attempt to refute LW's statements on a "cold universe" by pointing out Woolf's own attributes of warmth and humour, evident in his reviews.

Despite his strictures on bad writing style, LW's literary taste was flexible enough that he recognised that unusual writing must be judged by unusual standards. He objected to Drinkwater's insistence that poets write in traditional forms: "Modern poets have something to say which will not go into traditional forms" (C0535). While maintaining that some books are too poorly written to be read, he said that *Moby Dick* is a masterpiece despite its "execrable style" (C0412). In C0419 he praised Doughty's "rough writing" in *Travels in Arabia Deserta*, saying Doughty evolved a style so fitted to his subject that it makes his readers "see, feel, and understand . . . Arabia Deserta and the life of its nomadic Arabs."

LW held that nothing new is ever said in literature; what is important is the way it is said. This idea that form should be compatible with content is perhaps the basis of his aesthetic theory. It is similar to the theories of others in the Bloomsbury Group, Clive Bell's "significant form" (*Art*, 1914), Roger Fry's theory in *Vision and Design* (1920), and VW's more tentative theory in *A Room of One's Own* that women must devise new forms of fiction, even of the sentence, to convey the feminine experience. Because of his interest and curiosity about the new forms literature might take, LW permitted and encouraged authors to develop their own styles. This, together with VW's respect for his opinion, made him the ideal editor for her experimental works.

If LW's criteria for a good book were apparent in his reviews during the 1920s, so were his criteria for a good book review. These are implicit in his actual practice. He provided background about a subject to enable his readers to determine whether the book under review added anything to their knowledge of it. He compared the book to others of its kind. When relevant, he commented upon the author's qualifications. And he gave a candid opinion of the book.

From time to time LW also spelled out his theory of book-reviewing. In "The Art of Reviewing Books" (C0797), he said the two requirements of a book review are "a clear account of what is in the book [and] a clear account of what, in the reviewer's opinion, are the book's merits and defects." The latter is more difficult, he said, because books of lasting value should be judged by different standards than books of ephemeral interest. The reviewer needs to tell his reader what standards he is using despite the short space allotted to reviews.

This is a tall order. It shows that LW assumed that he and others who reviewed books were writing for literate, well-informed readers. He assumed that each reviewer must depend upon his own insights. He said it does not matter whether a reviewer likes or dislikes a book if he provides enough information for the reader to decide whether to read it. He really believed that book reviews were more important than advertising to the selling of books and that his own unfavourable, even scathing reviews were helpful to readers (see C0756). The fact that the Woolfs used unfavourable reviews in roughly the same proportion as favourable ones in their advertisements for Hogarth Press books supports this conclusion.

In the pamphlet entitled *Reviewing* (B35), the Woolfs publicly discuss the pros and cons of the book review. VW expresses her recurring disillusionment with the review process and with the negative effects unfavourable reviews have upon authors. She objects to the pressure of time involved in the writing of reviews and the shortness of space allotted which allows little room for criticism of value to the author. She suggests that reviews be abolished and that authors consult critics for advice on their writing.

In his "Note" at the end of Virginia's pamphlet, LW disagrees with some of her conclusions. He insists that mass production has made the review necessary to the publisher, to the buying public, and even to the author whether he likes it or not. The review is what sells his books "to the greater reading public and the circulating libraries". The author should not expect literary criticism in a book review because the reader will not pay for a critical journal if he can get his information from a newspaper. Having repeated his earlier criteria for a book review, he goes on to say that the reviewer is speaking to the reader not the author, but that when a reviewer encounters a real work of art he should provide true criticism as well as an overview.

In actual practice LW frequently criticised the style as well as the contents of a book, whether or not it was a work of art. He also frequently commented on the quality of the production. Of *The Works of George Borrow*, published by Constable, he said:

> In binding, type and paper it is exactly what an edition of "Complete Works" should be – no fuss or preciosity or artiness, but a finely printed book which invites you to take it up and handle it with pleasure which is only the prelude to the pleasure of reading it. . . . I have a prejudice in favour of book production which assumes that the main purpose of a book is to be read, and that is why the sight of these sixteen volumes of Borrow, in their green cloth, gives me a peculiar satisfaction. (See C0455).

He was quick to note the absence of an index in a work he felt needed one. He complained if a publication failed to mention the original title of a translation, especially if the wording differed from that in the English title. He consistently compared the works he was reviewing with other works in the same genre or on the same topic.

Despite disagreeing with VW on the place of reviewing in 1939, LW sometimes voiced some of the same objections, such as the shortness of space given to book reviews and the effect of journalism on the serious writer. To illustrate his thesis that the writing of ephemeral pieces to meet periodic deadlines can destroy an author's ability for creative writing, LW used the example of Desmond MacCarthy (C1400). He said that Desmond used the excuse of journalism to procrastinate writing more serious works. "When you write for an editor and a paper, particularly if you write what is unsigned, but even if your name appears, in a curious way you escape responsibility" (*Beginning Again* A41, p. 134). Later, in *Downhill all the Way* (A42, p. 57), he wrote that "despite her terrifying hypersensitivity, there was in Virginia an intellectual and spiritual toughness which Desmond lacked . . . and ultimately she had the courage of her convictions and published."

In his account of his work for Clifford Sharp of the *New Statesman* and H. W. Massingham of the *Nation (Beginning Again*, A41, p. 131) LW says he realized that he wrote quite differently for different editors, because of "the way in which a real or 'good' editor pervades his paper." Although LW allowed his reviewers and other writers more variety of opinion and style than some editors do, it is hard to tell which unsigned reviews are by him and which by another.

In addition to his full-length reviews LW wrote many short notices of books. Space limitations often precluded criticism in these. Furthermore, when writing for partisan papers designed to persuade readers to an explicit point of view, such as the *Fabian Quarterly*, LW was apt simply to describe the book and recommend it.

Some of LW's best writing is in his anecdotes and character sketches of the people he knew. His reviews, as well as the books he chose to retain in his library, show that he was especially fond of biographical writing: diaries, letters and memoirs. His comment (see C0618 and C0732) that autobiographies are seldom boring because their authors are nearly always interested in their subjects is a mild example of his wit. He was devastating in his criticism of poorly written biographies. He hated long official biographies. Of *Lord Rosebery,* by the Marquess of Crewe (C1061), he says, "If the reputation of an ex-Prime Minister has to be biographically buried in two volumes, Lord Crewe performs the operation admirably." He questioned the necessity of Sir Sidney Lee's making his biography of Edward VII (C0528) "quite so bad and so dull". Conversely, he pointed out the defects arising from misuse of the modern biographical method developed by Lytton Strachey. While restraining his public criticism of Strachey's writing, he deplored his influence on lesser writers, who seemed to have the impression that to be interesting one must always be entertaining. This, he said, led them to reduce history to comedy.

LW enjoyed reading satire, especially that of Voltaire and Swift. He indulged in writing satire, but the results sometimes surprised him. His comments on Samuel Butler's *The Fair Haven* (C0435) show that he was aware that an author who uses irony runs the risk of being misunderstood. Still, he made this mistake sometimes. His review of *The Diaries of John Bright* (C1036) is really a lament for the passing of the democratic era of which Bright was an important figure. In it LW gave full vent to his disillusionment, caused by the threat to democratic ideals of the rise of authoritarian governments. He asked whether it was worth publishing this book in an age when democracy is dead. F. E. Pollard wrote to the editor, 3 January 1931, objecting that Woolf had belittled Bright's achievements. LW replied that it was unsafe for a reviewer to write ironically (C1039). Meantime, a grandson of Bright, Paul Bernard Roth, took offence at Woolf's description of Bright wearing a frock-coat (January 24). Woolf replied (C1041) that he had merely reported the caricatures presented by the press during the statesman's lifetime. It is worth noting that another of Bright's grandsons, Roger Clark (letter, February 7), said Woolf's review was "an unusually discriminating appreciation of the character of John Bright."

The correspondence generated by LW's practice of fanning the flames of controversy makes for lively reading in the pages of the periodicals to which he contributed. Whether he persuaded them to his views or not, both he and his readers seem to have enjoyed the arguments.

In 1930 LW finally resigned from his post as Literary Editor of the *Nation & Athenaeum.* His employers had refused several earlier attempts to resign, persuading him to continue even when he repeatedly decreased his hours at the editorial offices. He helped to found the *Political Quarterly,* which began publication in 1930. In 1931 he became a joint editor, a post he held for many years. He was sole editor during World War II. The *Political Quarterly* was a more sophisticated periodical than either the *Nation* or the *New Statesman,* in that the articles are more for the political specialist than for the ordinary reader. LW also filled in occasionally for Kingsley Martin as editor of the *New Statesman and Nation.* His own writing became increasingly political and dovetailed with his committee work for the Labour Party. He wrote fewer reviews towards the end of his life when he devoted much time to editing some previously unpublished work by Virginia Woolf.

Index

Due to space constraints, this index cites only the following references: all titles of books and pamphlets written by LW (section A), titles of books and pamphlets to which he contributed (section B), and the most important manuscript collections containing his records (section D). Limited subject access is provided to all four sections.